CALLIMACHUS

FRAGMENTS

MUSAEUS

HERO AND LEANDER

LCL 421

CALLIMACHUS

AETIA · IAMBI · HECALE
AND OTHER FRAGMENTS

EDITED AND TRANSLATED BY
C. A. TRYPANIS

MUSAEUS

HERO AND LEANDER

EDITED BY
THOMAS GELZER

TRANSLATED BY
CEDRIC WHITMAN

HARVARD UNIVERSITY PRESS
CAMBRIDGE, MASSACHUSETTS
LONDON, ENGLAND

CALLIMACHUS

First published 1958
Reprinted 1968, 1975, 1978, 1989

MUSAEUS

First published 1975
Reprinted 1978, 1989

ISBN 0-674-99463-9

Printed in Great Britain by St. Edmundsbury Press Ltd,
Bury St. Edmunds, Suffolk, on wood-free paper.
Bound by Hunter & Foulis Ltd, Edinburgh, Scotland.

CONTENTS
CALLIMACHUS

	PAGE
INTRODUCTION	vii

AETIA—

| Introduction . . . . | 2 |

Text and Translation—

Book I	4
Book II	32
Book III	42
Book IV	68
Unplaced Fragments	88

IAMBI—

| Introduction . . . . . . | 103 |
| Text and Translation . . . . . | 104 |

LYRIC POEMS—

| Introduction . . . . . . | 159 |
| Text and Translation . . . . . | 160 |

HECALE—

| Introduction . . . . . . | 176 |
| Text and Translation . . . . . | 180 |

CONTENTS

PAGE

MINOR EPIC AND ELEGIAC POEMS—

Text and Translation 228

FRAGMENTS OF EPIGRAMS—

Text and Translation 246

FRAGMENTS OF UNCERTAIN LOCATION—

Text and Translation 252

INDEX 391

MUSAEUS

HERO AND LEANDER—

Preface 291

Introduction 297

Text and Translation 344

Index 421

CALLIMACHUS

INTRODUCTION

Very little is known about the life of Callimachus either from his own writings, or from other sources.[a] The available information, however, enables us to trace a bare outline.

The family of Callimachus came from Cyrene, and in fact the poet claimed to be descended from Battos, the founder of the city.[b] His parents were called Battos and Megatime,[c] and he himself was named after his grandfather, a Cyrenean general.[d] According to Suidas, he married the daughter of a Syracusan called Euphraios, but her name is not given, and we are not told whether any children resulted from the marriage.[e]

The date of the poet's birth is not known, and the

---

[a] The main source for the life of Callimachus is Suidas, s.v. Καλλίμαχος. For other sources see Pfeiffer, *Callimachus*, ii, pp. xcv ff.

[b] *Hymn* ii. 65 with *Diegesis* and scholia to the line ; Strabo xvii. 837.

[c] The name of his mother, as given by Suidas, is Mesatma. This was amended to Megatima by Hemsterhuys. See also Wilamowitz, *Hell. Dichtung* i, p. 170 ; and Call. *Epigr.* xxxv (xxxvii L.C.L.). The epigrams are numbered according to the Pfeiffer edition.

[d] Call. *Epigr.* xxi (xxiii L.C.L.).

[e] The name of Callimachus' father-in-law is given by Suidas as Euphrates. This was emended to Euphraios by Kaibel. Suidas also mentions a sister of the poet named Megatima, and a nephew called Callimachus.

only information about his arrival and establishment at Alexandria is that it took place during the reign of Ptolemy II (285-247 B.C.). He must have reached the capital of the Ptolemies poor,[a] for he worked as a school teacher—a proverbially poor profession—before he was introduced to the court.[b] [c] We do not know when, or by whom, he was brought into contact with the court circle, but his life seems to have changed completely after that. He was commissioned to prepare the *Pinakes*, the great catalogue of the books of the Alexandrian library [d]; his later court poetry betrays a close intimacy with the royal family.

Many modern scholars have seen Callimachus as the most characteristic representative of Alexandran poetry, in fact the man " who personified in the purest manner the Hellenistic spirit." [e] But although his highly polished verse is to modern eyes the most interesting form of poetry of that period, it may not have been the most popular, or even the most sig-

---

[a] It is not safe to assume with Wilamowitz (*Hell. Dichtung l.c.*) that Callimachus left for Alexandria after Ptolemy II had conquered Cyrene, because the wealth and splendour of Alexandria and her court were a constant attraction to poor and gifted men from all parts of the Hellenistic world.

[b] Certain of his epigrams, in which he complains against poverty, probably belong to this period.

[c] Hermocrates of Iasus, a famous authority on accents, is mentioned among the teachers of Callimachus, but we do not know where he attended his lessons. The older view that Callimachus may have visited Athens (see Mair, *Callimachus*, p. 2) is no longer tenable, now that Call. fr. 178. 32 f. has shown that he never travelled beyond the sea.

[d] As we can see from *P. Oxy.* 1241, col. ii. 1, Callimachus never became *Prostates* (director) of the Alexandrian library.

[e] Wilamowitz, *l.c.*

nificant, in the opinion of his contemporaries. The traditional long epic appears to have finally won the day, and continued to be written up to the early Byzantine period, long after the activities of Callimachus and his school had ceased.[a]

The literary controversy between the writers of long traditional epics and those who preferred the short and highly finished poem began before the days of Callimachus, probably with the poetry of Philetas, the great Coan scholar-poet and teacher of Ptolemy II, and continued long after the death of the Cyrenean master, if we are to judge from its echo in later epigrams.[b] The details of this dispute escape us, but the quarrel between Callimachus and his pupil Apollonius—later known as Apollonius Rhodius —seems to have been one of the important episodes in it. The freedom with which Apollonius took over and re-fashioned in his own style whole passages of Callimachean poetry [c] provides a likely explanation of the bitterness on the part of the older man, and suggests the turning of an objective literary discussion into a personal feud between teacher and pupil. However that may be, Apollonius is said to have left Alexandria for Rhodes on account of this quarrel, and not to have returned there for some years.[d] It was during this dispute that Callimachus wrote a poem " of studied obscurity and abuse " called *Ibis*, in which he attacked Apollonius, comparing him

[a] See Ziegler, *Das hellenistische Epos*, pp. 14 ff.

[b] *Cf. Anth. Pal.* xi. 347. 5 ff.; xi. 322; xi. 321; xi. 130.

[c] See Pfeiff. ii, p. xli, and vol. i *passim*.

[d] Tradition records a reconciliation of the two, and that their graves were placed side by side. *Cf. Vit. Apollon. Rhod.* A, in Schol. ed. C. Wendel, p. 2. 5.

with the bird Ibis, which was destructive and omnivorous " and polluted in every way what was clean and what was not its own." [a]

As the date of the birth of Callimachus is not known, and the statement of Suidas on his death is unfortunately corrupt beyond restoration,[b] it is only on the evidence of his own poems that we can rely for any more accurate dating. The only one of these to which a reasonably definite date can be attributed is the *Plokamos* (fr. 110). It treats of events of the year 246/5, and seems to have been written in its original form in the same year. But a *terminus post quem* can be found for three other Callimachean poems : (*a*) the *Galatea* (frs. 378-379), which speaks of the incursion of the Gauls into the Greek world in 278 B.C., must have been written after the event ; (*b*) the *Ektheosis Arsinoes* (fr. 228), which concerns the deification of Queen Arsinoë, must have been composed after her death in 270 B.C. ; and (*c*) Hymn iv, *On Delos*, which has a reference to Ptolemy II as θεὺς ἄλλος,[c] a second god, must also have been composed later than 270 B.C., for he was deified only after the death

---

[a] No fragments of the *Ibis* have survived. It was a short poem, but certainly not an epigram, as certain modern scholars believe, for it is included in the catalogue of the poet's works given by Suidas, in which no individual epigrams are mentioned. The curses which Callimachus pronounced there are not those which appear in Ovid's *Ibis*. The Greek original may well have been in elegiac metre ; it was certainly not an iambic poem. Ancient witnesses speak of Apollonius as the man attacked in the *Ibis* : it is not, however, impossible that the Ibis was some other of Callimachus' opponents. (*Cf.* Pfeiff. i, p. 307, fr. 382.)

[b] καὶ παρέτεινε (*sc.* his life) μέχρι τοῦ Εὐεργέτου κληθέντος Πτολεμαίου ὀλυμπιάδος δὲ †ρκζ' (272/69), ἧς κατὰ τὸ δεύτερον ἔτος ὁ Εὐεργέτης Πτολεμαῖος ἤρξατο τῆς βασιλείας.

[c] This hymn also refers to the Gauls in l. 173.

of the queen.[a] Besides these, fr. 387 of an elegy in
which the star of Berenice is mentioned may well
have been composed after the *Plokamos*. So from the
available evidence in the extant poems and fragments
of Callimachus it is clear that he was active as a poet
between the eighties and the forties of the third
century B.C. If indeed the *Sosibiou Nike* (fr. 384) was
written, as it appears, in honour of Sosibios, the future
minister of Ptolemy IV, Callimachus may have been
writing remarkable poetry even in the late forties of
that century. However that may be, he is to be seen
as one of the distinguished Alexandrian poets of the
first generation, slightly younger than Theocritus [b]
and Aratus,[c] and older than his pupil Apollonius,
whom, however, he may have survived.

The most famous Callimachean poems were the
Aetia and the *Hecale*. But his *Iambi* and his other
shorter works display the same mastery of form, and
occasionally a true poetic touch. On the whole the
purity of his style (in spite of the use of rare words
and forms), the variety and grace of his descriptions,
the search for novelty (in the use of local or non-
Panhellenic versions of myths, and the constant
adaptation—but never verbatim repetition—of Ho-
meric usages), and his peculiar irony, outweigh the
grammarian's love for detail, and the antiquarian's
taste for the rare and the unusual. For, in order to
appreciate the poetry of Callimachus, we should bear
in mind that he was a poet, a scholar and a critic, and
that the three qualities were equally developed in him.

[a] See U. Wilcken, *S.B. Berl. Akad.*, 1938, pp. 298 ff.

[b] See Pfeiff. ii, pp. xlii f., and Herter, *Gnomon* xix (1943),
pp. 325 ff.

[c] Achill. *Vit. Arat.* 4, p. 78. 22 M : μέμνηται γοῦν αὐτοῦ
καὶ Καλλίμαχος ὡς πρεσβυτέρου.

INTRODUCTION

For the modern world perhaps the most moving of his poems are certain of his epigrams, and those which appeal least are his hymns. But there are passages in the extant *Aetia* which are comparable to much of the great poetry written in the Greek language.

Callimachus was also famous in antiquity as a scholar. Of his prose works the most celebrated was the *Pinakes*, the catalogue of the books in the great library of the Museum of Alexandria. It included everything from the Homeric manuscripts to the last contemporary cookery book; the exact number of lines, as well as the beginning of every work, were quoted.[a] In view of the vast number of books then amassed in the library, the undertaking must have been enormous, influencing not only all subsequent bibliographers, but also the nature of the poetry of Callimachus. Besides the *Pinakes*, Callimachus wrote many other scholarly works,[b] *e.g.* a chronological register of the Athenian dramatic poets, a study of Democritus' writings and language, numerous encyclopaedias (about nymphs, birds, games, winds, rivers), collections of paradoxa and glosses. According to Suidas, on whose authority too much reliance, needless to say, should not be placed on this point, Callimachus wrote more than 800 books![c] His scholarly activities may also be judged from the

[a] See F. Schmidt, *Die Pinakes des Kallimachos*, 1922, and A. Koerte, *Hellenistic Poetry* (translated by J. Hammer and J. Hadas), pp. 84 ff.

[b] On these see Pfeiff. i, pp. 328 ff., and Herter, Pauly-Wissowa, *R.E.* Supplementband v, 1931, pp. 386 f. The prose fragments of Callimachus are not included in this volume.

[c] " Satyrical dramas, tragedies and comedies " are among the poems Suidas attributes to Callimachus. No trace of these, however, has been recovered in papyri or other sources.

xii

distinguished men numbered among his pupils ; they include Eratosthenes of Cyrene, Aristophanes of Byzantium, and Apollonius Rhodius.

It is probable that Callimachus produced at an advanced age a final full edition of his poetical works, which he prefaced with the famous *Answer to the Telchines* (fr. 1). It is the order of this edition which the present volume endeavours to follow. The hymns and epigrams were at the end of the complete works.[a] In fact, the epigrams may even have been collected by some later grammarian, and added to the corpus of the Callimachean poetry. From there a number of them passed on to the *Garland of Meleager*, and thence to the *Palatine* and *Planudean Anthologies*, and other authors who quote them.

The fame and popularity of Callimachus must have exceeded that of every other Alexandrian poet, if we judge by the great number of Callimachean papyri —even greater than those of Euripides—and the constant quotations found in grammarians, metricians, lexicographers and scholiasts of late antiquity.[b] To no other poet except Homer do the grammarians pay so much honour. Callimachus was studied by the Byzantine Greeks, and his poems seem to have survived till the fall of Athens to the Franks of the Fourth Crusade (A.D. 1205). After that only the hymns (which were included in the great collection of Homeric, Orphic and Proclean hymns) survived, and those of his epigrams included in the *Palatine* and *Planudean Anthologies* or quoted by some other author.

[a] In the Loeb Classical Library these are available in the edition of A. W. Mair.

[b] On the absence of Callimachean manuscripts among the Ptolemaic papyri see C. H. Roberts, " Literature and Society n the Papyri," *Museum Helveticum* 10 (1953), pp. 269 f.

INTRODUCTION

The oldest commentary known on the works of Callimachus belongs to the age of Augustus. It is by Theon, son of Artemidorus. Only one interpreter of Callimachus is known, called Salustius, who is of unknown date.

The *Diegeseis*, which have recently come to light, are of inestimable value for the knowledge of the subjects Callimachus treated in his poetry. Three separate *Diegeseis* have survived, all apparently going back to a common lost source, in which the arguments and other information on the poems of Callimachus were given.[a] Of these the so-called *Milan Diegeseis* are the best preserved, though the *Diegeseis* of *P. Oxy.* 2263 on the *Artemis of Leucas*, and the so-called *Scholia Florentina* are equally important for the parts of the poems of which they treat. Later lexicographers (Suidas, *Etymologicum Magnum*, etc.) draw on the works of such commentators and interpreters for much of the Callimachean material they include.

*　　*　　*　　*　　*

The present volume is a selection from the fragments of the poetry of Callimachus. It includes only those fragments which make sense and can be translated. The text is based to a large extent on the excellent edition of Pfeiffer (vols. i-ii, Oxonii, 1948 and 1953). As the Loeb Classical Library does not allow an elaborate apparatus I avoid mentioning the source of each fragment ; for this the reader should consult Pfeiffer.[b] Only very significant *variae lectiones*

---

[a] See Pfeiff. ii, p. xxviii and n. 1.
[b] For the Callimachean papyri till 1965 consult R. A. Pack, *The Greek and Latin Literary Papyri*, Ann Arbor, 1965².

are included, but the authors of supplements and emendations are always given.[a] All reasonably certain papyrus readings are accepted in the text without indication. The numbering of the fragments and the verses is that of Pfeiffer's edition, in order to facilitate quotations. This obviously entails certain gaps in the numeration, where fragments or parts of fragments are not included in this edition. Thick letters mark the beginning, and a thick dash the end of a poem.

The translation has no claims to literary qualities. It is intended only as a help to the understanding of the text.

The short introductions and notes which accompany the individual poems are again mainly based on Pfeiffer, unless otherwise indicated, and for that reason only rarely are the sources quoted.

After Theocritus Callimachus is the most privileged among the Alexandrian poets in the matter of editions. First Bentley's collection of the Callimachean fragments, then Schneider's *Callimachea*—a milestone in the study of Alexandrian poetry—, after that the editions of the *Hymns* and *Epigrams* by Wilamowitz, and finally Pfeiffer's great edition, without doubt the most significant work in the field of Hellenistic studies. Moreover, all the great scholars of the present and of the last century have worked on Callimachus. The accumulation of their work, together

---

[a] In the apparatus cod. = manuscript.

   P = papyrus.
   T = wooden tablet.
   L. = E. Lobel.
   Pf. = R. Pfeiffer.
   Wil. = U. v. Wilamowitz-Moellendorff.
   Hu. = A. S. Hunt.

with the many new papyrus fragments, has enabled us to recapture a more exact picture of the writings of this unique poet.

At this point I should like to express my thanks to Mr. E. A. Barber and Professor P. Maas for their valuable guidance and help.

C. A. TRYPANIS

EXETER COLLEGE
  OXFORD, 1957

Editorial note (1978) : Since this volume was revised for the 1968 reprint, more papyri containing poems of Callimachus have come to light. The occasion of another reprint now provides an opportunity of inserting some bibliographical first-aid against the day when the new material can be systematically incorporated. Professor Trypanis has very kindly given permission for this to be done, and the addendum which follows has been compiled by Mr. A. H. Griffiths of University College, London.

G. P. G.

FRAGMENTS OF CALLIMACHUS:
BIBLIOGRAPHICAL ADDENDUM

AETIA

Book I, fr. 17. 8-10 is now supplemented by *P. Mich.* inv. 3688, published by A. Henrichs in *Zeitschr. f. Papyrologie u. Epigraphik*, 4 (1969), pp. 23 ff.

Book II, fr. 46 : the remains of the middle portions of nine lines following this couplet are provided by *P. Sorb.* inv. 2248 fr. *a*, published by Cl. Meillier in *Rev. Ét. Greques*, 89 (1976), pp. 74 ff. ; fr. *b* gives a surrounding context of fourteen lines for fr. 475, which is thus also likely to belong to *Aetia* Book II.

Book III : substantial fragments, partly meshing with fr. 383, were published by Cl. Meillier in *Cahiers de Recherches de l'Institut de Papyrologie et d'Égyptologie de Lille*, 4 (1977) ; P. J. Parsons has shown in *Zeitschr. f. Papyrologie u. Epigraphik*, 25 (1977), pp. 1 ff. that the long poem (of perhaps 200 lines) whose outlines can be traced from these pieces, dealing with the victory in the Nemean Games of Queen Berenice's chariot team and including the story of the hospitality given to Heracles by Molorchus (frs. 55-59), very probably constituted the opening section of this book.

Book III, frs. 91-92 (the Melicertes story) : a previously unknown hexameter, possibly belonging to this *aetion*, was discovered in a palimpsest MS. of

BIBLIOGRAPHICAL ADDENDUM

Herodian by H. Hunger (*Jahrb. d. Oesterr. Byz. Ges.* 16 [1967], p. 12) ; corrections to the text of this, and of further fragments from the same source, are made by M. L. West in *Maia*, 20 (1968), p. 203.

HECALE

The codex-fragment *P. Oxy.* 2529 seems to present fr. 334 as preceding fr. 248 at an interval of one line.

The long fr. 260 has been carefully scrutinized and re-edited by H. Lloyd-Jones and J. R. Rea in *Harvard Studies in Class. Philol.* 72 (1968), pp. 125 ff.

FRAGMENTS OF UNCERTAIN LOCATION

Fr. 601 appears in *P. Ant.* 114 (*Antinoopolis Papyri*, vol. III), and may have come from the story of the Graces in *Aetia* I, frs. 3 ff.

Fr. 625 now appears in context in *P. Ant.* 113, and may also be ascribed to the *Aetia* : see the interpretation offered by A. W. Bulloch in *Class. Quart.* 20 (1970), pp. 269 ff.

Fr. 631 has turned up in a scrap of commentary published by F. Montanari in *Athenaeum*, 54 (1976), pp. 139 ff., and this new piece may help to establish the text.

A. H. G.

AETIA

INTRODUCTION

THE *Aetia* was an elegiac poem in four books, containing a series of aetiological legends connected with Greek history, customs and rites.[a] The whole work was made up of some 7000 lines, but the length of the individual aetia, or causes, varied greatly.[b]

The poet imagined himself carried in a dream from Libya to Mount Helicon, where the Muses instructed him in all manner of legendary lore. The extant fragments indicate that in the two first books the poet converses with the Muses, but that in Books III-IV the various stories were not connected by a fictitious dialogue, or by any other method.[c] [d] The

---

[a] Aetia, or the causes of myths, customs, etc., appear sporadically in many classical authors. Callimachus seems to have been the first to compile a whole work treating of them. The interest of the poet in aetia can be also seen from his *Iambi*, some of which are but aetia in iambic metre, and the *Hecale*, which is a grand " epic " aetion in hexameters.

[b] Compare, *e.g.*, fr. 64, *The Tomb of Simonides*, with frs. 67-75, *Acontius and Cydippe*.

[c] The title of the poem may refer to the first part of the work, a practice not unknown in antiquity, as can be seen from Cato's *Origines*, which begin with the origins of Italian cities but later deal with their subsequent history.

[d] See frs. 63*-64, 66-67 and 92*-93, 95-96. Ovid may have followed the example of *Aetia* i-ii in the structure of the *Fasti*, and Propertius in the fourth book of his elegies that of *Aetia* iii-iv.

* Fragment not included in this edition, but in Pfeiffer, *Callimachi Fragmenta*.

number of aetia contained in each book is unknown ; it is evident that they received very varied treatment. This variety, together with the lively personal and realistic touches, introduced into the narrative by the poet, never allowed the work to degenerate into an arid handbook of obscure mythology.

It is probable that Callimachus prepared a revised second edition of the *Aetia* to be included in the edition of his collected works. As the last aetion of this second edition we find the *Plokamos* (fr. 110), which must have been earlier published independently.[a] It was suitably altered to fit in with the general scheme of the revised edition.[b] To this also belongs the extant Epilogue (fr. 112), the last line of which would otherwise be unintelligible : αὐτὰρ ἐγὼ Μουσέων πεζὸν [ἔ]πειμι νομόν. This can only refer to the transition from the *Aetia* to the *Iambi*, which follow in the collected works.

As a general introduction to his collected works (and perhaps as a more special introduction to the *Aetia*) Callimachus composed the *Answer to the Telchines* (fr. 1). In it he expounds his final and most polemic views on poetry.

The subjects of the last few aetia of Book III, and possibly of all those included in Book IV, are now known from the *Diegeseis*.

---

[a] Cf. *P. Oxy.* 2258, no. 37.

[b] Lines 79-88 (they do not appear in *P. Oxy.* 2258, no. 37), which introduce the aetiological element, must have been added then, and the last couplet of the poem (lines 94ᵃ-94ᵇ Pf.) was also omitted to make way for the new general Epilogue (fr. 112).

[ΑΙΤΙΩΝ Α']

1

(IN TELCHINAS)

Οἶδ' ὅτ]ι μοι Τελχῖνες ἐπιτρύζουσιν ἀοιδῇ,
νήιδες οἳ Μούσης οὐκ ἐγένοντο φίλοι,
εἵνεκεν οὐχ ἓν ἄεισμα διηνεκὲς ἢ βασιλ[η
......]αs ἐν πολλαῖς ἤνυσα χιλιάσιν
5 ἢ .....]ους ἥρωας, ἔπος δ' ἐπὶ τυτθὸν ἑλ[ίσσω
παῖς ἅτε, τῶν δ' ἐτέων ἡ δεκὰς οὐκ ὀλίγη.
........] καὶ Τελχῖσιν ἐγὼ τόδε· '' φῦλον α[
......] τήκειν ἧπαρ ἐπιστάμενον,
......]ρεην [ὀλ]ιγόστιχος ἀλλὰ καθέλκει
10 ....] πολὺ τὴν μακρὴν ὄμπνια Θεσμοφόρο[s·

1 suppl. Vogliano.

ᵃ The Telchines were described as inhabitants of Crete,
Rhodes, Sicyon, Ceos or Cyprus. They were said to be the
first workers in metal, but of ill report as spiteful sorcerers.
Callimachus calls his literary enemies Telchines, using the
word in the sense of " spiteful backbiters." The *Scholia
Florentina* to this passage (Pfeiff. i, p. 3) give some of their
names ; among them are those of Asclepiades and Posidip-
pus, the famous Alexandrian poets (mainly known to us
through their epigrams in the *Palatine Anthology*), and of
Praxiphanes of Mitylene, a distinguished contemporary
grammarian and philosopher, against whom Callimachus
wrote (*cf.* fr. 460*).

ᵇ Θεσμοφόρος=Law-bringing Demeter.

ᶜ According to Pfeiffer's reading of the *Scholia Florentina*
in this mutilated passage (ll. 9 ff.) the short poems of Philetas
of Cos (born *c.* 320 B.C. and in a sense the founder of the

AETIA : BOOK I

1

(AGAINST THE TELCHINES)

(I know that) the Telchines,[a] who are ignorant and
no friends of the Muse, grumble at my poetry,
because I did not accomplish one continuous poem
of many thousands of lines on . . . kings or . . .
5 heroes, but like a child I roll forth a short tale,
though the decades of my years are not few. And I
(say) this to the Telchines : " . . . race, who know
how to waste away your heart. . . . of few lines, but
10 bountiful Demeter [b] by far outweighs the long [c] . . .,

Alexandrian school of poetry) and of Mimnermus of Colophon
(*fl. c.* 630 B.C.—he is supposed to have introduced the ama-
tory element into early Greek elegy) are compared with their
longer compositions and judged superior. The " bountiful
Demeter " could then be Philetas' narrative elegy *Demeter*,
which recounted the wanderings of the goddess ; the name of
the long poem, with which it was compared, is lost. The
" Large Woman " (l. 12) could be the *Nanno*, the famous
elegy of Mimnermus, named after the Lydian flute-girl he
is said to have loved (*cf.* Asclep. *Anth. Pal.* ix. 63), or even
his historical poem *Smyrneis*. The κατὰ λεπτὸν [ῥήσιες ?]
may possibly be the " opera minora " of the poet. Many
scholars, however, do not accept this interpretation and
believe that the short poems of Philetas and Mimnermus
are in this passage compared with long poems of other
poets, which cannot be as yet identified. The " Large
Woman " may in this case be the *Lyde* of Antimachus.
(See also M. Puelma, " Die Vorbilder der Elegiendichtung
in Alexandrien und Rom," *Museum Helveticum*, 11 (1954),
pp. 101 f.)

CALLIMACHUS

τοῖν δὲ] δυοῖν Μίμνερμος ὅτι γλυκύς, αἱ κατὰ λεπτόν

  . . . . . .] ἡ μεγάλη δ' οὐκ ἐδίδαξε γυνή.

  . . . . .]ον ἐπὶ Θρήϊκας ἀπ' Αἰγύπτοιο [πέτοιτο

  αἵματι Πυγμαίων ἡδομένη γέρανος,

15 Μασσαγέται καὶ μακρὸν ὀϊστεύοιεν ἐπ' ἄνδρα

  Μῆδον]· ἀ[ηδονίδες] δ' ὧδε μελιχρότεραι.

  ἔλλετε Βασκανίης ὀλοὸν γένος· αὖθι δὲ τέχνῃ

  κρίνετε,] μὴ σχοίνῳ Περσίδι τὴν σοφίην·

  μηδ' ἀπ' ἐμεῦ διφᾶτε μέγα ψοφέουσαν ἀοιδήν

20 τίκτεσθαι· βροντᾶν οὐκ ἐμόν, ἀλλὰ Διός.''

  καὶ γὰρ ὅτε πρώτιστον ἐμοῖς ἐπὶ δέλτον ἔθηκα

  γούνασιν, Ἀπόλλων εἶπεν ὅ μοι Λύκιος·

  '' . . . .] ἀοιδέ, τὸ μὲν θύος ὅττι πάχιστον

  θρέψαι, τὴ]ν Μοῦσαν δ' ὠγαθὲ λεπταλέην·

25 πρὸς δέ σε] καὶ τόδ' ἄνωγα, τὰ μὴ πατέουσιν

  ἄμαξαι

  τὰ στείβειν, ἑτέρων δ' ἴχνια μὴ καθ' ὁμά

  δίφρον ἐλ]ᾶν μηδ' οἷμον ἀνὰ πλατύν, ἀλλὰ κελεύθους

  ἀτρίπτο]υς, εἰ καὶ στεινοτέρην ἐλάσεις.

11 suppl. Housman.   12 ῥήσιες] suppl. Rostagni.
13 suppl. e.g. L. : init. fort. μακρ]ὸν Pf.   16 init. suppl.
Pf. : ἀ[ηδονίδες] Housman.   18 suppl. Housman.
24 θρέψαι suppl. Pf. : τὴ]ν Hu.   25 e.g. suppl. Hu.
26 δ' cod.   27 e.g. suppl. Hu.   28 suppl. Pf.

6

and of the two poems the small-scale . . . and not
the Large Woman taught that Mimnermus is a de-
lightful poet . . . let the crane, delighting in the
blood of the Pygmies,[a] fly (far) from Egypt to the
15 land of the Thracians and let the Massagetae [b] shoot
their arrows from a great distance at the Medes ;
but poems are sweeter for being short.[c] Begone, you
baneful race of Jealousy ! hereafter judge poetry
by (the canons) of art, and not by the Persian chain,[d]
20 nor look to me for a song loudly resounding. It is
not mine to thunder ; that belongs to Zeus." For,
when I first placed a tablet on my knees, Lycian [e]
Apollo said to me : " . . . poet, feed the victim to
be as fat as possible but, my friend, keep the Muse
25 slender. This too I bid you : tread a path which
carriages do not trample ; do not drive your chariot
upon the common tracks of others, nor along a wide
road, but on unworn paths, though your course be

[a] The Pygmies, a fabulous race of dwarfs on the upper
Nile, were said to have been warred on and destroyed by
cranes.

[b] The Massagetae were a Scythian people, to the east of
the Caspian Sea. Like the Medes, they were famous archers
and fought from a great distance " trusting their far-reaching
bows " (Herod. i. 214).

[c] If Housman's supplement ἀ[ηδονίδες] is right, it would
mean short poems. ἀηδών " nightingale " in the sense of
poem is used by Callimachus in *Epigr.* ii. 5.

[d] The Persian chain, the *schoenus*, was a (Persian) land-
measure used especially in Egypt ; its length was variously
reckoned from 30 to 60 stades.

[e] Epithet of Apollo, explained in various ways : the wolf-
slayer, the Lycian god, or the god of light. We are also told
that : " transfiguratus in lupum (λύκον) cum Cyrene con-
cubuit " (Serv. ad Verg. *Aen.* iv. 177 ; *cf. Schol. Lond.* in
Pfeiff. i, p. 7). Callimachus, who spent his early years in
Cyrene, must have learnt there how to read and write.

τεττίγω]ν ἐνὶ τοῖς γὰρ ἀείδομεν οἳ λιγὺν ἦχον

30 ‒‒‒ θ]όρυβον δ' οὐκ ἐφίλησαν ὄνων."

θηρὶ μὲν οὐατόεντι πανείκελον ὀγκήσαιτο

ἄλλος, ἐγ]ὼ δ' εἴην οὐλαχύς, ὁ πτερόεις,

ἃ πάντως, ἵνα γῆρας ἵνα δρόσον, ἣν μὲν ἀείδω

προίκιο]ν ἐκ δίης ἠέρος εἶδαρ ἔδων,

35 αὖθι τὸ δ' ἐκδύοιμι, τό μοι βάρος ὅσσον ἔπεστι

τριγλώχιν ὀλοῷ νῆσος ἐπ' Ἐγκελάδῳ.

‒‒‒ οὐ νέμεσις·] Μοῦσαι γὰρ ὅσους ἴδον ὄθματι παῖδας

μὴ λοξῷ, πολιοὺς οὐκ ἀπέθεντο φίλους.

29 suppl. Hu. 32 suppl. Hu. 34 προίκιο]ν *Schol. Theocr.* : πρώκιο]ν Th. Stanley. 37 init. suppl. Trypanis ex Call. *Epigr.* xxi. (xxiii L.C.L.) 5, cf. Call. *Hym.* iii. 64.

---

[a] The " voice " of the cicala is frequently used in Greek poetry as a simile for sweet sounds. The cicala, according

2

(SOMNIUM)

Ποιμένι μῆλα νέμοντι παρ' ἴχνιον ὀξέος ἵππου

Ἡσιόδῳ Μουσέων ἑσμὸς ὅτ' ἠντίασεν

μ]έν οἱ Χάεος γενεσ[

] ἐπὶ πτέρῃς ὑδα[

5 τεύχων ὡς ἑτέρῳ τις ἑῷ κακὸν ἥπατι τεύχει.

---

[a] The fountain Hippocrene on Mount Helicon. According to the myth it was created by the hoof of Pegasus, the winged horse of Bellerophon. It was there the Muses

more narrow. For we sing among those who love
30 the shrill voice of the cicala [a] and not the noise of
the . . . asses." Let others bray just like the long-
eared brute, but let me be the dainty, the winged
one. Oh, yes indeed ! that I may sing living on
35 dew-drops, free sustenance from the divine air ; that
I may then shed old age, which weighs upon me like
the three-cornered island [b] upon deadly Enceladus.
But never mind ! for if the Muses have not looked
askance at one in his childhood, they do not cast him
from their friendship when he is grey.

to Plato (*Phaedr.* 259), is the favourite of the Muses, and in
Alexandrian poetry poets are compared to, or called after it
(*e.g.* Theoc. i. 148 ; Posidip. *Anth. Pal.* xii. 98, etc.). The
cicala was thought to sing continually without food or drink,
or to subsist on a diet of air and dew ; like the snake it was
believed to cast away old age together with its dry skin.
 [b] The three-cornered island is Sicily, which Zeus is said
to have hurled upon the giant Enceladus.

2

(THE DREAM)

. . . when the bevy of Muses met the shepherd
Hesiod tending sheep by the foot-print of the fiery
horse [a] . . . (they told him ?) . . . the birth of
5 Chaos . . . (at the water) of the hoof . . . that
causing evil to another a man causes evil to his own
heart.[b]

appeared to Hesiod as he was tending his sheep. This
fountain is to be distinguished from the Aganippe, also in
Boeotia, mentioned by Callimachus in this part of the
Aetia.
 [b] An adaptation of Hesiod, *Op.* 265.

9

3–7. 14

(GRATIAE)

3

] κῶς ἄγ[ις αὐλῶν
ῥέζειν καὶ στεφέων εὔαδε τῷ Παρίῳ

1 suppl. Maas.

---

[a] As King Minos of Crete was sacrificing to the Graces in the island of Paros, the death of his son Androgeos was announced to him. He continued the sacrifice, but bid the flute-player cease playing, and removed the garland from his own head. Thereafter the Parians sacrificed to the

4

καὶ νήσων ἐπέτεινε βαρὺν ζυγὸν αὐχένι Μίνως

5

τὸ μὲν θύος ἤρχετο βάλλειν

6

οἱ δ' ἔνεκ' Εὐρυνόμη Τιτηνιὰς εἶπαν ἔτικτεν

---

[a] As we know from the *Scholia Florentina* (Pfeiff. i, p. 13), the Muse told Callimachus that the Graces were daughters of Dionysus and the Naxian nymph Coronis. The poet had previously mentioned three other traditions concerning their birth : the first that they were daughters of Zeus and

10

AETIA

3–7. 14

(THE GRACES)

3

. . . why did it please the Parians [a] to sacrifice (to the Graces) without flutes and garlands . . . ?

Graces without garlands and flutes. The source of Callimachus for this aetion (frs. 3–7. 14) was Agias and Dercylos, the former an old writer of " Argolica," to whom was also wrongly attributed the epic poem *Nostoi*, the latter an Alexandrian reviser of Agias' work. (See Jacoby, *Fr. Gr. Hist.* iii B, 1950, pp. 7-10 and add. p. 757.)

4

. . . and Minos stretched the heavy yoke over the neck of the islands.[a]

[a] A reference to the sea-power of King Minos of Crete.

5

(Minos) began to cast the first offering.[a]

[a] Refers to the hair cut from the victim.

6

. . . others said that Eurynome the Titan [a] gave birth (to the Graces).

Hera ; the second that they were daughters of Zeus and Eurynome (the daughter of the Titans Oceanus and Tethys), and the third that Zeus and Euanthe (the daughter of Ouranos) were their parents.

7

]ες ἀνείμονες ὡς ἀπὸ κόλπου
10   μητρὸς Ἐλειθυίης ἤλθετε βουλομένης,
ἐν δὲ Πάρῳ κάλλη τε καὶ αἰόλα βεῦδε᾽ ἔχουσαι
ἔστατ᾽,] ἀπ᾽ ὀστλίγων δ᾽ αἰὲν ἄλειφα ῥέει,
ἔλλατε νῦν, ἐλέγοισι δ᾽ ἐνιψήσασθε λιπώσας
χεῖρας ἐμοῖς, ἵνα μοι πουλὺ μένωσιν ἔτος.—

12 suppl. Maas.

7. 19–21

(ARGONAUTARUM REDITUS ET RITUS
ANAPHAEUS)

7. 19

Κῶς δέ, θεαί, [Φοίβῳ] μὲν ἀνὴρ Ἀναφαῖος ἐπ᾽ αἰ-
σ[χροῖς
20   ἡ δ᾽ ἐπὶ δυ[σφήμοις] Λίνδος ἄγει θυσίην,
η ... τηνε[. . . . . . τ]ὸν Ἡρακλῆα σεβίζῃ;
      ]επικ[. . . . .]ως ἤρχετο Καλλιόπη·
"Αἰγλήτην Ἀνάφην τε, Λακωνίδι γείτονα Θήρῃ,
π]ρῶτ[ον ἐνὶ μ]νήμῃ κάτθεο καὶ Μινύας,
25 ἄρχμενος ὡς ἥρωες ἀπ᾽ Αἰήταο Κυταίου
αὖτις ἐς ἀρχαίην ἔπλεον Αἱμονίην

19 [Φοίβῳ] suppl. Trypanis : αἰσ[χροῖς suppl. Körte.
20 suppl. Norsa et Vitelli.   21 ἥ[δισ]τ᾽ ἦν ἔ[σθοντα τ]ὸν
prop. Barber.   24 suppl. Norsa et Vitelli.

_____

ᵃ A small island in the Cretan Sea, revealed to the Argo-
nauts by Apollo, when caught by a storm on their way home
(cf. Ap. Rh. iv. 1694 f.).

7

9 . . . naked as with the goodwill of Eileithyia [a] you
came forth from your mother's womb, but in Paros
you stand wearing fineries and shimmering tunics,
and ointment always flows from your locks. Come
now and wipe your anointed hands upon my elegies
that they may live for many a year.

[a] The goddess of childbirth.

7. 19-21

(THE RETURN OF THE ARGONAUTS
AND THE RITE AT ANAPHE)

7. 19

AND, O Goddesses, how it is that a man of Anaphe [a]
20 sacrifices (to Apollo) with shameful (words), and the
city of Lindus [b] with blasphemy . . . pays honour
to Heracles ? . . . Calliope began : " First bring to
mind Apollo Aegletes [c] and Anaphe, neighbour to
25 Spartan Thera,[d] and the Minyans [e] ; begin when the
heroes sailed back to ancient Haemonia [f] from Aeëtes,
the Cytaean [g] . . . and he, when he saw the deeds

[b] Town in the island of Rhodes, said to have been founded
by Lindus, brother of Ialysus.
[c] The radiant one, epithet of Apollo, whom the Argonauts
invoked " because of the gleam seen from afar " (Ap. Rh.
iv. 1716 f.).
[d] The Aegean island now called Santorin.
[e] The Argonauts were also called Minyae in Greek
literature.
[f] Thessaly.
[g] King of Colchis, father of Medea. Cytaean here equals
Colchian.

CALLIMACHUS

]εν, ὁ δ' ὡς ἴδεν ἔργα θυγατρ[ός
] ἔλεξε τάδε·

.   .   .   .

31 σο[   ] ἐποιήσαντό με φόρτον
   σοῦσ[θε   νήιο]ν ὅ σφε φέρει
   αὔταν[δρον   ] Ἥλιος ἴστω
   καὶ Φᾶσις [ποταμῶν ἡμε]τέρων βασιλεύς

31 σο[ῦσθε prop. Barber-Maas.   32 σοῦσ[θε prop.
Barber-Maas : νήιο]ν e.g. suppl. Pf.   33 dub. suppl. Wil.
34 suppl. Ed. Schwartz : πα]τέρων Wil.

10

μαστύος ἀλλ' ὅτ' ἔκαμνον ἀλητύι

---

[a] In order to seize Jason and Medea, who fled from

11

οἱ μὲν ἐπ' Ἰλλυρικοῖο πόρου σχάσσαντες ἐρετμά
  λᾶα πάρα ξανθῆς Ἁρμονίης †ὄφιος†
5 ἄστυρον ἐκτίσσαντο, τό κεν " Φυγάδων " τις ἐνί-
    σποι
  Γραικός, ἀτὰρ κείνων γλῶσσ' ὀνόμηνε " Πόλας."
οἱ δ[

4 ὄφιος codd. : τάφιον coni. Bentley.

---

[a] The South-East Adriatic, off the shores of Illyria, modern
Albania.

14

31 of his daughter . . . said this . . . " Hasten . . .
they betrayed me. Hasten . . . (the ship) which
carries him with all its men . . . let the sun be my
witness and Phasis *a* the king of our rivers . . ."

a The main river in Colchis, which flows into the Black
Sea. It is in the Callimachean style to take an oath by the
river of one's fatherland. *Cf.* fr. 194. 106 ; fr. 201. The
sun was said to be the grandfather of Medea.

10

. . . but when (the Colchians) had tired of their
wandering and their searching *a* . . .

Colchis with the golden fleece. See The Oxford Classical
Dictionary, *s.v.* " Argonauts," for the main variants of the
story of the return of the Argonauts.

11

. . . one band, dropping their oars by the Illyrian
Strait,*a* built a small city near the stone of (the snake ?)
5 fair Harmonia *b* ; a Greek might call it " Of the
Exiles," but in their own tongue it was named
" Polae." The other band . . .

b Harmonia, daughter of Ares and Aphrodite, was wife
of Cadmus. She and her husband went in their old age to
Illyria, and were turned there into stone serpents. The story
of the return of the Argonauts is influenced by the geo-
graphical ideas of antiquity, as well as by the desire to bring
the Argonauts in contact with places traditionally " Minyan."

15

12

Φαιήκων ἐγένον[το
ἑσμὸν ἄγων ἑτέροις [
ἔκτισε Κερκυραῖον ἐδέθλιον, ἔνθ[εν ἀν' αὖτις
5 στάντες Ἀμαντίνην ᾤκισαν Ὠρικίην.
καὶ τὰ μὲν ὡς ἤμελλε μετὰ χρόνον ἐκτελέεσθαι

4 ἔνθ[εν suppl. L., cett. e.g. Pf.

15

ἀμφίδυμος Φαίηξ

^a Corcyra had a double harbour in antiquity, the port of

18

Τυ]νδαρίδαι
]ς Δία πρῶτον ἵκοντο
] ἄλλους ητεσαν ἀ[θ]ανάτους
ἀοσ]σητῆρας ἐυστείρ[. . . . .]ελέ . ο . . ·
5 ἀλλ' ὅγ' ἀνι]άζων ὃν κέαρ Αἰσονίδης
σοὶ χέρας ἤέρ]ταζεν, Ἰήιε, πολλὰ δ' ἀπείλει
ἐς Πυθὼ πέ]μψειν, πολλὰ δ' ἐς Ὀρτυγίην,
εἴ κεν ἀμιχθαλόεσσαν ἀπ' ἠέρα νηὸς ἐλάσσῃς·
] ὅτι σήν, Φοῖβε, κατ' αἰσιμίην

1 suppl. L.   2 Δία Pf.: διὰ L.   3 ἤτασαν?
Lobel: ἤτισαν? Pf.   4 νηὸς ἀοσ]σητῆρας ἐυστείρ[οιο τ]ε-
λε[ί]ο[υς]. prop. Pf.   5 suppl. Pf.   6 suppl. Pf.
7 suppl. L.

^a Castor and Polydeuces were sons of Zeus, according to

AETIA

12

. . . they (reached the island) [a] of the Phaeacians
. . . leading a swarm . . . (he) built a Corcyrean
5 settlement ; cast out again from there they founded
Amantine in the land of Oricus.[b] And these things
were to be fulfilled thus long after . . .

[a] Corcyra.
[b] Oricus, a seaport town of Illyria Graeca, opposite Cor-
cyra, now Ericho.

15

. . . the double Phaeacian (harbour).[a]

Alcinoüs and that of Hyllus. According to Ap. Rh. iv.
1125 the Argonauts came to the harbour of Hyllus.

18

. . . the Tyndaridae [a] . . . they first supplicated
Zeus . . . and they asked the other Immortals to
5 aid the ship of the well-built keel.[b] But the son of
Aeson,[c] grieving at heart, was lifting his hands to
you, Ieios,[d] and was promising to send many gifts to
Delphi and many to Delos,[e] if you would drive away
from the ship the misty cloud . . . that obeying
10 your oracle, Phoebus, they loosened the hawsers and

Hom. Hymn. 33. 1 : here, and in Hesiod, they are the sons
of Tyndareus and Leda. They were considered saviours of
sailors in peril.   [b] The *Argo.*
[c] Jason, the leader of the expedition.
[d] Epithet of Apollo derived from the invocation, *ἰή* or
ἰὴ παιών.
[e] " The Quail-island."

10   πείσματ᾿] ἔλυσαν ἐκληρώσαντό τ᾿ ἐρετμά
        ] πικρὸν ἔκοψαν ὕδωρ·
        ] ἐπώνυμον Ἐμβασίοιο
        ]εν .. Παγασαῖς

10 suppl. Pf.

ᵃ The Argonauts are said to have set out in obedience to

19

Μελαντείους δ᾿ ἐπὶ πέτρας

ᵃ The Melantean Rocks were near the island of Thera.
They were named after Melas, the founder of Naxos, who

20

ἐτμήγη δὲ κύφελλα

21

τόφρα δ᾿ ἀνιήσουσα λόφον βοὸς ἔγρετο Τιτώ
    Λαομεδοντείῳ] παιδὶ χροΐσσαμ[ένη
5   ] μετὰ δμωῇσι [
        ] ξείνιον Ἀλκινο[ο
  δ[   ] Φαιηκίδας, αἵ ῥα τ[
  τερπ .... υ .. ισ .. τινος ἡδομέναις

4 init. e.g. suppl. Pf., fin. suppl. L.   6 suppl. L.
7 δ[ώδεκα Μηδείη] e.g. prop. L.

ᵃ Eos, Dawn, who at night slept in the arms of Tithonus,
son of Laomedon.
ᵇ Ap. Rh. iv. 1219 f. tells us that King Alcinoüs and
Queen Arete of the Phaeacians gave many gifts to the
Argonauts, and among them twelve Phaeacian maidservants
for Medea. (According to Apollod. i. 9. 26. 2 they were a

18

allotted the oars [a] . . . they beat the bitter water
. . . (an altar) named after Apollo the Embarker
. . . in Pagasae . . .

an oracle of Apollo. An altar was set up to " Apollo the
Embarker " at Pagasae in Thessaly, the place where they
embarked.

19

. . . on the rocks of Melas.[a]

was shipwrecked there. *Cf.* Ap. Rh. iv. 1706 ff., who
describes Apollo in this episode as " swift to hear " the
prayers of the Argonauts, and coming " down from heaven
to the Melantean Rocks, which lie there in the (Cretan) sea."

20

. . . and the clouds were torn asunder.

21

But when Tito,[a] having slept with the son (of Lao-
medon), arose to set a chafing yoke on the neck of
5 the ox . . . (men ?) among the slave women [b] . . .
gift of (the wife of) Alcinoüs . . . (and) the Phaeacian
maids . . . amused . . . mocking . . . had hidden

gift of the queen to Medea, so the text may be here " the
wife of Alcinoüs.") These could not withhold their laughter
during the sacrifice at Anaphe, and " the heroes . . .
attacked them with taunting words, and merry railing and
contention flung to and fro were kindled among them. And
from that sport of the heroes such scoffs do the women fling
at the men in that island, whenever they propitiate with
sacrifices Apollo the gleaming god, the warder of Anaphe "
(Ap. Rh. iv. 1722 f.).

χλεύ .. δει .... ος ἀπεκρύψαντο λα[
10 νήστ[ι]ες ἐν Δηοῦς ἤμασι 'Ραριάδος

10 dub. suppl. L.

---

[a] The text is obscure but it appears that Callimachus is
comparing the rite of Anaphe with a similar unknown rite

22–23

(SACRIFICIUM LINDIUM)

22

τέμνοντα σπορίμην αὔλακα γειομόρον

[a] The outline of the story is that Heracles came upon a
ploughing Lindian peasant, and asked him for food ; when
the man refused Heracles took one of his oxen, killed it and
feasted on it, while the owner stood helplessly by cursing
him. The name of the Rhodian peasant is not known, but
in some of our sources the story of Thiodamas (frs. 24-25)

23

ἀστέρα, ναὶ κεραῶν ῥῆξιν ἄριστε βοῶν."
ὣς ὁ μὲν ἔνθ' ἠρᾶτο, σὺ δ' ὡς ἁλὸς ἦχον ἀκούει
Σελλὸς ἐνὶ Τμαρίοις οὔρεσιν 'Ικαρίης,
ἠιθέων ὡς μάχλα φιλήτορος ὦτα πενιχροῦ,
5 ὡς ἄδικοι πατέρων υἱέες, ὡς σὺ λύρης

---

[a] Possibly a description of the fine bull slain. Cf. Theocr.
xxv. 138 f.

10 . . . fasting on the sacred days of the Rarian De-
meter ^{a} . . .

in which χλευασμός appeared in the cult of Demeter. Demeter
was called Rarias from the field of Rarus, near Eleusis,
where tillage was " first " practised, and which was sacred
to Demeter.

22–23

(THE SACRIFICE AT LINDUS)

22

. . . a farmer cutting the seed furrow.^{a}

has been confused with that of the Lindian sacrifice, and
Thiodamas is quoted as the man whose ox Heracles killed in
Lindus. The citizens of Lindus are said to have sacrificed
to Heracles ever after with blasphemous words. The
" Lindian sacrifice " (according to others " The Rhodian
sacrifice ") became proverbial in the Greek world, and was
applied to those who sacrificed blasphemously to the gods.
E. A. Barber suggests that fr. 530 probably belongs to this
aetion.

23

. . . the star,^{a} yes, o greatest tearer of horned
oxen." Thus he was cursing there. But you as the
Selloi ^{b} on the mountain of Tmarus ^{c} hear the sound
of the Icarian Sea,^{d} or as the wanton ears of youths
5 hear a needy lover, or as unjust sons their fathers, or

^{b} Ancient inhabitants of Dodona, guardians of the oracle
of Zeus.
^{c} A mountain in Epirus near the sanctuary of Dodona.
^{d} The part of the Aegean Sea named after Icarus, son of
Daedalus, who on his flight from Crete was drowned there.

CALLIMACHUS

—ἐσσὶ] γὰρ οὐ μάλ' ἐλαφρός, ἃ καὶ λι . ος ουσε-
χελέξ . . —,
λυ]γρῶν ὧς ἐπέων οὐδὲν [ὀπιζόμ[εν]ος

. . . .

χαῖρε βαρυσκίπων, ἐπίτακτα μὲν ἑξάκι δοιά,
20 ἐκ δ' αὐταγρεσίης πολλάκι πολλὰ καμών.—

6 suppl. Pf., et totum versum parenthesin esse coni.:
Δ[ίν]ος οὔ σ' ἔχε λέξ[αι prop. Wil.   7 suppl. Wil.

24–25

(THIODAMAS DRYOPS)

24

σκῶλος ἐπεί μιν ἔτυψε ποδὸς θέναρ· αὐτὰρ ὁ πείνῃ
θυμαίνων λάχνην στήθεος εἷλκε σέθεν
δραξάμενος· τὶν δ' ὦνα γέλως ἀνεμίσγετο λύπῃ,
εἰσόκε τοι τρίπολον νειὸν ἀνερχομένῳ
5 ὠμογέρων ἔτι πουλὺς ἀνὴρ ἀβόλησε βοωτέων
Θειοδάμας· δεκάπουν δ' εἶχεν ἄκαιναν ὅγε,
ἀμφότερον κέντρον τε βοῶν καὶ μέτρον ἀρούρης·
. . . . . .]ου ξείνων χαῖρε [. . . . . .]μενων
. . . . .]η μέγ' ἀρητὲ προσ[. . . . . .]ς, αἶψα δ', ἄν-
ωγα,
10 εἴ τι κα]τωμαδίης οὐλάδ[ος ἐστὶ]ν ἔσω
τόσσο]ν ὅσον τ' ἀπὸ πα[ιδὶ κακὴν β]ούπειναν ἐ-
λά[σσαι,
ἔξελε]· καὶ φιλίης [μνήσομ' ἀεὶ δό]σιος.''

8 [συναντο]μένων prop. Wil.   9 οὗτος δ]ῆ suppl. Wil.
10-11 suppl. Wil.   12 ἔξελε suppl. Maas : οἶσον Wil.,
cetera suppl. Castiglioni.

22

as you hear the lyre—for you are not at all mild [a]
. . . thus taking no heed of the baneful words . . .
" Hail, armed with your heavy club, who performed
20 by command labours six times two,[b] and often many
of your own free choice."

[a] Linus, who instructed young Heracles in music, is said
to have been struck by his pupil with a lyre and killed.
[b] The twelve labours performed by Heracles at the com-
mand of Eurystheus. Lines 19-20 may well be part of a
prayer by a Lindian priest, in which Heracles is addressed.

24–25

(THIODAMAS THE DRYOPIAN)

24

. . . since a thorn had pricked him in the sole of his
foot.[a] But he,[b] raging with hunger, grasped your
chest and was pulling at the hair. And your laughter,
5 Sire, was mixed with sorrow, until sprightly old Thio-
damas, still a mighty man, while ploughing met you
crossing the thrice-turned fallow. He held a ten-foot
pole, both a goad for the oxen and a measure for the
land . . . " good day, of friends . . . greatly prayed
10 for . . . and at once, I bid you, if there is anything
in the bag hung from your shoulder just enough to
drive away great hunger from the child, bring it out ;
and I will always remember your friendly gift." But

[a] Heracles, on passing through the land of the Dryopes,
and being in want of food for his young son Hyllus, unyoked
and killed one of the oxen of King Thiodamas, whom he
found at the plough. War ensued, the Dryopes were de-
feated, and Hylas, son of Thiodamas, taken as hostage.
Hence Heracles got the epithet Bouthoinas, Feaster on oxen
(cf. Call. Hymn iii. 161).   [b] Hyllus, the son of Heracles.

CALLIMACHUS

αὐτὰρ ὅ]γ' ἀγρεῖον [καὶ ἀμείλιχον ἐξ]εγέλασσε

. . . .

17 οἵ κεν βρωσείοντες ἐμὸν παρίωσιν ἄροτρον
]ων
Λέπαργε

. . . .

20 ἔκλυε ⟨—⟩, τῶν μηδὲν ἐμοὺς δι' ὀδόντας ὀλίσθοι,
Πηλεύς

13 suppl. Wil.   20 ⟨καὶ⟩ add. Wil.: τοι Bentley, qui
scr. ὀλισθῇ: δὴ Meineke: τῶν ⟨οὐ⟩ μηδὲν—ὀλίσθη Porson.

25

δειλαίοις Ἀσινεῦσιν ἔπι τριπτῆρα πιάσσας

τριπτῆρος ἁπάσας vel τριπτῆρες ἁρπάσας codd.: τριπτῆρα
πιάσσας Barber.

---

[a] After the Dryopes were defeated they were forced to
establish themselves in the Peloponnese. They were then

26-28

(LINUS ET COROEBUS)

---

[a] According to the version of the myth we know, Psamathe,
daughter of Crotopus, king of Argos, became mother of
Linus by Apollo. In fear of her father she gave the child
away, and a shepherd reared it as his own boy. Linus was
killed by the king's dogs, and, when the secret of his birth
was known to Crotopus, he condemned his daughter to death.
In anger Apollo sent a plague upon Argos. When the

24

AETIA

17 he laughed in a coarse and callous way . . . whoever
go hungry past my plough . . . Lepargus [a] . . .
Peleus heard [b] . . . of which may none slip through
my teeth . . .

   [a] The name of the ox killed.
   [b] Peleus and Telamon, sons of Aeacus and Endeis, slew
their half-brother Phocus, son of Aeacus and Psamathe.
Peleus " heard things said about him," because the women
reproached him with the death of Phocus. Callimachus
seems here to have in mind Pind. *Nem.* v. 14 f. According
to the Schol. there was also a version that Peleus killed his
wife Antigone. The cries of Thiodamas against Heracles
seem to be compared with those of the women crying out
against Peleus. Ovid, *Met.* xi. 269, tells us that Peleus, guilty
of his brother's blood, went to Trachis (the fatherland of
Thiodamas).

25

. . . when he had pressed down the pestle upon the
wretched men of Asine.[a] [b]

called ἀσινεῖς = not harmful ; previously they had been con-
sidered destructive for plundering the land about Delphi.
We do not know what Callimachus means by the pestle.
   [b] Frs. 508, 528 A*, 705 and 784 may belong to this part of
the *Aetia*.

26–28

(LINUS AND COROEBUS) [a]

Argives consulted the Delphic oracle, they were told that
they must propitiate Psamathe and Linus. This they did,
and in addition to other honours women and maidens
lamented Psamathe and Linus, which gave rise to the Linus
song. They also named a month Lamb-month ('Aρνεῖος),
because Linus had been reared with the lambs, and held
a sacrifice and a Lamb-festival (ἑορτὴ ἀρνίς), on which day

25

they killed any dogs that they found.   As the plague did not cease, Crotopus, in accordance with an oracle, left Argos and founded a city in the Megarid which he called Tripodis-

26

.   .   .   .

   'Αρνεῖος μ[
'Αρνῆδας [
   καὶ θάνε [
τοῦ μενα[
5 καὶ τὸν ἐπὶ ῥάβδῳ μῦθον ὑφαινόμενον
ἀνέρες ε[
   πλαγκτὺν [
ἠνεκὲς ἀείδω δειδεγμένος
ουδεμενα[
10 νύμφης αι[
   παιδοφόνῳ [
ἦκεν ἐπ' 'Αρ[γείους
   ἤ σφεων [
μητέρας ἐξεκένωσεν, ἐκούφισθεν δὲ τιθῆναι
15 οὐχ οὕτω [
"Αργος ἀνα[

27

ἄρνες τοι, φίλε κοῦρε, συνήλικες, ἄρνες ἑταῖροι
   ἔσκον, ἐνιαυθμοὶ δ' αὐλία καὶ βοτάναι
26

AETIA

con and dwelt there. (*Cf.* frs. 26-31a *Diegesis*, ll. 18 f., Pfeiff.
ii, p. 108) The source of Callimachus was, as in frs. 3–7. 14,
Agias and Dercylos.

26

5 ARNEUS [a] . . . of the lambs [b] and died . . . and the
rhapsody woven . . . men . . . wandering . . . I
10 received and sing continuously . . . of the nymph [c]
. . . child-killer [d] . . . sent against the Argives [e] . . .
which . . . their . . . left the mothers with empty
hands, and their nurses were lightened from their
15 burden . . . not thus . . . Argos . . .

[a] The month of the Argives named after Linus.
[b] The days in which they held the Lamb-festival and
killed any dogs that they found or, according to certain
sources, any dog which approached the market.
[c] Psamathe.
[d] Probably Crotopus.
[e] Apollo sent Poine to punish the Argives. She carried
away the children from their mothers, until she was slain by
Coroebus.

---

5 ῥάβδων cod. v.l.   9 οὐδ' ἔμενα[ι vel οὐδὲ μὲν α[ut
v. 4 prop. Hu.   12 suppl. Wil. et Koerte.   14 ἐξε-
κένωσαν, ἐκούφισσαν (vel ἐκουφίσθησαν) δὲ τιθήνας codd. corr.
Bergk et Bernhardy.

27

LAMBS, sweet boy, were your playmates, lambs your
companions ; your sleeping-place the folds and the
pastures . . .

27

CALLIMACHUS

28

τόν σε Κροτωπιάδην

31 B

(DIANA LEUCADIA)

Τὼ]ς μὲν ἔφη· τὰς δ' εἶθαρ ἐμὸς πάλιν εἴρετο θυμός

suppl. L., at ὼ]ς excludi nequit.

---

a One of the Muses, as, *e.g.*, it was Calliope who spoke in fr. 7. 22, or Clio in frs. 4 f. and fr. 43. 56.

b The Muses.

c We now know what this aetion was about, from part of the *Diegesis* found in *P. Oxy.* 2263, which runs : " The wooden statue of Artemis in Leucas has a mortar on its head for the following reason. Inhabitants of Epirus . . . harassing . . . plundered Leucas. When they came to the sanctuary of Artemis they found the goddess crowned with a golden crown. In mockery they removed it, and put on (the head of) the goddess the mortar in which they had pounded garlic which they had eaten. . . . The Leucadians (a day

(Post fabulam *Dianae Leucadiae* neque fabularum neque fragmentorum ordo in lib. I constat.)

33

τετράενον Δαμάσου παῖδα Τελεστορίδην

37

οἵη τε Τρίτωνος ἐφ' ὕδασιν Ἀσβύσταο
Ἡφαίστου λόχιον θηξ[α]μένου πέλεκυν

2 suppl. Pf.

AETIA

28

. . . you, the descendant of Crotopus.[a]

    [a] Linus, the grandson of Crotopus.

31 B

(DIANA OF LEUCAS)

THUS she [a] spoke ; and straightway my heart asked them [b] again.[c]

later) made another crown, and put it on (the statue) instead of the mortar, and when it fell off they nailed it on to the wooden statue. Then again three days later the crown which was placed . . . " This story is otherwise unknown. But as E. Lobel suggests (*The Ox. Pap.* xx, p. 129) the Leucadians probably kept putting the crown back, but it would not stay there, so they consulted an oracle (*cf.* fr. 31 c* 5, Pfeiff. ii, p. 109) and were told to perpetuate the mortar.

(After fragment 31 B the sequence of the fragments attributed to the first book of the *Aetia* is unknown.)

33

TELESTORIDES, the four-year-old son of Damasus [a] . . .

    [a] The fragment is obscure. A child is a βρέφος up to the fourth year, when its first hair was dedicated.

37

. . . in such guise as, when Hephaestus had sharpened his axe to deliver you, you jumped in armour from

CALLIMACHUS

βρέγμ[α]το[ς] ἐκ δίοιο σὺν ἔντ[ε]σιν ἧλαο πατρός

3 suppl. L. : πατρός P, Παλλάς Maas.

---

[a] Athene is said to have been born from the head of Zeus, which Hephaestus opened by a blow of his axe. Ἀσβύστης is used by Callimachus to describe the boundaries of Cyrene (cf. fr. 384. 6 and Hymn ii. 76 with schol.), hence I translate " Libyan." Triton may here be either the god

41

γηράσκει δ᾽ ὁ γέρων κεῖνος ἐλαφρότερον,
κοῦροι τὸν φιλέουσιν, ἑὸν δέ μιν οἷα γονῆα
χειρὸς ἐπ᾽ οἰκείην ἄχρις ἄγουσι θύρην

2 νέοι δέ μιν οἷα τοκῆα, vel ἑὸν δέ μοι οἷα γονῆα codd. v.ll.

the divine head of your father by the waves of the Libyan Triton . . . [a]

of the Libyan lake Tritonis, or the Libyan river which joins the lake Tritonis with the sea. Ap. Rh. iv. 1309-1311, in imitation of Callimachus, describes Athene as washed after her birth by the Libyan nymphs in the waters of the Cyrenean Triton.

41

. . . that old man ages with a lighter heart, whom young boys love, and whom they lead up to his door by the hand like their own parent.[a]

[a] Cf. Tibull. i. 4. 79 f. Fr. 571 may belong to this part of the *Aetia*.

[ΑΙΤΙΩΝ Β′]

(De ordine fragmentorum huius libri non constat.)

43

(DE SICILIAE URBIBUS) (ll. 12–83)

. . . .

καὶ γὰρ ἐγὼ τὰ μὲν ὅσσα καρήατι τῆμος ἔδωκα
ξανθὰ σὺν εὐόδμοις ἁβρὰ λίπη στεφάνοις,
ἄπνοα πάντ' ἐγένοντο παρὰ χρέος, ὅσσα τ' ὀδόντων
15 ἔνδοθι νείαιράν τ' εἰς ἀχάριστον ἔδυ,
καὶ τῶν οὐδὲν ἔμεινεν ἐς αὔριον· ὅσσα δ' ἀκουαῖς
εἰσεθέμην, ἔτι μοι μοῦνα πάρεστι τάδε.—

. . . .

40   φθιν]οπωρίδες Ὧραι
†μὴ διὰ πεμφίγων ⟨αἰ⟩ὲν ἄγουσι νέα.
φήσω καὶ Καμάριναν ἵν' Ἵππαρις ἀγκύλος ἕρπει

. . . .

οἶδα Γέλα ποταμοῦ κεφαλῇ ἔπι κείμενον ἄστυ
Λίνδοθεν ἀρχαίη [σ]κιμπ[τόμενο]ν γενε[ῇ,

14 παρὰ χρέος pap. ut voluerat Naeke: παραχρῆμ' codd.
32

AETIA : BOOK II

(The sequence of the fragments in this book
is unknown.)

43

(ON THE SICILIAN CITIES)

12 . . . for certainly all the soft amber ointments and
the fragrant garlands I then put on my head swiftly
breathed no more, and of all that passed my teeth
and plunged into the ungrateful belly nothing re-
mained till the morrow; but the only things which
I still keep are those that I laid in my ears.

. . . .

40 . . . the Autumn season . . . I shall also tell of
Camarina,[a] where winding Hipparis crawls . . .

. . . .

46 I know of the city lying at the mouth of the river
Gelas, boasting its ancient descent from Lindus,[b]

[a] Camarina, a Dorian colony (founded in 599 B.C.) in
southern Sicily near modern Scoglitti.
[b] Gela, a Dorian colony in southern Sicily, founded by
Cretans and Rhodians (in 690 B.C.).

---

16 ἀκουὰς codd. : -αῖς Bentley.   40 suppl. Maas.   47-49
suppl. Hu.

CALLIMACHUS

Μινῴην καὶ Κρῆσσαν, ἵ[να ζείον]τα λοετ[ρά
χεῦαν ἐπ' Εὐρώπης υἱέϊ Κ[ωκαλί]δες·
50 οἶδα Λεοντίνους . δεδρα[
 καὶ Μεγαρεῖς ἕτερ[οι] τρὺς ἀ[πέ]νασσαν ἐκεῖ
Νισαῖοι Μεγαρῆες, ἔχω δ' Εὔβοιαν ἐνισπεῖν
 φίλατο κα[ὶ] κεστ[ο]ῦ [δ]εσπότ[ι]ς ἦν Ἔρυκα·
τάων οὐδεμιῇ γὰ[ρ ὅτ]ις πο[τὲ] τεῖχος ἔδειμε
55 νωνυμνὶ νομίμην ἔρχετ' ἐπ' εἰλαπίνην.''
 ὣς ἐφάμην· Κλειὼ δὲ τὸ [δ]εύτερον ἦρχετο μ]ύθ[ου
χεῖρ' ἐπ' ἀδελφειῆς ὦμον ἐρεισαμένη·
 '' λαὸς ὁ μὲν Κύμης ὁ δὲ Χαλκίδος, ὃν Περιήρης
ἤγαγε καὶ μεγάλου λῆμα Κραταιμένεος,
60 Τρινακρίης ἐπέβησαν, ἐτείχιζον δὲ πόληα
 ἅρπασον οἰωνῶν οὐχὶ φυλα[σσόμενοι
ἔχθιστον κτίστῃσιν, ἐρῳδιὸ[ς εἰ μὴ ἐφέ]ρπει·
 καὶ γὰρ ὁ βασκαίνει πύργον ἐ[γειρόμεν]ον,
γεωδαῖται καὶ σπάρτα διηνεκὲς εὖτε βάλωνται,
65 στείνεα καὶ λευρὰς ὄφρα τάμ[ωσιν ὁ]δούς.
 μέρμν[ο]υ μοι πτερύγεσσι [. . . . .]ου τε
  νέοιο,
 εἴ κοτετιξ[. . .]ην λαὸν ἔποικον ἄ[γοις.

51 suppl. Pf. 53-54 suppl. Hu. 61-62 suppl.
Hu.   63 suppl. Housman.   65 suppl. Hu.

and Cretan Minoa,[a] where the daughters of Cocalus
poured upon the son of Europa boiling water for his
50 bath.[b] I know of Leontini [c] . . . and the Megarians
sent out there by the other Megarians, those of
Nisa [d] ; and I can speak of Euboea [e] and Eryx, be-
loved by the mistress of the charmed girdle.[f] No one
whoever once built a wall for any of these cities comes
55 to its customary feast without being named." So I
said. And Clio went on to speak yet again, resting her
arm upon her sister's shoulder : " The people whom
Perieres and the great and arrogant Crataemenes
led came in part from Cyme and in part from Chalcis ;
60 they landed in Sicily and were building the walls of
a city without guarding themselves against the
harpasos,[g] which is the most hostile of birds for
builders if not followed by a heron ; for it has an
evil influence on a rising tower and on the measuring
65 cord, as the surveyors stretch it out to lay a narrow
alley and a flat street. . . . may you go . . . the wings
of a hawk . . . if you ever lead a people to a colony (in

[a] City on the south coast of Sicily, near Selinus.
[b] Minos pursued Daedalus to Sicily, where he found him
in the house of Cocalus, king of Camicus. He demanded
the surrender of Daedalus ; Cocalus, pretending to agree,
received Minos with a show of hospitality, and handed him
over to his daughters to be bathed in the Homeric fashion.
They killed him by pouring boiling water over him.
[c] Leontini, a colony of Naxos (founded *c.* 729 B.C.).
[d] Hyblaea Megara, near Syracuse, was founded by the
Nisean Megarians of the Greek mainland.
[e] Sicilian city near Syracuse.
[f] Aphrodite, patron of the city of Eryx.
[g] An unknown bird of prey.

66 πτερύγεσσι[ν ὑπ’ αἰγυπι]οῦ τε vel μετ’ ἰκτείν]ου τε suppl.
Housman : ἐπ’ αἰγυπι]οῦ Körte : ἐν αἰγυπι]οῦ Ehlers.   67
suppl. Housman : κοτ’ ἐ⟨π⟩ὶ ξ[ε]ῳην coni. Hu.

ἀλλ' ὅτε δὴ μόσσυνας ἐπάλξεσι [καρτυνθέ]ντας
οἱ κτίσται δρέπανον θέντο πε[ρὶ Κρόνιο]ν,
70 —κεῖθι γὰρ ᾧ τὰ γονῆος ἀπέθρισε μήδε' ἐκεῖνος
κέκρυπται γύπῃ ζάγκλον ὑπὸ χθονίῃ,—
ε[.]τισαν ἀμφὶ πόληος· ὁ μὲν θε[. . . . .]ε-
σθαι
. . . . .]ν, ὁ δ' ἀντίξουν εἶχε διχο[φροσύνην,
ἀλλήλοις δ' ἐλύησαν· ἐς Ἀπόλ[λωνα δ' ἰόν]τες
75 εἴρονθ' ὁπποτέρου κτίσμα λέγοιτ[ο νέον.
αὐτὰρ ὁ φῆ, μήτ' οὖν Περιήρεος ἄ[στυ]ρ[ον εἶ]ναι
κεῖνο πολισσούχου μήτε Κραταιμέ[νεος.
φῆ θεός· οἱ δ' ἀΐοντες ἀπέδραμον, ἐ̣[κ δ' ἔτι κεί]νου
γαῖα τὸν οἰκιστὴν οὐκ ὀνομαστὶ κ[αλε]ῖ,
80 ὧδε δέ μιν καλέουσιν ἐπ' ἔντομα δημιοεργοί·
" ἵλαος ἡμετέρην ὅστις ἔδειμε πόλιν
ἐρχέσθω μετὰ δαῖτα, πάρεστι δὲ καὶ δύ' ἄγεσθαι
καὶ πλέας· οὐκ ὀλ[ί]γως α̣[ἶ]μα βοὸς κέχυ[τ]αι."
ὣς ἡ μὲν λίπε μῦθον, ἐγὼ δ' ἐπὶ καὶ [τὸ πυ]θέσθαι
85 ἤθελον—ἦ γάρ μοι θάμβος ὑπετρέφετο—,
Κισσούσης παρ' ὕδωρ Θεοδαίσια Κρῆ[σσαν ἑ]ορτήν
ἡ πόλις ἡ Κάδμου κῶς Ἁλίαρτος ἄγει
καὶ στυρὸν ἐν μούνοισι πολίσμασι [. . . . .]δι[.]ο-
τωριϲ
καὶ Μίνω μεγάλοις ἄγγεσι γαῖα φ[ορεῖ,

68 e.g. suppl. Hu.   69 suppl. Hu.   72 ε[ἴ]τ'
ἴσαν Hu. : ἤρισαν L. : θέ[λεν οὔνομα θ]έσθαι Hu. : θέ[λεν ἄστυ
λέγ]εσθαι Ehlers : Kalinka.   73 τὸ σφὸ]ν Hu. : διχο[φροσύνην
vel [-στασίην suppl. Hu.   74 suppl. Hu. : δὲ βάν]τες Pf.
75 suppl. Hu.   76 ἄ[στυ] ῥ[εθῆ]ναι vel ἄ[στυ]ρ[ον εἶ]ναι
Hu.   77 suppl. Hu.   78 ἐ̣[κ δ' ἄρα κεί]νου Hu. : ἔτι Pf.
79 suppl. Hu.   83 ὀλ[ί]χῃς Hu. qui cetera suppl. : ὀλ[ί]-
36

a foreign land).   But when the builders made strong
the wooden towers with battlements, and placed them
70 around the sickle of Cronus *a*—for there in a cave is
hidden under the earth the sickle with which he cut
off his father's genitals—they quarrelled (?) about the
city.   The one wished (?) . . . and the other in op-
position disagreed.   They quarrelled with each other.
75 And they went to Apollo and asked to whom the new
foundation should belong.   And he said that the
town should have neither Perieres nor Crataemenes
as patron.   The god spoke, they heard and left ;
from then to this day the country does not invoke its
80 founder by name.   And the magistrates invite him
thus to the sacrifice : ' May he, whoever it was who
built our city, be gracious, and come to the feast :
he may bring two and more.   No little blood of an
ox has been spilt.' ''   So she stopped talking : and I
85 wanted to know this too—for my secret wonder grew :
'' Why does Haliartus,*b* the Cadmean city, celebrate
the *Theodaesia*, a Cretan festival, by the waters of
Cissousa ? *c*   And only in the cities incense . . . and
the land of Minos *d* brings it in great vessels . . . the

---

a The city of Zancle, founded *c.* 725 B.C. in north-east
Sicily, later renamed Messene. Zancle means sickle, and it
was said that Cronus hid there the sickle with which he had
cut off his father's genitals. The sickle-shape of the bay,
on which the city was built, is thought to have given rise to
the name Zancle.   *b* City of Boeotia.
   c Fountain in Boeotia, where the nymphs are said to have
washed Dionysus at his birth. The *Theodaesia* was a Cretan
festival in honour of Dionysus.
   d This may refer either to the whole of Crete, or to Cnossus
only.

γως Pf.   84 καὶ [τὸ vel καὶ [τι suppl. Hu.   86 suppl.
Hu.   89 suppl. Hu.

CALLIMACHUS

90 . .]ωθεδετι κρήνη ʽΡαδαμάνθυο[s . . . .]τ[. . .]ν
ἴχνια τῆς κείνου λοιπὰ νομογραφίης
. . . .]αμον· ἐν δέ νυ τοῖσι σοφὸν τόδε τηι[

90 Κλ]ῶθε Pf.

---

^a According to one tradition Rhadamanthys, son of Zeus,

44-47

(BUSIRIS—PHALARIS)

44

Αἴγυπτος προπάροιθεν ἐπ' ἐννέα κάρφετο ποίας

---

^a Busiris, an Egyptian king, slaughtered on the altar of
Zeus the foreigners who came to Egypt ; he is said to have
done so at the suggestion of the Cypriot seer Phrasios, who

45

τὴν κείνου Φάλαρις πρῆξιν ἀπεπλάσατο

κεινος φάληρον : κείνου φάλαρος : φάληρος codd. : corr.
Bentley. τάξιν v.l.

---

^a Phalaris, tyrant of Acragas (570–554 B.C.) was notorious
for his cruelty, especially for the hollow brazen bull in which

46

**πρῶτος ἐπεὶ τὸν ταῦρον ἐκαίνισεν, ὃς τὸν ὄλεθρον
εὖρε τὸν ἐν χαλκῷ καὶ πυρὶ γιγνόμενον**

38

90 fountain of Rhadamanthys *a* . . . remaining traces of his legislation *b* . . .''

had left Crete, and came to live with Alcmene in Boeotia, after the death of Amphitryon.

b Rhadamanthys was proverbial for his justice and one of the judges of the dead.

44–47

(BUSIRIS—PHALARIS)

44

EGYPT was dry for nine years formerly.*a*

foretold that the nine-year sterility of the Egyptian soil would cease, if a foreigner was sacrificed every year at the altar of Zeus. Phrasios was the first to be sacrificed by the king. Heracles is reputed to have killed Busiris.

45

PHALARIS followed his example.*a*

his victims were confined and roasted alive. The example he followed was that of the Egyptian king, Busiris. (See note to fr. 46.)

46

. . . because it was he that devised the death through bronze and fire, who first handselled the bull.*a*

a Perillos, who constructed the bronze bull, was the first person whom Phalaris had thrown into it. (See fr. 45, n. *a*.)

39

CALLIMACHUS

48

ὥς τε Ζεὺς ἐράτιζε τριηκοσίους ἐνιαυτούς

---

[a] In the reign of Cronus, Zeus is said to have made secret

49

Τάμμεω θυγατέρος

---

[a] There were three daughters of Tammes or Athamas, the Boeotian, or, according to other sources, Thessalian hero : Helle, Themisto and Euryclea. It is not known about

51

οὕνεκεν οἰκτείρειν οἶδε μόνη πολίων

48

. . . and how Zeus loved passionately for three hundred years.[a]

love to Hera for three hundred years. Hephaestus was the child of that union.

49

. . . (of) the daughter of Tammes.[a]

which of them Callimachus is speaking here. The poet may also be referring to Area, daughter of Athamas, the founder of Teos.

51

. . . since she is the only town which knows how to pity.[a]

[a] The reference is to Athens, often celebrated in Greek poetry for her humanity and hospitality.

[ΑΙΤΙΩΝ Γ′]

Ordo fabularum in posteriore huius libri parte narratarum (fr. 64–85) certus est ; cetera libri tertii fragmenta quae illis fabulis assignari nequeunt (fr. 55–59) ante illam seriem continuam collocavi.

55–59

(MOLORCHUS)

55

τὸν μὲν ἀρισκυδὴς εὖνις ἀνῆκε Διός
Ἄργος ἔθειν, ἴδιόν περ ἐὸν λάχος, ἀλλὰ γενέθλη
Ζηνὸς ὅπως σκοτίη τρηχὺς ἄεθλος ἔοι

---

[a] The lion of Nemea.
[b] Argos was sacred to Hera.
[c] Heracles was the son of Zeus and Alcmene. While on his way to kill the lion of Nemea, Heracles, we are told, came to Cleonae. There he was the guest of a poor man named Molorchus who, when about to sacrifice to the gods, was asked by the hero to put it off for thirty days : if by

57

αὐτὸς ἐπιφράσσαιτο, τάμοι δ᾽ ἄπο μῆκος ἀοιδῇ·
ὅσσα δ᾽ ἀνειρομένῳ φῆσε, τάδ᾽ ἐξερέω·

AETIA : BOOK III

(The sequence of the fragments in Book III is
unknown until fr. 63.)

55–59

(MOLORCHUS)

55

THE quick-tempered consort of Zeus unloosed him [a]
to ruin Argos, though her allotted portion,[b] and as a
hard labour to the unlawful offspring of Zeus.[c]

then Heracles did not return Molorchus was told to sacrifice
in his honour ; if on the other hand he did return the sacrifice
was to be in honour of Zeus the Saviour. Heracles came
back victorious upon the thirtieth day, and found Molorchus
preparing the sacrifice, which was then held in honour of
Zeus the Saviour. Heracles left Cleonae, and brought the
lion's body to Mycenae.

57

HE may suggest to himself,[a] and cut short the
song's length. But I will relate all he (*sc.* Heracles)
answered to the questions (of Molorchus) : " Father,

[a] Probably the reader of the poem.

" ἄττα γέρον, τὰ μὲν ἄλλα πα[ρὼν ἐν δ]αιτὶ μα-
θήσει,
νῦν δὲ τά μοι πεύσῃ Παλλὰ[ς   "

3 suppl. Wil.   4 Παλλὰ[ς ἔειπε θεή e.g. suppl. Wil.

58

ἄξονται δ' οὐχ ἵππον ἀέθλιον, οὐ μὲν ἐχῖνον
βουδόκον

59

5   καί μιν Ἀλητεῖδαι πουλὺ γεγειότερον
τοῦδε παρ' Αἰγαίωνι θεῷ τελέοντες ἀγῶνα
θήσουσιν νίκης σύμβολον Ἰσθμιάδος
ζήλῳ τῶν Νεμέηθε· πίτυν δ' ἀποτιμήσουσιν,
ἢ πρὶν ἀγωνιστὰς ἔστεφε τοὺς Ἐφύρῃ.
·   ·   ·   ·   ·   ·   ·   ·   ·   ·
νύκτα μὲν αὐτόθι μίμνεν, ἀπέστιχε δ' Ἄργος ἑῷος·
οὐδὲ ξεινοδόκῳ λήσαθ' ὑποσχεσίης,
20 πέμψε δέ οἱ τὸ[ν] ὀρῆα, τίεν δέ ἑ ὡς ἕνα πηῶν·
νῦν δ' ἔθ' [ἁ]γι[στείη]ν οὐδαμὰ παυσομένην

19 ξεινοδόκῳ Wil.: -δόκου P.   20 suppl. L.   δέ μιν ὡς
Maas.   21 e.g. suppl. Pf.

---

[a] The Corinthians, named after Aletes, the founder of
Corinth.

old man, the rest you will learn while present at the
feast, but now you will hear what Pallas (told me ? ") [a]

[a] Heracles is here repeating to Molorchus the prophecy
his protectress, Athene, had told him.

58

. . . and they will take as a prize not a racing horse,
not a cauldron large enough to contain an ox . . .
(but a wreath of celery).[a]

[a] Probably part of the prophecy concerning the Nemean
games, and the prizes awarded to the winners.

59

5 . . . " and the sons of Aletes,[a] holding games much
older than these at the sanctuary of the god Ae-
gaeon,[b] will set it [c] as a token of the Isthmian vic-
tory in rivalry with the Nemean games. And they
will remove from honour the pine-tree, which for-
merly crowned the competitors in the games of
18 Ephyra " [d] . . . he [e] spent there the night, but
walked away to Argos [f] at dawn. Nor did he forget
his promise to his host [g] ; he sent him the mule and
honoured him as one of his kin. And, still now, the
ritual, not about to cease . . .

[b] Posidon. The Isthmian games.
[c] The wreath of celery.
[d] Ancient name of Corinth.
[e] Probably Heracles, spending the night at Cleonae.
[f] Callimachus considered Heracles an " Argive."
[g] Molorchus. Nothing is otherwise known about the gift
of a mule by Heracles to Molorchus. Mules were, however,
a possible gift in return for hospitality. *Cf.* fr. 85. 5.

CALLIMACHUS

64

(SEPULCRUM SIMONIDIS)

Οὐδ' ἄν τοι Καμάρινα τόσον κακὸν ὁκκόσον ἀνδρός
  κινηθεὶς ὁσίου τύμβος ἐπικρεμάσαι·
καὶ γ]ὰρ ἐμόν κοτε σῆμα, τό μοι πρὸ πόληος
  ἔχ[ευ]αν
Ζῆν'] ᾿Ακραγαντῖνοι Ξείνι[ο]ν ἁζόμενοι,
5 ἶφι κ]ατ' οὖν ἤρειψεν ἀνὴρ κακός, εἴ τιν' ἀκούεις
  Φοίνικα πτόλιος σχέτλιον ἡγεμόνα·
πύργῳ δ' ἐγκατέλεξεν ἐμὴν λίθον οὐδὲ τὸ γράμμα
  ἠδέσθη τὸ λέγον τόν με Λεωπρέπεος
κεῖσθαι Κήϊον ἄνδρα τὸν ἱερόν, ὃς τὰ περισσά
10   καὶ] μνήμην πρῶτος ὃς ἐφρασάμην,
οὐδ' ὑμέας, Πολύδευκες, ὑπέτρεσεν, οἵ με μελάθρου
  μέλλοντος πίπτειν ἐκτὸς ἔθεσθέ κοτε
δαιτυμόνων ἄπο μοῦνον, ὅτε Κραννώνιος αἰαῖ
  ὤλισθεν μεγάλους οἶκος ἐπὶ Σκοπάδας.

3 suppl. L.   4 init. suppl. Pf.   5 suppl. Barber.
10 suppl. L., in init. ἤδη (=ἤδεα) καὶ dubitanter Pf.

---

[a] Lake near the city of Camarina in Sicily. An oracle
had advised the citizens " Μὴ κίνει Καμάριναν," " Do not
move lake Camarina," but they drained the lake, and the
city was later captured. In consequence this oracle became
a proverb used about men who do harmful things to them-
selves.
[b] Simonides of Ceos, the great lyric and elegiac poet (c.
556–468 B.C.), is supposed to be speaking here from his tomb.

AETIA

64

(THE TOMB OF SIMONIDES)

NOT even (the draining of) Camarina [a] would threaten
so great an evil as the removal of a pious man's
3 tomb. For once an evil man tore down by force my
tomb, which the citizens of Acragas threw up for
me before their city in awe of Zeus the Hospitable,[b]
Phoenix—you may have heard of him—the wicked
general of the city.[c] And he built my tombstone
into a tower, nor did he reverence the epitaph which
said that I, the son of Leoprepes, the sacred man of
10 Ceos was buried there, who (knew) rare things . . .
(and) was the first to devise a system of memory (?) [d];
nor did he fear you and your brother, Polydeuces,
who once called me alone of the banqueters out of
the hall which was about to fall, when alas! the
palace of Crannon fell upon the great Scopadae.[e]

He died in Sicily, and was buried outside the city of Acragas.

 [c] This war was between Syracuse and Acragas, but the
date is unknown, as well as any details about Phoenix.

 [d] Perhaps a reference to the system of memorizing that
Simonides is said to have invented. *Cf.* also Simon. fr.
78 Diehl[2].

 [e] When Simonides was entertained at a great banquet by
the powerful Scopadae of Crannon in Thessaly, two young
men are said to have stood at the door of the hall and called
him out. No sooner had the poet left the building than it
came crashing to the ground, killing hosts and guests alike.
The two young men were said to be Castor and Polydeuces,
the Dioscuri, who called the poet out in time to save him.

CALLIMACHUS

65–66

(FONTES ARGIVI)

65

Αὐτομά[της] εὐναὲς ἐπών[υμον, ἀλ]λ' ἀπὸ σ[εῖ]ο
λούονται λοχίην οἰκέτιν [. . . . . . .]ης

1 suppl. Vogliano. σ[εῖ]ο suppl. Maas.

 ᵃ Daughter of Danaus, who gave her name to a fountain
of Argos. Water was drawn from that fountain for washing
away the discharge after childbirth. The source of Calli-

66

ἡρῶσσαι [. . .]ιᾶς 'Ιασίδος νέπ[ο]δες·
νύμφα Π[οσ]ειδάωνος ἐφυδριάς, οὐδὲ μὲν "Ηρης
ἁγνὸν ὑφαινέμεναι τῆσι μέμηλε πάτος
στῆναι [πὰ]ρ κανόνεσσι πάρος θέμις ἢ τεὸν ὕδωρ
5 κὰκ κεφαλῆς ἱρὸν πέτρον ἐφεζομένας
χεύασθαι, τὸν μὲν σὺ μέσον περιδέδρομας ἀμφίς·
πότνι' 'Αμυμώνη καὶ Φυσάδεια φίλη
"Ιππη τ' Αὐτομάτη τε, παλαίτατα χαίρετε νυμφέων
οἰκία καὶ λιπαραὶ ῥεῖτε Πελασγιάδες.

1 [βαλ]ιᾶς (=βαλιῆς) Barber: suppl. L.   2 suppl. L.
4 suppl. L.   9 -γιάσιν ? Maas.

 ᵃ Iasis = Io the daughter of Iasus, and grand-daughter of
Argus.

48

AETIA

65–66

(THE FOUNTAINS OF ARGOS)

65

FAIR-FLOWING (water), called after Automate,[a] but from you they draw water for washing a slave who has given birth

machus for frs. 65-66 is probably again Agias and Dercylos (see n. *a* on fr. 3).

66

. . . heroines, children of . . . Io.[a] Nor was it proper, o water-nymph bride of Posidon, that the maidens that were to weave the pure robe of Hera should stand by the weaver's rods, before sitting on
5 the sacred rock about which you flow, and pouring your water over their head.[b] Venerable Amymone, and beloved Physadea and Hippe and Automate,[c] hail, most ancient homes of nymphs ; flow, brilliant Pelasgian [d] maidens.—

   [b] The fountain Amymone is addressed, and its part in the cult of Hera at Argos described.
   [c] Physadea, Hippe and Automate were all fountains of Argos, said to have been discovered by the daughters of Danaus, after whom they were named.
   [d] Pelasgian here means " Argive " maidens. The water of the fountains is called nymphs in true Alexandrian style.

CALLIMACHUS

67–75

(ACONTIUS ET CYDIPPA)

67

Αὐτὸς Ἔρως ἐδίδαξεν Ἀκόντιον, ὁππότε καλῇ
   ἤθετο Κυδίππῃ παῖς ἐπὶ παρθενικῇ,
τέχνην—οὐ γὰρ ὅγ' ἔσκε πολύκροτος—ὄφρα λέγο[
   τοῦτο διὰ ζωῆς οὔνομα κουρίδιον.
5 ἦ γάρ, ἄναξ, ὁ μὲν ἦλθεν Ἰουλίδος ἡ δ' ἀπὸ Νάξου,
   Κύνθιε, τὴν Δήλῳ σὴν ἐπὶ βουφονίην,
αἷμα τὸ μὲν γενεῆς Εὐξαντίδος, ἡ δὲ Προμηθ[ίς,
   καλοὶ νησάων ἀστέρες ἀμφότεροι.
πολλαὶ Κυδίππην ὀλίγην ἔτι μητέρες υἱοῖς
10 ἑδνῆστιν κεράων ᾔτεον ἀντὶ βοῶν·
κείνης ο[ὐ]χ ἑτέρη γὰρ ἐπὶ λασίοιο γέροντος
   Σιληνοῦ νοτίην ἵκετο πιδυλίδα
ἠοῖ εἰδομένη μάλιον ῥέθος οὐδ' Ἀριήδης
   ἐς χ]ορὸν εὐδούσης ἁβρὸν ἔθηκε πόδα·

3 fort. λέγοιτ[ο legi potest.   4 κουρίδιος, si λέγοιτο v.
3, exspectat L.   7 suppl. L.   11 suppl. L.   12 πη-
γυλίδα P : πηδυλίδα vel potius πιδυλίδα Pf.   14 suppl. L.

---

[a] Briefly the story is this. Acontius, a handsome youth
of Ceos, saw Cydippe with her nurse at the yearly festival at
Delos. Falling in love at sight, he followed her to the temple
of Artemis, where he threw in the way of her attendant an
apple inscribed with the words : ".I swear by Artemis to
marry Acontius." The attendant handed the apple to
Cydippe, who read the inscription, and, realizing the oath
by which she was unintentionally binding herself, threw it
50

AETIA

67–75

(ACONTIUS AND CYDIPPE) [a]

67

Eros himself taught Acontius the art, when the youth was ablaze with love for the beautiful maiden Cydippe—for he was not cunning—that he might gain for all his life the name of a lawful husband. For, Lord of Cynthus,[b] he came from Iulis [c] and she from Naxos to your ox-sacrifice in Delos ; his blood was of the family of Euxantius,[d] and she was a descendant of Promethus,[e] both beautiful stars of the islands. Many mothers asked for Cydippe, still a child, as bride for their sons, offering horned oxen as gifts. For no one with a face looking more like dawn came to the moist spring of old hairy Silenus, nor set her delicate foot in dance when Ariede [f] was asleep.

away. The father of Cydippe arranged a different marriage for his daughter ; but always when the time for the marriage arrived, Cydippe was seized by a mysterious illness. Three times this happened, but the fourth time the father went to Delphi to consult Apollo, and learnt that the whole mystery was due to the oath by which his daughter had unwittingly bound herself. By the advice of Apollo, Cydippe's father fulfilled his daughter's vow. *Cf.* Aristaenetus, *Ep.* i. 10, and Ovid, *Heroides* 20 and 21.

   [b] Apollo. Cynthus, the hill in Delos where Apollo was born.
   [c] City of Ceos, birthplace of Simonides and Bacchylides.
   [d] Son of Minos and Dexithea, some of whose children are supposed to have established themselves in Ceos.
   [e] Son of Codrus, the king of Attica ; after killing his brother Damasichthon, he fled to Naxos, where he is supposed to have died.
   [f] Ariadne, the daughter of Minos and Pasiphaë, who followed Theseus to Naxos, and who was honoured there. The spring of Silenus in Naxos is otherwise unknown

68

μέμβλετο δ' εἰσπνήλαις ὁππότε κοῦρος ἴοι
φωλεόν ἠὲ λοετρόν

69

πολλοὶ καὶ φιλέοντες Ἀκοντίῳ ἧκαν ἔραζε
οἰνοπόται Σικελὰς ἐκ κυλίκων λάταγας

1 Ἀκοντίῳ Maas : Ἀκόντιον cod.

---

[a] The reference is to the " cottabos," a game played in a
variety of ways with the last drop of wine in the cup, which

70

ἀλλ' ἀπὸ τόξου
αὐτὸς ὁ τοξευτὴς ἄρδιν ἔχων ἑτέρου

---

[a] The beauty of Acontius had wounded many with the

72

ἄγραδε τῷ πάσῃσιν ἐπὶ προχάνῃσιν ἐφοίτα

---

[a] Acontius was afraid to appear before his father and

73

ἀλλ' ἐνὶ δὴ φλοιοῖσι κεκομμένα τόσσα φέροιτε
γράμματα, Κυδίππην ὅσσ' ἐρέουσι καλήν.

---

[a] Lovers wrote the names of their favourites on trees and

52

68

. . . lovers noticed him,[a] when as a youth he went
to school or to the bath.

[a] Acontius. Perhaps fr. 534 refers to Acontius on his way
to the bath.

69

. . . and many lovers of Acontius, when drinking,
tossed from the cup to the ground in his honour the
last drops of wine in the Sicilian manner.[a]

was cast in reference to some beloved person, at the drinking
parties of antiquity. The form described here is otherwise
unknown.

70

. . . but the archer himself,[a] feeling the point of
an arrow from the bow of another.

arrows of love, until he was himself wounded by the beauty
of Cydippe.

72

. . . for that reason [a] he frequented the country-
side on every pretext.

would take every opportunity of going out into the country
to avoid him.

73

. . . but on your bark may you bear so many carved
letters as will say that Cydippe is beautiful.[a]

other objects together with the epithet *Kalos*, *Kalé*, " beauti-
ful."

74

λιρὸς ἐγώ, τί δέ σοι τόνδ' ἐπέθηκα φόβον;

τίδες, ὅταν δε cod. : corr. Bentley.   ἐπέσεισα Meineke :
ἐνέθηκα Schneider.

75

ἤδη καὶ κούρῳ παρθένος εὐνάσατο,
τέθμιον ὡς ἐκέλευε προνύμφιον ὕπνον ἰαῦσαι
ἄρσενι τὴν τᾶλιν παιδὶ σὺν ἀμφιθαλεῖ.
Ἥρην γάρ κοτέ φασι—κύον, κύον, ἴσχεο, λαιδρέ
5 θυμέ, σύ γ' ἀείσῃ καὶ τά περ οὐχ ὁσίη·
ὤναο κάρτ' ἔνεκ' οὔ τι θεῆς ἴδες ἱερὰ φρικτῆς,
ἐξ ἂν ἐπεὶ καὶ τῶν ἤρυγες ἱστορίην.
ἦ πολυιδρείη χαλεπὸν κακόν, ὅστις ἀκαρτεῖ
γλώσσης· ὡς ἐτεὸν παῖς ὅδε μαῦλιν ἔχει.
10 ἠῷοι μὲν ἔμελλον ἐν ὕδατι θυμὸν ἀμύξειν
οἱ βόες ὀξεῖαν δερκόμενοι δορίδα,
δειελινὴν τὴν δ' εἷλε κακὸς χλόος, ἦλθε δὲ νοῦσος,
αἶγας ἐς ἀγριάδας τὴν ἀποπεμπόμεθα,
ψευδόμενοι δ' ἱερὴν φημίζομεν· ἢ τότ' ἀνιγρή
15 τὴν κούρην Ἀίδεω μέχρις ἔτηξε δόμων.
δεύτερον ἐστόρνυντο τὰ κλισμία, δεύτερον ἡ πα[ῖ]ς
ἑπτὰ τεταρταίῳ μῆνας ἔκαμνε πυρί.

6 κάρ⟨θ⟩' coni. Hu. : ⟨μ⟩άργ' Wil.   7 ἐξ ἂν ἐπεὶ divisit
Housman.

---

[a] The reference is to the ἱερὸς γάμος, or secret marriage of
Zeus and Hera, first mentioned in the *Iliad*, xiv. 294 ff.

[b] The mysteries of Demeter.

[c] Μὴ παιδὶ μάχαιραν, " Do not give a knife to a child," was
a Greek proverb.

AETIA

74

. . . shameless I, why have I imposed upon you this fear ? [a]

> [a] Probably part of a soliloquy of Acontius.

75

. . . and already the maiden was bedded with the boy, as ritual ordered that the bride should sleep her prenuptial sleep with a boy whose parents were both alive. For they say that once upon a time Hera [a]—
5 dog, dog, refrain, my shameless soul ! you would sing even of that which is not lawful to tell. It is a great blessing for you that you have not seen the rites of the dread goddess,[b] or else you would have spewed up their story too. Surely much knowledge is a grievous thing for him who does not control his tongue ; this man is really a child with a knife.[c]
10 In the morning the oxen were to tear their hearts seeing before them reflected in the water the sharp blade.[d] But in the afternoon an evil pallor came upon her ; the disease seized her, which we banish on the wild goats and which we falsely call the holy disease.[e]
15 That grievous sickness then wasted the girl even to the Halls of Hades. A second time the couches were spread ; a second time the maiden was sick for seven months with a quartan fever. A third time they

> [d] The heads of the oxen were held over lustral water when about to be sacrificed. The reference is here to the prenuptial sacrifice which was to take place in the morning, but on the previous afternoon Cydippe fell ill.
> [e] Epilepsy. Κατ' αἰγας ἀγρίας was a wish for exorcizing sickness, by charming it away from men to wild animals.

τὸ τρίτον ἐμνήσαντο γάμου κάτα, τὸ τρίτον αὖτ[ε
Κυδίππην ὀλοὸς κρυμὸς ἐσῳκίσατο.
20 τέτρατον οὐκέτ' ἔμεινε πατὴρ ἐ[. . .]φ[. .]ο[
Φοῖβον· ὁ δ' ἐννύχιον τοῦτ' ἔπος ηὐδάσατο·
" Ἀρτέμιδος τῇ παιδὶ γάμον βαρὺς ὅρκος ἐνικλᾷ·
Λύγδαμιν οὐ γὰρ ἐμὴ τῆμος ἔκηδε κάσις
οὐδ' ἐν Ἀμυκλαίῳ θρύον ἔπλεκεν οὐδ' ἀπὸ θήρης
25 ἔκλυζεν ποταμῷ λύματα Παρθενίῳ,
Δήλῳ δ' ἦν ἐπίδημος, Ἀκόντιον ὁππότε σὴ παῖς
ὤμοσεν, οὐκ ἄλλον, νυμφίον ἐξέμεναι.
ὦ Κήϋξ, ἀλλ' ἤν με θέλῃς συμφράδμονα θέσθαι,
 . .]ν[. .] τελευτήσεις ὅρκια θυγατέρος·
30 ἀργύρῳ οὐ μόλιβον γὰρ Ἀκόντιον, ἀλλὰ φαεινῷ
ἤλεκτρον χρυσῷ φημί σε μειξέμεναι.
Κοδρείδης σύ γ' ἄνωθεν ὁ πενθερός, αὐτὰρ ὁ Κεῖος
γαμβρὸς Ἀρισταίου Ζηνὸς ἀφ' ἱερέων
Ἰκμίου οἷσι μέμ[η]λεν ἐπ' οὔρεος ἀμβώνεσσιν
35 πρηΰνειν χαλεπὴν Μαῖραν ἀνερχομένην,
αἰτεῖσθαι τὸ δ' ἄημα παραὶ Διὸς ᾧ τε θαμεινοί
πλήσσονται λινέαις ὄρτυγες ἐν νεφέλαις."

18 αὖτ[ις Hu.: αὖτ[ε Pf.   20 ἐς Δελφιον ἄρ[ας distinguere
sibi visus est Hu.   21 ἐμμύχιον coni. M. Pohlenz.
29 νῦ]ν γε? Pf.: ῥίμφα? Trypanis: πάντα Hu.   34
suppl. Hu.

thought of marriage ; a third time again a deadly
20 chill settled on Cydippe. A fourth time her father
could endure it no more, but (set off to Delphian ?)
Phoebus, who in the night spoke and said : " A
solemn oath by Artemis frustrates your child's
marriage. For my sister was not then vexing
Lygdamis,[a] neither in Amyclae's [b] shrine was she
weaving rushes, nor in the river Parthenios [c] was
25 she washing her stains after the hunt ; she was at
home in Delos when your child swore that she would
have Acontius, none other for bridegroom. But,
Ceyx, if you will take me for your counsellor, you
30 will fulfil the oath of your daughter. . . . For I say
that in the person of Acontius you will not be ming-
ling lead with silver, but electrum [d] with shining gold.
You, the father of the bride, are sprung from Codrus[e] ;
the Cean bridegroom springs from the priests of
Zeus Aristaeus the Icmian,[f] priests whose business
35 it is upon the mountain tops to placate stern Maera [g]
when she rises, and to entreat from Zeus the wind
whereby many a quail is entangled in the linen nets."

[a] A king of the Cimmerians, who burnt the temple of
Artemis at Ephesus, c. 670 B.C.
[b] In Laconia, by the river Eurotas.
[c] River in Pontus, a haunt of Artemis.
[d] Not amber, but the metallic alloy of gold and silver.
[e] The last king of Athens.
[f] Aristaeus, son of Apollo and Cyrene, who, when Ceos
was suffering from pestilence, owing to the heat of the Dog-
Star, went there and built an altar to Zeus Icmaeus or
Icmius, i.e. Zeus as God of Moisture, and established an
annual sacrifice for him and Sirius on the hills of the island.
Ever after Zeus caused the Etesian Winds to blow for forty
days after the rise of Sirius. Hence Aristaeus was worshipped
in Ceos as Zeus Aristaeus.
[g] The hound of Erigone. As a star = Sirius, or else Pro-
cyon.

CALLIMACHUS

ἦ θεός· αὐτὰρ ὁ Νάξον ἔβη πάλιν, εἴρετο δ᾽ αὐτήν
κούρην, ἡ δ᾽ ἀν᾽ ἑῶς πᾶν ἐκάλυψεν ἔπος

40 κῆν αὖ σῶς· [. . .] λοιπόν, ᾽Ακόντιε, σεῖο μετελθεῖν
. . . . . .]ηνιδίην ἐς Διωνυσιάδα.

χἠ θεὸς εὐορκεῖτο καὶ ἥλικες αὐτίχ᾽ ἑταίρης
εἶπον ὑμηναίους οὐκ ἀναβαλλομένους.

οὔ σε δοκέω τημοῦτος, ᾽Ακόντιε, νυκτὸς ἐκείνης

45 ἀντί κε, τῇ μίτρης ἥψαο παρθενίης,
οὐ σφυρὸν ᾽Ιφίκλειον ἐπιτρέχον ἀσταχύεσσιν
οὐδ᾽ ἃ Κελαινίτης ἐκτεάτιστο Μίδης
δέξασθαι, ψήφου δ᾽ ἂν ἐμῆς ἐπιμάρτυρες εἶεν
οἵτινες οὐ χαλεποῦ νήιδές εἰσι θεοῦ.

50 ἐκ δὲ γάμου κείνοιο μέγ᾽ οὔνομα μέλλε νέεσθαι·
δὴ γὰρ ἔθ᾽ ὑμέτερον φῦλον ᾽Ακοντιάδαι
πουλύ τι καὶ περίτιμον ᾽Ιουλίδι ναιετάουσιν,
Κεῖε, τεὸν δ᾽ ἡμεῖς ἵμερον ἐκλύομεν
τόνδε παρ᾽ ἀρχαίου Ξενομήδεος, ὅς ποτε πᾶσαν

55 νῆσον ἐνὶ μνήμῃ κάτθετο μυθολόγῳ,
ἄρχμενος ὡς νύμφῃσιν ἐναίετο Κωρυκίῃσιν,
τὰς ἀπὸ Παρνησσοῦ λῖς ἐδίωξε μέγας,
῾Υδροῦσσαν τῷ καί μιν ἐφήμισαν, ὥς τε Κιρώ[δης
.]ο[. .]θυσ[.]το[. .] ᾤκεεν ἐν Καρύαις·

40 ὅ τ[ε] Housman. lacun. inter 40 et 41 indicat Grain-
dor.   43 ειδον P : corr. Pf. ἦδον Wil.   45 τῇ G.
Murray : τῆς P.   58 e.g. suppl. G. Murray.   59 ἥ]ρως
ευσ[ί]τρις prop. Barber.
58

So spoke the god. And her father went back to
Naxos, and questioned the maiden herself ; and she
40 revealed in truth the whole matter. And she was well
again. For the rest, Acontius, it will be your business
to go . . . to Dionysias.[a] So faith was kept with the
goddess, and the girls of her age straightway said their
comrade's marriage-hymn, deferred no longer. Then,
45 I deem, Acontius, that for that night, wherein you
touched her maiden girdle, you would have accepted
neither the ankle of Iphicles [b] who ran upon the corn-
ears, nor the possessions of Midas of Celaenae.[c] And
my verdict would be attested by all who are not
50 ignorant of the stern god.[d] And from that marriage
a great name was destined to arise. For, Cean, your
clan, the Acontiadae, still dwell numerous and
honoured at Iulis.[e] And this love of yours we heard
from old Xenomedes,[f] who once set down all the
55 island in a mythological history, beginning with the
tale of how it was inhabited by the Corycian [g]
nymphs, whom a great lion drove away from Par-
nasus ; for that reason also they called it Hydrussa,[h]
60 and how Cirodes . . . dwelt in Caryae.[i] And how

<hr>

[a] *i.e.* Naxos.
[b] Iphiclus, or Iphicles, son of Phylacus, father of Podarces
and Protesilaus, was proverbial for his speed of foot. He
could run over a cornfield without bending the ears.
[c] Midas of Celaenae in Phrygia, proverbial for his
wealth.
[d] Eros.
[e] In Ceos, birthplace of Simonides and Bacchylides.
[f] Cean chronicler, who lived *c.* 450 B.C.
[g] Nymphs of the Corycian cave on Parnasus.
[h] "Having water."
[i] It is unknown who is supposed to have inhabited the
island between the Corycian nymphs and the Carians. No
connexion is mentioned between Ceos and any of the towns
called Caryae (in Laconia, Arcadia and Lycia).

60 ὥς τέ μιν ἐννάσσαντο τέων Ἀλαλάξιος αἰεί
    Ζεὺς ἐπὶ σαλπίγγων ἱρὰ βοῇ δέχεται
    Κᾶρες ὁμοῦ Λελέγεσσι, μετ᾽ οὔνομα δ᾽ ἄλλο βαλέ-
        σθ[αι
      Φοίβου καὶ Μελίης ἶνις ἔθηκε Κέως·
ἐν δ᾽ ὕβριν θάνατόν τε κεραύνιον, ἐν δὲ γόητας
65 Τελχῖνας μακάρων τ᾽ οὐκ ἀλέγοντα θεῶν
    ἠλεὰ Δημώνακτα γέρων ἐνεθήκατο δέλτοις
    καὶ γρηῦν Μακελώ, μητέρα Δεξιθέης,
    ἃς μούνας, ὅτε νῆσον ἀνέτρεπον εἵνεκ᾽ ἀλ[ι]τρῆς
      ὕβριος, ἀσκηθεῖς ἔλλιπον ἀθάνατοι·
70 τέσσαρας ὥς τε πόληας ὁ μὲν τείχισσε Μεγα-
      κ[λ]ῆς
    Κάρθαιαν, Χρυσοῦς δ᾽ Εὔπ[υ]λος ἡμιθέης
    εὔκρηνον πτολίεθρον Ἰουλίδος, αὐτὰρ Ἀκαῖ[ος
    Ποιῆσσαν Χαρίτων ἵδρυμ᾽ εὐπλοκάμων,
    ἄστυρον Ἄφραστος δὲ Κορή[σ]ιον, εἶπε δέ, Κεῖε,
75 ξυγκραθέντ᾽ αὐταῖς ὀξὺν ἔρωτα σέθεν
    πρέσβυς ἐτητυμίῃ μεμελημένος, ἔνθεν ὁ πα[ι]δός
    μῦθος ἐς ἡμετέρην ἔδραμε Καλλιόπην.—

62 βαλεισθ[P : βαλέσθαι L. : καλεῖσθ[αι coni. Hu.   68
suppl. Wil.   70 suppl. Hu.   71 Εὔπ[υ]λος Hu., sed possis

they settled in the country whose offerings Zeus
Alalaxius [a] always receives to the sound of trumpets
—Carians and Leleges [b] together ; and how Ceos,
son of Phoebus and Melia, caused it to take another
name. Withal the insolence and the lightning death
65 and therewith the wizards Telchines [c] and Demonax
who foolishly disregarded the blessed gods, the old
man put in his tablets, and aged Macelo, mother of
Dexithea, the two of whom the deathless gods alone
left unscathed, when for sinful insolence they over-
70 threw the island. And how of its four cities Megacles
built Carthaea, and Eupylus, son of the heroine
Chryso, the fair-fountained city of Iulis, and Acaeos
Poeessa, seat of the fair-tressed Graces, and how
75 Aphrastus built the city of Coresus.[d] And blended
therewith, (?) O Cean, that old man, lover of truth,
told of your passionate love ; from there the maiden's
story came to my Muse.

[a] Of the war-cry.
[b] Carians and Leleges (according to Herod. i. 171 the
Carians were " formerly called Leleges ") spread in pre-
historic times to the islands of the Aegean.
[c] The story in outline is that the Telchines, mythical
craftsmen and wizards, provoked the wrath of the gods.
So Zeus and Posidon " sent the land and all the host of the
people into the depths of Tartarus " (Pind. *Paeans* iv. 42 ff.),
but spared Dexithea and her sisters, daughters of Damon
(here called Demonax), because they had entertained Zeus
and Apollo. Macelo in the scholia on Ovid's *Ibis* is the
sister of Dexithea, not her mother. Dexithea became mother
of Euxantius by Minos of Crete.
[d] The founders of the Cean Tetrapolis are otherwise un-
known.

etiam Εὔπ[α]λος vel Εὔπ[ο]λος.   72 suppl. Pf. : Ἄκαι[ρος
von Arnim.   73 ἴδρῦμ' propos. Wil. : ἔίρυμ' (= ἔρυμ')
A. D. Knox.   74 suppl. Hu. fin. versus omnino in-
certus.   75 αὐταῖς P : ἀνίαις coni. Maas.

61

CALLIMACHUS

76–77

(ELEORUM RITUS NUPTIALIS)

76

Εἶπ' ἄγε μοι
εστιϲε Πιϲαίου Ζηνός οπιϲπ[. . .]ιθην

2 ἐς τί σε quaestio aetii prop. W. Morel: ἐς τί σε Πίσαίου
Ζηνὸς ὅπις π[αραβῇ; (quousque te praetereat Iovis P. vene-
ratio?) prop. Barber.

77

ᾙλιν ἀνάσσεσθαι, Διὸς οἰκίον, ἔλλιπε Φυλεῖ

[a] Apparently it was customary at some stage at Elis for
a bride-to-be to be visited before marriage by an armed
warrior. Callimachus explains the rite by a reference to the
following story. After Heracles had cleaned out Augeas'
stables, the king refused to pay him, and when Augeas' son
Phyleus, appointed to arbitrate, decided against his father,

78

(HOSPES ISINDIUS)

ᾮφελες οὐλοὸν ἔγ[χος, Ἰσίνδιε
μηδ[

1 ἔγ[χος Pf. Ἰσίνδιε Barber.

[a] Callimachus apparently explained here why the Ionians
barred the inhabitants of Isindus, also an Ionian city of
Asia Minor, from the festival of the Panionia. Aethalon, an

AETIA

76-77

(NUPTIAL RITE OF THE ELEANS)

76

COME tell me . . . Zeus of Pisa.[a]

[a] The Olympian Zeus. Pisa, a fountain at Olympia (Strabo viii. 3. 31), which gave a name to Olympia itself.

77

(Heracles) left Elis, the home of Zeus, to Phyleus to reign over.[a]

he was driven out of the country. Heracles marched against Elis, sacked it and installed Phyleus as king. But, as very many Elean men had been killed in battle, Heracles obliged their widows to sleep with his own soldiers. Thus a great number of children were born. He also established the Olympic games, and was said to have been the first to compete in them.

78

(THE ISINDIAN GUEST)

You should have . . . the destructive (weapon ?).[a]

Isindian, is said to have killed his guest. The gap in the *Diegeseis* suggests that a whole aetion may be lost between fr. 78 and fr. 79.

79

(DIANA LUCINA)

Τεῦ δὲ χάριν [.]ọ[κικλήσ]κουσιν

suppl. Maas.

 a Callimachus is explaining why women invoke Artemis at childbirth. According to the *Diegesis*: " The women who have difficulty in childbirth invoke Artemis, although a

80 + 82

(PHRYGIUS ET PIERIA)

10 αἰδοῖ δ' ὡς φοί[νικι] τεὰς ἐρύθουσα παρειάς
   ἤν]επες ὀφ[θαλμο]ῖς ἔμπαλι [. . . .]ομεν[

   .   .   .   .

16 ἦν γὰρ τοῖσι Μυ]οῦντα καὶ οἳ Μίλητον ἔναιον
   συνθεσί]η, μούν[ης νηὸν ἐς] Ἀρτέμιδος
   ξυνῇ π]ωλε[ῖσθαι Νη]ληΐδος· ἀλλὰ σὺ τῆμος
   βουκτ]ας[ι]ῶν ἀρ[τὺν πιστο]τέρην ἔταμες,
20 ἔνδει]ξας καὶ Κύπριν ὅτι ῥητῆρας ἐκείνου
   τεύχει τοῦ Πυλίου κρέσσονας οὐκ ὀλίγως·
   ἐξεσίαι πολέε[ς γὰρ ἀπ' ἀμφοτέροιο μο]λοῦσαι
   ἄστ]εος ἀπρήκτ[ους οἴκαδ' ἀνῆλθον ὁδούς

10-11 suppl. Pf.   16-23 suppll. Maas-Barber, praeter 19 βουκτ]ας[ι]ῶν ἀρ[τὺν Pf.

 a Apparently words spoken by Phrygius.   *b* Pieria.
c Ionian city in Asia Minor.   *d* Nestor.
e The story briefly is the following : The cities of Miletus

AETIA

79

(DIANA THE GODDESS OF CHILD-BIRTH)

For what reason do they invoke (?) [a]

maiden; either because . . . was born, or because Ilithyia,
at the command of Zeus, conferred this special honour upon
her, or because, when her mother was giving birth to Apollo,
it was she who relieved the pains."

80 + 82

(PHRYGIUS AND PIERIA)

10 But,[a] reddening your cheeks with shame, as with
16 scarlet dye, you [b] said with your eyes . . . There
was an agreement between the inhabitants of
Myus [c] and Miletus, that they could frequent in
common only the temple of Milesian Artemis. But
you then made a more trustworthy covenant than
20 that made by the sacrifice of oxen, and proved that
Cypris creates much greater orators than the famous
one of Pylos [d]; for many embassies, having come
from both the cities, returned to their homes un-
successful.[e]

and Myus were constantly at war, but even so the women
and maidens of Myus were allowed to take part in the pro-
cession in honour of Artemis at Miletus. At that festival
Phrygius, the son of Neleus, king of Miletus, fell in love
with Pieria, a noble maiden from Myus. As a result of this
love-affair the war between the two cities ceased, and
Aphrodite was proved a more eloquent statesman and
ambassador than all those the two cities had employed in
the past.

CALLIMACHUS

84–85

(EUTHYCLES LOCRUS)

84

Ἦλθες ὅτ' ἐκ Πίσης, Εὐθύκλεες, ἄνδρας ἐλέγξας

 a This story refers to the Locrians of southern Italy : the *Diegesis* says : " He (*sc.* Callimachus) says that Euthycles, the Olympic victor, who was sent as an envoy and returned home with some mules, the gift of a host, was falsely charged with receiving them on the understanding that he would do harm to the city. For that reason they voted to damage his statue. But, when a plague fell upon the city, the people

85

```
    ἔν]θεν ἀνερχόμε[νος] πάλιν [οἴκαδε
5   δῶ]ρον ἀπηναίους ἦλθες ὀρῆ[ας ἄγων·
    ὡς] δέ σ' ἐπὶ ῥήτρῃσι λαβεῖν κα[τὰ πατρίδος εἶπε
    δῆ]μος [ἐπ'] ἀφνειοῖς αἰὲν ἀπαγχόμενος,
    πά]ντες ὑπὸ ψηφῖδα κακὴν βάλον· ἦν δ' ἀπὸ [χαλκοῦ
    εἰκόν]α σὴν αὐτὴ Λοκρὶς ἔθηκε [πόλ]ις,
10     . . πλ]άσται Τεμεσαῖον ἔπειπ[
    ἔρ]γα μελισσάων ἀμφὶ σολοιτυπ[
    π]ολλά τε καὶ μακάρεσσιν ἀπεχ[θέα ῥέξαν ἀνι]γροί·
    τ]ῷ σφισιν ἐν χαλεπὴν θῆκ[ε τελεσφο]ρίην
    ὅν]τινα κικλήσκουσιν Ἐπόψ[ιον,] ὅστις ἀλιτρούς
15  αὐγάζειν ἰθαραῖς οὐ δύναται λογάσιν
```

4 init. suppl. L. : [οἴκαδε Barber-Maas.   5 suppl. L.
6 suppl. Barber-Maas.   7 δῆ]μος dub. suppl. L. [ἐπ']
suppl. Pf. : [ὑπ'] L.   8 init. suppl. Pf. : [χαλκοῦ Barber-
Maas.   9 [πόλ]ις dubitanter Pf.   10 suppl. dubi-
tanter Pf.   11 ἔρ]γα L.   12 suppl. Barber-Maas.
13 suppl. L.   14 sq. suppl. L.   15 καθαραῖς codd.

AETIA

84–85

(EUTHYCLES THE LOCRIAN)

84

EUTHYCLES,[a] when you came from Pisa,[b] having defeated men (at the games).[c]

learned from Apollo that it had been sent on account of the dishonour done to Euthycles. Therefore they honoured his statue equally to that of Zeus, and, moreover, they set up an altar . . . at the beginning of the month."

Callimachus has drawn upon other occasions on stories of the Epizephyrian or Western Locrians, *cf.* frs. 635* and 669.

  [b] Pisa = Olympia.   [c] He was winner of the pentathlon.

85

4 . . . from there,[a] returning (home), you came bringing driving-mules as a gift. And when the people, who always choke with indignation against the rich, said that you received them on condition to harm your fatherland, they all voted secretly against you. And to the (bronze) statue, which the Locrian city

10 itself had set up in your honour . . . [b] the villains did many things that the gods hate. For that reason,

15 he who is called Epopsios,[c] who cannot look upon the sinful with glad eyes, set upon them an evil harvest (?)

  [a] From the city to which he was sent as an ambassador.

  [b] Probably the material and the method of construction of the statue were described in ll. 10-11. Temesa, a city in Bruttium, was famous in antiquity for its bronze, and was at one stage conquered by the Epizephyrian Locrians.

  [c] "The Watcher from Above," adjective of Zeus and Apollo, and even collectively of all the gods (ἐπόψιοι θεοί, Soph. *Philoct.* 1040).

Fr. 114 may well belong to Book III.

ΑΙΤΙΩΝ Δ΄

(The sequence of the aetia in Book IV is known from the *Diegeseis*. But as the papyrus of the *Diegeseis* is mutilated at the beginning the *Delphic Daphnephoria* may not have been the first aetion of this

86 (?)–87

(DAPHNEPHORIA DELPHICA)

86

Μοῦ]σαί μοι βασιλη[ἀεί]δειν

init. suppl. Norsa-Vitelli, fin. Maas.

87

Δειπνιὰς ἔνθεν μιν δειδέχαται

ᵃ After Apollo had killed the serpent at Delphi, he and his comrades are said to have cleansed themselves in the river Peneus. Then the god cut a branch off a bay-tree which grew in the vale of Tempe, made a garland from the same tree and returned to Delphi (*cf.* fr. 89 Pf.). In com-

AETIA : BOOK IV

book. One, and even two, may have preceded it, and
fr. 177, *The Mousetrap*, may have well been one of
these ; *cf.* Pfeiff. i, p. 501 and p. 503, Addenda to
frs. 84-86 and 177. 4-6.)

86 (?)-87

(THE DELPHIC DAPHNEPHORIA)

86

MUSES, sing for me . . . the king (?)

87

. . . thereafter Deipnias (the village) has welcomed
him.[a]

memoration of this the Delphians sent yearly to Tempe an
architheoros accompanied by noble youths, who after sacrific-
ing to the god returned to Delphi wearing garlands of bay-
leaves. The village Deipnias was in Thessaly near Larissa,
and it was alleged to have been the place where Apollo first
tasted food (ἐδείπνησεν) on his way back from Tempe after he
had cleansed himself from the slaughter of the serpent.

CALLIMACHUS

90

(ABDERA)

Ἔνθ’, Ἄβδηρ’, οὗ νῦν [. . . .]λεω φαρμακὸν ἀγινεῖ

μ[ε π]λέω⟨ν⟩ tempt. Barber.

---

[a] According to the *Diegesis* : " In Abdera a slave, bought
in the market, is used to purify the city. Standing on a
block of grey stone, he enjoys a rich banquet, and so fed to
the full he is led to the gates called Prurides. Then he goes
round the walls in a circle purifying in his own person the
city, and then the *basileus* and the others throw stones at

91

(MELICERTES)

Ἀ[όνι’ ὦ] Μελικέρτα, μιῆς ἐπὶ πότνια Βύνη

suppl. Maas.

---

[a] According to the *Diegesis* : " After Ino threw herself
into the sea with her child Melicertes, the body of the child
was washed up on a shore of Tenedos. The Leleges, who
once lived there, set up an altar in his honour. On it the
city performs the following sacrifice when in great danger :
a woman kills her baby and at once blinds herself. This
practice was abolished later, when the descendants of Orestes
inhabited Lesbos." Ino, daughter of Cadmus, was driven

93

(THEUDOTUS LIPARENSIS)

Νέκταρος α[. . . . . .]ν γλύκιον γένος ηραπεδο[
κ[. .] δονηδυ[. . . . .]ς ἀμβροσίης

---

[a] The story Callimachus treated in this aetion refers to a
siege of Lipara (the city of the largest of seven volcanic

AETIA

90

(ABDERA)

THERE, Abderos, where now . . . leads (me) a scape-
goat.[a]

him until he is driven beyond the boundaries." Abdera was
a Greek city in Thrace near the mouth of the river Nestos.
In this fragment Ἄβδηρ' may be either Ἄβδηρε, the epony-
mous hero of the city, or Ἄβδηρα the city itself. The slave
who was used as scapegoat appears to be speaking in this
fragment.

91

(MELICERTES)

AONIAN Melicertes, Queen Byne on one (anchor ?)
. . .[a]

mad by Hera together with her husband Athamas. Upon
seeing her husband kill Learchus, one of her two sons, she
jumped into the sea carrying her other son Melicertes. They
were both transformed into deities. Melicertes is called
Boeotian (Aonian = Boeotian) presumably because Ino was
the daughter of Cadmus, king of Thebes. The form *Byne*
is Boeotian, used here instead of Ino. Children were said to
be the " anchors," the safeguards, of the parents ; a ship
riding on one anchor was not considered safely moored (*cf.*
fr. 191. 47 and Herodas i. 41).

93

(THEUDOTUS OF LIPARA)[a]

A RACE sweeter than nectar . . . ambrosia. The

islands off north-eastern Sicily) by the Tyrrhenians, during
which they promised to sacrifice to Apollo the most coura-
geous Liparian warrior. After their victory they sacrificed
one called Theudotus.

CALLIMACHUS

ὑμέας γαῖ’ ἀνέδ[ωκε, τ]ὰ καὶ τερπνίστατα πά[ντων
νεῖσθε διὰ γλῶσ[σαν γλεύ]κεος ὅσσα πέρα.
5 δείλαιοι, τυ[τθόν] μιν ἐπὶ πλ⟨έ⟩ον ἢ ὅσον ἄ[κρον
χεῖλος ἀναγλ[. . . . . . .]π[.]ρ ἀναινομένου
ἀνδρὸς ανουν[. . . . .]s ἐπέτασσεν [

94

(LIMONIS)

94

Τὸν νεκρ[ὸ]ν [. . . . .] τ[. . . .]υβατονιστιναευω

---

[a] The two extant fragments of this aetion (94-95*) are untranslatable. According to the *Diegesis*, the first line of which is also badly mutilated, Hippomenes, a descendant of

96

(VENATOR GLORIOSUS)

Θεοὶ πάντες κομποῖς νεμεσήμονες, ἐκ δέ τε πάντων
Ἄρτεμις α[

---

[a] According to the *Diegesis*: "A huntsman . . . upon killing a boar said that it was not fitting for those who

97

(MOENIA PELASGICA)

Τυρσηνῶν τείχισμα Πελασγικὸν εἶχέ με γαῖα
πελαργικὸν cod.

---

[a] The Pelasgi seem to have been a north Aegean people, uprooted by Bronze Age migrations. The Greeks came to use their name for all "aboriginal" Aegean populations,

earth sent you up and most delightful of all things,
that are beyond sweet new wine, you go across the
5 tongue. Poor wretches, a little further than the tip
of the lip . . . a man refuses . . .

3-5 e.g. suppl. L.

94–95

(LIMONIS) [a]

Codrus, king of Athens, " shut up his daughter Limone,
who had been secretly seduced, in a chamber with a horse,
and by this means killed her. And for this reason in Athens
there is a place called ' The Horse and the Girl.' And the
father struck with a spear the man who had seduced her,
and tied his body to a horse, which dragged it through the
city."

96

(THE BOASTING HUNTSMAN)

ALL the gods are angry with braggarts, but most of
all Artemis . . . [a]

surpass Artemis to dedicate (their trophies) to her ; so he
dedicated the boar's head to himself, hanging it on a black
poplar. He lay down to sleep under the tree, and the head
fell and killed him."

97

(THE PELASGIAN WALLS)

THE land held me, a Pelasgian wall, built by the Tyr-
rhenians.[a]

and they were sometimes identified with the Tyrrheni. This
aetion, according to the *Diegesis*, spoke " of the boundaries
(?) set round Athens by the Pelasgi, and of the wall which
they made."

73

CALLIMACHUS

98

(EUTHYMUS)

Εὐθύμου τὰ μὲν ὅσσα παραὶ Διὶ Πῖσαν ἔχοντι

[a] The extant fragment is too incomplete to be translated. According to the *Diegesis*: " In Temese, a hero who was left behind from the ship of Odysseus laid a tribute upon the people of the place and their neighbours that they should bring him a bed and a maiden ready for marriage and with-

100

(IUNONIS SAMIAE SIMULACRUM ANTIQUISSIMUM)

οὔπω Σκέλμιον ἔργον ἐύξοον, ἀλλ' ἐπὶ τεθμόν
  δηναιὸν γλυφάνων ἄξοος ἦσθα σανίς·
ὧδε γὰρ ἱδρύοντο θεοὺς τότε· καὶ γὰρ Ἀθήνης
  ἐν Λίνδῳ Δαναὸς λιτὸν ἔθηκεν ἕδος

---

1 εἰσοξόανα vel εἰς ξόανον codd.: em. Bentley. τεθμοῦ Is. Voss, Bentley. 2 δὴ νεό///γλυφον ὦναξ θεᾶς codd.: δηναιοῦ γλυφάνῳ ἄξοος Bentley: γλυφάνων Toup: δηναιὸν (ad τεθμόν) Bergk. 4 λίθον vel λεῖον codd.: em. Is. Voss.

---

[a] Scelmis is said to be the first to carve a statue for Hera at Samos. He is otherwise unknown.
[b] Danaus was held to be a descendant of Zeus, who, upon quarrelling with Aegyptus, fled with his daughters to Argos. There are many versions of the myth.

AETIA

98

(EUTHYMUS) [a]

out looking back go their ways. In the morning her parents
would take her away a woman and no longer a maid.
Euthymus, the boxer, did away with this tribute . . . ''
Temese was a city of Bruttium founded by the Ausonians.
The name of the companion of Odysseus is said to be Polites
(or according to Paus. vi. 6. 11 Lycus). Euthymus was three
times an Olympic victor in boxing (Ol. 74, 76 and 77). There
was a Greek proverb referring to this story, Ὁ ἐν Τεμέσῃ
ἥρως, The hero of Temese.

100

(THE OLDEST STATUE OF THE SAMIAN HERA)

. . . the well-carved work of Scelmis [a] had not yet
(been dedicated), but according to the old custom
you were a plank not carved by chisels ; for thus
did they then set up the (effigies of the) gods. In
fact Danaus [b] had placed at Lindus [c] the simple
statue of Athene . . . [d]

[c] City of Rhodes.
[d] According to the *Diegesis* : " . . . the wooden image
of Hera took the form of a statue when Procles was *archon
basileus*. The wood out of which it was shaped . . . they
say from Argos . . . was brought over in old days still no
more than a plank and quite unfashioned, because the art
of statuary was not then advanced any further."

CALLIMACHUS

101

(IUNONIS SAMIAE SIMULACRUM ALTERUM)

"Ηρη τῇ Σαμίῃ περὶ μὲν τρίχας ἄμπελος ἕρπει

---

[a] According to the *Diegesis*: " It is said that the Hera of Samos has a vine winding round her hair and a lion's skin at her feet. They were spoils, as it were, of Heracles and Dionysus, the unlawful children of Zeus." We do not

102

(PASICLES EPHESIUS)

'Ηισύμνας 'Εφέσου, Πασίκλεες, ἀλλ' ἀπὸ δαίτης

---

[a] According to the *Diegesis* : " He (*i.e.* Callimachus) says that Pasicles, archon of Ephesus, was attacked when leaving a banquet. The assailants were in difficulty on account of the darkness, but when they approached the temple of Hera,

103

(ANDROGEOS)

"Ηρως ὦ κατὰ πρύμναν, ἐπεὶ τόδε κύρβις ἀείδει

---

[a] The *Diegesis* explains : " The so-called ' Hero of the Stern' is Androgeos. For in days of old, before the Piraeus was built, the anchorage of Phaleron was where ships used

AETIA

101

(THE OTHER STATUE OF HERA
AT SAMOS)

A VINE-BRANCH runs round the hair of the Samian Hera.[a]

know if this is supposed to describe the work of Scelmis, or some other statue dedicated to Hera at Samos. On Samian coins of *c.* 600 B.C., on which the wooden statue of Hera is depicted on the one side, there is also a plant that might well be a vine, and on the other a lionskin.

102

(PASICLES OF EPHESUS)

You were archon of Ephesus, Pasicles, but from a banquet.[a]

Pasicles' mother, who was a priestess (there), heard the noise of the pursuit, and ordered a lamp to be brought out. And in this way they got a light and killed her son."

103

(ANDROGEOS)

O HERO of the stern, since a pillar sings this.[a]

to anchor." Nothing is known about this pillar or its inscription. Androgeos was said to be the son of Minos, and a guardian of the stern of ships.

CALLIMACHUS

104

(OESYDRES THRAX)

Οἰσύδρεω Θρήϊκος ἐφ' αἵματι πολλὰ Θάσοιο

[a] The reference may be to the wars between the Parians

105

(SYRMA ANTIGONES ?)

.]δε[. . . . .]ν[. . . . .]ιδετωνδ[

[a] Pfeiffer suggests that this quotation in the very muti-
lated *Diegesis* may refer to an aetion on the " Syrma of
Antigone," a place at Thebes, where Antigone was thought

106

(GAIUS ROMANUS)

Ὧδ' ἐ[σθλοὶ] γείνεσθε, Πανελλάδος ὧδε τελέσσαι

ἐ[σθλοὶ] suppl. Barber.

[a] According to the *Diegesis* : " (Callimachus) says that,
during the siege of Rome by the Peucetii, the Roman Gaius
leapt from the walls and killed their leader. He was wounded
in the thigh, and later was complaining that he limped.
But when his mother rebuked him, he ceased worrying."
Nothing is certain about the war, or the person of Gaius to
whom Callimachus is here referring. It is, however, possible

78

AETIA

104

(THE THRACIAN OESYDRES)

BECAUSE of the blood of the Thracian Oesydres many
(evils befell the people of ?) Thasos.[a]

and the Thracians in Thasos, which took place in the 7th
century B.C.

105

(THE " SYRMA " OF ANTIGONE ?) [a]

to have dragged the body of Polynices to the pyre of his
brother Eteocles. Even the flames of the pyre are said to
have split into two.

106

(THE ROMAN GAIUS) [a]

THUS be brave, (on behalf) of Greece thus . . . to
accomplish . . .

that the Peucetii are the Etruscans, in which case the lame
hero would be Horatius Cocles (*cf.* Dion. Hal. *A.R.* v. 25. 3
and Clem. Al. *Strom.* iv. 56. 3 (vol. ii, p. 274. 10 St.)). From
other similar stories appearing in later Greek and Roman
writers it can be concluded that the mother told her son
something to the effect of : " Do not worry, my son ; every
step you take will remind you of your own valour."

CALLIMACHUS

108

(ANCORA ARGUS NAVIS CYZICI RELICTA)

Ἀργὼ καὶ σέ, Πάνορμε, κατέδραμε καὶ τεὸν ὕδωρ

παροσμε P : corr. W. Morel.

---

[a] According to the *Diegesis* : " He (*i.e.* the poet) says that when the Argonauts went ashore at Cyzicus to fetch drinking-water they left there the stone which they had been using as an anchor, because it was too light, and took on a heavier one. The first was later dedicated to Athene." Cyzicus, the Milesian colony on the " island " of Arctonnesus among the Myso-Phrygian populations, was a great commercial centre. Practically all the shipping of the Propontis came to its two harbours in order to avoid the inhospitable northern shore. It was connected with the myth of the Argonauts in the manner described by the *Diegesis*. The

110

(COMA BERENICES)

Πάντα τὸν ἐν γραμμαῖσιν ἰδὼν ὅρον ᾗ τε φέρονται

. . . .

7 κἠμὲ Κόνων ἔβλεψεν ἐν ἠέρι τὸν Βερενίκης
βόστρυχον ὃν κείνη πᾶσιν ἔθηκε θεοῖς

. . . .

7 ἦ με codd. : κἠμὲ (?) Maas.

---

[a] *The Lock of Berenice* is mainly known from the translation by Catullus (66). The *Diegesis* summing up the poem writes : " He (*i.e.* Callimachus) says that Conon set the lock of Berenice among the stars, which she had promised to dedicate to the gods on (her husband's) return from the Syrian war." Berenice was the daughter of Magas, king of Cyrene, who was the son of Berenice I, wife of Ptolemy I. The Syrian war referred to is the Third Syrian War (247–246 B.C.). Upon

AETIA

108

(THE ANCHOR OF THE ARGO ABANDONED AT CYZICUS)

AND to you also, Panormus, came Argo, and your water.[a] [b]

" Panormus " mentioned in the fragment might be either the city Cyzicus, or its eponymous hero. The fountain from which the Argonauts are said to have drawn water at Cyzicus was called " Artacia."

[b] The *Lock of Berenice* and the Epilogue were probably added to the second edition of the *Aetia*. If this is so, in its original form the work may have finished with an aetion referring to the story of the Argonauts (108), as it also began with a similar story (fr. 7. 19 ff.).

110

(THE LOCK OF BERENICE) [a]

1 HAVING examined all the charted (?) sky,[b] and where
7 (the stars) move . . . Conon saw me also in the air, the lock of Berenice, which she dedicated to all the gods

the departure of Ptolemy III for that war, Berenice, his wife, vowed to the gods to dedicate a lock of her hair on his safe return. This she dedicated in the temple of Arsinoë Aphrodite at Zephyrium, from where the lock mysteriously disappeared. Thereupon Conon, the court astronomer, pretended to identify it with the group of stars, thenceforth known as Coma Berenices, lying within the circle formed by Ursa Major, Bootes, Virgo and Leo. The title of the poem is conjectural, and the fragments are assigned to their place on the evidence of Catullus. The lock is speaking in the style of certain dedicatory epigrams, in which the offering itself speaks.

[b] On the charts of the stars the sky was divided by lines into sections. This is probably the meaning of ἐν γραμμαῖσιν.

40   σήν τε κάρην ὤμοσα σόν τε βίον

. . . .

ἀμνάμων Θείης ἀργὸς ὑπερφέρεται,
45 βουπόρος Ἀρσινόης μητρὸς σέο, καὶ διὰ μέσσου
Μηδείων ὀλοαὶ νῆες ἔβησαν Ἄθω.
τί πλόκαμοι ῥέξωμεν, ὅτ' οὔρεα τοῖα σιδήρῳ
εἴκουσιν; Χαλύβων ὡς ἀπόλοιτο γένος,
γειόθεν ἀντέλλοντα, κακὸν φυτόν, οἵ μιν ἔφηναν
50   πρῶτοι καὶ τυπίδων ἔφρασαν ἐργασίην.
ἄρτι νεότμητόν με κόμαι ποθέεσκον ἀδελφεαί,
καὶ πρόκατε γνωτὸς Μέμνονος Αἰθίοπος
ἵετο κυκλώσας βαλιὰ πτερὰ θῆλυς ἀήτης,
ἵππος ἰοζώνου Λοκρίδος Ἀρσινόης,
55 . .]ασε δὲ πνοιῇ με, δι' ἠέρα δ' ὑγρὸν ἐνείκας
Κύπριδος εἰς κόλπους [   ] ἔθηκε   ·
αὐτή μιν Ζεφυρῖτις ἐπὶ χρέος
. . . . Κ]ανωπίτου ναιέτις α[ἰγιαλοῦ.
ὄφρα δὲ] μὴ νύμφης Μινωίδος ο[
60   . . . . .]ος ἀνθρώποις μοῦνον ἐπι[,

55 η[ρπ] lacuna capere non videtur. tamen vix aliud atque
ῆ[ρπ]ασε in textu et ἁρπασθῆναι in scholiis fuisse potest.
57 in fine hex. (aut init. pentam. ?) suppleri potest (ἔ)πεμψε
vel (προέ)ηκε(ν) Pf.   58 suppl. Vitelli.   59 init. suppl.
Vitelli, sed fort. σῆμα δὲ] et ὅ[φρα ? Pf.   60 in fine inter-
punxit L., etsi nullum exemplum coniunctionis ἀλλά quinto
loco positae exstare videtur.

---

[a] The lock swears by the head and life of the queen that
it has been cut off against its will.

[b] This may refer either to the Sun, who was a son of
Theia and Hyperion, or to Boreas, a grandson of Theia.

[c] Probably refers to Mount Athos; it would be, strictly
speaking, the obelisk of Queen Arsinoë II (cf. fr. 228. 47).

AETIA

40 . . . I took an oath by your head and by your life [a]
. . . the bright descendant of Theia [b] is carried over
45 . . . the obelisk of Arsinoë your mother,[c] and through
the middle of Athos the destructive ships of the Per-
sians sailed.[d] What can we do, locks of hair, when such
mountains succumb to the iron ? Oh that the whole
50 race of the Chalybes [e] would perish, who first brought
it to light, an evil plant rising from the earth, and
who taught (men) the work of the hammer ! When
(I was) newly shorn my sister-locks were mourning
for me. At once the brother of Memnon the Aethio-
pian, the gentle breeze, the steed of Locrian Arsinoë
of the violet girdle,[f] moving his swift wings in
55 circles dashed and seized me with his breath, and
carrying me through the humid air he placed me . . .
in the lap of Cypris. Aphrodite Zephyritis who
dwells on the shore of Canopus [g] (chose) him herself
. . . for that purpose. And so that not only the
. . . of the Minoan bride [h] . . . should (cast its
60 light) on men, but I too, the beautiful lock of Berenice,

βουπόρος means " ox-piercing." We do not know why it was
called thus.
   [d] Xerxes on his way to Greece cut a canal through the
isthmus joining Mount Athos with the Chalcidice, so that
his ships could avoid the rough seas off the promontory.
   [e] A Scythian race established near the river Thermodon,
reputed to be the inventors of ironwork.
   [f] Zephyr, who was a half-brother to Memnon. They
were both sons of Eos. Queen Arsinoë is here called Locrian,
because of her temple at Zephyrium, the promontory near
Canopus.
   [g] Queen Arsinoë after her deification was called Aphro-
dite Zephyritis.
   [h] A reference to the constellation called the Crown of
Ariadne. Ariadne, daughter of Minos, was abandoned by
Theseus in Naxos. Dionysus is said to have loved her, and
set up a crown of stars in her memory.

CALLIMACHUS

φάεσ]ιν ἐν πολέεσσιν ἀρίθμιος ἀλλ[ὰ
  καὶ Βερ]ενίκειος καλὸς ἐγὼ πλόκαμος,
ὕδασι] λουόμενόν με παρ' ἀθα[νάτους ἀνιόντα
Κύπρι]ς ἐν ἀρχαίοις ἄστρον [ἔθηκε νέον.

  •   •   •   •   •   •

67 πρόσθε μὲν ἐρχομεν .. μετοπωρινὸν Ὠκεανόνδε

  •   •   •   •   •   •

75 οὐ τάδε μοι τοσσήνδε φέρει χάριν ὅσσον ἐκείνης
  ἀσχάλλω κορυφῆς οὐκέτι θιξόμενος,
ἧς ἄπο, παρθενίη μὲν ὅτ' ἦν ἔτι, πολλὰ πέπωκα
  λιτά, γυναικείων δ' οὐκ ἀπέλαυσα μύρων.

61 φάεσι]ν Eitrem : τείρεσι]ν Maas, Kuiper (prob. longius
spatio). in fin. φαείνω L. : φανείην Vitelli : γένωμαι Maas.

112

(EPILOGUS)

. . . . .]ιν ὅτ' ἐμὴ μοῦσα τ[. . . . .]άσεται
. . .]του καὶ Χαρίτων [. . . . . .]ρια μοιαδ' ἀνάσσης
. . .]τερης οὔ σε ψευδομ[ένῳ στό]ματι

1 ἀεί]δειν Platt. τ[ι κομπ]άσεται G. Murray : τ[ι τεχν]άσεται
vel κωμ]άσεται Coppola.   2 πλού]του καὶ Χαρίτων [κοσ-
μήτ]ρια, μαῖα δ' ἀνάσσης A. Platt de Venere cogitans (πλου)
longius spatio) : Βάτ]του (?) E. Bignone : [κηδεύτ]ρια, μαῖα
Coppola, de Cyrene : [κομμώτ]ρια Gallavotti, de Calliope
Musa.   3 ἡμε]τέρης G. Murray, cett. : ὑμε]τέρης von Arnim
et Wil. Iovem in vv. 1-7 loqui arbitrati : ψευδον[P emend. et
suppl. Maas : ψεῦδον [ἐπ' οὐνό]ματι G. Murray (ὅτ' οὔ. Platt) :
[ὅτε στό]ματι Ellis : [ὄναρ στό]ματι Coppola : [ὕδος πό]ματι
Gallavotti : ἔπος στό]ματι Barber.

84

be counted among the many stars. Washed in the
waters (of the Ocean), and rising close to the im-
mortals, Cypris set me to be a new star among the
37 ancient ones . . . Proceeding to the Ocean . . . late
75 autumn . . . The joy of these honours cannot out-
weigh the distress which I feel that I no longer shall
touch that head, from which when (Berenice was) still
a maiden I drank so many frugal scents, but did not
enjoy the myrrh of the married woman's (hair).[a] [b]

[a] Married women used stronger perfumes.
[b] In Catullus (ll. 79-88) there is a nuptial rite, which pro-
bably comes from the second edition of the *Plokamos*, pre-
pared when the poem was added as a last aetion to the *Aetia*.

62 suppl. Vitelli.   63 ὕδασι] Vogliano : κύμασι] Vitelli
(fort. longius, δάκρυσι non capit lacuna).   fin. et 64 suppl.
Vitelli.

112

(EPILOGUE) [a]

" . . . when my Muse . . . and of the Graces . . .
and (mother) of our queen [b] . . . not with a false (?)

[a] The epilogue is highly problematic. Besides Zeus
another deity is invoked, as can be seen from ll. 7 ff. Various
suggestions have been made (*e.g.* Platt suggested Aphrodite,
Gallavotti the Muse Calliope), but Coppola's, that the poet
is here invoking Cyrene (nymph and city), appears the most
probable. On various other views see H. Herter, *Zeitbericht
über die Fortschritte der Klass. Altertumswissenschaft* (*Bur-
sian*), cclv (1937), pp. 140 ff.
[b] It is not clear which queen is here addressed, Arsinoë
or Berenice. The mention of the Graces recalls the beginning
of the *Aetia* (frs. 3-7).

πάντ' ἀγαθὴν καὶ πάντᾳ τ[ελ]εσφόρον εἶπεν [
5   κείν .. τῷ Μοῦσαι πολλὰ νέμοντι βοτά
σὺν μύθους ἐβάλοντο παρ' ἴχνιον ὀξέος ἵππου·
χαῖρε, σὺν εὐεστοῖ δ' ἔρχεο λωϊτέρη.
χαῖρε, Ζεῦ, μέγα καὶ σύ, σάω δ' [ὅλο]ν οἶκον ἀνά-
κτων·
αὐτὰρ ἐγὼ Μουσέων πεζὸν [ἔ]πειμι νομόν.—

10   ΚΑΛΛΙΜΑΧΟΥ ΑΙΤΙΩΝ Δ'

4 εἶπέ μ[οι ὥσπερ Coppola : εἶπεν [ἀοιδός] | κεῖν[ος Mair et
Maas : εἶπ' ἐν [ἀοιδῇ Barber.   5 fort. κείν[ου—πελλὰ coni.
Maas.   7 -τέρη Gallavotti.   8 [ὅλο]ν suppl. Hu. :
[ἐμὸ]ν Ellis et Wil.   9 potius πεζὸν (quam ος) in P legit
L. : suppl. Hu.   νόμον Kapsomenos.

86

(mouth ?) fully good and fully fruitful he said you
(were) . . . to whom the Muses, as he tended his
5 many sheep by the footprint of the fiery horse, told
stories.ᵃ Fare well, and return with greater pros-
perity.ᵇ Hail greatly thou too, Zeus, and save all
the house of the kings. But I will pass on to the
prose pasture of the Muses.ᶜ

ᵃ The reference is again to Hesiod, as in fr. 2.
ᵇ The goddess invoked, probably Cyrene (nymph and
city), or the Muse Calliope.
ᶜ This can only mean the *Iambi*, which followed in the
collected works of Callimachus, and indicates that the whole
epilogue (fr. 112) was written for the final edition of the
Aetia. *Cf.* Horat. *Sat.* ii. 6. 17 " Musa pedestris " and
Epist. ii. 1. 250.

FRAGMENTA INCERTI LIBRI
AETIORUM

114

(STATUA APOLLINIS DELII)

" **Δήλιος ὠπόλλων;** "] " ναί, Δήλιος." " ἦ σύ γε
   πῃ[χέων
5   ἐννέα δίς; " " τόσσων,] ναὶ μὰ τὸν αὐτὸν ἐμέ."
" χρύσεος ἐπλάσθης; "] " ναί, χρύσεος." " ἦ καὶ
   ἀφα[ρής; "
      " ναί, μοῦνον περί με] ζῶμα μέσον στ[ρέφεται."
" τεῦ δ' ἕνεκα σκαιῇ μὲν ἔ]χεις χερὶ Κύνθιε τ[όξον,
   τὰς δ' ἐπὶ δεξιτερῇ] σὰς ἰδανὰς Χάριτας; "
10 "   ] ἵν' ἄφρονας ὕβρ[ιος ἴσχω
             τοῖς ἀ]γαθοῖς ὀρέγω."

4-5 suppl. Maas.   6 χρύσεος ἐπλάσθης] Maas : ἀφα[ρὴς Pf.
7 ναί, μοῦνον (Pf.) περί με] Barber : στ[ρέφεται L.   8 τεῦ—μὲν
suppl. Pf., cett. L.   9 τὰς—δεξιτερῇ] suppl. Pf.   10 suppl.
Maas.   11 suppl. L. Maas.

---

[a] The statue of Apollo at Delos held the Graces in the
right hand and the bow in the left. The explanation given

FRAGMENTS FROM THE AETIA
WHICH CANNOT BE ATTRIBUTED
WITH CERTAINTY TO ANY
SPECIAL BOOK

114

(THE STATUE OF APOLLO AT DELOS)

" ARE you the Delian Apollo ? " " Yes, I am the
5 Delian." " Are you eighteen cubits high ? " " That
is right, by me (the god)." " Made of gold ? "
" Yes, made of gold." " And unclad ? " " Yes,
only a belt goes round the middle of me." " For
what reason in your left hand, Cynthian, do you hold
the bow, and in your right hand your comely
10 Graces ? " [a] " . . . To hold back the stupid from
being insolent . . . I offer to the good."

was that the god was more inclined to offer blessings than to
inflict punishment. Apollo is called Cynthian after Cynthus,
the mountain of Delos. The poet is addressing the statue in
this fragment. On this aetion see R. Pfeiffer, " The Image
of the Delian Apollo and Apolline Ethics," *Journal of the
Warburg and Courtauld Institutes*, xv (1952), pp. 21 f.

115

(ONNES)

[. . . . . .]υνη· λάθρη δὲ παρ' Ἡφαίστοιο καμίνοις
ἔτραφεν αἱράων ἔργα διδασκόμενοι.
Ὄννης μὲν νῦν ηχ[   ]εισιμ[
    λαοῖσιν, τότε δ' ην ψ[   ]αν[
15 ἧστο τεὴν κάθοδον θηεύμενο[ς
    τω δὲ σιδηρείας ἱμα[. .]ς ἀντυγάδ[ας
    ἃς αὐτοὶ χάλκευσαν ἐπ' ἄκμοσιν Ἡφ[αίστοιο
    γεντ[. .]κ[. .]τειν νεκ[   ]υσ[

119

Μηκώνην μακάρων ἕδρανον αὖτις ἰδεῖν,
ἧχι πάλους ἐβάλοντο, διεκρίναντο δὲ τιμάς
πρῶτα Γιγαντείου δαίμονες ἐκ πολέμου·

---

[a] Mecone is the old name for Sicyon, the city on the
northern coast of the Peloponnese; Zeus, Posidon and

177

(MUSCIPULA)

5 ἀστὴρ δ' εὖτ'] ἄρ' ἔμελλε βοῶν ἄπο μέσσαβα
    [λύσειν
    αὔλιος], ὃς δυθμὴν εἶσιν ὑπ' ἠελίου
    ] ὣς κεῖνος Ὀφιονίδῃσι φαείνει
    ] θεῶν τοῖσι παλαιοτέροις,

5 ἀστὴρ εὖτ'] et [λύειν suppl. Norsa-Vitelli, δ' propter spa-
tium et [λύσειν Pf.   6 suppl. Blomfield.

AETIA

115

(ONNES)

11 AND they [a] grew up secretly by the furnaces of He-
phaestus, learning the art of the hammer . . . Onnes
now . . . but then . . . sat looking out for your re-
16 turn . . . iron shields which they themselves forged
on the anvils of Hephaestus.

[a] The story is not clear, and otherwise unknown. It may
well be that Onnes and Tottes are here identified with the
Cabiri, the non-Hellenic deities, who promoted fertility and
protected sailors, and the historic centre of whose worship
was Samothrace.

119

. . . to see again Mecone, seat of the Blessed Ones,
where the gods drew lots and first distributed the
honours after the war against the Giants.[a]

Pluto are said to have drawn lots there for the kingdoms of
the Earth, the Sea and Hades.

177

(THE MOUSETRAP) [a]

5 AND when the evening-star [b] which comes at sunset
was about to release the leather straps from the
necks of the oxen . . . as he (*sc.* the sun) shines on
the descendants of Ophion [c] . . . the older gods

[a] Nothing is known about the invention of the mouse-
trap. We do not know what the story in this aetion is about,
or who the persons mentioned in it are.
[b] αὔλιος = bringing to the fold ; the planet Venus.
[c] The gods overthrown by Zeus lived ever after in dark-
ness. Ophion was ruler of the universe before Cronos.

]τηρι θύρην· ὁ δ' ὅτ' ἔκλυεν ἠχ[ήν,
10]ιῆς ἴαχ' ἐπ' οὖς ἐλάφου
..]υμνο[....]μεν ὅσσον ἀκουέμεν, ἦκα δ' ἔλ[εξεν·
" ὀχληροὶ τί πο[τ'] αὖ γείτονες ἡμέτερον
ἦκατ' ἀποκνα[ί]σοντες, ἐπεὶ μάλα [γ'] οὔ τι φέ-
ρο[ντες;
ξ[εί]νοις κωκυμοὺς ἔπλασεν ὕμμε θεός."
15 ὣς ἐνέπων τὸ [μ]ὲν ἔργον, ὅ οἱ μετὰ [χερ]σὶν
ἔ[κειτο,
ῥῖψ]εν, [ἐ]πεὶ σμίνθοις κρυπτὸν ἔτευχε δόλον·
ἐν δ' ἐτίθει παγίδεσσιν ὀλέθρια δείλατα δοιαῖς
...]ιν[.....]ε[...] μίγδα μάλευρον ἑλών
..]ντ[...]ωιτα[.]α[.........] θάνατόνδε κά-
λ[εσσε
20 ...]γειη[.....]α[.]ωσιν ἔπι
..]ημ[....]σκί[........]ατιρε[
πολλάκις ἐκ λύχνου πῖον ἔλειξαν ἔαρ
ἀλκαίαις ἀφύσαντες, ὅτ' οὐκ ἐπὶ πῶμ[α τεθείη
..]μαις και[..]άλη[.]ι[..] πότ' ἐξ ἑτέρου
25 ..]λησ[....]λοιο τά τ' ἀνέρος ἔργα πενιχροῦ
...]οιον[...]σπληρους κυπ[.....]συπ .
..]εισμορα [....... ὠ]ρχήσαντο
βρέγματι, καὶ κανθῶν ἤλασαν ὦρον ἄπο.
ἀλλὰ τόδ' οἱ σίνται βρα[χέ]ῃ ἔνι νυκτὶ τέλεσσαν
30 κύνατον, ᾧ πλεῖστ[ον] μήνατο κεῖνος ἔπι,
ἄμφ[ιά] οἱ σισύρην τε κακοὶ κίβισίν τε διέβρον·
τοῖσι δὲ] διχθαδίους εὐτύκασεν φονέας,
ἱπόν τ' ἀνδίκτην τε μάλ' εἰδότα μακρὸν ἁλέσθαι.

AETIA

. . . the door. But he, as he heard the noise (of the
mice), like the (dappled ?) hind to whose ears comes
the cry of (a lion-cub) from afar . . . and he said
12 softly : " Tiresome neighbours, why did you come
again to ravage our house ? for certainly you bring
nothing (good). God created you to be a bane to
15 the guests (?)." Saying this he put down the work
he was doing, for he was preparing a secret (imple-
ment) to trick the mice. And in the two traps he
placed a fatal bait . . . taking flour mixed with
. . . called them to death. . . . Often they drew
the fat oil from the lamp with their tails, and licked
it when the lid was not in place . . . from another
25 . . . the tasks of a poor man . . . they danced on
(his) head and drove away sleep from his eyes. But
30 this was the most shameless deed, and the one for
which he was most angry, that the thieves achieved
within a short night. The rogues gnawed at his pau-
per's rags, the goat's hair cloak and the wallet. He
prepared for them a double killer, a mousetrap, and
a catch which is able to make a long jump[a] . . .

---

[a] Presumably the kind of trap which knocks the mouse
on the head as he nibbles the bait.

---

9 in init. e.g. ξῦσέ τι δὴ κνησ]τῆρι temptavit Pf. : finem
suppl. Norsa-Vitelli.   10 βαλ]ιῆς Maas : ὀκνη]ρῆς Norsa-
Vitelli.   ὡς ὅτε τις βαλ]ιῆς prop. Barber.   11 fort. σκ]ύμνο[ς
Pf. : σκ]ύμνο[ς, [με]ῖ[νε] μὲν prop. Barber.   ἐλ[εξεν suppl. Maas.
12 suppl. Pf. (aut τό[δ'] ?).   13 suppl. Pf.   14 ξ]είνοις
Pf. : δ]εινούς Barber.   15 τὸ [μ]ὲν L.   [χερ]σὶν ἔ[κειτο
suppl. Maas.   16 ρῦψ]εν e.g. suppl. L. : ἧκ]εν (sc. ἐκ
χειρῶν) Pf.   19 suppl. Barber.   23 exit. e.g. suppl.
Körte.   πώμ[ατ' ἔκειτο Norsa-Vitelli.   25 σύ]λησ[αν πί]-
λοιο Maas.   27 κλ]εισμὸν i.e. κλισμὸν Pf. : exit. suppl.
L.   29 βρα[χέ]η et τέλεσσαν Maas : τελέσσαι Norsa-Vitelli.
30 ᾧ πλεῖστ[ον dist. et suppl. L.   31 ἄμφ[ιά] suppl. Maas.
32 e.g. suppl. Maas.

93

CALLIMACHUS

178-184

(ICUS)

178

ἠὼς οὐδὲ πιθοιγὶς ἐλάνθανεν οὐδ' ὅτε δούλοις
ἦμαρ Ὀρέστειοι λευκὸν ἄγουσι χόες·
Ἰκαρίου καὶ παιδὸς ἄγων ἐπέτειον ἀγιστύν,
Ἀτθίσιν οἰκτίστη, σὸν φάος, Ἠριγόνη,
5 ἐς δαίτην ἐκάλεσσεν ὁμηθέας, ἐν δέ νυ τοῖσι
ξεῖνον ὃς Αἰγύπτῳ καινὸς ἀνεστρέφετο
μεμβλωκὼς ἴδιόν τι κατὰ χρέος· ἦν δὲ γενέθλην
Ἴκιος, ᾧ ξυνὴν εἶχον ἐγὼ κλισίην
οὐκ ἐπιτάξ, ἀλλ' αἶνος Ὁμηρικός, αἰὲν ὁμοῖον
10 ὡς θεός, οὐ ψευδής, ἐς τὸν ὁμοῖον ἄγει.
καὶ γὰρ ὁ Θρηϊκίην μὲν ἀπέστυγε χανδὸν ἄμυστιν
οἰνοποτεῖν, ὀλίγῳ δ' ἥδετο κισσυβίῳ.

11 ἀπέστυγε P codd.: ἀνήνατο cod. v.l.   12 ζωροποτεῖν
codd. v.l.

---

[a] In Egypt Callimachus was the guest of Pollis, an
Athenian, who had settled in that country. In his home
Pollis scrupulously kept the festivals of his native Athens.
On this particular occasion, the festival celebrated was that
of the *Aiora*, which was instituted in connexion with the
epidemic of suicide among the women of Attica after Erigone,
daughter of Icarius, hanged herself. Among the guests of
Pollis was a merchant, Theogenes, from the small island of
Icos, one of the Magnesian islands. Callimachus questions
him about the cult of Peleus in Icos, and the relations of
that island with Thessaly.

[b] The *Pithoigia* were the first day of the *Anthesteria*.

[c] The "Feast of the Pitchers" was celebrated on the
second day of the *Anthesteria*. The *Anthesteria* were cele-
brated on the 11th (*Pithoigia*), 12th (*Choes*) and 13th
(*Chytroi*) of the month Anthesterion. The myth was that
Orestes came to Athens during the celebration of a public

94

AETIA

178–184

(ICOS) [a]

178

Nor did the dawn of the Opening of the Jars [b] pass
unheeded, nor the day whereon the Pitchers of Ores-
tes bring a white day for the slaves.[c] And when he
kept the yearly ceremony of Icarius' child, your day,
5 Erigone, lady most lamented by Attic women,[d] he
invited to a banquet his friends, and among them a
stranger who was newly visiting Egypt, having come
on some private business. He was an Ician [e] by
birth, and I shared a couch with him—not by design,
10 but the saying of Homer is not false that God ever
brings like to like.[f] For he too hated the greedy
Thracian draught [g] of wine, and liked a small cup.

festival, and the king of Athens ordered that a pitcher of
wine (χοῦς) be given to each guest separately, so that he
would not appear inhospitable, but at the same time an un-
purified murderer would not eat and drink with the others.
On that day slaves enjoyed great licence, hence " a white
day " for the slaves.
    [d] Icarius, an Athenian, was taught the knowledge of the
vine by Dionysus. He was killed by some peasants to whom
he had given wine. His daughter Erigone, guided by her
dog Maera, found his grave on Mt. Hymettus. In her grief
she hanged herself on a tree over her father's grave. Erigone
became the constellation Virgo, her father Bootes or Arcturus,
and Maera became Sirius. Dionysus caused a plague of
madness to fall upon the Athenian women, who hanged
themselves as Erigone had done. To end the plague the
festival of the *Aiora* was founded, which was called " Eu-
deipnos."
    [e] Icos, an island off Thessalian Magnesia.
    [f] *Od.* xvii. 218.
    [g] The custom of draining the cup was considered Thracian
and barbarian.

τῷ μὲν ἐγὼ τάδ' ἔλεξα περιστείχοντος ἀλείσου
τὸ τρίτον, εὖτ' ἐδάην οὔνομα καὶ γενεήν·
15 " ἦ μάλ' ἔπος τόδ' ἀληθές, ὅ τ' οὐ μόνον ὕδατος
αἶσαν,
ἀλλ' ἔτι καὶ λέσχης οἶνος ἔχειν ἐθέλει.
τὴν ἡμεῖς—οὐκ ἐν γὰρ ἀρυστήρεσσι φορεῖται
οὐδέ μιν εἰς ἀτ[ενεῖ]ς ὀφρύας οἰνοχόων
αἰτήσεις ὁρόων ὅτ' ἐλεύθερος ἀτμένα σαίνει—
20 βάλλωμεν χαλεπῷ φάρμακον ἐν πόματι,
Θεύγενες· ὅσσα δ' ἐμεῖο σέθεν πάρα θυμὸς ἀκοῦσαι
ἰχαίνει, τάδε μοι λέξον [ἀνειρομέν]ῳ·
Μυρμιδόνων ἐσσῆνα τ[ί πάτριον ὕ]μμι σέβεσθαι
Πηλέα, κῶς Ἴκῳ ξυν[ὰ τὰ Θεσσαλι]κά,
25 τεῦ δ' ἕνεκεν γήτειον ἰδ[. .]υτ[. . . .]ρτον ἔχουσα
ἥρωος κα[θ]όδου πα[ῖς
εἰδότες ὡς ἐνέπου[σιν
κείνην ἢ περὶ σὴν [
οὔθ' ἑτέρην ἔγνωκα· τ[
30 οὔατα μυθεῖσθαι βουλομέν[οις ἀνέχων."
τ[αῦτ'] ἐμέθεν λέξαντο[ς
" τρισμάκαρ, ἦ παύρων ὄλβιός ἐσσι μέτα,
ναυτιλίης εἰ νῆϊν ἔχεις βίον· ἀλλ' ἐμὸς αἰών
κύμασιν αἰθυίης μᾶλλον ἐσῳκίσατο

13 τόδ' cod. v.l.   15 ἦ γὰρ cod. v.l. : ἦν ἄρ' Porson.
18 suppl. Grenfell-Hu. (vel ἀτ[ρεμεῖ]ς, ἀτ[ρόμου]ς, ἀτ[ρόπου]ς).
22 suppl. Grenfell-Hu.   23 suppl. Grenfell-Hu.   24 suppl.
e.g. L.   25 ἄ]ρτον suppl. Grenfell-Hu. : fort. κα]ρτὸν? i.e.

184
οὐδ' ἔτι τὴν Φθίων εἶχεν ἀνακτορίην
εἶλεν cod. v.l.

AETIA

To him I said this, as the beaker was going round for
the third time, when I had learnt his name and de-
15 scent : " Verily this is a true saying that wine requires
not only its portion of water, but also its portion of
talk. So—for talk is not handed round in ladles, nor
will you ask for it by gazing at the haughty brows of
the cup-bearers, at a time when the free man favᵘns
20 upon the slave—let us, Theogenes, put talk in the
cup to mend the tedious draught ; and do tell me in
answer to my question what my heart yearns to
hear from you : Why is it the tradition of your
country to worship Peleus, king of the Myrmidons ?
30 What has Thessaly to do with Icos ? [a] . . . holding
ears ready for those who want to tell a story."
When I had thus spoken . . . " Truly, thrice blessed
one, you are happy as few are, if you lead a life
which is ignorant of sea-faring. But the home of my
life is more among the waves than the sea-gull."

[a] It appears that in Icos it was customary to celebrate the
day of the death of Peleus, who is reputed to have been killed
there.

---

sectivum porrum Pf.   26 suppl. Grenfell-Hu. (vel
πα[ρθένος) : κα[θ]’ ὁδοῦ Wil.   27 suppl. Grenfell-Hu.
28 ἢ Grenfell-Hu. : ἢ περὶ σὴν [δέδρομε νῆσον, ἅλα e.g. Pf.
30 -μέν[οις ἀνέχων vel παρέχων vel ὑπέχων e.g. Pf.   31 suppl.
Grenfell-Hu.   32 ἐστι codd. : corr. F. Jacobs.   μέγα
codd. : corr. Bentley.   33 ναυτιλίησιν ἣν ἔχεις codd. :
ναυτιλίης ὃς νῆιν Bentley : εἰ A. Nauck.

184

. . . nor was he yet ruler of the inhabitants of
Phthia.[a]

[a] The reference is probably to Peleus.

186

(HYPERBOREI)

]σιν ἐτήσια, σὺν δ[ε]κ[α]τ[α]ίῳ
4   ]ουσιν δῖα πέτευρα [φόρ]ῳ

.   .   .   .

]ν υἷες Ὑπερβορέων
Ῥιπαίου πέμπουσιν ἀπ' οὔρεος, ἧχι μάλιστα
10   τέρπουσιν λιπαραὶ Φοῖβον ὀνοσφαγίαι·
Ἑλλήν]ων τά γε πρῶτα Πελασγικο[ὶ Ἑλλοπιῆες
ἐξ Ἀριμα]σπείης δειδέχαται κο[μ]ι̣[δῆς.
ἔνθεν] ἐπὶ πτόλιάς τε καὶ οὔ[ρεα Μαλίδος αἴης
στέλλο]υσιν Νάου θῆτες ἀ̣[νιπτόποδες
15   ] ὅτις φηγοῦ [

3 suppl. L.   4 suppl. L.   11 init. suppl. L.:
fin. suppl. J. D. P. Bolton; cf. Hes. fr. 134 et fr. 212, etiam
Steph. Byz. v. Ἑλλοπία.   12 suppl. L.   13-14 suppl.
Barber-Maas.

---

[a] The Hyperboreans were a legendary race of Apollo-
worshippers living in the far north, highly revered by the
Greeks. Offerings from them arrived at the Delian shrine,
not carried by the Hyperboreans themselves, but passed
" from city to city " until brought to Delos by the men of
Tenos. They were said to sacrifice donkeys in honour of
Apollo.

186

(THE HYPERBOREANS) [a]

3 . . . yearly, along with the tribute of the tenth . . .
they (send) the divine planks . . . the sons of the
Hyperboreans send from the Rhipaean [b] Mountains
10 where the rich sacrifice of donkeys pleases Phoebus
particularly. Of the Greeks the Pelasgian Ellopians [c]
first accept these conveyed by the Arimaspi.[d] From
there, the servants of Zeus Naios [e] with unwashen
feet send them to the cities and the mountains of
the land of Malis [f] . . .

[b] The Rhipaean Mountains were east of the river Istrus
(Danube).

[c] By these Callimachus means the " Dodonaeans " (*cf.*
Herod. iv. 33. 2). There were, as J. D. P. Bolton pointed
out, two districts called *Ellopia*, one around Dodona, the
other in Euboea (*cf.* Steph. Byz. *s.* 'Ελλοπία). For the former
cf. Hes. fr. 134, called Pelasgic (*cf.* Hes. fr. 212) here, to
distinguish it from the Euboean or " Abantian " Ellopia
(*cf.* Hes. fr. 186 and Call. *Hymn* iv. 20).

[d] The Arimaspians are said to have been a tribe of the
Hyperboreans, or, according to other sources, their neigh-
bours.

[e] The Zeus of Dodona was also called Zeus Naios. The
Selloi, the priests of the Dodonaean Zeus, were called ἀνιπτό-
ποδες, " with unwashed feet."

[f] The area of the Greek mainland which faces the north-
western tip of Euboea.

IAMBI

INTRODUCTION

A BOOK of iambic poems, of approximately one thousand lines, followed the *Aetia*.[a] It consisted of thirteen poems of miscellaneous content and character. They were included in one book because the metres in which they were written were all iambic or choliambic.[b] There is no internal or external evidence for the dating of any of these poems or in support of Dawson's view that *Iambi* i and xiii were written at a later date as an introduction and epilogue to this group of poems.[c]

[a] See fr. 112. 9.
[b] Even *Iambus* xii, which is written in a catalectic trochaic trimeter, would have been considered as written in an " iambic " metre by certain ancient metricians; *cf*. Hephaest. vi. 2, p. 18. 11 C. In fact, " iambic " is here used as a generic term, in contrast with the elegiac and melic metres of other Callimachean " books."
[c] C. M. Dawson, *The Iambi of Callimachus*, especially p. 143, and Pfeiff. ii, p. xxxvii.

ΚΑΛΛΙΜΑΧΟΥ ΙΑΜ[ΒΟΙ

IAMBUS I

Iambus i is in its present condition an obscure poem. It appears to be a dramatic monologue by Hipponax of Colophon, to whom tradition ascribes the invention of the choliambic metre, in which the poem is written. The content of *Iambus* i is given thus by the *Diegesis* :

(Callimachus) imagines the dead Hipponax as summoning the scholars to the shrine of Parmenion, called the Sarapideum. When they came in droves (Hipponax) bade them not to be jealous of one another, telling them how the Arcadian Bathycles on his deathbed disposed of all his property, and in particular of a golden cup, which he handed over to Amphalces, his middle son, to give to the greatest of the seven sages. Amphalces came to Miletus and offered the cup to Thales, but Thales sent it to Bias of Priene, and he to Periander of Corinth. Periander passed it on to Solon of

---

ᵃ Dawson, *Yale Class. Studies*, xi (1950), p. 148, believes that *Iambi* i and xiii are later works, written when Callimachus prepared the final edition of his collected works. There is, however, very little evidence in support of this view : the "tone of assured pre-eminence and self-confidence with which the poet speaks," and the fashion of finishing a "book" with a poem on literary criticism, hardly prove the point.

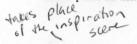
takes place
of the inspiration scene

’Ακούσαθ’ ‘Ιππώνακτος· οὐ γὰρ ἀλλ’ ἥκω

ᵃ Callimachus is a Hipponax *redivivus*, who comes from

IAMBI

IAMBUS I

Athens, who passed it on to Chilon the Lacedaemonian ; he dispatched it to Pittacus of Mitylene and he to Cleobulus of Lindus. Then from Cleobulus the cup came back again to Thales, who, having received the award twice, dedicated it to Didymean Apollo. Accordingly (Hipponax) said (you scholars should not be so critical) of one another . . . or quarrel (so bitterly ?) . . .

At the end of the poem Hipponax returns to Hades (ll. 96 ff.).

There is no indication as to the date of the poem [a] ; the dialect is a literary Ionic. Callimachus derived the story of the cup of Bathycles from Leandrios of Miletus, a writer of *Milesiaca.*[b] With the exception of Euhemerus,[c] no other person mentioned can be identified, though no doubt they must have been well-known literary or comic figures of the day.

Neither Euhemerus, called " old," nor the " Sarapideum before the walls " can help in dating *Iambus* i, as the date of Euhemerus is uncertain (see Pauly-Wissowa, *R.E.* vi. 952 f.), and the Sarapideum mentioned here is not one of the known Alexandrian sanctuaries of Sarapis (see Pfeiff. ii, pp. xxxix f.).

[b] *Cf.* Diog. Laert. i. 28. The exact date of Leandrios is unknown, as well as any details about his life.

[c] See note on l. 11.

LISTEN to Hipponax,[a] for indeed I have come from Hades to admonish the Alexandrian scholars. Hipponax of Ephesus, *c.* 550 B.C., famous iambographer.

ἐκ τῶν ὅκου βοῦν κολλύβου πιπρήσκουσιν,
φέρων ἴαμβον οὐ μάχην ἀείδοντα
τὴν Βουπάλειον [

ἐς τὸ πρὸ τείχευς ἱρὸν ἁλέες δεῦτε,
10 οὗ τὸν πάλαι Πάγχαιον ὁ πλάσας Ζᾶνα
γέρων λαλάζων ἄδικα βιβλία ψήχει.

26 ὤπολλον, ὤνδρες, ὡς παρ᾽ αἰπόλῳ μυῖαι
ἢ σφῆκες ἐκ γῆς ἢ ἀπὸ θύματος Δελφοί,
εἰληδὸν [ἐσ]μεύουσιν· ὦ Ἑκάτη πλήθευς.
ὁ ψιλοκόρσης τὴν πνοὴν ἀναλώσει
30 φυσέων ὅκως μὴ τὸν τρίβωνα γυμνώσῃ·
σωπῇ γενέσθω καὶ γράφεσθε τὴν ῥῆσιν.
ἀνὴρ Βαθυκλῆς Ἀρκάς—οὐ μακρὴν ἄξω,
ὦ λῶστε μὴ σίμαινε, καὶ γὰρ οὐδ᾽ αὐτός
μέγα σχολάζω· δεῖ με γὰρ μέσον δινεῖν·
35 φεῦ φ]εῦ Ἀχέροντος—τῶν πάλαι τις εὐδαίμων
ἐγένετο, πάντα δ᾽ εἶχεν οἷσιν ἄνθρωποι
θεοί τε λευκὰς ἡμέρας ἐπίστανται.
ἤδη καθίκ[ειν οὗτ]ος ἡνίκ᾽ ἤμελλεν

2 ὅκου P : ὅκο vel οἴκων codd. corr. Bentley.   28 suppl.
Pf.   35 suppl. Pf. : σοὶ Ζ]εῦ L.   38 καθίκ[ειν Pf.,
Snell.   οὗτ]ος Knox, L.

---

[a] The cheapness of things in Hades was proverbial. Cf.
Call. Epigr. xiii. (xv L.C.L.) 6.
[b] The sculptors Bupalos and Athenis of Clazomenae were
attacked by Hipponax.
[c] This, according to the Diegesis, is τὸ Παρμενίωνος καλού-

the place where they sell an ox for a penny,[a] armed
with iambic verses, which do not sing the feud with
Bupalos,[b] but . . . come, gather at the shrine out-
10 side the walls,[c] where the old man who invented the
ancient Panchaean Zeus babbles and scribbles his im-
26 pious books [d] . . . O Apollo, the men swarm round in
droves like flies about a goatherd, or wasps from the
ground, or the Delphians returning from a sacrifice,[e]
what a crowd, O Hecate ![f] The bald man will exhaust
30 his breath blowing, that he may not be left without his
threadbare cloak (?).[g] Silence ! and write down my
tale : " A man of Arcadia, Bathycles—I will not tell
a long story (don't turn up your nose at me, my good
fellow), for not even I have much time to spare, as I
35 must whirl back to the heart of Acheron,[h] oh dear, oh
dear—was one of the happy men of old times ; he had
all those things by which men and gods know a lucky
day.[i] When he was about to sink into long (sleep ?)[j]—

μένον Σαραπίδειον. It is, therefore, none of the known sanc-
tuaries of Sarapis in Alexandria.

[d] Euhemerus of Messene claimed to have sailed down the
Red Sea, and round the south coast of Asia. In his book
Ἱερὰ Ἀναγραφή, the island of Panchaea was described with
its cities and temples and the stele on which Zeus was sup-
posed to have inscribed his *res gestae*, but the author was
attacked as a godless liar.

[e] The Delphians were said to hang around the altar and
carry away huge slices of the animals sacrificed, so that the
actual person sacrificing was often left without anything to
eat.

[f] Ancient chthonian goddess, frequently confused with
Artemis and Selene.

[g] This passage is still obscure.

[h] River of Thesprotia in southern Epirus, reputed to lead
to Hades.

[i] The λευκαὶ ἡμέραι (the white, the happy days) were cele-
brated in Attica. *Cf.* fr. 178. 2.   [j] Death.

CALLIMACHUS

ἐς μακρὸν [ὕπνον]—καὶ γὰρ ἐ[σθλ]ὸς ἔζωσε—,
40 τῶν′ [. . . . .] τοὺς μὲν ἔνθα, τοὺς δ′ ἔνθα
ἔστησε τοῦ κλιντῆρος· εἶχε γὰρ δεσμ[ό]ς
⟨ . . . . ⟩
μέλλοντας ἤδη παρθένοις ἁλινδεῖσθαι.
μόλις δ′ ἐπά[ρας] ὡς ποτῆς ἐπ′ ἀγκῶνα
. . . . .]ν ὁ Ἀρκ[ὰς κ]ἀνὰ τὴν στέγην βλέψας

46 ἔ]πειτ′ ἔφ[ησε
" ὦ παῖδες ὦ ἐμαὶ τὠπιόντος ἄγκυραι

. . . .

[Desunt versus fere 15 in P]

ἔπλευσεν ἐς Μίλητον· ἦν γὰρ ἡ νίκη
Θάλητος, ὅς τ′ ἦν ἄλλα δεξιὸς γνώμην
καὶ τῆς Ἁμάξης ἐλέγετο σταθμήσασθαι
55 τοὺς ἀστερίσκους, ᾗ πλέουσι Φοίνικες.
εὗρεν δ′ ὁ Προυσέληνος αἰσίῳ σίττῃ
ἐν τοῦ Διδυμέος τὸν γέροντα κωνίῳ
ξύοντα τὴν γῆν καὶ γράφοντα τὸ σχῆμα,
τοὐξεῦρ′ ὁ Φρὺξ Εὔφορβος, ὅστις ἀνθρώπων
60 τρίγωνα καὶ σκαληνὰ πρῶτος ἔγραψε
καὶ κύκλον ἐπ[. . .] κἠδίδαξε νηστεύειν

39 [ὕπνον] Trypanis (cf. *Anth. Pal.* vii. 91. 4) : [ἄλσος] e.g.
Pf. : [Ἀΐδην] Snell : ἐ[σθλ]ὸς Pf. 41 post v. 41 lacunam
vidit Maas. 43 suppl. L. 44 Ἀρκ[ὰς suppl. Pf. :
κ]ὰ L. 46 ἔ]π suppl. Hu. ἔφ[η Crusius : ἔφ[ησε Pf.,
Snell. 53 ὃς τὸν ἄλλα vel ὃς τἄλλα codd. : ὅς τ′ ἦν ἄλλα
Bentley. 61 ἔπ[λασε propos. Maas : ἔπ[αγε tempta-
verat Pf.
108

IAMBI

for he had lived virtuously (?)—. . . he placed his sons
some on the one side and some on the other of the bed
41 —for he was held down by arthritis . . . ready by
42 now to take their brides. Lifting himself with an
effort up on his elbow, as one who drinks . . . the
46 Arcadian man, and looking at the ceiling . . . he
then said : " Children, anchors of me who am passing
away . . .

[About 15 lines missing]

52 he [a] sailed to Miletus. For Thales [b] was the winner :
he was clever in other things, and was also said to
55 have mapped out the little stars of the Wain, [c] by which
the Phoenicians sail their ships. And the Arcadian [d]
by happy chance found the old man in the shrine of
Didymean Apollo, [e] scratching the earth with a staff,
drawing the figure which the Phrygian Euphorbos [f]
60 had devised, who was the first to draw both unequal-
sided triangles and the circle . . . and taught men to

[a] Amphalces, son of Bathycles.
[b] Thales of Miletus, the earliest Greek philosopher. His
most famous feat in astronomy was his prediction of the
solar eclipse of 28th May 585 B.C.
[c] Ursa Minor, the Lesser Bear, by which the Phoenicians
sailed, while the Greeks sailed by Ursa Major.
[d] The word used here means " Prelunar," for the Arca-
dians were said to be " older than the moon."
[e] The temple of Apollo at Didyma, or Didymi, near
Miletus. See fr. 229.
[f] Euphorbos was a Trojan, slain by Menelaus, of whom
Pythagoras of Samos declared himself to be a reincarnation
The mathematical achievements here attributed to Pytha-
goras are referred to with such brevity that the meaning is
exceedingly obscure. The figure which Thales is found
drawing appears to be the inscribing of a right-angled tri-
angle with its corners in a semi-circle, which was attributed to
Thales or Pythagoras, in other words the demonstration of the
theorem that " the angle in a semicircle is a right angle."

τῶν ἐμπνεόντων· οἱ δ' ἄρ' οὐχ ὑπήκουσαν,
οὐ πάντες, ἀλλ' οὓς εἶχεν οὗτερος δαίμων.
πρὸς δή μιν ὧδ' ἔφησε . [

65 ἐκεῖ[νο] τοὐλόχρυσον ἐξ[ελὼν πήρης·
" οὑμὸς πατὴρ ἐφεῖτο τοῦ[το τοὔκπωμα
δοῦ[ναι], τίς ὑμέων τῶν σοφ[ῶν ὀνήιστος
τῶν ἑπτά· κἠγὼ σοὶ δίδωμι πρωτῆον."
ὁ δ' ἦκα τῷ] σκίπωνι τοὐδα[φος ξύων

70 καὶ τ]ὴν ὑπήνην τητέρη [καταψήχων
ἐξεῖπε· " τὴν δόσιν μὲν [οὐκ ἔγωγ' ἄξω·
σὺ δ' εἰ τοκεῶνος μὴ λό[γοις ἀπειθήσεις,
Βίης [

[Desunt versus fere 20 in P, quorum hi quattuor
alias afferuntur]

Σόλων· ἐκεῖνος δ' ὡς Χίλων' ἀπέστειλεν

· · · · · · ·

75 πάλιν τὸ δῶρον ἐς Θάλητ' ἀνώλισθεν

· · · · · · ·

" Θάλης με τῷ μεδεῦντι Νείλεω δήμου
δίδωσι, τοῦτο δὶς λαβὼν ἀριστῆον."

· · · · · · ·

ἀλλ' ἢν ὅρῃ τις, " οὗτος 'Αλκμέων " φήσει
79 καὶ " φεῦγε· βάλλει· φεῦγ' " ἐρεῖ " τὸν ἄνθρωπον."

· · · · · · ·

62 οἱ τάδ' οὐδ' codd. : οἱ δ' ἄρ' οὐχ Niebuhr.   63 ἔσχεν
codd.   64 παῖς Βαθύκλης e.g. suppl. Diels.   65 ἐκεῖ[νο]
suppl. Hu., fin. e.g. suppl. Pf.   66 suppl. Pf. e *Dieg.* vi. 8.
67 δοῦ[ναι] suppl. Housman. fin. suppl. Hu.   68 e.g.
suppl. Pf.   69 ὁ δ' ἦκα τῷ] et [ξύων suppl. Maas : ἔτυψε
δὲ]—τοὐδα[φος πρέσβυς Pf. : alii alia.   70 init. suppl. Hu.,

abstain from living things *a* . . . but they did not
obey him; not all, but only they who were possessed
65 by the evil spirit. To him he said thus . . . having
drawn from his bag the cup of solid gold: " My
father bade me give this cup to the wisest of you
seven (sages) ; and I give you the prize." And he,
70 scratching calmly the ground with his stick, and
stroking his beard with his other hand, answered :
" (I for one will not accept) the gift ; if you are not
74 going to disobey your father's command, Bias *b* . . .

[About 20 lines missing in the papyrus, of which
4 are known from other sources]

75 Solon.*c* And he sent it to Chilon *d* . . . and again the
gift returned to Thales. . . . " Thales dedicates this
prize, which he was awarded twice, to the protector
of Neleus' people " *e* . . . But if one sees him he *f*
will cry : " He is mad as Alcmeon," *g* and " Flee," he
82 will say, " he strikes, flee the man " . . . and the

a According to some, Pythagoras enjoined abstention from
all animal food, according to others, he limited his prohibition
to the ploughing ox and the ram.
b Son of Teutamos from Priene, one of the " seven sages."
c The great Athenian statesman and poet (*c*. 640–560 B.C.),
one of the " seven sages."
d The Spartan ephor (556/5 B.C.), later accepted as one
of the " seven sages."
e According to Attic tradition, Neleus, the son of Codrus,
was the founder of Miletus. Ll. 76-77 quote the dedicatory
epigram on the votive offering.
f We do not know about whom Callimachus is speaking.
g Alcmeon, son of Amphiaraus and Eriphyle, and Orestes
were the proverbial madmen and matricides of the Euripidean
tragedies.

---

finem Pf.   71 e.g. suppl. Diels.   72 e.g. suppl.
Pf.   75 πάλιν cod. : πολὺ v.l.

82 ὁ δ' ἐξόπισθε Κω[ρ]υκαῖος ἐγχάσκει
τὴν γλῶσσαν †ελων ὡς κύων ὅταν πίνῃ,
καί φησι

83 εἰλῶν Hu. : ἕλκων Maas.

> [a] Probably the man mentioned in ll. 78 ff. The inhabitants
> of Corycus in Asia Minor were notorious for mingling with

IAMBUS II

THE content of *Iambus* ii is given by the *Diegesis* as follows:

All other animals shared speech with mankind, until the
swan went to the gods with the request that old age should
be abolished, and the fox ventured to assert that Zeus was
not ruling justly. From that time Zeus transferred their
power of speech to men, and they became loquacious. He

> [a] The basic elements of the story are also to be found in
> " Aesop " (*Fab.* 383 Halm); but more light is shed by
> Philo (*De confus. lingu.* 6 ff. (ii, p. 231 C.-W.)), who
> seems to have had Callimachus, or his source, in mind when
> writing: " there is another (fable) . . . about the com-
> munity of language of the animals . . . for it is said that all
> animals of the land, sea and air had once a common language,
> and spoke to one another in the manner in which Greeks
> speak to the Greeks and the barbarians to the barbarians,
> until a surfeit of the good things they enjoyed landed them
> in a desire to acquire the impossible : they sent ambassadors

192

῏Ην κεῖνος οὐνιαυτός, ᾧ τό τε πτηνόν

> [a] Animals are said to have possessed speech under the
> rule of Cronos.

eavesdropper [a] behind, gapes curling (?) his tongue
like a drinking dog, and says . . .

the captains of ships at anchor in the harbour, and then,
having overheard where the ship was sailing for, attacking
and plundering the vessel. Consequently " any busybody,
or anyone, who tries to listen in on those who are conversing
privately and in secret, is called a Corycian " (Strabo xiv.
644).

IAMBUS II

(*i.e.* the poet) says, mocking at them, that Eudemos acquired
a dog's, and Philton a donkey's voice.

The outline of the fable [a] and the satirical turn Callimachus
gives to it are clear, but neither Eudemos nor Philton has
been as yet identified. [b]

The metre is choliambic, and the dialect a literary Ionic.

---

demanding immortality, the abolition of old age and eternal
youth. They said that already one kind of animal, the snake,
had received this gift, for it divested itself of old age and
acquired its former youth. They also said that it was not
proper that the higher animals should be in an inferior posi-
tion to any baser animal, or all to one. They were duly
punished for their insolence by the immediate gift of many
languages. From that moment they cannot hear one another,
on account of the division of their common language into
many tongues."

[b] Even if Eudemos were the Eudemos of Call. *Epigr.* xlvii
(xlviii L.C.L.), as Coppola suggested (*Cirene*, pp. 45 and 82),
or the man who " curls his tongue like a drinking dog " of
Iambus i. 82 f., we still have no definite information about
him.

192

It was the time [a] when birds and creatures of the

CALLIMACHUS

καὶ τοὐν θαλάσσῃ καὶ τὸ τετράπουν αὔτως
ἐφθέγγεθ' ὡς ὁ πηλὸς ὁ Προμήθειος

. . . .

[Non plus quam 17 vv. deesse possunt inter 3 et 4]

τἀπὶ Κρόνου τε καὶ ἔτι τὰ πρὸ τη[
5 λ[. .]ουσα και κως [.]υ σ[.]νημεναις [
δίκαιος ὁ Ζεύς, οὐ δίκαια δ' αἰσυμνέων
τῶν ἑρπετῶν μὲν ἐξέκοψε τὸ φθέ[γμα,
γένος δὲ τ[.]υτ[. . .]ρον—ὥσπερ οὐ κάρτος
ἡμέων ἐχόντων χήτεροις ἀπάρξασθαι—
10 . . .]ψ ἐς ἀνδρῶν· καὶ κυνὸς μὲν Εὔδημος,
ὄνου δὲ Φίλτων, ψιττακοῦ δὲ [ῥητῆρες
οἱ δὲ τραγῳδοὶ τῶν θάλασσαν οἱ[κεύντων
ἔχουσι φωνήν· οἱ δὲ πάντες [ἄνθρωποι
καὶ πουλύμυθοι καὶ λάλοι πεφ[ύκασιν
15 ἐκεῖθεν, ὠνδρόνικε· ταῦτα δ' Αἴσωπος
ὁ Σαρδιηνὸς εἶπεν, ὅντιν' οἱ Δελφοί
ᾄδοντα μῦθον οὐ καλῶς ἐδέξαντο.—

2 αὔτως Pf. : αὐτῷ vel οὕτως codd. 3 Προμηθέως
codd. : Προμηθεῖος Blomfield (-ηος ?) : ⟦Προμηθῆος Bentley :
Προμηθεῖος (gen.) Bergk. 4 τῆ[σδ' ἀρχῆς ? Pf. : τῆ[ς Ῥείης
Barber. 5 λ[έγ]ουσα καὶ κῶς [ο]ὐ σ[υ]νῆμεν αἰσ[χύνη Kapsomenos. 7 suppl. von Arnim et Platt. 8 τουτο cum vestigiis
non convenit, post υτ fort. η : [χ]ῆρον ? Pf. 10 ἐτρε]ψ'
von Arnim : ἡμει]ψ' Platt. 11 suppl. von Arnim. 12
suppl. Wil. 13 sq. suppl. Platt.

IAMBUS III

The *Diegesis* sums up the poem as follows :

He criticizes the period as valuing wealth more than virtue,

114

sea and four-footed animals could talk in the same
way as the Promethean clay *a* . . .

[Not more than 17 lines missing] *b*

4 in the time of Cronus, and even before . . . Just is
Zeus, yet unjust was his ruling when he deprived
the animals of their speech, and—as though we
were not in a position to give part of our voice to
10 others *c*—(diverted) it to the race of men (defective
in this way ?). Eudemos, therefore, has a dog's voice,
and Philton a donkey's, (the orators) *d* that of a parrot,
and the tragedians have a voice like the dwellers in
the sea.*e* And for this cause, Andronicus,*f* all men
15 have become loquacious and wordy. Aesop of Sardis
told this, whom the Delphians did not receive well *g*
when he recited his tale.

a Man, who according to the myth was fashioned by
Prometheus out of clay.
b In this lacuna (of *c.* 17 lines) must have fallen the em-
bassy of the swan to Zeus, of which we hear in the *Diegesis*.
c Man has always spoken more than he should, according
to the poet.
d In view of the fact that the *Diegesis* does not mention
any other name, the supplement by von Arnim of ῥητῆρες,
the orators, is very probable, for oratory, like dramatic poetry,
was in decline in the days of Callimachus.
e The fish.
f Andronicus, to whom the poem is addressed, is unknown.
g Aesop is said to have rebuked the Delphians for hanging
about the altar and carrying away large slices of the sacrificed
animals ; the infuriated populace forced him over a cliff,
pelting him with stones. *Cf.* also fr. 191. 26 ff.

IAMBUS III

and accepts the preceding period (as superior), in which the
opposite view prevailed. He also criticizes a certain Euthy-

CALLIMACHUS

demos for exploiting his youth and beauty for profit, after
being introduced to a rich man by his mother.

Callimachus alludes to Hesiod (*Op.* 174), who considered
the past superior to the present, and begins the poem with
a wish (l. 1) that he had lived in that better past. We do
not know who Euthydemos was, but it appears he was a young

---

^a Other rivals appear in *Iambi* iv (Simos) and v (Apollonius or Cleon) and in *Epigr.* xxviii (xxx L.C.L.).

193

Εἴθ' ἦν, ἄναξ ὤπολλον, ἡνίκ' οὐκ ἦα

]αι καὶ σὺ κάρτ' ε[. .]μασθε

.   .   .   .

] . ν μοι τοῦτ' ἂν ἦν ὀνήϊσ[το]ν

35   . . .] Κ[υβή]βῃ τὴν κόμην ἀναρρίπτειν

Φρύγα πρὸς αὐλὸν ἢ ποδήρες ἕλκοντα

Ἄδωνιν αἰαῖ, τῆς θεοῦ τὸν ἄνθρωπον,

ἰηλεμίζειν· νῦν δ' ὁ μάργος ἐς Μούσας

ἔνευσα· τοίγαρ ἦν ἔμαξα δεν[. . .]σω.—

2 φίλαι τε Μοῦσα]αι Maas. ε[τι]μᾶσθε Puelma.   34 suppl.
Hu.   35 suppl. L.

---

^a i.e. in other, older times.
^b Cybebe, the Lydian form for Cybele, the great mother-
goddess of Anatolia. Primarily she was a goddess of fertility,
but also cured disease, gave oracles and protected her people

116

man whom Callimachus admired, and who was lured away by the wealth of a rival.[a] The poem ends on a pessimistic note (ll. 34 ff.): a life devoted to the Muses can never bring the wealth which is necessary in a materialistic age.[b]

The metre is choliambic, and the dialect a literary Ionic, similar to that of *Iambi* i and ii.

---

[b] On Callimachus' poverty see *Epigr.* xxxii. (xxxiv L.C.L.) 1, *Epigr.* xxviii (xxx L.C.L.) and *Epigr.* xxxi (xxxiii L.C.L.), and Wilamowitz, *Hell. Dichtung* i, pp. 171 ff.

193

LORD Apollo, would that I had lived when I was not [a] (and the . . . Muses) and you were greatly
34 honoured (?) . . . it were better for me . . . tossing my hair, to honour Cybebe [b] to the sound of the Phrygian flute [c] or in trailing robe, alas !, to mourn Adonis,[d] the slave of the goddess.[e] But now, fool that I was, I inclined to the Muses. I will, therefore, have to eat (?) the dough I kneaded.[f]

in war. The Greek world associated her with Demeter, and perhaps with a native Μήτηρ Θεῶν, Mother of the Gods.

[c] Ecstatic states, inducing prophetic rapture and insensibility to pain, were characteristic of the worship of Cybele. The Phrygian music played on the flute, said to have been invented by Marsyas, was thought to induce ecstatic and Bacchic rapture.

[d] Adonis, son of Cinyras, king of Cyprus, by an incestuous union with his daughter Myrrha, beloved by Aphrodite, who was killed while hunting by a boar. Lamentation at the death of Adonis was a feature of the annual festival in his honour.

[e] Aphrodite.

[f] Probably a reference to the proverb : ἤν τις ἔμαξε μᾶζαν, ταύτην καὶ ἐσθιέτω, " one eats the dough one kneads," equivalent to : " I have made my bed, and I must lie on it."

CALLIMACHUS

IAMBUS IV

THE *Diegesis*, which is not complete, gives the following information about *Iambus* iv :

The poet was disputing with one of his rivals, and a certain Simos, who happened to be close by, broke in on their discussion, trying to show himself their equal. Callimachus says he is a Thracian . . . he is a thief of beautiful boys. And he adds the tale about the dispute for supremacy between the laurel and the olive which grew side by side on Mount Tmolus. They recounted their different useful qualities ; then, as the dispute continued, an old bramble-bush—for she was growing near by—said : " Cease, before we become a source of joy to our enemies." The laurel stared at it . . . and said : " You foul disgrace, as though you were one of us ! . . . "

Nothing is known about Simos, the son of Charitades.[a] The theme of this tree-fable—modest merit competing with arrogant self-assertion—is a usual folk-tale motif. In its simplest form we can find it in " Aesop." [b] In the framework

---

[a] He was not necessarily of Thracian origin. The word is used as an insult, and perhaps even because of the paederastic associations with Orpheus. See Pohlenz, *Philol.* xc

194

Εἶς—οὐ γάρ;—ἡμέων, παῖ Χαριτάδεω, καὶ σύ

· · · · · · ·

6 ἄκουε δὴ τὸν αἶνον· ἔν κοτε Τμώλῳ
δάφνην ἐλαίῃ νεῖκος οἱ πάλαι Λυδοί
λέγουσι θέσθαι· καὶ γὰ[ρ
καλόν τε δένδρεον

8 καὶ γὰ[ρ Hu.

118

IAMBI

IAMBUS IV

of the fable Callimachus introduces the device of εἰρωνεία, which enables the olive-tree to enumerate its virtues and avoid the charge of arrogance by attributing the details of its defence to a pair of birds, chattering in its branches ; he also employs the technique of the ἀγών.

But the poet does not follow closely any formal ἀγών-scheme, for the laurel's points are not refuted one by one by the olive, which only after receiving the final insults turns them to her advantage, and enumerates—apparently in reverse order—her merits.

The language is a literary Ionic dialect, and the metre choliambic. As certain points in this poem recall the *Hecale* (l. 77 the meal of Theseus at Hecale's hut, fr. 248 ; ll. 61 f. the chattering birds, those of the *Hecale*, fr. 260. 15 f.), it has been assumed that it was written later than the famous epyllion ; but that is not certain.

(1935), p. 121, n. 3. Simos of Call. *Epigr.* xlviii (xlix L.C.L.) appears to be another man.

ᵇ *Fab.* 385 and *Fab.* 116 (Halm).

194

You also (claim)—is that not so ?—son of Charitades,[a]
6 to be one of us. . . . Well, listen to this tale. Once upon a time the ancient Lydians [b] say the laurel had a quarrel with the olive on Tmolus [c] . . . a beautiful tree

[a] The name of the man was Simos, as we know from the *Diegesis*. He is otherwise unknown.

[b] Lydia was a territory in the west of Asia Minor, centred in the lower Hermus and the Caÿster valleys.

[c] Mountain of Lydia.

119

CALLIMACHUS

10 σείσασα τοὺς ὄρπηκας

[Desunt in P fort. non plus quam 9 versus]

. . . .

15 τάλαινα[
ἐμεῦ πα[
τῇ δ' αὖτι[ς
" ὤφρων ἐλαίη
ἐγὼ δεμ[
20 ὁ Δῆλον ο[ἰκέων
καί μευ τ[

. . . .

ὠριστερὸς μὲν λευκὸς ὡς ὕδρου γαστήρ,
ὁ δ' ἡλιόπληξ ὃς τὰ πολλὰ γυμνοῦται.
τίς δ' οἶκος οὗπερ οὐκ ἐγὼ παρὰ φλιῇ;
25 τίς δ' οὔ με μάντις ἢ τίς οὐ θύτης ἕλκει;
καὶ Πυθίη γὰρ ἐν δάφνῃ μὲν ἵδρυται,
δάφνην δ' ἀείδει καὶ δάφνην ὑπέστρωται.
ὤφρων ἐλαίη, τοὺς δὲ παῖδας οὐ Βράγχος
τοὺς τῶν Ἰώνων, οἷς ὁ Φοῖβος ὠ[ργίσθη,
30 δάφνῃ τε κρούων κἦπος οὐ τομ[   ]s
δὶς ἢ τρὶς εἰπὼν ἀρτεμέας ἐποίησε;
κ]ἢγὼ μὲν ἢ 'πὶ δαῖτας ἢ 's χορὸν φ[οι]τέω
τὸν Πυθαϊστήν· γίνομαι δὲ κἄεθλον·
οἱ Δωριῆς δὲ Τεμπόθεν με τέμνουσιν
35 ὀρέων ἀπ' ἄκρων καὶ φέρουσιν ἐς Δελφούς,
ἐπὴν τὰ τὠπόλλωνος ἱρ' ἀγινῆται.
ὤφρων ἐλαίη, πῆμα δ' οὐχὶ γινώσκω
οὐδ' οἶδ' ὁκ[οίη]ν οὐλαφηφόρος κάμπτει,
120

IAMBI

10 . . . after shaking her young boughs . . . (she said ?)

[Not more than 9 lines missing]

22 . . . the left *ᵃ* side is white like the belly of a water-
snake, the other, which is mostly exposed, scorched
by the sun. What house is there where I am not
25 beside the doorpost ? What seer or priest fails to
carry me ? In fact the Pythian priestess has her
seat on laurel, laurel she sings, and she has laurel
for a couch. Stupid olive, did not Branchus *ᵇ* make
whole the sons of the Ionians, with whom Phoebus
30 was angry, by striking them with laurel, and ut-
tering two or three times his mystic spell (?) ? And
I go too to the feasts and Pytho's dance,*ᶜ* and I
35 am the prize of victory.*ᵈ* The Dorians cut me on the
hill-tops of Tempe and carry me to Delphi, whenever
Apollo's festival is celebrated.*ᵉ* Stupid olive, I know
no sorrow nor the path trod by the carriers of the

ᵃ The reference is to the olive and the difference of colour
between the upper and under surface of the leaves. The
laurel is poking fun at the olive, which is here compared to a
slave wearing an ἐξωμίς, a garment which left the right
shoulder exposed to the sun.

ᵇ Branchus the seer (see fr. 229) is supposed to have
cleansed the Milesians from a pest by throwing laurel
branches over their heads, and chanting a mystic chant.

ᶜ The Athenians sent an embassy (θεωρία) to Delphi, the
participants in which were called Πυθαϊσταί.

ᵈ The crown at the Pythian games was originally of oak-
leaves, and later of laurel to commemorate the purification
of Apollo.

ᵉ *Cf.* frs. 86 f. Every ninth year laurel-bearing boys led
by an ἀρχιθέωρος carried from Tempe in Thessaly laurel
branches to Delphi to commemorate the purification of
Apollo at Tempe after slaying the snake Python (*cf.* fr. 87).

20 suppl. Pf.   29 suppl. Wil.   30 suppl. Pf.
32 suppl. Hu.   38 suppl. Wil.

121

ἁγνὴ γάρ εἰμι, κοὐ πατεῦσί μ' ἄνθρωποι,
40 ἱρὴ γάρ εἰμι· σοὶ δὲ χὤπότ' ἂν νεκρὸν
μέλλωσι καίειν ἢ [τά]φ[ῳ] περιστέλλειν,
αὐτοί τ' ἀνεστέψ[αντο χ]ὑπὸ τὰ πλευρά
τοῦ μὴ πνέοντ[ος . . .]παξ ὑπ[έ]στ[ρωσαν.''
ἡ μὲν τάδ', οὐκέτ' ἄλλα· τὴν δ' ἀπήλ[λαξε
45 μάλ' ἀτρεμαίως ἡ τεκοῦσα τὸ χρῖμα·
" ὦ πάντα καλή, τῶν ἐμῶν τὸ κ[άλλιστον
ἐν τῇ τελευτῇ κύκνος [ὡς
ἤεισας· οὕτω μὴ κάμοιμ[
ἐγὼ μὲν ἄνδρας, οὓς "Αρη[ς ἀνήλωσε
50 συνέκ τε πέμπω χὐ[πὸ
. . .]ων ἀριστέων, οἳ κα[
ἐγὼ] δὲ λευκὴν ἡνίκ' ἐς τάφον Τηθύν
φέρουσι παῖδες ἢ γέροντα Τιθωνόν,
αὐτή θ' ὁμαρτέω κἠπὶ τὴν ὁδὸν κεῖμαι·
55 γηθέω δὲ πλεῖον ἢ σὺ τοῖς ἀγινεῦσιν
ἐκ τῶν σε Τεμπέων. ἀλλ' ἐπεὶ γὰρ ἐμνήσθης
καὶ τοῦτο· κῶς ἄεθλον οὐκ ἐγὼ κρέσσων
σεῦ; καὶ γὰρ ὠγὼν οὖν 'Ολυμπίῃ μέζων
ἢ 'ν τοῖσι Δελφοῖς· ἀλλ' ἄριστον ἡ σωπή.
60 ἐγὼ μὲν οὔτε χρηστὸν οὔτε σε γρύζω
ἀπηνὲς οὐδέν· ἀλλά μοι δύ' ὄρνιθες
ἐν τοῖσι φύλλοις ταῦτα τινθυρίζουσαι
πάλαι κάθηνται· κωτίλον δὲ τὸ ζεῦγος.
τίς δ' εὗρε δάφνην; γῆ τε καὶ κα[. . .]σ[
65 ὡς πρῖνον, ὡς δρῦν, ὡς κύπειρον, ὡς πεύκην.

41 suppl. Hu.   42 suppl. Hu.   43 εἰσά]παξ
temptavit Hu. : fort.—ὦ πό]παξ—interiectio indignantis Pf.
cett. suppl. Hu.   44 suppl. L.   46 suppl. von Arnim.
47 [ὡς 'Απόλλωνος e.g. suppl. Pf.   48 [ι ποιοῦσα dub.
122

40 dead, for I am pure, and men do not tread on me, for
I am holy. But you, whenever men are to burn a
corpse or lay it in a grave, they use for wreaths to
wear, and (alas ! (?)) they strew you under the sides
of him who breathes no more." So much the one said
and no more. But the oil-bearing tree got rid of her
45 opponent ^a (?) very quietly : " Friend, fair in all
respects, like the swan ^b . . . you sang my greatest
beauty at the end of your song. May I never tire
50 doing thus. I escort the men whom Ares slays (?),
and beneath . . . of princes, who . . . and when
the children carry to the grave a white-haired Tethys,^c
or some old Tithonus,^d it is I who go with them and
55 lie strewn on the path ; and I find more joy in this
than you in those who bear you from Tempe. But
since you spoke of this too, am I not better than you
as a prize ? For certainly the Olympic ^e games are
greater than those held at Delphi. Silence is best.
60 For my part I say no word of praise or blame for you.
But two birds which have long been perched in my
leaves mutter all this—they are a chattering couple :
' Who brought forth the laurel ? ' ' Earth and . . .
65 just like the ilex, the oak, the galingale and the pine.'

---

^a ἀπαλλάξαι τοὺς κατηγόρους was a term used in the law-
courts, meaning to get rid of one's opponents.
^b The swan was supposed to sing its sweetest song just
before its death.
^c Daughter of Earth and Heaven, sister of Ocean ; be-
came consort of Ocean and bore the Rivers and the three
thousand Oceanids ; here used as an example of longevity.
^d Tithonus, type of extreme longevity.
^e The crown at the Olympic games was of wild olive, the
Kotinos.

---

suppl. Pf. : [ἀκούουσα e.g. L.   49 suppl. e.g. Trypanis.
52 suppl. Hu.

τίς δ' εὗρ' ἐλαίην; Παλλάς, ἦμος [ἤρ]ιζ[ε
τῷ φυκιοίκῳ κἠδίκαζεν ἀρχαίοις
ἀνὴρ ὄφις τὰ νέρθεν ἀμφὶ τῆς Ἀκτῆς.
ἐν ᾗ δάφνη πέπτωκε. τῶν δ' ἀειζώων
70 τίς τὴν ἐλαίην, τίς δὲ τὴν δάφνην τιμᾷ;
δάφνην Ἀπόλλων, ἡ δὲ Παλλὰς ἣν εὗρε.
ξυνὸν τόδ' αὐταῖς, θεοὺς γὰρ οὐ διακρίνω.
τί τῆς δάφνης ὁ καρπός; ἐς τί χρήσωμαι;
μήτ' ἔσθε μήτε πῖνε μήτ' ἐπιχρίσῃ.
75 ὁ τῆς δ' ἐλαίης ἐν μὲν †αλιτιτω† μάσταξ
ὃ στ[έμφυλο]ν καλεῦσιν, ἐν δὲ τὸ χρῖμα,
ἐν [δ' ἡ κολ]υμβὰς ἣν ἔπωγε χὠ Θησεύς·
τ[ὸ δ]εὔ[τερ]ον τίθημι τῇ δάφνῃ πτῶμα.
τεῦ γὰρ τὸ φύλλον οἱ ἱκέται προτείνουσι;
80 τὸ τῆς ἐλαίης· τὰ τρί' ἡ δάφνη κεῖται.
(φεῦ τῶν ἀτρύτων, οἷα κωτιλίζουσι·
λαιδρὴ κορώνη, κῶς τὸ χεῖλος οὐκ ἀλγεῖς;)
τεῦ γ]ὰρ τὸ πρέμνον Δήλιοι φυλάσσουσι;
τὸ τῆς ἐλαίης ᾗ ἀνέπαυσε τὴν Λητώ.

---

66 suppl. Wil.   76 suppl. Diels.   77 init. suppl.
Knox : κολ]υμβὰ[ς iam Diels. ἔγωγε (vix ἔτρωγε) L. : ἔπιγε
(vix ἔτρωχε) Knox.   78 suppl. Hu.   83 suppl. Hu.

---

[a] The reference is to the story of the contest between
Athena and Posidon for the possession of Attica. Posidon
124

' Who brought forth the olive ? ' ' Pallas, when she
contended for Attica with the Sea-weed Dweller in
old times, with a snake-tailed man as judge.' *a* ' One
70 fall against the laurel.' *b* ' Which god honours the
laurel, which the olive-tree ? ' ' Apollo honours the
laurel, Pallas the olive, which she herself discovered.'
' This is a tie, for I do not distinguish between gods.'
' What is the laurel's fruit ? What use can I make of
it ? ' ' Do not use it for food or drink or ointment.
75 But the olive's fruit is first the food (of the poor ?),
the olive-cake, as they call it, second (it produces)
oil, and third the pickled olive which even Theseus
swallowed.' *c* ' I count this a second fall for the
laurel.' ' Whose is the leaf that suppliants offer in
80 appeal ? ' ' The olive's.' ' The laurel has had three
falls now.' (Alas ! those creatures, how they chat-
ter on ! Shameless crow, does not your lip grow
sore ?) ' Whose trunk do the Delians preserve ? '
84 ' The olive's, which gave rest to Leto . . .' *d* . . .

smote a rock on the Acropolis and produced a salt pool
(θάλασσα). Then Athena, calling Cecrops, who was repre-
sented as having the lower part of his body in snake form,
to witness her possession (κατάληψις), produced an olive.
Finally Zeus appointed the twelve gods as arbiters, who
decided in favour of Athena.

In this passage, however, Cecrops is said to be the only
judge.

b The picture comes from the wrestlers who were beaten
when thrown thrice on the ground.

c The κολυμβάς, which was offered by Hecale to Theseus.
Cf. fr. 248.

d According to a rarer version of the myth Leto, when
giving birth to Apollo in Delos, rested against the trunk of an
olive tree. *Cf.* Call. *Hymn* iv. 262. No satisfactory supple-
ment of lines 85-91 has been suggested. It seems, however,
probable that there the olive took up in reverse order the
first three claims of the laurel to superiority.

CALLIMACHUS

85   ....]οι πολῖται κ[   ]τι τῷ δήμῳ
       ]τανουν ἔστεφέν μιν ἡ δάφνη
       ]α θαλλῷ καλλίνικος ἡλαίη
       ]υφανητε κἠπὶ τὴν ὄγχνην
       ]τερην τιν' αἰνεῖται
90   ]ικουτεκοι μάντεις
       ]ν οὔτ' ἐπὶ φλιῆς
       φ]ημι τὴν δάφνην."
ὣς εἶπε· τῇ δ' ὁ θυμὸς ἀμφὶ τῇ ῥήσει
ἤλγησε, μέζων δ' ἢ τὸ πρόσθεν ἠγέ[ρ]θη
95 τ]ὰ δεύτερ' ἐς τὸ νεῖκος, ἔστε τιν̣[
βάτος τὸ τρηχὺ τειχέων π[..]δ[..]να
ἔλεξεν (ἦν γὰρ οὐκ ἄπωθε τῶν δενδρέων)·
" οὐκ ὦ τάλαιναι παυσόμεσθα, μὴ χαρταί
γενώμεθ' ἐχθροῖς, μηδ' ἐροῦμεν ἀλλήλας
100 ἄνολβ' ἀναιδέως, ἀλλὰ ταῦτά γ' [.]β[..]μ[.];"
τὴν δ' ἄρ' ὑπόδραξ οἷα ταῦρος ἡ δάφνη
ἔβλεψε καὶ τάδ' εἶπεν· " ὦ κακὴ λώβη,
ὡς δὴ μι' ἡμέων καὶ σύ; μή με ποιῆσαι
Ζεὺς τοῦτο· καὶ γὰρ γειτονεῦσ' ἀποπνίγεις
105]ς οὐ μὰ Φοῖβον, οὐ μὰ δέσποιναν,
τῇ κ]ύμβαλοι ψοθεῦσιν, οὐ μὰ Πακτ[ωλόν

IAMBUS V

Accoʀᴅɪɴɢ to the *Diegesis* :

He (*i.e.* Callimachus) attacks in iambics a school-teacher called Apollonius, or according to others one named Cleon, for shamefully abusing his own pupils, bidding him in the guise of a well-wisher not to do this, lest he be caught.

Clearly Callimachus did not mention the name of the teacher in his poem. This iambus was written, at least in parts, in

126

93 So she spoke ; and the other was pained by her
speech, and roused in her heart more than before to
95 fight a second time, until . . . a bramble-bush spoke,
the thorny . . . of the walls—for it was not far off
from the trees : " Wretches, let us stop, lest we
100 should give pleasure to our foes ; let us not rashly
say evil (things) of one another ; but . . . " The
laurel-tree looked grimly at it like a wild bull and
said : " You disgraceful wretch, you pass yourself
off as one of us ? Preserve me, Zeus, from that !
105 For even having you near me stifles me. . . . No, by
Phoebus, by the Lady for whom the cymbals clash,[a]
no, by Pactolus [b] . . ."

[a] Cybele, see fr. 193, note b.
[b] River in Lydia whose sources are in Mount Tmolus.
To swear by the river of your fatherland is in the Callimachean
style ; cf., e.g., frs. 7. 34, and 201.

---

86 κα]τὰ νοῦν L.   92 suppl. Hu. : ἄπαντα πίπτειν ταῦτα
φ] e.g Crusius. 94 ἠχέ[ρ]θη Pf. : ἤχε[ιρ]εν L.   95 fines
versuum 95 sq. valde incerti.   106 suppl. Pf.

IAMBUS V

an allegorical quasi-oracular style, which provided Choero-
boscus and others [a] with an adequate example of ἀλληγορία,
i.e. the technique of saying one thing while implying another
in matters too delicate to be treated openly in public. It is

[a] Cf. Spengel, Rhet. Gr. iii. 245. 6 and Pfeiffer's notes on
ll. 23-29.

not known who this Apollonius (or Cleon) was, nor is there
any indication as to the date of the poem.[a]

---

[a] It is not clear if Pittheus (l. 33) is a reminiscence of
Hecale fr. 237*, which would point to a later date for this
poem.

195

Ὦ ξεῖνε—συμβουλὴ γὰρ ἔν τι τῶν ἱρῶν—
ἄκουε τἀπὸ καρδ[ίης,
ἐπεί σε δαίμων ἄλφα βῆτ[α
οὐχ ὡς ὀνήιστον . [

. . . .

22 ὡς δ᾽ ἄν σε θωιὴ λάβοι·
τὸ πῦρ δὲ τὠνέκαυσας, ἄχρις οὐ πολλῇ
πρόσω κεχώρηκεν φλογί,
25 ἀλλ᾽ ἀτρεμίζει κἠπὶ τὴν τέφρην οἰ[χ]νεῖ,
κοίμησον. ἴσχε δὲ δρόμου
μαργῶντας ἵππους μηδὲ δευτέρην κάμψῃς,
μή τοι περὶ νύσσῃ δίφρον
ἄξωσιν, ἐκ δὲ κύμβαχος κυβιστήσῃς.
30 ἆ, μή με ποιήσῃς γέ[λω.
ἐγὼ Βάκις τοι καὶ Σίβυλλα καὶ δάφνη
καὶ φηγός. ἀλλὰ συμβαλεῦ

2 sq. suppl. Roberts.   25 suppl. Norsa-Vitelli.   30
suppl. Norsa-Vitelli.

---

[a] Apollonius or Cleon, see introduction.
[b] Callimachus uses here ironically the proverb : ἱερὸν
συμβουλή, "advice is a sacred thing," which was said about
those who give advice " with a pure heart, and with no
fraud."

128

IAMBI

The dialect is a literary Ionic, and the metre a choliambic trimeter followed by an iambic dimeter.[b]

Frs. 210* and 213* may belong to this iambus.

---

[b] On this see Pfeiff. *Philol.* lxxx (1933), p. 268. We now know that Hipponax composed poetry in the same metre. *Cf.* Fraenkel, *C.Q.* xxxvi (1942), pp. 54 f.

195

LISTEN, friend [a]—for advice is held one of the sacred things [b]—to my heartfelt warning [c] . . . since Fate (has decreed that) you (teach) abc . . . not as the
22 best . . . you would thus be punished. But as long as the fire [d] you kindled has not grown into a great
25 flame, but still lies calm and moves among the ashes, quench it. Hold back from their running the wild horses, and do not race a second time round the course, lest they should shatter your chariot on the
30 turning-post,[e] and you tumble forth headlong. Ah ! make me not a laughing-stock. For you I am Bacis,[f] Sibyl,[g] the laurel-tree and the oak.[h] Come, solve the

---

[c] ἄκουε τἀπὸ καρδίας, " listen to my heartfelt warning," is a second proverb woven into the beginning of the poem.

[d] The fire of love.

[e] The turning-post in the racecourse was the most dangerous point.

[f] A Boeotian prophet.

[g] The Sibyl was originally a single prophetic female variously localized, and legends of her wanderings account for her presence at different spots. As early as Heraclides Ponticus (*c.* 390–310 B.C.) she became pluralized, and the term gradually became generic.

[h] The laurel-tree and the oak were the two prophetic trees of antiquity. The one was sacred at the oracle of Apollo in Delphi, the other at the oracle of Zeus at Dodona.

CALLIMACHUS

τὦνιγμα, καὶ μὴ Πιτθέως ἔχε χρείην·
ἄον]τι καὶ κωφεῖ λόγος.

34 suppl. Maas; cf. Aesch. *Eum.* 322 ff. : λύει] τι Barber.

> [a] The soothsayer (*cf.* fr. 237*) and diviner who solved

IAMBUS VI

THE *Diegesis* reads thus :

(Callimachus) describes to an acquaintance of his, who was sailing to see the statue of Olympian Zeus at Elis, the length, height and width of the pedestal, the throne, the footstool and of the actual (statue of the) god ; in addition he states the amount it cost, and that the Athenian Phidias, son of Charmides, was the sculptor.

Iambus vi was a *propemptikon*, a poem to wish " bon voyage " to a departing friend. As far as we can see there is little poetic inspiration here : the object is the display of a great deal of erudite detail, as well as a peculiar sense of humour in setting that kind of material in immaculate verse. The sources of the poet are unknown.[a] Phidias, the great Athenian sculptor of the 5th century B.C., was the artist of the famous gold and ivory statue of the Olympian Zeus. He represented the god seated, his bending head almost touching the roof of the cella of the temple : at the top of his throne were two three-figure groups, the Graces and the Horae. The excavations of Olympia have uncovered the site where the statue stood, and it is now clear that the base of the

> [a] Probably some earlier *Periegesis* of Elis, or even a copy of the official records of the construction of the famous statue.

IAMBI

riddle and seek no Pittheus *a* to explain it . . .
speech (benefits) both the hearing and the deaf man.

the oracle given to Aegeus, to whom he gave his daughter in
marriage. He was also the teacher of Theseus, who was
born from that marriage.

IAMBUS VI

statue was 6·65 m. broad ; consequently Callimachus used
in his description a foot of *c.* 0·330 metre. According to
modern calculations based on this iambus the throne must
have been 9·90 m. high and the god 12·375 m. high.*b* The
proportion of throne to statue was therefore three to five, and
that is what can be also seen on the extant Elean coins on
which the statue is represented. One interesting point
emerges from the measurements Callimachus gives. The
groups of the Horae and the Graces do not seem in the iambus
to protrude above the head of the god, whereas in the descrip-
tion of Pausanias (v. 11. 7) they are expressly said to do so.
The description of Strabo (viii. 353. 4), on the other hand,
supports Callimachus. Each figure of these groups was *c.*
six feet high, so the two groups must have been most impres-
sive and substantial.*c*

The dialect of *Iambus* vi is literary Doric, and the metre
iambic trimeters alternating with ithyphallics, the metre
employed in *Iambus* vii.

---

b On these, as well as the other measurements derived
from this iambus, see Pfeiff. *J.H.S.* lxi (1941), pp. 4 ff.
c If the throne was 9·90 m. high, and the Graces and
Horae 1·98 m., the two together would be 11·88 m. as against
the height of the statue, 12·375 m.

196

'Αλεῖος ὁ Ζεύς, ἁ τέχνα δὲ Φειδία

. . . .

37 αὐτὸς δ' ὁ δαίμων πέντε τᾶς ἐφεδρίδος
παχέεσσι μάσσων·
].τεῖ δὲ Νίκα [

. . . .

παρθένοι γὰρ Ὧραι.
τᾶν ὀργυιαιᾶν ὅσσον οὐδὲ πάσ[σα]λο[ν
φαντὶ μειονεκτεῖν.
45 τὸ δ' ὧν ἀναισίμωμα—λίχνος ἐσσὶ γάρ
καὶ τό μευ πυθέσθαι—
. . . .] μὲν [ο]ὐ [λ]ογιστὸν οὐδ [. .]ε[

. . . .

61   ] δ' ὁ Φειδία πατήρ.
προσκύσας] ἀπέρχευ.—

43 suppl. L.   47 suppl. L.   62 suppl. Maas,
cf. Soph. *Philoct.* 1408.

---

[a] The celebrated Athenian sculptor, born *c.* 490 B.C., who
was commissioned to design the marble sculptures of the

IAMBUS VII

THE *Diegesis* reads :

Hermes Perpheraios is worshipped in Aenus, the Thracian
city, for the following reason : Epeus [a] carved before the
wooden horse a Hermes, which the Scamander swept away

---

[a] Epeus, the mythical sculptor of the Wooden Horse of
Troy, is said to have carved other statues of Hermes too. *Cf.*
Paus. ii. 19. 6.

IAMBI

196

(The statue of) Zeus is in Elis, the art is that of
37 Phidias [a] . . . and (the image of) the god himself is
five cubits [b] higher than the throne . . . and a Nike [c]
42 . . . for the maiden Horae [d] say that they are not
a peg smaller than (the Graces ?), six feet [e] high . . .
45 and as for the cost, for in your thirst for knowledge
you ask this too from me . . . it is impossible to
61 calculate, nor . . . and the father of Phidias. . . .
(having made obeisance), go.[f]

Parthenon. He was primarily a bronze-worker, but acquired
much of his fame from his skill at chryselephantine statues,
most famous of which were the Athena Parthenos and the
Zeus of Olympia. Phidias must have gone to Elis after 432,
when the Parthenon was completed. He went there in exile
owing to political charges against him by the opponents of
Pericles.
    [b] The statue itself was therefore 12·375 m.
    [c] Zeus was represented holding a Nike, a winged victory,
in the palm of his hand.
    [d] Goddesses of the Seasons in Greek mythology.
    [e] The foot Callimachus uses is probably the so-called
" Phidonian foot," *c.* 330 mm. long.
    [f] These words (*cf.* Call. *Epigr.* xl. [xli L.C.L.] 6), as well as
the first lines of the poem, are addressed directly to his de-
parting friend.

IAMBUS VII

in a large flood. The statue was carried from there to the
sea off Aenus, where some fishermen hauled it up in their
net. When they saw it they grumbled about the catch, and
attempted to split it up into firewood and build themselves a
fire ; but they succeeded in doing no more than make a
wound-like dent in the shoulder when they struck it ; they
were unable to split it up completely. And so they tried to

burn it whole, but the fire flowed around it (without burning
it). They gave up, and threw it into the sea, but when they
hauled it up in their nets again they believed it to be divine,
or to belong to some divinity, and established a shrine for it on
the shore, and offered the first fruits of their catch, (passing)
the image around from one to the other. And in accordance
with an oracle of Apollo they (received) it into their city and
honoured it like a god.

This poem is an aetion, explaining the name *Perpheraios* as
derived from the ritual of passing the statue from man to

---

[a] *Cf.* Call. *Epigr.* v, xxi, xxiv (vi, xxiii, xxvi L.C.L.). This
poem and *Iambus* ix are the only two extant Greek poems

197

Ἑρμᾶς ὁ Περφεραῖος, Αἰνίων θεός,
  ἔμμι τῶ φυγαίχμα
ἐκ Φωκίδος] πάρεργον ἱπποτέκτον[ος·
  δεξιὸς] γὰρ [ὡ]νὴρ
5 ◡ – ◡ – σκέπαρνον

3-4 suppl. Maas : [ὡ]νὴρ suppl. L.

---

[a] Callimachus in this iambus wishes to explain the name
of the god as derived from the ritual of passing the statue
from man to man.

IAMBUS VIII

According to the *Diegesis*, *Iambus* viii was:

An epinician poem for Polycles of Aegina, who won the
Diaulos Amphorites in his native land. The contest is as
follows : At the end of the stadium is placed an amphora
full of water up to which the contestant runs empty-handed ;
he picks up the amphora and retraces his steps, and if he
arrives first he wins. This contest derived from the following

IAMBI

man. In a sense it is also an *aretalogy*, in which Hermes makes his power manifest by relating the story. The statue itself is speaking here in the style of certain sepulchral dedicatory epigrams.[a]

The nterest of Callimachus in local traditions or rarer versions of panhellenic myths is manifest here again. The figure of Hermes appears on the coins of Aenus.

The dialect of the poem is basically Doric, but certain Aeolic, perhaps Cyrenean, elements are also evident. The metre is iambic trimeters alternating with ithyphallics.

---

which in the style " of a speaking monument " extend beyond the epigram, or " short " elegy.

197

I AM Hermes Perpheraios,[a] the god of Aenus,[b] a by-product of the man of Phocis who shunned the fight,[c] (but) built the horse. For the man was clever (in using ?) the carpenter's axe.

' City in Thrace.
[e] Epeus, the traditional constructor of the wooden horse of Troy, was notorious for his cowardice.

IAMBUS VIII

fact : The Argonauts landed at Aegina and strove to outdo one another while procuring water. The contest is called the *Hydrophoria*.

Iambus viii appears to have been one further effort on the part of Callimachus to adapt the traditional epinician ode to simpler recitative metres,[a] and to add the aetiological element

---

[a] *Cf.* fr. 384 and fr. 383, both in elegiacs.

to this type of poetry.[a] Apollonius, who mentions this contest as the last event in the Argonauts' journey home, is presumably following Callimachus.[b]

---

[a] Probably he followed in this the precedent of Bacchylides (*cf.* Snell, *Hermes*, lxvii (1932), pp. 1 f.).
[b] *Argon.* iv. 1765 f. The festival in which this contest

198

'Αργώ κοτ' ἐμπνέοντος ἤκαλον νότου

---

[a] In Apollonius Rhodius too (*Argon.* iv. 1769), the fair breeze made the Argonauts compete in bringing water to the

---

IAMBUS IX

THE content of *Iambus* ix is given as follows by the *Diegesis* :

The lover of a handsome youth called Philetadas saw the ithyphallic statue of a Hermes in a small palaestra, and asked if his condition was not due to Philetadas. But the Hermes answered that he was of Tyrrhenian descent, and that he was ithyphallic because of a mystic story. On the other hand (he said) his questioner loved Philetadas with evil intent.

We do not know who Philetadas was, or whether, as Koerte suggested,[a] he was a favourite of Callimachus, in which case the lover of *Iambus* ix would be the poet himself. The mocking and satirical tone, however, points rather to a rival, or an

---

[a] *Arch. f. Papyr.* xi (1935), p. 240.
[b] *Cf., e.g.,* fr. 97.

IAMBI

The dialect of *Iambus* viii was a literary Ionic and the metre probably a stichic iambic trimeter.[c] Frs. 220, 222, 223 and 596* may belong to this poem.

---

took place (at Aegina) was called the *Hydrophoria* ; it was in honour of Apollo and was celebrated in the local month Delphinios. The water was drawn from the fountain Asopis.

[c] As only the first line has survived we cannot be certain if it is a stichic iambic trimeter, or an epodic metre.

198

THE Argo once, the south wind gently blowing.[a]

ship. This competition gave rise to the contest of the *Hydrophoria* (see introduction).

IAMBUS IX

enemy of the poet. Herodotus (ii. 51) speaks of the Pelasgian origin of the ithyphallic Hermes. Pelasgians were frequently identified with Tyrrhenians in antiquity and even by Callimachus himself.[b]

The mystic story explaining the origin of the ithyphallic Hermes is unknown. The poem is composed in the form of a dialogue between the lover of Philetadas and the Hermes. This form was used by Callimachus in his epigrams and also in the *Aetia* (fr. 114. 4 f.).

The dialect is presumably a literary Doric and the metre a catalectic iambic trimeter. Fr. 221 may belong to this poem.[c]

---

[c] The similarity of *Iambus* ix to *Iambus* vii is clear ; they both treat of the cult of Hermes, and in both instances the statue is the source of information.

CALLIMACHUS

199

Ἑρμᾶ, τί τοι τὸ νεῦρον, ὦ Γενειόλα,
ποττὰν ὑπήναν κού ποτ' ἴχνι[ον   ;

2 suppl. L.   in fine fort. βλέπει Maas.

IAMBUS X

THE *Diegesis* says :

At Aspendus in Pamphylia a boar is sacrificed to Aphrodite Castnia for the following reason : Mopsus, a leader of the Pamphylians, when setting out to hunt vowed to her that, if he were lucky, he would sacrifice whatever he caught first. And so, when he caught a wild boar, he fulfilled his promise. From then to this day the Pamphylians do the same. For, if it had not pleased the goddess, Mopsus would never have hunted the boar. The poet also commends Artemis of Eretria because she rejects nothing that is sacrificed to her.

The sacrifice of swine to Aphrodite was not universal among the Greeks, but, in spite of what Callimachus asserts in l. 4, in Argos a festival was held called *Hysteria*, The Slaying of Pigs, in which that animal was sacrificed to the goddess.[a] The tradition that Aspendus in Pamphylia (which was near Mount Castnion, whence Aphrodite Castnietis derived her name) was an Argive colony, established there by Mopsus,

200 A

Τὰς 'Αφροδίτας—ἡ θεὸς γὰρ οὐ μία—
ἡ Καστνιῆτις τῷ φρονεῖν ὑπερφέρει
πάσας,
ὅτι μόνη παραδέχεται τὴν τῶν ὑῶν θυσίαν.

2 sq. in versus redegit Meineke.   4 de his verbis in versus redigendis nondum constat.

138

IAMBI

199

LONG-BEARDED Hermes, why is your penis (pointing ?)
to your beard and not to your feet [a] . . . ?

[a] Statues of ithyphallic Hermae stood at the entrances of
palaestrae in antiquity.

IAMBUS X

may well link the cult of the Castnian goddess with that of
Argos. The hatred of the goddess towards swine was ex-
plained by her hatred of the animal that killed her favourite
Adonis. As we can see from the *Diegesis*, Callimachus is
again [b] treating two similar cults in the same poem. After
Aphrodite Castnietis, he spoke about the cult of Artemis
Colaenis, worshipped at Amarynthus in Euboea, near Eretria.
The cult of the latter goddess seems also to have been popular
in Attica, and various efforts have been made to explain the
derivation of the name Colaenis. Callimachus appears to
have favoured the suggestion that the origin of the name was
due to the sacrifice of a mutilated ram (κριὸς κόλος) by Aga-
memnon on his way to Troy.

The dialect is a literary Ionic, and the metre iambic tri-
meters.

---

[a] Athen. iii. 95 f.   [b] *Cf. Aetia* frs. 22-25.

200 A

THE Aphrodite of Mount Castnion [a]—for the goddess
4 is not one—is the wisest of all (as she alone allows the
sacrifice of swine).[b]

[a] Mountain in Pamphylia in Asia Minor. On a relevant
inscription see D. Hereward, *J.H.S.* lxxviii (1958), pp. 64 f.
[b] Line four as printed in the text is in prose.

CALLIMACHUS

200 B

τὴν ὠγαμέμνων, ὡς ὁ μῦθος, εἴσατο,
τῇ καὶ λίπουρα καὶ μονῶπα θύεται

---

^a Of Artemis Colaenis (see introduction).

IAMBUS XI

THE *Diegesis* runs :

The proverb " The goods of Connarus are anyone's prey " is
wrongly quoted. You should say " Connidas." For this is
the source of the proverb : Connidas, a settler from abroad
in Selinus, acquired wealth as a brothel-keeper, and in his
lifetime used to say that he would divide his property between
Aphrodite and his friends. But, when he died, his will was
found to say : " The goods of Connidas are anyone's prey."
Consequently the people left the theatre, and plundered the
property of Connidas. Selinus is a city of Sicily.

This is another aetiological poem, describing the origin of the
proverb " The goods of Connidas are anyone's prey." At

---

^a See also *Iambus* iv, where from the address to the son of

201

Ἀλλ' οὐ τὸν Ὑψᾶν, ὃς τὸ σᾶμά μευ

---

^a Connidas (on whom see introduction) is speaking from
his tomb on the bank of the river Hypsas, now called Belice,

IAMBUS XII

THE *Diegesis* states :

This (poem) is written for the seventh-day celebration of the
birth of a little girl whose father Leon was a friend of the

140

IAMBI

200 B

. . . whose effigy,[a] as the story goes, Agamemnon dedicated, and to whom even tail-less and one-eyed animals are sacrificed.

IAMBUS XI

the same time Callimachus takes the opportunity of showing the scholarly character of his poetry by correcting the popular misquotation of the proverb. The poem starts by Connidas speaking from his tomb, in the style of certain sepulchral epigrams. In all probability it later developed into a direct narrative by the poet.[a] [b]

The word σᾶμα of l. 1 points to the use of a Doric literary dialect, appropriate for a story from Selinus. The metre is a brachycatalectic iambic trimeter, an unusual Greek metre.

Charitades the poet proceeds to the direct narrative of the dispute of the laurel and the olive.

[b] The source of Callimachus in this story may have well been Timaeus of Tauromenium (c. 356–260 B.C.), because his version agrees with that given by the *Diegesis*. *Cf.* fr. 148* ; Jacoby, *Frag. Gr. Hist.* iii B (1950), p. 642.

201

BUT nay, by Hypsas, you who (pass) my tomb.[a]

which flowed by the city of Selinus to the south-west coast of Sicily. In true Callimachean fashion Connidas swears by the river of his motherland (see note b on *Iambus* iv. 106).

IAMBUS XII

poet ; in it he says that the hymn sung by Apollo was superior to all the gifts brought to Hebe by the other gods.

141

CALLIMACHUS

This is a birthday poem, unique in its kind in Greek litera-
ture.[a] The occasion was the *Amphidromia*, a rite accord-
ing to which a child was carried round the hearth on the
fifth, seventh or tenth day after its birth, and gifts were pre-
sented by relatives and friends.[b] The divine example intro-
duced by the poet adds to the importance of this poem. The
festival for the *Hebdoma* of Hebe is, however, not men-
tioned elsewhere. The object of the poem is firstly to pay a

---

[a] It has nothing in common with the brief birthday poems
in the *Palatine Anthology*.

[b] The naming of the child could also take place upon that
occasion. The celebration for the child of Leon fell upon the
seventh day, a day sacred to Apollo.

[c] See Lobel (*Hermes*, 1935, p. 42) and Maas (*Gnomon*, xii,
1936, p. 97); poems in trochaic metres, used already from

202

Ἄρτεμι Κρηταῖον Ἀμνισοῦ πέδον
ἤ τε Δικτ[υνναῖον ἀμφέπεις ὄρος
τιμίη [
ἤ σε του[
5 ἱ]στίη Λ[έοντος

    ·   ·   ·

9 καὶ ὔ]μμες ὦ κά[λ]λιστα νήθουσαι μυ[

    ·   ·   ·

15 ἔστιν οἰκ[   ]ι[   ] ἀψευδέα λέγων
καὶ τάφο[ν τὸ]ν Κ[ρ]ῆτα γινώσκειν κενόν
φησὶ καὶ πατρῷον οὐ κτείνειν ὄφιν·

142

IAMBI

compliment to his friend Leon—who is otherwise unknown—and secondly to praise poetry. and point out its superiority over any form of material wealth.

As the gift of Callimachus was this poem, it is a rather obvious compliment to himself that he is presenting the best gift of all. The poet must have given the final touches to the poem in the seven days between the birth and the *Hebdoma* of the child, for he speaks in l. 20 about a "little maid."

The metre is a catalectic trochaic trimeter :

$$-\cup-\widehat{\cup}-\mid\cup\mid-\widehat{\cup}-\cup\underset{\smile}{\smile}$$

and the dialect a literary Ionic.[c]

Fr. 204* may possibly belong to this poem.

the days of Archilochus by iambographers, were included in the Alexandrian editions of their iambic works.

202

1 ARTEMIS [a] (who dost haunt) the Cretan plain of Am-
9 nisus and (Mount) Dicte [b] . . . honoured . . . and you,
15 most beautifully spinning, . . . speaking true words
and he says he knows the Cretan tomb (of Zeus) [c] is
empty, and that he did not kill his father's snake (?).[d]

[a] Invoked here as Artemis Ilithyia, goddess of childbirth.
[b] Mountain sacred to Zeus in eastern Crete.
[c] The "tomb" of Zeus was alleged to be in Crete. *Cf.* Call. *Hymn* i. 8.
[d] The passage is obscure.

2 e.g. suppl. Pf.   5 ἱ]στίη L. : Λ[έοντος Pf.   9 suppl. Barber.   15 οἰκ[ιστ]ῆρσιν Barber.   16 suppl. L.

τοὔνεκ' ἀντήσ[αιτε], πρηεῖαι θεαί,
τῆσδ' ἐτῆς εὐχῇσι . . .]αεισομαι
20 Μοῦσα τῇ μικκῇ τι τε[. .]ηναι μελ[
ἡνίκ' ἀρ[τύο]υ[σ]α τὴν γενεθλίην
ἑβδόμην Ἥρ[η] θ[υγ]ατρὸς ἡμέρην
ἦ[γε]ν οἱ δ' Ὄλυμπον ἦρ[ι]σαν θεοί
ἦ[μεν]ο[ι] τίς παῖδ[α καλ]λίστη δόσει
25 πρ[επ]τὰ τιμήσει τ[. . . . .]ερο[
Ζεὺς πατὴρ οὐ φαυ[
πολλὰ τεχνήεντα ποικ[ίλ]α γλ[υφῇ
παίχνια Τριτωνί; ἤνεικεν κόρ[η
πολλὰ [καὶ Ἀπ]ίου πυλωρὸς αὐχένος

. . . .

33 παίχνια χρυσοῖο τιμηέσ[τ]ερ[α

. . . .

45 οἱ δ' ι[. . . γ]λυκεῖαν ἀλλήλοις ἔριν
θέντες ἡμιλλῶντο δω[τί]νη[ς πέρι.
Δ]ήλι' ὤπολλον, σὺ δ' ἐσκλ[. . .]ευμ[
ὅσσα] τοι Πυθῶνος ἀρχα[ίης ἔ]σω
δω]μάτων ἔκειτο [. . . .]ιπον ρυ[

. . . .

] ἐφ[θέγ]ξω τ[ά]δε
" .]χεισθ[. . .]οισ[. . . .]οισιν α[.]τε[. . . .]ιρια
55 .]εσθ', ἐγὼ δ' ἄλλην τιν' ο[. .]ησ[ω . . .]ιν.
χρεὼ σοφῆς ὦ Φοῖβε πε[ιρ]ᾶσθαι τέχνης,
ἥτις Ἡφαίστεια νικήσει καλά.

18 suppl. Maas.   19 suppl. L.   ἐτῆς divisit et ι sub-
scripsit Pf.   21 suppl. Smiley.   23 ἦ[γε]ν Barber.   ἦρ[ι]-
144

IAMBI

Wherefore, accept, gentle goddesses,[a] this earnest
19 request . . . Muse, I will sing for the little maid
. . . once when Hera was celebrating the feast of the
seventh day of her daughter's [b] birth, the gods sitting
on Olympus quarrelled, who would honour the child
with the most beautiful gift . . . Father Zeus . . .
27 Tritonis [c] brought many toys of cunning workman-
ship shrewdly carved, and many came from the
33 guardian of the (Apian) Isthmus,[d] . . . toys more
45 precious than gold. . . . The gods in amicable rivalry
vied with one another in offering gifts. But you,
Delian Apollo, . . . all your treasures which were
stored in the house of ancient Pytho [e] . . . you said
56 the following . . . " Phoebus, you must try your
skilful art which will surpass the masterpieces of

---

[a] The goddesses of birth, presumably here the Fates, as
can be surmised from the ὦ κά[λ]λιστα νήθουσαι of l. 9.

[b] Hebe, see introduction.

[c] Athene. According to an old legend the goddess was
born from, or at the banks of the Libyan lake Τριτωνίς, or
from Triton, a torrent in Boeotia, or from a spring of the
same name in Arcadia ; the name Τριτωνίς is also connected
with the word τριτώ, which in Aeolic means head. Cf. also
fr. 37.

[d] Posidon, master of the Corinthian Isthmus. The Pelo-
ponnesus was called Ἀπία after Apis, a mythical king of
Argos.

[e] The sanctuary of Delphi was famous for the rich offerings
it had received from Greeks and Orientals.

σαν Pf.   24-25 suppl. Pf.   27 sq. suppl. Hu.   γλ[υφῇ
Barber.   28 κόρ[η Hu.   κόρ[η puellae nuper natae vel
fort. κόρ[ας pupas ? Pf.   29 suppl. Barber.   45 ἴσ[οι Pf.
in contentione pares ἡμιλλῶντο (cf. ἰσάμιλλοι).   46 δω-
[τί]νη[ς πέρι suppl. Maas.   48 ὅσσα suppl. Pf. : τῶν ἃ L.
cett. suppl. L.   49 suppl. Barber : κτη]μάτων L.   54 ff.
Apoll. loquitur.   55 ὁ[κχ]ήσ[ω δόσ]ιν feram vel ὁ[πλ]ήσ[ω
praeparabo e.g. Pf.   56 suppl. L.

145

αὐτίκα χρυσὸν μὲν Ἰνδικοὶ κύνες
βυσσόθεν μύρμηκες ο[ἴσου]σι πτεροῖς·
60 πολλάκις καὶ φαῦλον οἰκήσει δόμον
χρυσός, ἀρχαίους δ' ἀτιμήσει [. . . . . .]ς.
καὶ Δίκην καὶ Ζῆνα καὶ [. . .]ου[.]α[.]ας
ὑπτίῳ παίσαντες ἄνθρωποι ποδί
χρυσὸν αἰνήσουσι τίμιον κ[ακόν.
65 τὴν Ἀθηναίης δὲ καὶ ἑτέρων δόσιν,
καίπερ εὖ σμίλησιν ἠκριβωμένην,
ὁ πρόσω φοιτέων ἀμαυρώσει χρόνος·
ἡ δ' ἐμὴ τῇ παιδὶ καλλίστη δόσις,
ἔστ' ἐμὸν γένειον ἁγνεύῃ τριχός
70 καὶ ἐρίφοις χαίρωσιν ἅρπαγ[ες λ]ύκ̣[ο]ι "

59 suppl. C. Bonner.   61 [τρόπου]ς Barber, Morel :
[τόπου]ς vel [νομού]ς Bonner : [νόμου]ς Trypanis.   62 καὶ
Νόμου σέβας temptavit Bonner.   64 κάλλιστον κακόν v.l. P.
68 καλλίστη suspectum editoribus.   70 κηρίφων χαίρωσιν
ἅρπαγ[ῇ prop. Maas.

IAMBUS XIII

ACCORDING to the *Diegesis* :

In this poem, in answer to those who criticized him for the
variety of the poetry he writes, (Callimachus) says that he
is copying the tragic poet Ion. Indeed neither does one
criticize a craftsman for producing utensils of different kinds.

This poem, which concludes the book of the *Iambi*, deals
with literary criticism, and, though in a fragmentary con-
dition, betrays the polemical spirit of its author. Callimachus
defended himself against the criticism of πολυείδεια, of com-

146

Hephaestus.[a] For example the ants, the Indian
dogs,[b] will bring gold from the depths of the earth on
30 their wings, and often shall the home in which it
settles be base : it will pay no regard to ancient
(customs ?).   Mankind, kicking with spurning foot
both Dike [c] and Zeus and . . . will praise gold, an
35 honoured evil (?) ; the gift of Athene, and of the
others,[d] though splendidly chiselled, will lose its lustre
as time passes on. But my most beautiful gift to the
child,[e] while my cheeks and chin are still smooth
40 and free of hair, while the ravening wolves delight in
kids . . . "

[a] The songs of Apollo will surpass even the most excellent
goldsmith's work of Hephaestus.   From ll. 54 ff. Apollo
appears to be speaking.
[b] The Indian ants were said to be " larger than foxes, but
smaller than dogs " (Herod. iii. 102).   The sand they dug
up, when making their nests, was said to be full of gold.
[c] The personification of Order and Right.
[d] We do not know what these are.
[e] The song.   The poet compares the immortality of (great)
poetry with the transitory splendour of material gifts.

IAMBUS XIII

posing poems in too many genres, by putting forward the
" classical " example of Ion of Chios (born c. 490 B.C.) who
was admired in Alexandria and included in the Alexandrian
canon of the tragedians ; he also wrote comedies, dithyrambs,
lyric poetry, paeans, hymns, encomia, elegies, epigrams,
scolia and a number of prose works.[a]
Neither the *Diegesis*, nor the legible fragments of the

[a] See A. von Blumenthal, *Ion von Chios* (1939), and F.
Jacoby, *C.Q.* xli (1947), pp. 1 ff.

iambus, give any indication as to who were the critics Calli-
machus attacked here. No doubt Apollonius Rhodius and
the Telchines of *Aetia* fr. 1 should be counted among them.

203

Μοῦσαι καλαὶ κἄπολλον, οἷς ἐγὼ σπένδω

. . . .

7   ὁ Μίμν[ερμος

. . . .

11 ἐκ γὰρ [. . . . . οὔτ'] ᾿Ιωσι συμμείξας
οὔτ' ῎Εφεσον ἐλθών, ἥτις ἐστι [.]αμ[
῎Εφεσον, ὅθεν περ οἱ τὰ μέτρα μέλλοντες
τὰ χωλὰ τίκτειν μὴ ἀμαθῶς ἐναύονται·
15 ἀλλ' εἴ τι θυμὸν ἢ 'πὶ γαστέρα πνεῡσ[
εἴτ' οὖν ἐπ[. . .] ἀρχαῖον εἴτ' ἀπαι[,
τοῦτ' ἐμπέπλεκται καὶ λαλευσ[
᾿Ιαστὶ καὶ Δωριστὶ καὶ τὸ σύμμεικτον.
τεῦ μέχρι τολμᾷς; οἱ φίλοι σε δήσ[ουσι,
20 κἢν νοῦν ἔχωσιν, ἐγχέουσι τὴν [
ὡς ὑγιείης οὐδὲ τῷννυχι ψαύεις

. . . .

31 σὺ πεντάμετρα συντίθει, σὺ δ' ἡ[ρῷο]ν,
σὺ δὲ τραγῳδεῖν ἐκ θεῶν ἐκληρώσω;
δοκέω μὲν οὐδείς, ἀλλὰ καὶ το[.]δ[. .]κεψαι

[Inter vv. 33 et 34 9 vel 10 versus desunt]

40 τὰ νῦν δὲ πολλὴν τυφεδῶνα λεσχαίνεις

. . . .

IAMBI

The dialect is a literary Ionic, and the metre a stichic choliambic trimeter.

Frs. 215 and 218 may belong to this poem.

203

1 FAIR Muses and Apollo, to whom I make libations
7 (with my songs ?) . . . Mimnermus[a] . . . neither
11 having mixed with the Ionians, nor having come to
Ephesus (of many tongues (?)), Ephesus which in-
15 spires those who will write scazons skilfully.[b] But if
something (appeals) to the heart or the stomach,
. . . this has been interwoven and they (?) speak
. . . Ionic and Doric and a mixture of both. How
far dare you go ? Your friends will bind you, and,
20 if they have sense, will pour out (a libation to Sanity),
as you don't touch sanity even with your finger-tips
31 . . . who said " Do you compose pentameters and you
epics ; the gods have allotted that you write trage-
dies " ? Nobody, I believe, but . . .

[9 or 10 lines missing in the papyrus between
lines 33 and 34]

40 but now you chatter much nonsense . . . poet is

[a] The great poet of Colophon ; see fr. 1. 11.
[b] The writers of choliambs or scazons take Hipponax of Ephesus as their model.

---

7 suppl. Crusius.   11 suppl. L.   12 πάμφ[υλος
vel πάμφ[ωνος ? Pf.   16 ἀπαρτη[θέν L. Radermacher:
ἐτ[ῶς]—ἀπαρ[τισθέν Barber.   31 suppl. Crusius, Knox.
33 τό[δ]ε σκέψαι Knox.

52   ] ἀοιδὸς ἐς κέρας τεθύμωται
κοτέω]ν ἀοιδῷ κἠμὲ δει[. .]ταπραχ[
      ] δ[ύ]ρηται τὴν γενὴν ἀνακρίνει
55 καὶ δοῦλον εἶναί φησι καὶ παλίμπρητον
καὶ τοῦ πρ[. . . . . .]ου τὸν βραχίονα στίζει,
ὥστ' οὐκ αικε[. . . . .]υσιν α[.]λ[. .]υσαι
φαύλοις ὁμιλέω[. . . . .]ν παρέπτησαν
καὐταὶ τρομεῦσαι μὴ κακῶς ἀκούσωσι·
60 τοῦδ' οὕνεκ', οὐδὲν πῖον, ἀλλὰ λιμηρά
ἕκαστος ἄκροις δακτύλοις ἀποκνίζει,
ὡς τῆς ἐλαίης, ἢ ἀνέπαυσε τὴν Λητώ.
μηθ[. . . . .]ν ἀείδω
οὔτ' Ἔφεσον ἐλθὼν οὔτ' Ἴωσι συμμείξας,
65 Ἔφεσον, ὅθεν περ οἱ τὰ μέτρα μέλλοντες
τὰ χωλὰ τίκτειν μὴ ἀμαθῶς ἐναύονται.

53 suppl. Knox.   54 suppl. L.

150

IAMBI

52 angry against poet to the point of assaulting him.
. . . examines his descent, and says he is a slave,
and a good for nothing slave, passing from hand to
hand, and . . . brands his arm so that . . . to
associate with vile people . . . they, too, flew past
60 him, fearing lest they be spoken of badly . . . There-
fore, each one scrapes off with the tips of his fingers
not rich things, but hungry morsels, like those
scraped off the olive-tree that gave Leto rest.[a] Nor
do (?) I sing,[b] either having come to Ephesus, or
65 having mixed with the Ionians, Ephesus which inspires
those who will write scazons skilfully.

[a] The sacred olive-tree, which gave rest to Leto (see note
on fr. 194. 84), was shown in Delos, and visitors scraped off
tiny bits of the trunk.

[b] Callimachus is here speaking about himself, and pro-
bably uses the very words with which his opponents assailed
him.

151

IAMBORUM FRAGMENTA INCERTAE
SEDIS, 215-223

215

ἥτις τραγῳδὸς μοῦσα ληκυθίζουσα

---

^a May belong to fr. 203. ληκυθίζω means to declaim in a hollow voice as though speaking into a λήκυθος, an oil-flask.

216

ἔβηξαν οἷον ἀλίβαντα πίνοντες

οἶνον cod. v.l.

218

Μούσῃ γὰρ ἦλθον εἰς ὄβδην

219

οὐ πρῶν μὲν ἡμῖν ὁ τραγῳδὸς ἤγειρε

220

καὶ τῶν νεήκων εὐθὺς οἱ τομώτατοι

(IAMBIC FRAGMENTS WHICH CANNOT BE ATTRIBUTED WITH CERTAINTY TO ANY OF THE IAMBI, 215-223)

215

. . . the tragic muse, which making a booming noise.[a]

216

. . . they coughed like those who drink vinegar.

218

. . . for they came in sight of the Muse (?)

219

. . . the tragedian did not stir for us (?) . . . just now.[a]

a May belong to fr. 203.

220

. . . and the most ardent youths at once.[a]

a Possibly from fr. 198.

CALLIMACHUS

221

αἰτοῦμεν εὐμάθειαν Ἑρμᾶνος δόσιν

222

οὐ γὰρ ἐργάτιν τρέφω
τὴν Μοῦσαν, ὡς ὁ Κεῖος Ὑλίχου νέπους

ᵃ Simonides of Ceos, the great lyric and elegiac poet (c. 556–468 b.c.) was proverbial for his stinginess. Hylichu

223

κοὐχ ὧδ' Ἀρίων τὠπέσαντι πὰρ Διί
ἔθυσεν Ἀρκὰς ἵππος

ᵃ Arion is the famous horse of Adrastus, reputed to be the offspring of Posidon and Demeter, when she in equine form

IAMBI

221

. . . we ask for zeal for learning, the gift of Hermes.[a]

[a] Probably comes from fr. 199. Hermes was a general patron of literature.

222

. . . for I do not bring up my Muse a labourer as the Cean descendant of Hylichus (did).[a]

was the founder of the family τῶν Ὑλιχιδῶν, to which Simonides belonged.

223

ARION, the Arcadian horse, did not rage thus at the shrine of Apesantian Zeus.[a]

was seeking her daughter near Thelpusa in Arcadia. Apesas is a hill near Nemea. This may belong to fr. 198.

LYRIC POEMS

LYRIC POEMS

INTRODUCTION

THE *Diegeseis* place four lyric poems between the *Iambi* and the *Hecale*. Three of these are quoted in antiquity under their own titles, but are never mentioned as part of a separate book of Callimachean ΜΕΛΗ. Pfeiffer suggests Πρὸς τοὺς Ὡραίους, *To Beautiful Boys*, as title for the first.[a] The other three are the Παννυχίς, *The Night-Festival*, the Ἐκθέωσις Ἀρσινόης, *The Deification of Arsinoë*, and Βράγχος, *Branchus*.

---

[a] He quotes the *Diegesis*. This poem is never mentioned by any ancient author.

[ΜΕΛΗ ?]

[ΠΡΟΣ ΤΟΥΣ ΩΡΑΙΟΥΣ ?]

The title, *To Beautiful Boys*, is by no means certain, but is suggested by Pfeiffer because of ll. 1 f. of the *Diegesis*:

(The poet) addresses the beautiful boys. Lemnos, happy of old, became unhappy when the women attacked the men. Therefore, you (plural), too, should have regard to the future.

As we can see from the *Diegesis*, the poem referred to the myth that the women of Lemnos murdered all the men of the island, because they had taken to themselves concubines (or possibly in this version beautiful boys) from Thrace, after Aphrodite had plagued the women with a foul odour, because

226

Ἡ Λῆμνος τὸ παλαιόν, εἴ τις ἄλλη

---

a *i.e.* before the women attacked and slew the men.

ΠΑΝΝΥΧΙΣ

The title of the poem, *Pannychis*, means night-festival, or vigil. The *Diegesis* describes it as:

A drinking-song in honour of the Dioscuri. He (*i.e.* Callimachus) also celebrates Helen, and asks her to accept the sacrifice. He also exhorts the fellow-drinkers to lie awake.

LYRIC POEMS

TO BEAUTIFUL BOYS (?)

they had neglected her rites. Hypsipyle, daughter of King Thoas, governed the island, and received the Argonauts, with whom she and her women mated, and thus the island was repopulated. The admonition to the beautiful boys in this poem remains obscure. It can either be " carpite diem," for bad fortune succeeds happiness, or else beware of neglected women, for they may harm you.

The metre is phalaecean, probably stichic. There is no evidence as to the length or the date of the poem.

226

LEMNOS in ancient times,[a] if ever there was a (happy) island, (was happy) . . .

PANNYCHIS

The metre is epodic, described in antiquity as " Fourteen-syllable Euripidean " (Εὐριπίδειον τεσσερεσκαιδεκασύλλαβον). There is no indication as to the length or date of the poem.

227

Ἔνεστ' Ἀπόλλων τῷ χορῷ· τῆς λύρης ἀκούω·
καὶ τῶν Ἐρώτων ἠσθόμην· ἔστι κἀφροδίτη.

    ·   ·   ·   ·   ·   ·   ·

θυμηδίην [   ] δεῦτε παννυχ[
5 ὁ δ' ἀγρυπνήσας [ἠνεκὲς] μέχρι τῆς κο[ρώνης
τὸν πυραμοῦντα λήψεται καὶ τὰ κοττάβεια
καὶ τῶν παρουσῶν ἣν θέλει χὢν θέλει φιλήσει.
ὦ Κάστορ [ἵππων δμήτορες] καὶ σὺ Πωλύδ[ευκες
καὶ τῶν ἀ[οίκων ῥύτορες] καὶ ξένω[ν ὁδηγοί

4 παννυχ[ίζειν vel παννυχ[ισταί Wil.   5 [ἠνεκὲς] suppl.
Pf. : fin. suppl. Wil.   7 χον P : corr. Pf.   8 [ἵππων
δμήτορες] e.g. Maas. fin. suppl. Wil.   9 ἀ[οίκων Wil. ῥύ-
τορες e.g. Maas. ξένω[ν Wil. ὁδηγοί e.g. Maas.

---

   [a] The epiphany of the gods Apollo, Aphrodite and the
Erotes (in the plural, in true Alexandrian manner), gives a
realistic touch to the beginning of the poem, reminiscent of
Call. *Hymn* ii. We do not know how many lines are missing
between ll. 2 and 4.
   [b] It is not known what the κορώνη was. The word literally
meaning " crow " seems here to be used in the sense of
" culmination " or " fulfilment." The fragment speaks of
the cottabos game, which was of Sicilian origin and played

ΕΚΘΕΩΣΙΣ ΑΡΣΙΝΟΗΣ

THE poem is a lament on the sudden death of Queen Arsinoë,
sister and wife of Ptolemy II Philadelphos. The title *Ektheo-
sis Arsinoes* is preserved by the *Diegesis*, which reads :

Deification of Arsinoë. (The poet) says that she was snatched
up by the Dioscuri, and that an altar and a holy enclosure
were established in her honour near the Emporion.[a]

APOLLO is in the choir ; I hear the lyre. I also felt
2 the presence of the Erotes ; Aphrodite too is here ^a
4 . . . come hither, revellers (?), and he who has kept
awake till the height of the festival (?) ^b will take the
cake of roasted wheat and honey, and the cottabos
prize ^c ; and he will kiss whom he wishes of the girls
and boys present. O Castor, and you, Polydeuces,^d
(tamers of horses), (protectors of the homeless) and
(guides) of the guests . . .

at banquets after the tables were cleared away. One of its
more popular forms consisted of throwing heel-taps into a
metal basin, but there were many variations of the game, as
can be seen in its description by Athenaeus, xv. 665 d ff.
There we are also told (xv. 668 c) that " they used to keep
themselves awake as long as possible by dancing " (cf. fr. 69
with note).

^c We do not know what the cottabos prizes were in this
instance. According to Athenaeus (xv. 667 d) eggs, cakes,
nuts, raisins, or (xv. 668 d) ribbons and apples and kisses
were presented as prizes. Here the cottabos prize seems to
be different from the πυραμοῦς, a kind of bread covered with
sesame, and the kisses.

^d Castor and Polydeuces, the Dioscuri, sons of Tyndareus
and Leda, brothers of Helen (cf. fr. 64. 11, with note).

THE DEIFICATION OF ARSINOË

As the queen died on the 9th of July 270 B.C., the poem can-
not have been written very much later.

Apollo is invoked and asked to lead the chorus of the
Muses, without whose aid the poet proclaims he is unable to
sing. The mutilated condition of the papyrus does not al-
low us to follow the exact development of the poem, but in

---

^a A quarter of the city of Alexandria near the harbour.

CALLIMACHUS

ll. 40 ff. we find the queen's younger sister Philotera, who was already dead and honoured as a goddess (l. 52), asking Charis to fly to the top of Mount Athos in order to find out the origin of the huge column of smoke that came rolling across the surface of the Aegean Sea. Charis complied with the request of the goddess, and then told Philotera that the smoke came from the funeral pyre of her sister Arsinoë, who had just died, and that all the Egyptian cities were mourning for the death of the queen. The papyrus breaks off at that

228

Ἀγέτω θεός—οὐ γὰρ ἐγὼ δίχα τῶνδ' ἀείδειν
        π]ροποδεῖν Ἀπόλλων
        ]κεν δυναίμαν
       κατ]ὰ χεῖρα βᾶσαι.
5 νύμφα, σὺ μὲν ἀστερίαν ὑπ' ἄμαξαν ἤδη
Ἀνάκων ὕπο κλεπτομέν]α παρέθει⟨ς⟩ σελάνᾳ
διχομήνιδι - ⌣ ⌣ -] ἀτενεῖς ὀδυρμοί
        ] μία τοῦτο φωνά
      Ἀρσινόα] βασίλεια φροῦδα
10   ἀστὴρ ⌣ ⌣ | - ⌣ ⌣ - τ]ί παθὼν ἀπέσβη;
       ἁ δ]ὲ χύδαν ἐδίδασκε λύπα
       ] μέγας γαμέτας ὁμεύνῳ
       ]αν πρόθεσιν πύρ' αἴθειν

1 ἔχω v.l. codd.   2 suppl. Wil.   4 αχείραβαμοισαι P : suppl. e schol. et corr. Wil.   6 Ἀνάκων ὕπο Barber. κλεπτομέν]α (sc. Arsinoe) e schol. et e.g. ἀνετείλαο vel ἐπανέρχεο Pf. : παρέθει⟨ς⟩ Wil.   7 suppl. Wil.   9 Ἀρσινόα] Barber : ἀμετέρα] Pf. e.g.   10 ἀστὴρ suppl. Barber : τ]ί suppl. Wil.   11 suppl. e schol. Wil.   12 μέγας Pf.

point, so we do not know whether the formal deification of Arsinoë was described here, or whether the poem concluded with the setting up of the altar and precinct in her honour.

The metre is a stichic archebouleion:

$$\overset{\smile}{\underset{\smile}{}} - \smile\smile \;\Big|\; - \smile\smile - \;\vdots\; \smile\smile - \smile - -$$

A diaeresis appears after the third anapaest, and a caesura after the two short syllables of the second anapaest.[a]

---

[a] In ll. 41 and 57 we find the caesura after the first short syllable. The last syllable of the line is usually long.

228

Let the god[a] lead—for without them[b] I (cannot) sing
— . . . Apollo to show the way . . . I could . . .
5 stepping in accord with his hand[c] . . . O bride,[d]
already up under the stars of the Wain, . . . snatched
away (by the Dioscuri), you were speeding past the
(full) moon . . . loud laments . . . one voice (said
10 this) . . . Queen (Arsinoë) has gone . . . having
suffered what, was (our star) quenched ? . . . and
over-flowing grief taught . . . the great husband[e]
for his wife . . . to light fires as an offering (?) . . .

[a] Apollo.
[b] The Muses and Apollo.
[c] The Muses dancing and singing with Apollo are here visualized by the poet as described in the Introduction to Hesiod's *Theogony* (ll. 1 ff.).
[d] The queen, or rather the soul of the queen, is imagined here as snatched away by the Dioscuri and travelling beside the full moon under the stars of the Wain.
[e] The king, Ptolemy II Philadelphos.

165

```
                            ] λεπτὸν ὕδωρ
15                     Θέτ]ιδος τὰ πέραια βωμῶν
                            ]ωδε Θήβα .
```

. . . .

```
                            ] πόλις ἄλλα τευξεῖ·
35                     ]φέρει θάλασσαν
                       ]ᾶ παναγὴς ε[ . . . . ]ς̅
                       ]ν τὰ τάλαντα [ . . . . .
                       ]ων τὰ καλὰ πτ[ . . . . ]ᾶ
       Πρωτῆϊ μὲν ὧδ᾽ ἐτύμοι κατάγο[ντο φᾶμαι.
40  σαμάντριαν ἆ δὲ πυρᾶς ἐνόησ᾽ ἰ[ωάν,
    ἂν οὖλα κυλινδομέναν ἐδίωκ[ον αὖραι
```

⟨ .   .   .   .   .   . ⟩

```
    ἠδ᾽ ἂμ μέσα Θρηϊκίου κατὰ νῶτα [πόντου
    Φιλωτέρα· ἄρτι γάρ οἱ Σικελὰ μὲν Ἔννα
    κατελείπετο, Λαμνιακοὶ δ᾽ ἐπατεῦ[ντο βουνοί
45  Δηοῦς ἄπο νεισομένᾳ· σέο δ᾽ ἦν ἄπ[υστος,
    ὦ δαίμοσιν ἁρπαγίμα, φάτο δ᾽ ἡμιδ[
    '' ἕζευ Χάρι τὰν ὑπά[τ]αν ἐπ᾽ Ἄθω κολώ[ναν,
    ἀπὸ δ᾽ αὐγασαι, ἐκ πεδίου τὰ πύρ᾽ αἱ σαπ[
    τ]ίς ἀπώλετο, τίς πολίων ὁλόκαυτος α[ἴθει.
50  ἔνι μοι φόβος· ἀλλὰ ποτεῦ· νότος αὐ[τὸς οἰσεῖ,
    νότος αἴθριος· ἦρά τι μοι Λιβύα κα[κοῦται; ''
    τάδ᾽ ἔφα θεός· ἁ δ᾽ ὁπότε σκοπιὰν ἐπ[έπτα
    χιονώδεα, τὰν ἀπέχειν ἐλάχιστ[ον ἄρκτου
```

15 suppl. Wil. e schol.   39 suppl. Wil.   40 suppl.
Wil.   41 suppl. Wil. inter 41 et 42 versum deesse in P
vidit Wil.   42 suppl. Wil.   44 suppl. Wil.   45 νεισο-
μενας· P : corr. Maas. ἄπ[υστος suppl. Wil.   47 suppl.
Wil.   49 suppl. Wil.   50 e.g. suppl. Barber.   52 ἀλλ᾽
P : ἁ δ᾽ Maas. fin. suppl. Wil.   53-57 e.g. suppl. Wil.

15 shallow water . . . that faces the altars of Thetis [a]

39 . . . Thebes [b] . . . Thus the true report was carried
down to Proteus.[c] But she, Philotera,[d] noticed the
smoke, the indicator of the funeral pyre, which was
carried by the breezes as it rolled curling . . . and
along the mid-surface of the Thracian [e] Sea. For a
short time ago she had left Sicilian Enna,[f] and was
walking on the hills of Lemnos returning from her
45 visit to Deo.[g] But she knew not of you [h] (sc. of your
death), O stolen by the gods, and said . . . " Charis,[i]
sit on the top of Mount Athos, and see if the fire
comes from the . . . plain . . . which city has perished,
50 which city all on fire sends forth this light ? I am
anxious. But fly off. The south wind, the clear
south wind will itself carry you. Can it be that my
Libya is being harmed ? " Thus spoke the goddess.
And she (i.e. Charis), when she flew onto the snow-
covered peak, which is said to be the nearest to the

---

[a] According to the scholia the altar of Thetis was " on an
island near Alexandria," probably the island of Pharos itself.

[b] The Egyptian Thebes. These lines may refer to the
chain of fires that were lit from the Pharos to Thebes at the
death of the queen. In the following lines (17 ff.) the scholia
seem to suggest that the great qualities of the dead queen were
mentioned. Lines 34-38 are too fragmentary to translate.

[c] According to Homer (Od. iv. 355) Proteus, a minor sea-
god, herdsman of the flocks of the sea, lived on the island of
Pharos. This was at the entrance to the great harbour of
Alexandria.

[d] Philotera was the younger sister of Queen Arsinoë, and
had died before her, and was already deified when the poem
was written.   [e] The Aegean Sea.

[f] City of Sicily with a famous temple of Demeter.

[g] Demeter. Philotera is here treated as a " synnaos " or
" synhedros " of Demeter.   [h] Arsinoë.

[i] Charis, wife of Hephaestus, lived with her husband on
the island of Lemnos.

167

ἥκει λόγος, ἐς δὲ Φάρου περίσαμο[ν ἀκτάν
55 ἐσκέψατο, θυμολιπὴς ἐβόα[σε
" ναὶ ναὶ μέγα δή τ[ι
ἁ λίγνυς ἀφ' ὑμετ[έρας πόλιος φορεῖται."
ἁ δ' ἤνεπε ταῦτα [
τάν μοι πόλιν ᾷ με [
60 κείρουσιν· ὁ δ' ἐς φιλι[
πόσις ᾤχετο πενθερ[
ἄκουσά τε Μακροβίω[ν
ὄφρα δύσποδας ὣς ἑ π[
θεὸς ἔδραμεν· αὐτίκ[α
65 ἥξεῖ δόμον." ἁ μὲν [
οὐκ ἤδεε· τᾷ δὲ Χάρ[ις βαρὺν εἶπε μῦθον·
" μή μοι χθονός—οὐχὶ [τεὰ Φάρος ἁθάλωται—
περικλαίεο· μηδέ τι[
ἄλλα μέ τις οὐκ ἀγαθ[
70 θρῆνοι πόλιν ὑμετέρ[αν
οὐχ ὡς ἐπὶ δαμοτ[έρων
χθών· ἀλλά τι τῶ[ν] μεγάλων ἐξ[,
τάν τοι μίαν οἰχομ[ένα]ν ὁμόδελφυν [αὐτάν
κλαίοντι· τὰ δ' ᾷ [κεν ἴ]δῃς, μέλαν [ἀμφίεσται
75 χθονὸς ἄστεα· ν[ωῖτ]έρων τὸ κρατ[

ΒΡΑΓΧΟΣ

BRANCHUS, son of a Delphian called Smicrus and a Milesian mother (but whose lineage went back to Daites on his father's, and to Apollo on his mother's side), was beloved of Apollo, who gave him the gift of prophecy. He founded at Didyma or Didymi, near Miletus, a temple of Apollo with a cult similar to that of the Delphic oracle. It was consulted by

55 Pole-star,[a] and cast her eyes towards the famous
(coast) of Pharos, cried out faint at heart. . . . " Yes,
yes, a great . . . the smoke is coming from your city [b]
66 . . . " . . . Charis said sad words to her : " Please do
not weep for your land—your Pharos has not been
70 burnt—nor for . . . other evil . . . your city (is
full of) lament . . . not as though a person of lower
rank (were dead ?), . . . but one of the great ones
. . . they are weeping over your one and only sister
dead. Wherever you glance the cities of the land
75 are clad in black. Of our . . .

> [a] The height of the mountain is thus stressed.
> [b] Alexandria.

---

61 πενθερ[ὸν ὃν vel πενθερ[ικὸν prop. Wil., fort. πενθερ[ικὰν,
i.e. Eurynomen, Pf.   66 e.g. suppl. Wil.   67 sqq.
e.g. suppl. Wil.

BRANCHUS

Croesus, the Cumaeans and certain kings of Egypt, who also
dedicated rich offerings there. The temple was pillaged and
burnt by the Persians in 494 B.C., but was rebuilt on a scale
so huge that it remained unroofed.

There is no indication as to the date or the length of the
poem.[a]

The metre is a catalectic choriambic pentameter, with
(probably) a diaeresis after the second choriambus :

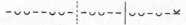

---

[a] The *Diegesis* summarizes the *Branchus* thus : Apollo
comes from Delos to a place near Miletus called the Sacred
Grove, where Branchus was.

169

229

Δαίμονες εὐυμνότατοι, Φοῖβέ τε καὶ Ζεῦ, Διδύμων
  γενάρχα
  .   .   .   .
μηδ᾽ ἀγέλαις τετρ]απόδων λοιμὸς ἐπέλθῃ κατάρατος
  ἅρπαξ,
κοῦρε ποθήτ᾽] ᾧ τρὶς ἐμο[ί]· χὠ μὲν [. .]λείτας ἀπό
  κεν τράποιτο,
μῆλα δ᾽ ὑπ᾽ εὐ]ηπε[λ]ίης πείονα χλωρὴν βοτάνην
  νέμοιτο·
5 β]αίτη[ς] ἑτέρ[ῳ] τῆσδε μελέσθω· [σὺ] δὲ καὶ
    προπάππων
  ]ρδ[.]κ[.]υσλ[. .]θιν ὁμαρτεῖν· ἐπ[εὸ]ν γάρ
    ἐστιν
ἡ γενέθλη] τοι πατρόθεν τῶν ἀπὸ Δαίτε[ω], τὸ δὲ
  πρὸς τεκούσης
αἷμ᾽ ἀνάγεις ἐ]ς Λαπίθην α[. . . .] δ᾽ ἕλκεις μία⟨ν⟩
  εὐγένει[α]ν.
Φοῖβε, σὺ μὲν] το[ιά]δ᾽ ἔφη[ς· το]ῦ δ᾽ ἐπὶ δώ[ροις]
  ἀνέπαλτ[ο θ]υμός·
10 αὐτίκα δή τ]οι τέμ[ε]ν[ο]ς [κα]λὸν ἐν ὕλῃ, τόθι πρῶ-
    τον ὤφθης,
εἴσατο κρην]έων δ[ιδύ]μων ἐγγύθι, δάφνης κατὰ
  κλῶνα πήξας.

1-7 suppl. Barber-Maas, praeter τετρ]απόδων L. et β]αίτη[ς]
ἑτέρ[ῳ] Barber.   3 χὠ μὲν (sc. λοιμὸς) ὁπλίας ἀπό κεν
τράποιτο dub. prop. Trypanis ; apud Hesych. ὁπλίας· Λοκροὶ
τοὺς τόπους ἐν οἷς συνελαύνοντες ἀριθμοῦσι τὰ πρόβατα καὶ τὰ
βοσκήματα : χὠ μὲν [ὁπ]λείτης Barber-Maas.   8 suppl.
Barber.   9 suppl. Barber-Maas praeter ἀνέπαλτ[ο θ]υμός

229

O GODS, who are well worthy of song, Phoebus and
Zeus, the founders of Didyma [a] . . . " The accursed
and snatching plague [b] shall (?) never fall upon the
3 flocks of animals, O youth thrice beloved to my heart ;
and it (the plague) would turn away, from . . . and
the fat flocks would graze in prosperity on the green
5 grass. Let another take care of this shepherd's coat
of skins . . . For it is true that your family on your
father's side is descended from that of Daites, [c] and
on your mother's side (you trace back your blood to)
Lapithes [d] and from . . . you derive one (equal)
nobility." (Phoebus), you said such words, and his
10 heart was raised by the gifts. [e] And (at once), where
you [f] first appeared in the wood (he [g] dedicated to
you) a beautiful holy precinct near the double foun-
tain, [h] and stuck in the earth the branch of the bay-

[a] Didyma, or Didymi, the oracle near Miletus dedicated
to Apollo and Zeus.
[b] These words are spoken (till l. 8) by Apollo. Branchus
could cleanse those affected by " the snatching plague " ;
see fr. 194. 28 f.
[c] Machaereus, a priest of Apollo at Delphi, who killed
Neoptolemus, was the father of Daites, and forefather of
Branchus.
[d] Lapithes was a son of Apollo and Stilbe, daughter of
Peneus.
[e] We are told that when Branchus was kissed by Apollo
in the wood, and had received the gifts of a crown and a
bay-tree branch, he began to utter prophesies. The " sacred
crown " was later kept in the adyton of the temple at Didyma.
[f] Apollo.   [g] Branchus.
[h] The etymology of the name Didyma is explained by the
double fountain.

L. [σ]οῦ Pf.   10 τέμ[ε]ν[ο]ς [κα]λὸν L. cett. Barber-Maas.
11 εἴσατο Barber-Maas.   cett. Pf.

εἴλαθι, Δελφ]ίνι' ἄ[ν]αξ· οὔν[ο]μα γά[ρ] τοι τόδ' ἐγὼ
    κατάρχω,
εἴνεκεν Οἰκούσ]ιον εἰς ἄ[σ]τυ σε δελφὶς ἀπ' ἔβησε
    Δήλου.

12-13 suppl. Pf. praeter εἴλαθι Barber-Maas.

---

[a] Apollo Delphinius was worshipped in the outskirts of the city of Miletus.

tree. May you be propitious, Lord Delphinius [a]; for I begin from this name of yours, because a Dolphin brought you [b] from Delos to land at the city of Oecus [c] . . .

[b] Once again tracing the etymology of a name back to a myth.

[c] If the supplement is correct then the city of Oecus must be another name for Miletus, or the oldest part of the city, founded by the hero Miletus, son of Apollo.

HECALE

INTRODUCTION

THE *Hecale*, an epic poem, described the victory of
Theseus over the bull that devastated the district of
Marathon in Attica. But in the foreground Callima-
chus set the figure of Hecale, an aged, impoverished
woman of noble descent, in whose hut Theseus took
refuge from a storm, while on his way to Marathon
to overcome the bull. The main source which the
poet used was an *Atthis* (a chronicle of the history of
Attica), possibly that of Philochorus on which Plu-
tarch also relied for the same story, related by him
in the *Life of Theseus* 14 :

Theseus, wishing to be actively employed, and at the same
time to win the favour of the people, went out against the
Marathonian bull, which was causing no small annoyance
to the inhabitants of the Tetrapolis, and he overcame the
bull, and drove it through the city to exhibit it, after which
he sacrificed it to Apollo Delphinius. Hecale, and the legend
of her reception and entertainment (of Theseus), seem to be
not quite without some portion of truth. For the demes
round about used to meet and hold a Hecalesian festival in
honour of Zeus Hecalus, and honoured Hecale, whom they
called by the pet name Hecaline, because when she enter-
tained Theseus, who at the time was quite young, she ad-
dressed him as an old woman would, and greeted him with
that sort of pet names. When Theseus was setting out to
the contest she vowed on his behalf to offer a sacrifice to
Zeus if he came back safe. She died, however, before his
return, and received the above-mentioned honours in return

for her hospitality, by order of Theseus, as Philochorus relates.[a]

But this story was treated by Callimachus in a free and poetic manner, as we can see from the *Diegesis*, which runs :

Theseus, after escaping the treacherous plot of Medea, was carefully guarded by his father, to whom the stripling had been restored unexpectedly from Troezen. Wishing to set out and overcome the bull that ravaged the country round Marathon, and being detained, he secretly left his house at evening. As an unexpected rainstorm broke out, he noticed on the edge of the land a small hut belonging to an old woman called Hecale. (He took refuge there) and was entertained as a guest. He rose at early dawn, set out for Marathon, overcame the bull, and returned to Hecale. To his astonishment he found her dead, and, sighing for the hopes that were belied, what he had promised after her death he would do to repay her hospitality, this he did. He established a deme which he named after her, and set up a sanctuary to Zeus Hecaleios.

It is impossible to reconstruct the course of Callimachus' narrative in any detail. It appears, however, that the emphasis fell on the visit of Theseus to the humble hut of Hecale, which is in accordance with the practice of Alexandrian poetry, in which the great heroes of the past were on the whole represented in scenes of their ordinary everyday life (to which realistic and humorous touches were added), and not when performing great " heroic " deeds. The description of Theseus' visit to Hecale was considered very successful in late antiquity and often imitated by other poets (*e.g.* Ovid, *Met.* viii. 620 f. ; Ps.-Vergil, *Moretum*, etc. See Wilamowitz, *Hell.*

[a] Philochorus of Athens, the most famous of the *Atthidographers*, who lived at the end of the 4th and the beginning of the 3rd century B.C.

Dichtung, i, p. 189). In fact the *Hecale* became very famous and was read, copied, paraphrased and commented on up to the thirteenth century A.D.

The conversation between Hecale and Theseus gave the opportunity to Callimachus to introduce a number of stories about the birth, childhood [a] and deeds of Theseus, and other narratives about the former life and position of Hecale. It appears that the actual struggle with the bull was treated briefly; the reception of Theseus by the countryfolk after his victory has survived in frs. 259 and 260. 1-15.

The pleasure Callimachus took in narrating independent episodes can be also seen from fr. 260. 16 ff., which includes the story of Erichthonius and the daughters of Cecrops, as well as the story of the wrath of Pallas against the crows, on account of the bad news they brought to her, and how Apollo turned the raven from white to black. We do not know, however, how these stories were connected with the general trend of the narrative. When Theseus returned the next day victorious to Hecale's hut, he found her dead, and instituted the Δεῖπν' Ἑκαλεῖα in her memory. He also set up a sanctuary to Zeus Hecaleios and established a deme which was named after her. Thus Callimachus ends the *Hecale* in an aetion which explains these three events.

[a] The story was that Aegeus, king of Athens, being childless, consulted the oracle at Delphi. To interpret the oracle which he received, he went to consult Pittheus of Troezen. Here he became father of Theseus by Aethra, daughter of Pittheus. Leaving Troezen before the birth of Theseus, Aegeus hid his sword and shoes under a rock, telling Aethra that, when their son was able to raise the rock and remove the sword and shoes, she was to send him to Athens with these tokens of recognition. This duly took place, and Theseus was recognized as the son of Aegeus.

HECALE

The scholiast to Callimachus, *Hymn* ii. 106 says :
ἐγκαλεῖ διὰ τούτων τοὺς σκώπτοντας αὐτὸν μὴ δύνασθαι
ποιῆσαι μέγα ποίημα, ὅθεν ἠναγκάσθη ποιῆσαι τὴν
Ἑκάλην. (" In these verses he attacks those who
mocked him for not being able to write a long poem ;
for this reason he was forced to compose the *Hecale*.")
How far the *Hecale* was a " big poem " is, of course,
unknown. In the complete edition of the poet's
works it did not fill more than one book, and can
therefore not have exceeded by much the 1000 lines
which on the average were the length of a Calli-
machean " book." Nothing is known about the date
of its composition, but, if it was an answer to his
critics, it must have been written after the first
edition of the *Aetia* had circulated. Moreover, the
highly finished style of the extant fragments points
to a work of full maturity. The parts of the *Iambi*
that seem to depend on the *Hecale* (*e.g.* fr. 194. 61 ff.)
are of little help in this matter, because the dates of
the *Iambi* are equally uncertain. The *Argonautica* of
Apollonius Rhodius depend on the *Hecale* in many
points (see Pfeiffer i, *passim*), and this refutes the
view that the *Hecale* was composed as an answer to
Apollonius in the great (and apparently later) con-
troversy between him and his teacher Callimachus.

ΕΚΑΛΗ

(Fr. 230–263 ad ordinem
narrationis)

230

Ἀκταίη τις ἔναιεν Ἐρεχθέος ἔν ποτε γουνῷ

---

^a Fabulous king of Athens, son of the Earth and reared by Athene. " A hill of Erechtheus "=a hill in Attica. The demos of Hecale was probably situated on the eastern slopes

231

τίον δέ ἑ πάντες ὁδῖται
ἧρα φιλοξενίης· ἔχε γὰρ τέγος ἀκλήιστον

---

^a Hecale, who was proverbial for her hospitality. The myth gave rise to the false etymology of the name which we

232

ἡ δ' ἐκόησεν,
τοὔνεκεν Αἰγέος ἔσκεν

---

^a Medea.

233

ἴσχε τέκος, μὴ πῖθι
180

HECALE

(The fragments follow the sequence of the narrative till fr. 263.)

230

ONCE on a hill of Erechtheus [a] there lived an Attic woman.

of Mount Brilessos, somewhere near the present village " Koukounari."

231

. . . and all wayfarers honoured her [a] for her hospitality ; for she kept her house open.

find in Suidas (*s.v.* Ἑκάλη) ἡ πρὸς ἑαυτὴν καλοῦσα, and in *Etym. Gen.* A (Reitz. *Ind. lect.* Rostock, 1890/1, p. 14) παρὰ τὸ εἰσκαλεῖν ἢ εἰς καλιήν.

232

. . . (but) she [a] understood that he [b] was the son of Aegeus.

[b] Theseus. The fragment comes from the " Μηδείας ἐπιβουλή."

233

. . . hold back, child, do not drink.[a]

[a] The poison, which Medea attempted to give Theseus. These are probably words spoken by Aegeus to Theseus.

CALLIMACHUS

234

παρὲκ νόον εἰλήλουθας

<hr>

^a Probably words spoken after the " recognition " by

235

ἐν γάρ μιν Τροιζῆνι κολουραίῃ ὑπὸ πέτρῃ
θῆκε σὺν ἁρπίδεσσιν

<hr>

^a Aegeus.

236

εὖτ' ἂν ὁ παῖς ἀπὸ μὲν γυαλὸν λίθον ἀγκάσσασθαι
ἄρκιος ᾖ χείρεσσιν, ἑλὼν Αἰδήψιον ἆορ
⟨   καὶ τὰ⟩ πέδιλα, τὰ μὴ πύσε νήχυτος εὐρώς

3 suppl. Naeke.

<hr>

^a Theseus ; see introduction. Probably quoting words
spoken by Aegeus to Aethra.

238

4 τῷ ⟨ῥα⟩, πάτερ, μεθίει με, σόον δέ κεν αὖθι δέχοιο

[10 versus desunt]

15 ὄφρα μὲν οὖν ἔνδιος ἔην ἔτι, θέρμετο δὲ χθών,
τόφρα δ' ἔην ὑάλοιο φαάντερος οὐρανὸς ἦνοψ
οὐδέ ποθι κνηκὶς ὑπεφαίνετο, πέπτατο δ' αἰθήρ
ἀννέφελος· σ[
μητέρι δ' ὁππ[ότε
20 δειελὸν αἰτίζουσιν, ἄγουσι δὲ χεῖρας ἀπ' ἔργου,
τῆμος ἄρ' ἐξ[

4 ⟨ῥα⟩ Kassel : ⟨νν⟩ Nickau.   19 suppl. L.

182

HECALE

234

. . . you have come unexpectedly.[a]

Aegeus to Theseus, about his unexpected arrival from Troezen ; see introduction.

235

. . . for in Troezen he [a] put it [b] under a hollow stone together with the (soldier's) boots.

[b] The sword ; see introduction. The sword and the boots were the γνωρίσματα, the tokens of recognition.

236

. . . whenever the child [a] should be strong enough to lift up with his arms the hollow stone ; having seized the sword of Aedepsos [b] . . . and the boots, which the abundant dripping mould had not rotted . . .

[b] City of Euboea. Euboea was well known in antiquity for its iron and copper mines. According to a tradition copper was first found there.

238

4 . . . therefore father, let me go ; you would again receive me alive and well . . .[a]

[10 lines missing]

15 . . . while then it was still midday, and the earth was warm, for so long the brilliant sky was clearer than glass, nor was a wisp of vapour to be seen, and cloudless stretched the heavens . . but when to (?)
20 their mother . . . (the daughters) ask for the evening meal, and take their hands from work,[b] then . . .

[a] See K. Nickau, *Philologus*, cxi (1967), pp. 126 f. Probably part of a dialogue between Theseus and his father before he set out for Marathon ; cf. *Dieg.* x. 26.
[b] Spinning and weaving.

πρῶτον ὑπὲρ Πά[ρνηθος,] ἐπιπρὸ δὲ μᾶσσον ἐπ'
    ἄκρου
Αἰγαλέως θυμόεντος, ἄγων μέγαν ὑετόν, ἔστη·
τῷ δ' ἐπὶ διπλόον [
25 τρηχέος Ὑμηττ[οῖο
ἀστεροπαὶ σελάγι[ζον
οἷ[ο]ν ὅτε κλονέ[
Αὐσόν[ι]ον κατὰ π[όντον
ἡ δ' ἀπὸ Μηρισοῖο θοὴ βορέαο κατᾶιξ
30 εἰσέπεσεν νεφέλ[ῃσιν

| 22 suppl. L. | 25 suppl. L. | 26 suppl. L. |
| 28 suppl. L. | 30 suppl. Pf. | |

239

διερὴν δ' ἀπεσείσατο λαίφην

240

τὸν μὲν ἐπ' ἀσκάντην κάθισεν

241

αὐτόθεν ἐξ εὐνῆς ὀλίγον ῥάκος αἰθύξασα

242

παλαίθετα κᾶλα καθήρει

---

[a] Hecale.

first over Parnes,[a] and then farther forward and
larger on the summit of thyme-covered Aegaleos,[b]
stood (the cloud ?) bringing much rain . . . and
25 thereupon a double . . . of rugged Hymettus [c] . . .
lightning was flashing [d] . . . as when . . . on the
Ausonian Sea [e] . . . and the swift northern squall
30 from Merithus [f] fell upon the clouds.

[a] The highest mountain of Attica, situated to the north of
Athens.
[b] A low mountain range of Attica to the west of Athens.
[c] The celebrated mountain of Attica to the east of Athens.
[d] This can only be the description of the storm that obliged
Theseus to take refuge in the hut of Hecale.
[e] The sea of Sicily. According to Strabo (ii. 123) the
Ausonian Sea extended from Sicily to Crete.
[f] Mountain of Thrace. The north wind coming from
Thrace was famous for its violence in ancient Greece.

239

. . . and he [a] cast off his wet garment.

[a] Theseus. This and fr. 240 have *Od.* xiv. 48 ff. as their
pattern.

240

. . . she [a] made him [b] sit on the humble couch.

[a] Hecale.   [b] Theseus.

241

. . . having at once snatched a small tattered garment
from the bed.

242

. . . and (she) [a] took down wood stored away a long
time ago.

CALLIMACHUS

243

δανὰ ξύλα [   ] κεάσαι

244

αἶψα δὲ κυμαίνουσαν ἀπαίνυτο χυτρίδα κοίλην

^a Probably warming the water for the foot-bath of Theseus.

245

φράσον δέ μοι, εἰς ὅ τι τεῦχος
χεύωμαι ποσὶ χύτλα καὶ ὁππόθεν

^a Theseus is speaking to Hecale.

246

ἐκ δ' ἔχεεν κελέβην, μετὰ δ' αὖ κερὰς ἠφύσατ' ἄλλο

247 ^a

^a See fr. 284 A.

248

γεργέριμον πίτυρίν τε καὶ ἦν ἀπεθήκατο λευκήν
εἰν ἁλὶ νήχεσθαι φθινοπωρίδα

^a Hecale. Frs. 248 and 251 are part of the description of
the meal Hecale offered Theseus. *Cf.* fr. 194. 77. Cabbage
186

HECALE

243

. . . dry wood . . . to cut.[a]

[a] Cf. Od. xiv. 418.

244

. . . (she) swiftly took off the hollow, boiling pot.[a]

Cf. Od. x. 360 f.   Frs. 244-246 are all that is left from the scene of the foot-bath.

245

. . . but tell me into what vessel am I [a] to pour the water for my feet, and from where.

246

. . . she [a] emptied the tub, and then she drew another mixed draught.

[a] Hecale.

247 [a]

[a] See fr. 284 A.

248

. . . olives which grew ripe on the tree, and wild olives, and the light-coloured ones, which in autumn she [a] had to put to swim in brine.

and wild vegetables were also offered to Theseus during the rustic meal.

CALLIMACHUS

251

ἐκ δ' ἄρτους σιπύηθεν ἅλις κατέθηκεν ἑλοῦσα
οἴους βωνίτῃσιν ἐνικρύπτουσι γυναῖκες

ᵃ Hecale.

253

ἐ]ς Μαραθῶνα κατέρχομαι ὄφρα κ[ ]π̣α̣ρ̣[.
    Παλλὰς] δὲ καθηγήτειρα κελεύθου.
τὼς ἄρ' ἐμεῦ μεμάθ]ηκας ἅ μ' εἴρεο· καὶ σύ [γε]
    μαῖα
λέξον, ἐπεὶ καὶ ἐμο]ί τι ποθὴ σέο τυτθὸν ἀκοῦσαι
5] γρηῢς ἐ[ρη]μαίη ἔνι ναίεις

[32 fere versus desunt]

δινομένην πέρι βουσὶν ἐμὴν ἐφύλασσον ἄλωα.
τὸν δ' ἀπ' Ἀφιδνάων ἵπποι φ[έρον
εἴκελον, οἵ τ' εἶεν Διὸς υἱέϊ[ς,
10 μέμνημαι καλὴν μὲν α̣[
ἄλλικα χρυσείῃσιν ἐεργομένην ἐνετῆσιν,
ἔργον ἀραχνάων [

1 init. suppl. Vitelli. fort. κ' [ἀ]π̣ᾶ̣ρ̣[ω Pf.   2 suppl.
Vitelli.   3 sq. e.g. suppl. Vitelli.   σύ [γε] suppl. Pf.
5 suppl. T. Lodi.   8 φ[έρον suppl. Vitelli.   ἢ βασιλεῦσιν
e.g. prop. Pf.   9 ἢ θεῷ αὐτῷ e.g. suppl. Pf.

ᵃ Fragments 253-256 are parts of the conversation Theseus
had with Hecale, probably during and after their meal.
Theseus is speaking in ll. 1-6.

254

οὐ γάρ μοι πενίη πατρώιος, οὐδ' ἀπὸ πάππων
εἰμὶ λιπερνῆτις· βάλε μοι, βάλε τὸ τρίτον εἴη

251

. . . and from the bread-box she [a] took and served loaves in abundance, such as women put away for herdsmen.

253

. . . " I [a] go down to Marathon, so that . . . and (Pallas) leads the way. (You have thus learnt from me) what you asked me. And you, good mother, (tell me, for I also) wish to hear you for a while (speaking)
5 . . you live an old woman in a lonely . . . "

[About 32 lines missing]

"they guarded my threshing floor, trod in a circle by the oxen.[b] Horses (brought) him from Aphidnae,[c] looking
10 like . . . and who were Zeus' sons . . . I remember the beautiful . . . mantle held by golden brooches, a work of spiders " [d] . . .

[b] Fr. 255 Pf. *Cf.* V. Bartoletti, *Studi di fil. cl.* xxxi (1959), p. 3.
[c] Probably Hecale is speaking here. We do not know about whom she is speaking. Aphidnae was one of the demes of Attica.
[d] May refer to patterns woven in the cloth, like the work of Arachne (*cf.* Ovid, *Met.* vi. 5 ff.), the Lydian woman, daughter of Idmon of Colophon, so skilled in weaving that she challenged Athene to a competition. When Athene destroyed her web, she hanged herself, and the goddess turned her into a spider.

254

. . . " for poverty was not in my family, nor was I a pauper from my grandparents.[a] O that I, O that I had a third of . . . "

[a] Hecale is here speaking, presumably about her earlier life.

CALLIMACHUS

255 [a]

[a] See fr. 253, l. 7.

256

λέξομαι ἐν μυχάτῳ· κλισίη δέ μοί ἐστιν ἑτοίμη

[a] Hecale, speaking to Theseus. In all probability, if we are to judge by the Homeric pattern of Odysseus at the hut

257

ὡς ἔμαθεν κἀκεῖνον ἀνιστάμενον

---

[a] Hecale.

258

θηρὸς ἐρωήσας ὀλοὸν κέρας

---

[a] Fragments 258–260. 1-15 treat of the fight of Theseus with the bull and his victory over it.

259

ὁ μὲν εἷλκεν, ὁ δ' εἵπετο νωθρὸς ὁδίτης

260

. . . . . .] ἑτέρην περίαπτε καὶ εἰν ἄορ ἧκεν [
ὡς ἴδον, ὡς ἅμα πάντες ὑπ[έ]τρεσ[α]ν ἠδ[ὲ φόβη]θεν

1 omnia incertissima.   2 ἠδ[ὲ φόβη]θεν e.g. suppl. Pf.

HECALE

255 [a]

[a] See fr. 253, l. 7.

256

... I [a] will sleep in a corner (of my hut) ; a couch
is ready for me.

of Eumaeus, Theseus slept by the fire, and Hecale is referring
here to her own usual bed.

257

... as she [a] saw him [b] also getting up.

[b] Theseus, who also woke up early in the morning to set
out against the bull of Marathon.

258

... having bent to the earth the terrible horn of
the beast.[a]

259

... he was dragging (the bull), and it was following,
a sluggish wayfarer.

260

.. the other (strap) he fastened (?) and put in his
sword ... when they saw it they all trembled and

ἄνδρα μέγαν καὶ θῆρα πελώριον ἄντ[α ἰ]δέσθαι,
μέσφ' ὅτε δὴ Θησεύς φιν ἀπόπροθι μακρὸν ἄυσε·
5 " μίμνετε θαρσήεντες, ἐμῷ δέ τις Αἰγέϊ πατρί
νεύμενος ὅς τ' ὤκιστος ἐς ἄστυρον ἀγγελιώτης
ὧδ' ἐνέποι—πολέων κεν ἀναψύξειε μεριμνέων—·
Θησεὺς οὐχ ἑκὰς οὗτος, ἀπ' εὐύδρου Μαραθῶνος
ζωὸν ἄγων τὸν ταῦρον." ὁ μὲν φάτο, τοὶ δ' ἀίοντες
10 πάντες ἰὴ παιῆον ἀνέκλαγον, αὖθι δὲ μίμνον.
οὐχὶ νότος τόσσην γε χύσιν κατεχεύατο φύλλων,
οὐ βορέης οὐδ' αὐτὸς ὅτ' ἔπλετο φυλλοχόος μείς,
ὅσσα τότ' ἀγρῶσται περί τ' ἀμφί τε Θησέϊ βάλλον,
οἵ μιν ἐκυκλώσαν]το περισταδόν, αἱ δὲ γυναῖκες
15   στόρνησιν ἀνέστεφον

[22 fere versus desunt]

" καί ῥ' ὅτ' ἐποφ[. . . . .] ἐφ' ὃν ἄν τιν' ἕκαστοι
Οὐρανίδαι . ἐπάγοιεν ἐμῷ πτερῷ· ἀλλά ἑ Παλλάς
τῆς μὲν ἔσω δηναιῳ̣αφη δρόσον Ἡφαίστοιο
20 μέσφ' ὅτε Κεκροπίδ[ῃσιν] επ[. . . . .] λ[ᾶ]αν
λάθριον ἄρρητον, γενεῇ δ' ὅθεν οὔτε νιν ἔγνων
οὔτ' ἐδάην, φήμη δὲ κατ' ὠγυγίους εφαν[.]υται

3 suppl. Gomperz.   7 ὡς T : corr. Pf.   14 suppl.
Gomperz.   17-19 multa adhuc incerta.   19 δηναιὸν
ἀφῇ Gomperz.   20 suppl. Gomperz : ἐπ[αλέα θήκατο]
prop. Barber.

---

[a] Exclamation of joy (hurrah !), especially used in the
cult of Apollo.

[b] The φυλλοβολία was the custom of pelting the victors in
games with leaves, or leafy crowns, as a token of applause.

[c] The reference is to the birth of Erichthonius, son of

shrank from looking face to face on the great hero
and the monstrous beast, until Theseus called to
5 them from afar : " Have courage and stay, and let
the swiftest go to the city to bear this message to my
father Aegeus—for he shall relieve him from many
cares : ' Theseus here is close at hand bringing the
bull alive from Marathon rich in water.'" So he said,
10 and, when they heard, they all cried out : " IE
PAIEON " [a] and stayed there.   The south wind
does not shed so great a fall of leaves, nor the north
wind, even in the month of falling leaves, as those
which in that hour the countryfolk threw all around
and over Theseus,[b] the countryfolk who . . . encir-
15 cled him, while the women . . . crowned him with
girdles . . .

[About 22 lines missing]

18 " . . . But Pallas left him,[c] the seed of Hephaestus,
long (?) within (the chest), until for the sons of
Cecrops . . . the rock, . . . secret, unutterable, but
I neither knew, nor learnt whence he was by descent,
but a report (spread ?) among the primeval birds,

Hephaestus. Athena wished to rear him secretly. She
therefore " shut him up in a chest (κίστη) and gave him to
the daughters of Cecrops, Agraulos, Pandrosos and Herse,
with orders not to open the chest until she herself came.
Having gone to Pellene, she was bringing a hill in order to
make a bulwark in front of the Acropolis, when two of
Cecrops' daughters opened the chest, and saw two serpents
with Erichthonius. As Athene was bringing the hill which is
now called Lycabettus, a crow (κορώνη) met her, and told her
that Erichthonius was discovered. Athena, when she heard
it, threw down the hill where it now is, and told the crow
that, for her bad news, she must never enter the Acropolis "
(Amelesagoras in Antig. Caryst. Hist. Mirab. c. xii, cf.
Apollod. iii. 14, Ovid, Met. ii. 551 ff.).

CALLIMACHUS

οἰωνούς, ὡς δῆθεν ὑφ᾽ Ἡφαίστῳ τέκεν Αἶα.
τουτάκι δ᾽ ἡ μὲν ἑῆς ἔρυμα χθονὸς ὄφρα βάλοιτο,
25 τήν ῥα νέον ψήφῳ τε Διὸς δυοκαίδεκά τ᾽ ἄλλων
ἀθανάτων ὄφιός τε κατέλλαβε μαρτυρίῃσιν,
Πελλήνην ἐφίκανεν Ἀχαιίδα· τόφρα δὲ κοῦραι
αἱ φυλακοὶ κακὸν ἔργον ἐπεφράσσαντο τελέσσαι,
κίστης [   ] δεσμά τ᾽ ἀνεῖσαι.

[22 fere versus desunt]

οὕτως ἡμετέρην μὲν ἀπέπτυσεν, οὐδὲ γενέθλην
40   ] ἀλλὰ πέσοιο
μηδέ ποτ᾽ ἐκ θυμοῖο. βαρὺς χόλος αἰὲν Ἀθήνης·
αὐτὰρ ἐγὼ τυτθὸς παρέ[ην γ]όνος· [ὀ]γδ[ο]άτ[η] γάρ
ἤδη μοι γενεὴ πέλ[εται], δεκάτη δὲ τοκεῦσι

[8 fere versus desunt]

γαστέρι μοῦνον ἔχοιμι κακῆς ἀλκτήρια λιμοῦ

[3 versus mutili sequuntur]

46 καὶ κρῖμνον κυκεῶνος ἀποστάξαντος ἔραζε·
48   ]ν[ ] κακάγγελον· εἴθε γὰρ [εἴης
κεῖνον ἔτι] ζώουσα κατὰ χρόνον, ὄφρα τ[όδ᾽ εἰδ]ῇς
50 ὡς Θριαὶ τὴν γρηῢν ἐπιπνείουσι κορώνην.

25 δε T : τε Gomperz.   39-41 οὕτως ἢ χ᾽ ἑτέρην μὲν
ἀπέρτυχεν οὐδὲ γενέθλην | ἡμετέρην ἔκλεινε [τό]ϲ[ο]ν [θεό]ϲ· ἀλλὰ
πέσοιο | μηδέποτ᾽ ἐκ θυμοῖο· prop. Barber.   42-43 suppl.
Gomperz.   48 e.g. suppl. Pf. : φήμην Ἀπόλλω]ν[ι] prop.
Barber.   49 e.g. suppl. Pf. : τ[ό γ᾽ εἰδ]ῇς Barber.

The reference is to the story of the contest between
Athena and Posidon for the possession of Attica. See note
on fr. 194. 66 ff. The speaker appears to be the crow.

The crow is still speaking. According to Hesiod (fr. 171
Reitz.) the crow lives the length of ten human generations.
Aegeus was thought to be the eighth successor of Cecrops,
so the dating seems to fit in admirably.

194

that Earth forsooth bore him to Hephaestus. Then
she, that she might set up a bulwark for her land,
25 which she had newly obtained by vote of Zeus and
the twelve other immortals,[a] and by the witness of
the snake, was coming to Pellene in Achaia. Mean-
while, the maidens that watched the chest planned to
do an evil deed . . . undoing the fastenings (of the
chest) . . .

[About 22 lines missing]

39 thus she rejected our (race ?), nor . . . But may you
never fall from her favour ; the anger of Athene is
ever grievous. But I was present as a little one,
for this is my eighth generation,[b] but the tenth for
my parents.

[About 8 lines missing]

may I have (this ?) alone as protection for my belly
against evil hunger [c] . . .

[3 mutilated lines follow]

46 and barley-groats, that dripped from the posset [d] upon
48 the earth . . . messenger of bad news [e] . . . O that
you were still alive then to know this : how the
51 Thriae [f] inspire the old crow

[c] Fr. 346 Pf. ; cf. P. Oxy. nos. 2437 and 2398.
[d] Here the reference seems to be to the barley-groats, that
had dropped on the ground from the posset, the potion in
which barley-oats, grated cheese, wine, honey and certain
" magical " drugs were mixed. Barley, we are told by
ancient sources, was a food eaten by crows.
[e] On the bad news the crow brought to Apollo and how
it was punished, see note d on p. 197.
[f] The Thriae were nymphs of Mount Parnasus, three in
number, who had nursed Apollo when young, and who were
considered teachers of divination.

CALLIMACHUS

ναὶ μὰ τόν—οὐ γὰρ πάντ' ἤματα—ναὶ μὰ τὸ ῥι-
  κνὸν
σῦφαρ ἐμόν, ναὶ τοῦτο τὸ δένδρεον αὖον ἐόν περ,
οὐκ ἤδη ῥυμόν τε καὶ ἄξονα κανάξαντες
ἠέλιοι δυσμέων εἴσω πόδα πάντες ἔχουσι·
55 δεί]ελος ἀλλ' ἢ νὺξ ἢ ἔνδιος ἢ ἔσετ' ἠώς,
εὖτε κόραξ, ὃς νῦν γε καὶ ἂν κύκνοισιν ἐρίζοι
καὶ γάλακι χροιὴν καὶ κύματος ἄκρῳ ἀώτῳ,
κυάνεον φῆ πίσσαν ἐπὶ πτερὸν οὐλοὸν ἕξει,
ἀγγελίης ἐπίχειρα, τά οἱ ποτε Φοῖβος ὀπάσσει,
60 ὁππότε κεν Φλεγύαο Κορωνίδος ἀμφὶ θυγατρός
  "Ἰσχυϊ πληξίππῳ σπομένης μιερόν τι πύθηται."
τὴν μὲν ἄρ' ὣς φαμένην ὕπνος λάβε, τὴν δ' ἀίουσαν.
καδδραθέτην δ' οὐ πολλὸν ἐπὶ χρόνον, αἶψα γὰρ
  ἦλθεν
στιβήεις ἄγχαυρος, ὅτ' οὐκέτι χεῖρες ἔπαγροι
65 φιλητέων· ἤδη γὰρ ἑωθινὰ λύχνα φαείνει·
ἀείδει καί πού τις ἀνὴρ ὑδατηγὸς ἱμαῖον·
ἔγρει καί τιν' ἔχοντα παρὰ πλόον οἰκίον ἄξων
τετριγὼς ὑπ' ἄμαξαν, ἀνιάζουσι δὲ †πυκνοι †
δμῶοι χαλκῆες κωφώμενοι ἔνδον ἀκουήν

. . . .

51 ναὶ μὰ τόν = fr. 351 Pf.   51-54 P. Oxy. 2398.   55
suppl. Gomperz.   64 αγκουρος T: corr. Pf.   67 παρα-
πλοον T: περίπλοον cod.: corr. Gomperz.   68 πυκνοὶ
Gomperz, fort. πυκνοῖς (Pf.).   69 ultima linea lectu diffi-
cillima, satis incerta.

---

[a] The name of the god is not mentioned out of piety.

[b] We do not know who is speaking. There is some indi-
cation (ἀ]λλ' εκαλ[in P. Oxy. 2398. 3, and the Suda s.v. ναὶ μὰ

261

ἡ μὲν ἀερτάζουσα μέγα τρύφος ὑψίζωνος

1 ὑψιζώνου codd.: corr. Bentley.

196

Yes by [a] — ? — yes by my old shrivelled skin,[b] yes by
this tree though dry, all the suns have not yet dis-
appeared in the West with a broken pole and axle.[c]
55 But it shall be evening or night, or noon, or dawn,
when the raven,[d] which now might vie in colour
even with swans, or with milk, or with the finest
cream of the wave, shall put on a sad plumage, black
as pitch, the reward that Phoebus will one day give
60 him for his message, when he learns terrible tidings
of Coronis, daughter of Phlegyas, that she has gone
with Ischys, the driver of horses." While she spoke
thus, sleep seized her and her hearer.[e] They fell
asleep, but not for long; for soon the frosty early
dawn came, when the hands of thieves are no longer
65 seeking for prey; for already the lamps of dawn
are shining; many a drawer of water is singing the
Song of the Well,[f] and the axle creaking under
the wagons wakes him who has his house beside the
highway, while many (?) a blacksmith slave, with
hearing deafened, torments the ear . .

τὸν . . . καὶ Ἑκάλη εἶπε) that it may be Hecale. If that
were so, the dry tree may be the staff she was holding (*cf.* fr.
292 and *Iliad* i. 234 f.).
    [c] Presumably a way of saying either (a) that the speaker
is not yet dead, or (b) that the end of the world has not yet
come.
    [d] Ll. 55-61, however, seem to be the prophecy of the old
crow, in which it predicted the turning of the raven's plumage
from white to black as a punishment for the news which it
brought to Apollo regarding Coronis, who, being with child
by Apollo, sinned with Ischys, son of Elatos.
    [e] Another bird, possibly a younger crow, hearing the old
crow speaking throughout the night?
    [f] The Ἱμαῖον was the song of the drawers of water.

. . . and she (*sc.* Athene), high-girdled, was going up

CALLIMACHUS

ἄστυρον εἰσανέβαινεν, ἐγὼ δ' ἤντησα Λυκείου
καλὸν ἀεὶ λιπόωντα κατὰ δρόμον Ἀπόλλωνος

ᵃ Fragment from the narrative of the crow. This should probably be placed in the lacuna that follows fr. 260. 29.

262

τίνος ἠρίον ἵστατε τοῦτο ;

ᵃ May be part of the words Theseus spoke to the neigh-

263

ἴθι, πρηεῖα γυναικῶν,
τὴν ὁδόν, ἣν ἀνίαι θυμαλγέες οὐ περόωσι.
⟨   ⟩ πολλάκι σεῖο,
μαῖα, ⟨   ⟩ φιλοξείνοιο καλιῆς
5 μνησόμεθα· ξυνὸν γὰρ ἐπαύλιον ἔσκεν ἅπασιν

2 θυμοφθόροι v.l. codd.   3 sic distrib. vers. 3-4 Maas.

ᵃ Probably part of the farewell speech over the body, or the tomb, of Hecale. This may have been spoken either by

(Fr. 266-377 secundum fontium ordinem alphabeticum)

266

πολυπτωκές τε Μελαιναί

267

γίνεό μοι τέκταινα βίου δαμάτειρά τε λιμοῦ

to the city carrying a great fragment ; and I met her by the beautiful ever-brilliant gymnasium of the Lycean Apollo.[a]

The famous Lycean Gymnasium at Athens was situated between the Gates of Diochares and the hill called Lycabettus.

262

. . . whose tomb is this you are building ? [a]

bours of Hecale, when he found her dead on his return from Marathon.

263

. . . go, gentle woman, the way which heart-gnawing worries do not traverse. . . . Often, good mother . . . will we remember your hospitable hut, for it was a common shelter for all.[a]

Theseus, or by one (or many) of the neighbours of Hecale. It may even be part of the words spoken at the Δεῖπν' 'Εκαλεῖα, held in memory of Hecale by the inhabitants of the new deme.

(The remaining fragments of the *Hecale* [not all of 266-377 being included here] no longer follow the sequence of the narrative, but are placed according to the alphabetical order of the sources from which they come.)

266

. . . and Melaenae,[a] abounding in hares.

[a] Deme of Attica on the borders of Attica and Boeotia.

267

. . . become my life-giver, my overcomer of hunger.

CALLIMACHUS

268

ἔστιν ὕδος καὶ γαῖα καὶ ὀπτήτειρα κάμινος

269

ὁππότε λύχνου
δαιομένου πυρόεντες ἄδην ἐγένοντο μύκητες

ᵃ This occurs, we are told, before a storm.

270

γέντο δ' ἀλυκρά

271

σὺν δ' ἡμῖν ὁ πελαργὸς ἀμορβεύεσκεν ἀλοίτης

ᵃ May be part of the crows' talk (cf. frs. 260. 16 ff. and 261). It is uncertain why the stork is called ἀλοίτης, an

272

ἄνδρες ἐλαιηροὺς Δεκελειόθεν ἀμπρεύοντες

ἐλα οὶ vel -οί codd. : ἐλαιηροὺς Barber : ἄνδρες δ' ἠλαιοὶ Sylburg : ἄνδρες δ' Εἰλέσιοι Rutherford : ἐλαστροῦσιν? Reitzenstein : ἐλαιολόγοι Diels : δεἰλαιοι Pf., sed potius obiectum exspectes.

273

Ἀπόλλωνος ἀπαυγή

HECALE

268

. . . there is water and earth and a baking furnace.[a]

[a] May refer to the simple household utensils of Hecale.
Cf. frs. 341 and 344.

269

. . . when plenty of red-hot snuffs of the wick had
been formed as the lamp was burning.[a]

270

. . . they became warm.

271

. . . and the avenging stork was journeying with us.[a]

avenger, possibly because in parts of Greece he who killed a
stork was condemned to death. *Cf.* Plin. *Nat. Hist.* x. 31.

272

. . . men hauling from Decelea (jars ?) of oil.[a]

[a] After ἐλαιηρούς Barber, *e.g.*, suggests κεράμους (*cf.* Hip.
Mul. ii. 114 ἐλαιηρὰ κεράμια) in the following line.

273

. . . the brilliant light of Apollo.

CALLIMACHUS

274

ἁρμοῖ που κἀκείνῳ ἐπέτρεχε λεπτὸς ἴουλος
ἄνθει ἑλιχρύσῳ ἐναλίγκιος

1 ἐπέτρεχεν ἁβρὸς codd. v.l.

275

πάσχομεν ἄστηνοι· τὰ μὲν οἴκοθε πάντα δέδασται

276

δέκα δ' ἄστριας αἴνυτο λάτρον

αἴνυτο codd. : prob. ἄρνυτο Pf.

277

βόες ἧχι γέγειαι
ἄνθεα μήκωνός τε καὶ ἤνοπα πυρὸν ἔδουσι

278

τοὔνεκα καὶ νέκυες πορθμήιον οὔτι φέρονται
μούνη ἐνὶ πτολίων, ὅ τε τέθμιον οἰσέμεν ἄλλους
δανοῖς ἐν στομάτεσσι

1 νέκυος cod. v.l.   2 sq. ἐπιπτολίοτε θυμιώνησσε μεν.
ἀλλ' οὐ σάνοις codd. : ἐνὶ—ἄλλους corr. Casaubonus.   3
⟨δ⟩ανοῖς Pf.

HECALE

274

. . . a delicate down, like the blossom of the gold-flower,[a] was just spreading, I ween, on his cheeks too.

[a] ἐλίχρυσος also means the flower of the ivy; *cf.* fr. 253. 8. We do not know about whom this is said.

275

. . . we miserable paupers suffer; and at home all our belongings have been divided out.

276

. . . he took ten knuckle-bones as a prize.[a]

[a] This must be a child, but we do not know who is referred to.

277

. . . where ancient cows eat the flowers of the poppy and shining wheat.

278

. . . that is why in this city [a] alone even the dead receive no coin as fare, which it is the custom for others to carry in dry mouths.

Argolid. But Suidas (*s.v.* πορθμήϊον) tells that the people of Aegialos, near Sicyon, were excused by Demeter from the fare paid to Charon for transport across the river Acheron. This was because the inhabitants of that region informed the goddess about the fate of Persephone, when Hades had snatched her away.

CALLIMACHUS

279

αὐτίκα Κενθίππην τε πολύκρημνόν τε Πρόσυμναν

> [a] Part of Argos, so called (according to the traditional false etymology of the name) because Bellerophon there ἐκέντησε τὸν Πήγασον. *Cf. P. Oxy.* xxx (1964), p. 91.

280

καὶ δόνακι πλήθοντα λιπὼν ῥόον Ἀστερίωνος

> [a] A river near the Heraion of Argos. We do not know

281

τὺ δ' ἐγκυτὶ τέκνον ἐκέρσω

> [a] Theseus, when visiting Delphi, is supposed to have shorn the front part of his head. This style of cutting the

282

ὀκκόσον ὀφθαλμοὶ γὰρ ἀπευθέες, ὅσσον ἀκουή
εἰδυλίς

283

ἵν' ἔλλερα ἔργα τέλεσκεν

ἔργα codd. : πολλά v.l.

284 [a]

> [a] See fr. 284 A.

279

. . . presently Centhippe [a] and craggy Prosymna.[b]

  [b] Region near the Heraion of Argos.

280

. . . and having left the stream of Asterion,[a] full of reeds.

who left the stream of Asterion. It might have been Theseus on his way to Athens from Troezen.

281

Bᴜᴛ you have been shorn to the skin, child.[a]

hair (which was dedicated to the god) was later called θησηΐς.

282

. . . for the ears are as well informed as the eyes are ignorant.[a]

  [a] *Cf.* fr. 43. 16 f. and fr. 178. 30.

283

. . . where he did harmful deeds.[a]

  [a] The reference is probably to the harm the bull had caused to the Tetrapolis of Marathon.

284 [a]

  [a] See fr. 284 ᴀ.

CALLIMACHUS

284 A

$$(=337 + 366 + 247 + 284 + 350 + 294 + 368 + 639 + 327)$$

τὼ μὲν ἐγὼ θαλέεσσιν ἀνέτρεφον οὐδέ τις οὕτως
                ] γενέθλην
                ] ῥυδὸν ἀφνύονται
              ]ετο νη .. ς·
5   ] τινθαλέοισι κατικμήναιντο λοετροῖς
            ]ανε παῖδε φερούσῃ.
τώ μοι ἀναδραμέτην ἅτε κερκίδες, αἵτε χαράδρης
         [Desunt versus fere 15]

ἠρνεόμην θανάτοιο πάλαι καλέοντος ἀκοῦσαι
μὴ μετὰ δὴν ἵνα καὶ σοὶ ἐπιρρήξαιμι χιτῶνα;
          [Desunt versus 3]

10 Κέρκ[υον   ] παλαίσμασι πε[
φθει[   ] ἄστεος, ὅς ῥ᾽ ἔφυγεν μέν
Ἀρκαδίην, ἡμῖν δὲ κακὸς παρενάσσατο γείτων
          [Desunt versus 2]

τοῦ π[
αὐτὴ [   ] ζώοντος ἀναιδέσιν ἐμπήξαιμι
15 σκώλους ὀφθαλμοῖσι καί, εἰ θέμις, ὠμὰ πασαίμην.

              *   *   *

ἵππους καιτάεντος ἀπ᾽ Εὐρώταο κομίσσαι
          ] κῦμα κ[
          ]εια .. ν ὁθιδ[
         ] αἰθυίης γὰρ ὑπὸ πτερύγεσσιν ἔλυσαν
20 πείσματα· τῆ⟨ς⟩ μήτ᾽ αὐτ[ὸς
μ]ήθ᾽ ὅτις ἄμμι βεβουλ[

1=fr. 337.   3=fr. 366.   4 νηδύς vel νηλής L.
5=fr. 247.   7=fr. 284.   8-9=fr. 350.   12=fr.
206

HECALE

284 A†

(= 337 + 366 + 247 + 284 + 350 + 294 + 368 + 639 + 327)

THESE two I brought up on dainties, nor did anybody
else in such a manner . . . abundantly rich . . .
5 they should be drenched in a warm bath . . . carry-
ing the children . . . these two of mine ran up like
aspens, which in a ravine (?) . . .

[About 15 lines missing]

was I refusing to hear death calling me a long time
ago, that I might soon tear my garments over you
too (dead) . . . ?

[3 lines missing]

10 Cercyon *a* (?) . . . wrestlings . . . city, who fled from
Arcadia and took up residence near us, a bad neigh-
bour . . .

[2 lines missing]

15 may I pierce his impudent eyes with thorns while he
is still alive, and, if it be not a sin, eat him raw
16 . . . to bring horses from the Eurotas plentiful in
mint . . . the wave . . . for they unloosened the
20 hawsers under the wings of the sea-gull ; with this
omen may I neither myself (set sail), nor a person
who has (undertaken a commission ?) for me.

† The text of fr. 284 A is based on *P. Oxy.* 2376 and 2377.
These papyri show that probably a woman, whom we can-
not yet identify, is speaking, but the content of her speech is
still obscure. They show also that fr. 639 belongs to the
Hecale, and what the correct metre of fr. 327 was. It is not
known whether lines 1-15 precede lines 16-21 or if they
immediately follow them.
   a Probably a reference to the robber Cercyon, who had
come from Arcadia, and was killed by Theseus near Eleusis.

---

294.   14-15 = fr. 368.   14 τοῦ μὲν ἐγὼ ζώοντος
codd.   16 = fr. 639.   19-20 = fr. 327.

CALLIMACHUS

285

Δηώ τε Κλυμένου τε πολυξείνοιο δάμαρτα

<hr>

[a] Clymenus is Hades, his wife Persephone, and Deo is

286

αὖτις ἀπαιτίζουσαν ἑὴν εὐεργέα λάκτιν

287

ἡ ἄφαρον φαρόωσι, μέλει δέ φιν ὄμπνιον ἔργον

ἀφαρόωσι vel ἀφαρώσι codd. σφιν vel σφίσιν codd.: corr.
Bentley. Ὀμπνίου Hecker.

288

Σκύλλα γυνὴ κατακᾶσα καὶ οὐ ψύθος οὔνομ' ἔχουσα
πορφυρέην ἤμησε κρέκα

<hr>

[a] Nisus, legendary king of Megara, had a lock of purple
hair on his head, on which depended his life and the fate of
the city. His daughter Scylla cut this off, and betrayed the

289

ἀλλὰ σὺ μὲν σιπαλός τε καὶ ὀφθαλμοῖσιν ἔφηλος

208

HECALE

285

. . . and Deo, and the wife of Clymenus *a* the hospitable.

Demeter. This fr. may be connected with the cult of Demeter in Hermione. *Cf.* fr. 278 and fr. 705.

286

. . . demanding again her well-made ladle.

287

. . . or (?) they plough unploughed land and they are at work on the corn.

288

Scylla, a whore, having no untrue name, cut the purple lock.*a*

city to Minos, king of Crete, who had besieged it. Nisus was turned into a sea-eagle, Scylla into a bird *ciris* pursued by him (on *ciris* see D'A. Thompson, *Gloss. of Gk. Birds*, *s.v.*; fr. 113*, Ps.-Virgil, *Ciris*, Ovid, *Met.* viii. 1 ff.

289

. . . but you are hideous and your eyes have white spots on them.

291

ἡνίκα μὲν γὰρ †φαίνεται τοῖς ἀνθρώποις ταῦτα†
[αὐτοὶ μὲν φιλέουσ', αὐτοὶ δέ τε πεφρίκασιν,]
ἑσπέριον φιλέουσιν, ἀτὰρ στυγέουσιν ἑῷον

1 ἡνίκα μὲν γὰρ ταῦτα (ταὐτὸ Barber) φαείνεται ἀνθρώποισιν
Hecker, alia alii.   3 ἀτὰρ στ. codd. : ἀποστ. v.l.

292

ἔπρεπέ οἱ προέχουσα κάρης εὐρεῖα καλύπτρη,
ποιμενικὸν πίλημα, καὶ ἐν χερὶ χαῖον †ἔχουσα†

293

στάδιον δ' ὑφέεστο χιτῶνα

294 [a]

[a] See fr. 284 ʌ.

295

σὺν δ' ἄμυδις φορυτόν τε καὶ ἴπνια λύματ' ἄειρεν

ἀείρας codd. v.l.

298

ἐπεὶ θεὸς οὐδὲ γελάσσαι
ἀκλαυτὶ μερόπεσσιν ὀιζυροῖσιν ἔδωκεν
210

291

. . . but when the same star (?) [a] appears to men [the selfsame people love and loathe] ; at eventide they [b] love, but at dawn they hate it.

[a] Possibly the morning and the evening stars.
[b] Bentley thought the reference was to the newly-wed.

292

. . . the wide hat, stretching out beyond the head, a shepherd's felt headgear, suited her, and in her hand a stick.[a]

[a] Probably part of the description of Hecale.

293

. . . and under he wore a long tunic.[a]

[a] Probably part of the description of Theseus, when he arrived at Athens.

294 [a]

[a] See fr. 284 A.

295

. . . and together he collected the rubbish and the dung.

298

. . . for god did not give miserable mortals even the possibility of laughing without crying.

CALLIMACHUS

299

Αἴσηπον ἔχεις, ἑλικώτατον ὕδωρ,
Νηπείης ἥ τ' ἄργος, ἀοίδιμος 'Αδρήστεια,[a]

2 ἠδ' cod. v.l. : ἦτ' Bentley.

[a] Adrastea, a name for Nemesis, daughter of Zeus and
Ananke, one of the most puzzling of Greek goddesses, owing

300

ἔκ με Κολωνάων τις ὁμέστιον ἤγαγε δήμου
τῶν ἑτέρων

1 ἐκ μὲν codd.: corr. Porson et Buttmann.

[a] Meaning and text are as yet obscure. τῶν ἑτέρων may
not refer to Κολωνάων, but to δαίμων (according to Naeke's

301

βουσόον ὅν τε μύωπα βοῶν καλέουσιν ἀμορβοί

302

οἵ νυ καὶ 'Απόλλωνα παναρκέος 'Ηελίοιο
χῶρι διατμήγουσι καὶ εὔποδα Δηωίνην
'Αρτέμιδος

[a] Daughter of Demeter. *Cf.* Serv. in Verg. *Ecl.* iii. 26 :
novimus eandem esse Proserpinam quam Dianam. And in
magical papyri we meet with " Artemis-Persephone." We

HECALE

299

. . . you who are mistress of Aesepus, the very black water, and the plain of Nepea, Adrastea, famous in song.[a]

to the wide divergence between her mythology and her position in cult and morals. Aesepus was a river near Cyzicus in Asia Minor, and the plain of Nepea was near by.

300

. . . and from the deme of the other Colonae somebody brought me to live in the same house.[a]

emendation of δήμου), one of the evil daemons (cf. fr. 191. 63). If it refers to the deme of Colonos, there were two in ancient Attica, the Ἀγοραῖος in the city, and the Ἵππειος to the west of the city of Athens : we do not know to which the fragment refers, nor who is speaking here.

301

. . . the ox-driving gadfly, which the herdsmen call the goad.

302

. . . who distinguish Apollo from the sun that shines on all alike, and fair-footed Deoine [a] from Artemis.

do not know about whom the poet is speaking, nor what his views on the matter were. Hecate was also said to be a daughter of Demeter by Zeus (cf. fr. 466*), and the identification of Artemis-Hecate was made in Ephesus.

CALLIMACHUS

304

ἀμφὶ δέ οἱ κεφαλῇ νέον Αἱμονίηθεν
μεμβλωκὸς πίλημα περίτροχον ἄλκαρ ἔκειτο
ἴδεος ἐνδίοιο

305

Λιμναίῳ δὲ χοροστάδας ἦγον ἑορτάς

^a In the days of Theseus, the oldest festivals in honour of
Dionysus were said to have been held ἐν Λίμναις, a marshy
area to the south of Athens.

309 (dub.)

ποσσὶ δ᾽ ἀνελθεῖν
ἄγκος ἐς ὑψικάρηνον ἐδίζετο· πᾶσα δ᾽ ἀπορρώξ
πέτρη ἔην ὑπένερθε καὶ ἄμβασις οὔ νύ τις ἦεν.

1 ποσὶ δ᾽ αὖ ἐλθεῖν codd.: corr. Toup et Valckenaer.

^a The subject of ἐδίζετο is unknown. Bergk considers

310

ἀείπλανα χείλεα γρηός

312

ἄκμηνον δόρποιο

313

ἁλυκὸν δέ οἱ ἔκπεσε δάκρυ

214

304

. . . and there encircled his head a round felt hat,
lately come from Haemonia *a* ; it was a guard against
the midday heat.

a Thessaly. Hats from Thessaly were large. It is not
known to whom the fragment refers.

305

. . . they held feasts celebrated with choral dances
in honour of the Dionysus of Limnae.*a*

309

. . . on foot (he ?) *a* tried to climb the high-peaked
hill. All the rocks below were sheer, and there was
no path upwards.

this fragment spurious, and attributes it to the *Mythica* (*cf.*
Babrius, p. 219 Cr.), and indeed the style of l. 3 is most un-
like Callimachus.

310

. . . the lips of an old woman are never still.

312

. . . without having tasted food.

313

. . . a salt tear fell from him.

CALLIMACHUS

318

σχέτλιαι ἀνθρώπων ἀφραστύες

319

ἠέρος ἀχλύσαντος

320

βέβυστο δὲ πᾶσα χόλοιο

321

γαμβρὸς Ἐρεχθῆος

---

[a] Boreas, who carried off his bride Orithyia, daughter of King Erechtheus, from the Areopagus, or the banks of the

322

γέντα βοῶν μέλδοντες

βοὸς cod. v.l.

327 [a]

[a] See fr. 284 A.

328

ἧχι κονίστραι
ἄξεινοι λύθρῳ τε καὶ εἴαρι πεπλήθασι

---

[a] This may refer to the " palaestra of Cercyon " near

329

νυκτὶ δ᾽ ὅλῃ βασιλῆας ἐλέγχομεν

HECALE

318

. . . evil stupidities of men.

319

. . . the air having become dark.

320

. . . she was stuffed with anger.[a]

[a] *Cf.* fr. 374.

321

. . . the son-in-law of Erechtheus.[a]

Ilyssus, or, according to a rarer version of the myth, from Mount Brilessos in Attica.

322

. . . cooking the limbs of oxen.

327 [a]

[a] See fr. 284 A.

328

. . . where unfriendly wrestling-arenas are full of gore and blood.[a]

Eleusis, where the robber is supposed to have wrestled with the passers-by, and killed them. *Cf.* fr. 284 A.

329

. . . we abuse kings all night long.[a]

[a] *Cf.* fr. 275 (and fr. 284 A). It is possible that, as in Hesiod, unjust kings were attacked.

330 + 325

πότμον ἐλινύσειε, δύην ⟨δ'⟩ ἀπόθεστον ἀλάλκοι

coniunxit Dilthey.

331

ἐπήλυσιν ὄφρ' ἀλέοιτο

φώριον

333

ἐπικλινές ἐστι τάλαντον

―――――――――――――

ᵃ Cf. Π. xix. 223.

334

εἰκαίην τῆς οὐδὲν ἀπέβρασε φαῦλον ἀλετρίς

335

ἠέρος ὄγμοι

336

ἑρπετὰ δ' ἰλυοῖσιν ἐνέκρυφεν

337 ᵃ

ᵃ See fr. 284 ᴀ.

HECALE

330 + 325

. . . that (he ?) might stop misfortune,[a] and ward off despised misery.

[a] It possibly refers to Theseus, who, by conquering the bull of Marathon, saved the inhabitants of the Tetrapolis.

331

. . . that he might avoid an attack by robbers.

333

. . . the scales are tipped.[a]

334

. . . (flour) taken at random, from which the mill-woman did not clear the dross.[a]

[a] *Cf.* fr. 260. 46.

335

. . . the paths of the air.[a]

[a] Or the mist, the haze.

336

. . . the reptiles hid in their holes.[a]

[a] This may refer to the time of the year, or even to the storm.

337 [a]

[a] See fr. 284 A.

338

Θείας ἀμνάμων

339

Κλεωναίοιο χάρωνος

341

Κωλιάδος κεραμῆες

342

τοῦτο γὰρ αὐτήν
κωμῆται κάλεον περιηγέες

1 αὐτῆς vel αὐτῇ vel αὐτοί codd.: αὐτήν Hemsterhuys,
Ruhnken.

343

οὐδ᾽ οἷσιν ἐπὶ κτενὸς ἔσκον ἔθειραι

344

λάτριν ἄγειν παλίνορσον ἀεικέα τῷ κεραμῆι
220

HECALE

338

. . . a descendant of Theia.[a]

[a] The winds were the progeny of Theia. *Cf.* fr. 110. 44, where the same words appear in reverse order.

339

. . . of the lion of Cleonae.[a]

[a] Place in the Argolid. Here the reference seems to be to the lion of Nemea.

341

. . . potters of Colias.[a]

[a] Part of Attica where pottery was made. *Cf.* frs. 268, 344.

342

. . . for that is what the neighbours around called her.[a]

[a] The reference is to Hecale. The fragment can belong either to the beginning, or to the end, of the poem.

343

. . . nor they who had hair at their penis.

344

. . . to bring a shameful slave (or hired servant) back to the potter.

345

τοιοῦτον γὰρ ὁ παῖς ὅδε λῆμα φαείνει

ᵃ If, as has been suggested by P. Maas, the reference is

346 ᵃ

ᵃ See fr. 260, l. 45.

348

τὸ δέ μοι μαλκίστατον ἦμαρ

350 ᵃ

ᵃ See fr. 284 ᴀ.

355

γέντο δ' ἐρείκης
σκηπάνιον ⟨   ⟩ ὃ δὴ πέλε γήραος ὀκχή

2 ⟨χείρεσσιν⟩ Naeke.

358

εἰ δὲ Δίκη σε
πὰρ πόδα μὴ τιμωρὸς ἐτείσατο, δὶς τόσον αὖτις
ἔσσεται, ἐν πλεόνεσσι παλίντροπος,

359

εἷλε δὲ πασσαγίην, τόδε δ' ἔννεπεν

HECALE

345

· . . for this boy shows such a spirit.[a]

to Theseus, it should be connected with the Troezen period of his life.

346 [a]

[a] See fr. 260, l. 45.

348

. . . this is the coldest day for me.

350 [a]

[a] See fr. 284 A.

355

. . . she got hold of a stick of heath . . . which was the support of her old age.[a]

[a] Probably about Hecale. *Cf.* fr. 292. 2. The heath is *erica arborea*.

358

. . . and if avenging Dike has not punished you at once, she will be twice as severe returning among the majority.[a]

[a] The dead. Dike is the personification of Justice.

359

. . . he seized the panoply and said this :

CALLIMACHUS

366 [a]

[a] See fr. 284 A.

368 [a]

[a] See fr. 284 A.

371

Αἴθρην τὴν εὔτεκνον ἐπ᾽ ἀγρομένης ὑδέοιμι

ἐν ἀγρ. Bernhardy, Hecker, Wil.

374

ἡ δὲ πελιδνωθεῖσα καὶ ὄμμασι λοξὸν ὑποδράξ
ὀσσομένη

1 fort. ὄθμασι scr., ut semper in *Aetiis.*

[a] The fragment may refer either to Medea, or to Athene

375

θῆκε δὲ λᾶαν

σκληρὸν ὑπόκρηνον

376

ὅς τε φόβῃσι

ξανθοτάταις ἐκόμα

HECALE

366 [a]

[a] See fr. 284 A.

368 [a]

[a] See fr. 284 A.

371

. . . may I celebrate the fruitful Aethra [a] among all those women gathered (here).

[a] Daughter of Pittheus and mother of Theseus (see introduction). The speaker of this encomium is unknown.

374

. . . and she, turned pale, and her eyes looking grimly askance.[a]

at the time when she was told that Erichthonius was discovered (fr. 260. 16 ff.).

375

. . . and (he ?) placed a hard stone under (his ?) head.[a]

[a] We do not know to whom this refers.

376

. . . who had very fair hair.[a]

[a] Who is here described is unknown.

MINOR EPIC AND ELEGIAC POEMS

(No *Diegesis* has survived for any of these poems. Their full content, therefore, as well as their exact place in the edition of the poet's collected works, is unknown.)

CARMINA EPICA ET ELEGIACA MINORA

ΓΑΛΑΤΕΙΑ

A poem by Callimachus called *Galatea* is quoted by Athenaeus (vii. 284 c). It appears that the Galatea of this poem is the Nereid, with whom the Cyclops had fallen in love,[a] but we know nothing about the manner in which Callimachus treated the story. As the poem was in hexameters, it may well have been an epic poem, and for that reason Pfeiffer attributed to the same work the epic fragment 379, which speaks about the Gauls. The Γαλάται, the Gauls, were said to be descended from Galates, the son of the Nereid Galatea, and there is no other epic poem by Callimachus of

378

ἢ μᾶλλον χρύσειον ἐν ὀφρύσιν ἱερὸν ἰχθύν
ἢ πέρκας ὅσα τ' ἄλλα φέρει βυθὸς ἄσπετος ἅλμης

1 ἐπ' coni. Meineke, Schneider.

379

οὓς Βρέννος ἀφ' ἑσπερίοιο θαλάσσης
ἤγαγεν Ἑλλήνων ἐπ' ἀνάστασιν,

---

[a] The leader of the Gauls in their expedition against Greece in 279/8 B.C. He was wounded at Delphi, and com-

228

MINOR EPIC AND ELEGIAC
POEMS

GALATEA

which we know, except the *Hecale*, to which this fragment
certainly does not belong. If this view is correct, then the
poem must have treated of the legend of Galatea, of Galates
and the expedition of the Gauls against Greece in 279/8 B.C.,
an expedition which Callimachus also mentions in his Hymn
on Delos.[b] This would establish a *terminus post quem* for
the dating of the poem. Fragment 592, in which Athene
Pronaos of Delphi is mentioned, may belong to the same
poem.

---

[a] *Cf.* Theocr. *Id.* xi and Call. *Epigr.* xlvi. (xlvii L.C.L.) 1.
[b] *Hymn* iv. 171 ff.

378

Or rather the sacred fish with golden brow,[a] or the
perch, and all other things the ineffable depth of the
sea bears.

[a] Probably the gilthead, *Chrysophrys aurata*.

379

. . . those whom Brennus [a] led from the western sea
to the destruction of the Greeks.

mitted suicide during the general retreat of the Gauls north-
wards, when they were attacked by the Thessalians.

ΓΡΑΦΕΙΟΝ

THE only mention of a work by Callimachus called Γραφεῖοι
occurs in an anonymous treatise on metres (Anonym. Am-
brosian. *De re metrica, Anecd. Var. Graec.*, 1886, p. 224. 5 f.),
which also quotes the only extant fragment. The meaning
of the title, as indeed the nature and length of the work, is

380

εἵλκυσε δὲ δριμύν τε χόλον κυνὸς ὀξύ τε κέντρον
σφηκός, ἀπ' ἀμφοτέρων δ' ἰὸν ἔχει στόματος

2 στόματος Schneider et Bergk : στομάτων codd.

---

^a The fragment refers to Archilochus (*fl. c.* 725 B.C.), the

[ELEGIA IN VICTORIAM NEMEAEAM ?]

THIS appears to be an epinician poem, composed in elegiacs
like *The Victory of Sosibios* (fr. 384), which follows. It is on
a victory in the chariot race at Nemea, but we do not know
who the victor was. Sosibios, or even Queen Berenice, the
daughter of Magas, has been suggested. It may well be
that this and the poem on the victory of Sosibios are en-

383

Ζηνί τε καὶ Νεμέῃ τι χαρίσιον ἔδνον ὀφείλω,
  νύμφα κα[
ἡμ[ε]τερο[
  ἁρμοῖ γὰρ Δαναοῦ γῆς ἄπο βουγενέων (?)

2 Κα[νωπῖτ- ? Pf.   3 suppl. L.   4 γῆς ἀπὸ βου-
γενέσεως vel γῇ ὡς ἀπὸ βουγεέως vel γῆς ἐπὶ γενέας codd. : γῆς
ἄπο βουγενέων (?) Pf. : γῆς ἐπὶ βουγενέος Schneidewin.

GRAPHEION

unknown. Γραφεῖον in the days of Callimachus meant "archive," and various views as to the content of the work have been expressed. Some believe it was a collection of epigrams on poets, others a kind of criticism of poets, a work of a literary-historical nature. Dilthey (*Cydippe*, p. 17, n. 1) compared it to the *Imagines* of Varro.

380

. . . he drew (?) the keen anger of the dog and the sharp sting of the wasp ; his mouth has the venom of both.[a]

iambic and elegiac poet of Paros, the alleged inventor of the iambic metre.

[ELEGY ON A NEMEAN VICTORY ?]

deavours of Callimachus to revive the ancient lyric epinician ode in a " modern " elegiac metre. As in the poem on the victory of Sosibios, the narrative may have moved from the events at the games of Greece to events in Egypt.

The length, date and title of the poem are unknown.

383

1 . . . I owe to Zeus and Nemea some token of grati
4 tude[a] . . . for lately from the (bee-producing[b] (?))

[a] The opening line is in the Pindaric manner. Nemea was, like Olympia, sacred to Zeus.
[b] Bees were called βουγενεῖς, because it was thought that they were born from the bones of bulls. The passage is, however, obscure and the text as yet uncertain ; one source, however, mentions that bees were thus produced in Nemea.

CALLIMACHUS

5 εἰς Ἑλένη[ς νησῖδα

. . . .

ἄσθμασι χλι[αίνοντες ‿ – ‿ ‿] ἀλλὰ θεόντων
10 ὡς ἀνέμων οὐδεὶς εἶδεν ἁματροχιάς.

. . . .

16 εἰδυῖαι φαλιὸν ταῦρον ἰηλεμίσαι

5 εισελενη[P.: εἰς Ἑλένη distinxit L.: εἰς Ἑλένη[ς νησῖδα
Barber.   9 suppl. Maas.

ΣΩΣΙΒΙΟΥ ΝΙΚΗ

THIS is an encomiastic elegy on Sosibios. In the extant frag-
ments we are told that Sosibios won the boys' double race (di-
aulos paidon) at games, presumably the Ptolemaea in Egypt
(l. 41), established in honour of Ptolemy I; that later he
won the men's contest in wrestling at the Panathenean games,
although he was not yet a full-grown man but still) an
ageneios, i.e. under 20 (ll. 37 f.); and that finally, as a man
of great wealth and importance (cf. ll. 53 ff.), he won the
chariot races at the Isthmian and at the Nemean games.
Moreover, he was the first Egyptian Greek to win this double
victory, for which the river Nile expresses its satisfaction
(ll. 27 ff.). We can also gather that the votive offerings of
Sosibios to temples in Greece and Egypt were mentioned
(ll. 44 ff.) in the poem, presumably offerings to commemorate
his victories in the great Greek games.
    This Sosibios can be no other than the famous minister of

---

ᵃ Sosibios was responsible for the murder of Queen Bere-
nice, the queen repeatedly celebrated in the poetry of Calli-
machus. But this poem on Sosibios may have been written

9 land of Danaus [a] (to Helen's island [b] (?)) . . . hot
and panting . . . but as they ran no one saw their
chariot-tracks, invisible like those of the winds . . .
16 Knowing how to bewail the white-foreheaded bull.[c]

[a] The land of Danaus is Argos ; Nemea belonged to the
Argives.
[b] Probably the island now called Nelson's Island, near
the mouth of the Nile.
[c] Apparently the maidens of the Nile are here described
as bewailing Apis, the sacred bull worshipped in Egypt, *cf.*
Tib. i. 7. 28 te (*sc.* Nile) canit atque suum pubes miratur
Osirim | barbara, Memphiten plangere docta bovem.

THE VICTORY OF SOSIBIOS

Ptolemy IV, later *Pseudepitropos* of Ptolemy V. Already a
man of importance in the reign of Ptolemy III, he became a
leading figure in Alexandrian politics under Ptolemy IV,
and is even said to have forged the king's testament at his
death. But he did not survive the king long, for he is sup-
posed to have died *c.* 202, shortly after the new king's acces-
sion. If, according to the poem, Sosibios won the *diaulos
paidon* in the *Ptolemaea*, he must have been a boy after
279/8, when the games were established, and a man of great
importance in the forties of the third century B.C., when the
poem could have been written by Callimachus as an old
man. In the forties Egypt and Cyrene were under the same
rule and so the river Cinyps (ll. 24 f.) could have been men-
tioned as a definition of the western extremities of the king-
dom. Moreover, the general tone of flattery fits in with
Callimachus' servility towards the powerful,[a] and in Polybius

---

before the event. It is, however, noteworthy that no mention
of living Ptolemies occurs in any of its extant fragments.

v. 37. 11 there is a reference to the love of Sosibios for horses.[a]
There can be little doubt that Callimachus, when writing this
elegy, had in mind the great epinician odes of Pindar,
Simonides, Bacchylides and possibly that of Euripides on
the many victories of Alcibiades (cf. Plut. Vit. Alcib. 11 (p.

---

[a] The points of style that led Wilamowitz and Pfeiffer to
suggest an early date for this poem are by no means con-
vincing, and the reference in Athenaeus iv. 144 e is not clear
or definite enough to over-rule the other internal evidence

384

Καὶ [

. . . .

ᾧ τὸ μὲν ἐξ Ἐφύρης ἅρμα σελινοφόρον
5 νεῖον ἀπ' οὖν μέμβλωκεν· ἔτι χνόον [οὔασι κείνου
ἄξονος Ἀσβύστης ἵππος ἔναυλον ἔχει.
σημερινὸν δ' ὡσεί περ ἐμὸν περὶ χεῖλος ἀΐσσει
τοῦτ' ἔπος ἡδείη λεχθὲν ἐπ' ἀγγελίη·
" δαῖμον ὃς ἀμφοτέρωθεν ἁλιζώνοιο κάθησαι
10 στείνεος, ἀρχαίοις ὅρκιε Σισυφίδαις,
ἐν ποδὶ ληγούσης Πελοπηΐδος ἱερὸν ἰσθμόν,
τῇ μὲν Κρωμνίτην τῇ δὲ Λέχαιον ἔχων,

5 suppl. Barber.

---

[a] νεῖον = νεωστί can be used not only about things which
" recently " took place, but also about events which hap-
pened some years ago ; cf. Plat. Gorg. 503 c Περικλέα τὸν
νεωστὶ (more than twenty years ago) τετελευτηκότα.
[b] Ephyra was the old name of Corinth. The reference is

196 B)). If, as has been suggested, Callimachus was de-
liberately trying in this poem to remould in the " new style "
the old epinician ode, the complete absence of the mytho-
logical element in any of the extant fragments is indeed
striking.

---

for a late dating. See Maas, *Pancarpeia*, *Mélanges Henri
Grégoire*, i, p. 447 (Annuaire de l'Institut de Philologie et
d'Histoire Orientales et Slaves, ix, 1949).

384

1 AND . . . for whom (*i.e.* Sosibios) in the past the chariot
5 had come back [a] (to Egypt) from Corinth, bringing
the celery wreath [b] ; the Asbystian [c] horse still hears
the sound of (that) axle ringing in its (ears). And,
as though it were to-day, these words that were said,
when the sweet news came, jump to my lips : " O god,
who art seated on either side of the sea-girt pas-
10 sage,[d] and by whom the old Corinthians [e] swore ;
thou, master of the sacred isthmus at the extremity
of the land of Pelops, with Cromna on the one side
and Lechaeon on the other,[f] where ability in hand

to the victory of Sosibios at the chariot-race of the Isthmian
games, where the prize was a celery wreath.

[c] The Asbystae lived in Cyrenaica, but the word is loosely
used as an equivalent of Libyans. Libyan horses were
famous for their speed.

[d] Posidon, master of the Isthmus of Corinth. Here he
may be invoked as " hippeios," master of horses.

[e] The Corinthians were called Sisyphidae, after Sisyphus
the mythical founder of the city.

[f] In historic times the two sea-ports of Corinth were
called Lechaeon (on the gulf of Corinth) and Cenchreae, pre-
sumably here called Cromna (on the Saronic Gulf).

CALLIMACHUS

ἔνθα ποδῶν ἵνα χειρὸς ἵνα κρίσις ὀξέο̣[ς ἵππου
ἰθυτάτη, χρυσὸν δ' εὐδικίη παραθεῖ,
15 χρυσὸν ὃν ἀνθρώποισι καλὸν κακὸν ἔτραφ[ε μ]ύ[ρ-
μη]ξ."

[Desunt versus fere 5 in P]

ἐς Νεμέην ἔσπε]υσεν, ἐπ' αὐτίκ[α δ' ἄλ]λα σέλινα
τοῖς ἀπὸ Πειρήνης ἤγαγεν 'Α[ργο]λικά,
ὄφρα κε Σωσίβιόν τις 'Αλεξάνδρου τε πύθηται
γῆν ἐπὶ καὶ ναίων Κίνυφι διστεφέα
25 ἀμφοτέρῳ παρὰ παιδί, κασιγνήτῳ τε Λεάρχου
καὶ τὸ Μυριναῖον τῷ γάλα θησαμένῳ,
θηλύτατον καὶ Νεῖλο̣[ς ἄ]γων ἐνιαύσιον ὕδωρ
ὧδ' εἴπῃ· " καλά μοι θρεπτὸς ἔτεισε γέρα
. . . . . . ού] γάρ πώ τις ἐπὶ πτόλιν ἤγαγ' ἄεθλον
30 διπλόον ἐκ] ταφίων τῶνδε πανηγυρίων
κ]αὶ πουλύς, ὃν οὐδ' ὅθεν οἶδεν ὁδεύω
θνητὸς ἀνήρ, ἐνὶ γοῦν τῷδ' ἔα λιτότερος
κε[ίνω]ν, οὓς ἀμογητὶ διὰ σφυρὰ λευκὰ γυναικῶν
καὶ πα]ῖς ἀβρέκτῳ γούνατι πεζὸς ἔβη "

[Desunt versus fere 8]

13 suppl. L.   15 μ]ύ[ρμη]ξ Pf. : conf. Paul. Silent.
Ecphr. St. Soph. 768 (Friedl.) ἤροσε μύρμηξ Trypanis.   ἔ-
τραφ[ε Maas, cf. Call. fr. 110. 49.   21 ἐς Νεμέην ἔσπε]υσεν
suppl. Barber, cett. suppl. L.   22 suppl. L.   27 suppl.
Maas.   29 suppl. Hu.   30 suppl. Trypanis.   31 κ]αὶ (vix
ν]αὶ) Pf.   33 suppl. Pf. : ἄλλων] Früchtel.   34 suppl. L.

^a At the Isthmian games.
^b If the supplement ἔτραφ[ε μ]ύ[ρμη]ξ is correct, there is an
allusion here to the story that the Indian ants, when making
their nests, turned up sand full of gold. Cf. fr. 202. 58 f.
^c The prize at the Nemean games was also a celery wreath.
^d Pirene, the sacred fountain of Corinth, is here men-
tioned instead of the city of Corinth and the Isthmian games.

236

and foot and fiery horse is most fairly judged [a]—and
15 fair judgement outruns gold, gold a beautiful evil the
ants (reared [b] ?) for man . . ."

[About 5 lines missing]

21 he (hurried to Nemea) and swiftly he added more
celery from the Argolid [c] to that he had gained from
Pirene,[d] so that the people of Alexandria and those
living on the banks of the river Cinyps [e] may learn
25 that Sosibios received two crowns near-by the two
sons—the brother of Learchus and the child that the
woman of Myrina suckled [f]—and so that the Nile may
say as it brings each year its most fertilizing water :
" A beautiful reward has my nursling [g] paid back to
30 me . . . for till now no one had brought a (double ?)
trophy to the city from these sepulchral festivals [h]
. . . and, great though I am, I, whose sources no
mortal man knows, in this one thing alone was more
insignificant than those streams which the white
ankles of women cross without difficulty, and children
pass over on foot without wetting their knees . . . [i] "

[About 8 lines missing]

[e] The river Cinyps flowed at the western end of the king-
dom of the Ptolemies ; beyond it stretched the land of the
Carthaginians.
[f] The " brother of Learchus " was Melicertes, in whose
honour the Isthmian games are said to have been established.
The " child that the woman of Myrina suckled " is Opheltes-
Archemoros, who was commemorated by the games of
Nemea. He was the foster-child of Hypsipyle, daughter of
Myrina, after whom the town Myrina of Lemnos was named.
[g] Sosibios was born in Egypt.
[h] All great Greek athletic games and festivals were said to
have been established in commemoration of the death of
mythical kings and heroes.
[i] The rivers of Greece, Italy and the islands could, of
course, not compare with the Nile in wealth of water or fame.

CALLIMACHUS

35 " —καὶ παρ' Ἀθηναίοις γὰρ ἐπὶ στέγος ἱερὸν ἧνται

κάλπιδες, οὐ κόσμου σύμβολον, ἀλλὰ πάλης—

ἄνδρας ὅτ' οὐ δείσαντες ἐδώκαμεν ἡδὺ βοῆσαι

νηὸν ἔπι Γλαυκῆς κῶμον ἄγοντι χορῷ

Ἀρχιλόχου νικαῖον ἐφύμνιον· ἐκ δὲ διαύλου,

40 Λαγείδη, παρὰ σοὶ πρῶτον ἀεθλοφορεῖν

εἰλάμεθα, Πτολεμαῖε, τεῇ π[άτε]ρ ἡνίκ' ἐλεγχ[. "

[Desunt versus fere 13]

" ἀμφοτέρων ὁ ξεῖνος ἐπήβολος· οὐκέτι γυμνάς

45 παῖδας ἐν Ἡραίῳ στήσομεν Εὐρυνόμης."

ὣς φαμένῳ δώσει τις ἀνὴρ ὁμόφωνον ἀοιδήν.

τοῦτο μὲν ἐξ ἄλλων ἔκλυον ἱρὸν ἐγώ,

κεῖνό γε μὴν ἴδον αὐτός, ὃ πὰρ ποδὶ κάτθετο Νείλου

νειατίῳ, Κασίην εἰς ἐπίκωμος ἅλα·

---

41 suppl. L.   46 ομοφρονος P : ὁμόφωνον Hu. (Wil.) :
ὁμόφωνος ἀμοιβήν coni. L.   49 κασιου P : Κασίην Wil.

---

[a] Amphorae, full of oil, were prizes at the Panathenean games.

[b] At the Panathenean games παῖδες, boys, ἀγένειοι, youths under 20, and ἄνδρες, men, took part. It appears that Sosibios, while still a youth under 20, took part in the wrestling contest of the full-grown men at Athens and was victorious.

[c] It appears that Sosibios is speaking here. Ll. 35-36 must be one of the usual Callimachean parentheses.

[d] *Glauce* is here equivalent to γλαυκῶπις, *i.e.* Athene. This custom of a Κῶμος, an ode sung at a festive procession to celebrate the victory, was apparently Athenian.

35 "for in Athens too the jars are kept in a sacred temple,
not as ornaments, but as a token of prowess at wrest-
ling *a*—when not fearing the full-grown men *b* we *c*
gave to the chorus, leading a revel to the temple of
Glauce,*d* the opportunity to sing a sweet ode, the song
40 of victory by Archilochus.*e* Ptolemy, son of Lagus,*f*
near-by you first we chose to win a prize of victory for
the double course,*g* when . . ."

[About 13 lines missing]

" . . . the stranger *h* has been victorious in both.
45 We will no longer set up the (statues of the) daughters
of Eurynome *i* nude in the temple of Hera."*j* After
he has said this someone will (sing in concert with
him ?). I heard from others *k* about that offering,
but I saw myself the one he (*i.e.* Sosibios) dedicated
at the outermost branch of the mouth of the Nile
50 . . . on a visit to the Casian Sea.*l* " From Cyprus a

e The song of victory by Archilochus with the refrain
τήνελλα καλλίνικε was also sung in honour of the victors at
Olympia.

f The reference is to the *Ptolemaea*, the games established
in 279/8 B.C. in Egypt in honour of Ptolemy I Soter.

g This is the *diaulos paidon*, a race of two laps round the
stadium, in which boys competed. It must have been the
first victory of Sosibios at athletic games.

h Sosibios, who was not born in Greece but in Egypt. We
do not know who is speaking here.   *i* The Graces.

j The famous Heraion at Argos. The offering is much
more likely to have been statues of the Graces robed than
garments for extant nude statues of the daughters of Eury-
nome. (On the representation of the Graces as nude see
fr. 6.) This offering may well have been in commemoration
of his victory at Nemea, for the Nemean games were for a
time under the control of the Argives.

k Callimachus had never travelled beyond Egypt.

l This votive offering must have been set up near the
temple of Zeus Casios, which was situated near Pelusium.

CALLIMACHUS

50 " Κυπρόθε Σιδόνιός με κατήγαγεν ἐνθάδε γαῦλος "

[Desunt versus fere 13]

καὶ τὸν ἐφ' οὗ νίκαισιν ἀείδομεν, ἄρθμια δήμῳ
εἰδότα καὶ μικρῶν οὐκ ἐπιληθόμενον,
55 παύριστον τό κεν ἀνδρὶ παρ' ἀφνειῷ τις ἴδοιτο
ᾧτινι μὴ κρείσσων ἦ νόος εὐτυχίης·
οὔτε τὸν αἰνήσω τόσον ἄξιος οὔτε λάθωμαι
— δείδια γὰρ δήμου γλῶσσαν ἐπ' ἀμφοτέροις —,

54 ειδοταουκεπιμικρων P : καὶ μικρῶν G. Murray et L. : τὸν
μικρῶν Hu.

---

[a] The votive offering, probably a chariot, speaks in the
well-known style of certain dedicatory epigrams.   It pro-

384 A

ἱερά, νῦν δὲ Διοσκουρίδεω γενεή

[ELEGIAE FRAGMENTUM INCERTAE SEDIS]

WE do not know from which poem this fragment comes.

388

Φωκαέων μέχρις κε φανῇ μέγας εἰν ἁλὶ μύδρος,
10 ἄχ]ρι τέκῃ Παλλὰ[ς κῆ γάμος] Ἀρ[τ]έμιδι,
. . . .]ς ἀεὶ πανάριστ[α μέ]νειν α[. . . .] Βερενίκῃ
· · · · · · · · ·

9 μεῃη P codd. : φανῇ corr. Maas.   10 ἄχ]ρι Pf., cett.
(γάμος vel πόσις) suppl. Hu.

---

[a] When Phocaea, the most northern Ionian city in Asia

240

Sidonian merchant-ship brought me here . . ." [a]

[About 13 lines missing]

and him [b] we celebrate for his victories, friendly to
55 the people, and forgetting not the poor, a thing so
rarely seen in a rich man, whose mind is not superior
to his good fortune. I will not praise him as much as
he deserves, nor forget him—for I am afraid of the
people's tongue in either case— . . .

bably said that the bronze used for the offering was brought
from Cyprus by a Phoenician ship.
    [b] Sosibios.

384 A

. . . sacred, but now the family of Dioscorides.[a]

    [a] Dioscorides was the father of Sosibios.

[UNPLACED FRAGMENT OF AN ELEGY]

It has been suggested that it may belong to a poem on Magas
and his daughter Berenice, the wife of Ptolemy III.

388

9 . . . till the great red-hot iron of the Phocaeans, sunk
in the sea, appears,[a] till Pallas gives birth to a child,
and Artemis enters wedlock [b] . . .

Minor, was besieged by a Persian army in 540 B.C., the in-
habitants decided to leave the city for the west, and, throwing
a red-hot lump of iron in the sea, vowed never to return as
long as the lump rested under water (Herod. i. 165).
    [b] Athene and Artemis, the virgin goddesses, were the
proverbial examples of perpetual virginity.

241

CALLIMACHUS

[IN ARSINOES NUPTIAS ?]

THE fragment indicates that the poem started by celebrating the wedding of Arsinoë to Ptolemy II, which probably took place in 275/4 B.C. Scholars have attributed it to an epitha-

---

^a The only other epithalamion in Greek elegiacs we know of was probably also on the wedding of Queen Arsinoë. It was written by the poet Posidippus (*cf.* Milne, *Catalogue of*

392

Ἀρσινόης, ὦ ξεῖνε, γάμον καταβάλλομ᾽ ἀείδειν

[ON THE WEDDING OF ARSINOË ?]

lamion for the occasion, but that is by no means certain. It
may have been written either in hexameters or elegiacs.[a]

---

the Lit. Pap. Brit. Mus., 1927, no. 60). But Callimachus
may here again be trying to compose in " modern " elegiacs
a kind of poem which was traditionally written in lyric
metres or hexameters.

392

I START, O stranger, singing of the wedding of
Arsinoë.

FRAGMENTS OF EPIGRAMS

(The following fragments are quoted by various writers from
the *Epigrams* of Callimachus. There is some ground for
supposing that Callimachus published a separate volume
under this title.)

EPIGRAMMATUM FRAGMENTA

393

αὐτὸς ὁ Μῶμος
ἔγραφεν ἐν τοίχοις " ὁ Κρόνος ἐστὶ σοφός."
ἠνίδε καὶ κόρακες τεγέων ἔπι " κοῖα συνῆπται "
κρώζουσιν καὶ " κῶς αὖθι γενησόμεθα."

2 σοφός cod. : καλός v.l.   3 κου codd. : κοὶ Wil. : καὶ
Fabricius.

---

[a] Momos, the personification of reproach.

[b] Just as lovers used to write the names of their favourites
on walls, accompanied by the adjective *kalos* (beautiful), so
here even Momos praises Diodorus, and calls him " wise."

[c] Cronos was the nickname of Diodorus, son of Aminias,
from Iasos, one of the later philosophers of the Megarian
school.   The nickname indicated " an old fogey."

394

θεὸς δέ οἱ ἱερὸς ὕκης

398

Λύδη καὶ παχὺ γράμμα καὶ οὐ τορόν

---

[a] The elegy written by Antimachus of Colophon (born

FRAGMENTS OF EPIGRAMS

393

Momos [a] himself used to write on the walls [b] : " Cronos [c] is wise." Look, even the crows on the roofs [d] croak: " what (different) things are joined together ? " [e] and " how shall we be hereafter ? " [f]

[d] The epigram implies that his doctrines were so current that even the crows on the roofs discussed them.

[e] This refers to the classification of sentences or propositions into simple (ἁπλᾶ), and adjunct (συνημμένα) and complex (συμπεπλεγμένα). An adjunct sentence (κοῖα συνῆπται) is, *e.g.* : " If it is daytime, there must be light."

[f] This refers to Diodorus' argument for immortality, which was connected with the denial of the possibility of motion.

394

. . . the sacred hykes [a] (was ?) a god to him.

[a] A sea fish, possibly the red mullet or the rainbow-wrasse. *Cf.* fr. 378.

398

. . . the *Lyde* [a] (is) a fat and inelegant book.

c. 444 B.C.) on the Lydian girl he loved, which was greatly admired by the opponents of the Callimachean school.

CALLIMACHUS

399

Ἔρχεται πολὺς μὲν Αἰγαῖον διατμήξας ἀπ' οἰνηρῆς
   Χίου
ἀμφορεύς, πολὺς δὲ Λεσβίης ἄωτος νέκταρ οἰνάνθης
   ἄγων

1 διατμήξας cod. : διανήξας v.l.   2 Λεσβίην cod. : corr.
Bentley. ἄωτοννέκταρ cod. : corr. Pf.   init. v. 3 fort. στάμνος
Maas.

400

Ἁ ναῦς, ἃ τὸ μόνον φέγγος ἐμὶν τὸ γλυκὺ τᾶς ζόας
ἅρπαξας, ποτί τε Ζανὸς ἱκνεῦμαι λιμενοσκόπω

401

Ἡ παῖς ἡ κατάκλειστος,
τὴν οἵ φασι τεκόντες
εὐναίους ὀαρισμούς
ἔχθειν ἶσον ὀλέθρῳ·

4 ἔχειν codd. : corr. Scaliger.

399

MANY a two-handled jar comes, having cut through the Aegean from wine-bearing Chios, and many a jar without handles bringing the nectar of the Lesbian vine.

400

SHIP, that snatched from me the only sweet light of my life, I entreat you by Zeus, watcher of harbours

401

THE cloistered maiden who, her parents say, hates marriage talk even as death.

FRAGMENTS OF UNCERTAIN
LOCATION

FRAGMENTA INCERTAE SEDIS

467

ἐδείμαμεν ἄστεα μορτοί

468

γράμματα δ' οὐχ εἴλισσεν ἀπόκρυφα

471

Μοῦσαί νιν ἑοῖς ἐπὶ τυννὸν ἔθεντο
⟨γούνασι⟩

2 suppl. Toup.

475

αἰεὶ τοῖς μικκοῖς μικκὰ διδοῦσι θεοί

480

ἀρχόμενοι μανίην ὀξυτάτην ἔχομεν

483

μή με τὸν ἐν Δωδῶνι λέγοι μόνον οὕνεκα χαλκόν
ἤγειρον

---

[a] There was a proverb about the garrulous : τὸ Δωδωναῖον

FRAGMENTS OF UNCERTAIN
LOCATION

467

WE mortals built cities.

468

BUT he did not unwind secret writings.

471

THE Muses sat him a small child on their (knees).

475

THE gods always give small things to small men.

480

OUR madness is most acute at the start.

483

MAY he not say this of me, that I only beat the bronze at Dodona.[a]

χαλκίον, the bronze gong at Dodona, the ancient oracle of Zeus in Epirus.

CALLIMACHUS

485

ὁ δ' ἀείδων Μαλόες ἦλθε χορός

ᵃ There was a sanctuary of Maloeis Apollo outside the

486

δημεχθέα Χέλλωνα κακόκνημόν τε Κόμητα

ᵃ Neither Chellon nor Comes is otherwise known.

488

Ἀτράκιον δἤπειτα λυκοσπάδα πῶλον ἐλαύνει

ᵃ If the line does not refer to a chariot at some race, ἐλαύνει should mean " rides."

489

οἷοί τε βιοπλανὲς ἀγρὸν ἀπ' ἀγροῦ
φοιτῶσιν

ᵃ This fragment may come from the *Hecale*.

491

μεῖον ἐδάκρυσεν Τρωίλος ἢ Πρίαμος

ᵃ Troïlus, son of Priam, who was slain by Achilles. (If

492

Φοῖβος Ὑπερβορέοισιν ὄνων ἐπιτέλλεται ἱροῖς

ᵃ A legendary race of Apollo-worshippers, living in the far north. Offerings from them arrived at Delphi and Delos. In Delphic legend Apollo spent the winter months with the

FRAGMENTS OF UNCERTAIN LOCATION

485

. . . and the Lesbian [a] chorus came singing.

city of Mitylene in the island of Lesbos, in a place called Μαλόεις (τόπος).

486

CHELLON, whom the people hated, and ugly-shinned Comes.[a]

488

. . . afterwards he drives [a] a Thessalian foal by the wolf-bit.[b]

[b] A jagged bit for hard-mouthed horses was called a λύκος, a wolf.

489

. . . like those who wander from field to field to get their vagabond living.[a]

491

TROILUS [a] wept less than Priam.

you die young and soon, you will weep less than if you live long.)

492

PHOEBUS visits the Hyperboreans [a] for the sacrifice of asses.

Hyperboreans, who sacrificed asses in his honour. *Cf.* fr. 186.

CALLIMACHUS

493

εἴ σε Προμηθεύς
ἔπλασε, καὶ πηλοῦ μὴ ’ξ ἑτέρου γέγονας

^a Prometheus, one of the Titans, the ancient and popular demi-god, developed in common belief into a supreme crafts-man. As master-craftsman he is supposed to have made

494

ἄκαπνα γὰρ αἰὲν ἀοιδοί
θύομεν

495

Νισαίης ἀγλῖθες ἀπ’ Ὀργάδος

^a Possibly among the things offered to Theseus by Hecale in the *Hecale*.

498

τῷ περὶ δινήεντ’ Ἀκμονίδην ἔβαλεν

περιδινήεντ’ Bentley.

499

ἀλλ’ ἐπακουούς
οὐκ ἔσχεν

500

φοιτίζειν ἀγαθοὶ πολλάκις ἤιθεοι
εἰς ὄαρους ἐθέλουσιν

FRAGMENTS OF UNCERTAIN LOCATION

493

. . . if Prometheus has moulded you, and you are not made of another clay.[a]

man from clay, or, according to another version of the myth, from clay and parts of other animals.

494

. . . for we singers always sacrifice [a] without burnt offerings.

[a] To the Muses.

495

. . . heads of garlic [a] from Nisaean Orgas.[b]

[b] Nisa was the port of Megara and Orgas a place in the Megarid.

498

. . . round which he placed (?) the revolving son of Acmon.[a]

[a] Ouranos was the son of Acmon ; Acmon was the aether, or, according to another version of the myth, Oceanus.

499

. . . but he did not have listeners.

500

. . . noble youths often like to indulge in love-talk.

CALLIMACHUS

502

ἦν μο⟨ύ⟩νη ῥύετο παῖς ἀμαλή

508

ὅσον βλωμοῦ πίονος ἠράσατο

512

καὶ γλαρίδες σταφύλη τε καθιεμένη τε μολυβδίς

515

ξεῖνος Ἐχιδναῖον νέρθεν ἄγων δάκετον

ᵃ Heracles, who dragged Cerberus, the monstrous dog,

516

τῶν ἔτι σοὶ δεκάφυια φάτο ζωάγρια τείσειν

519

ἀλλὰ θεῆς ἥτις με διάκτορον ἔλλαχε Παλλάς

ᵃ The owl, which served as messenger to Athene.

520

εἰ δέ ποτε προφέροιντο διάσματα, φάρεος ἀρχήν

προφοροῖντο coni. Schneider.

502

. . . whom [a] the tender maiden alone was protecting.

[a] Probably a city, or a land.

508

. . . as much as he [a] desired a rich morsel of bread.

[a] About a person or animal that was hungry.

512

. . . and the chisels and the plummet of a level and the sinking plumb of a mason's line.

515

. . . the foreigner.[a] bringing the monstrous son of Echidna from below.

guardian to the entrance of the lower world, away. Cerberus was the offspring of Typhon and Echidna.

516

HE said he would still pay you tenfold ransom for them.

519

. . . but of the goddess, her, Pallas, who received me [a] by lot as her messenger.

520

. . . if ever they were to set the warp in the loom, the beginning of a cloth.

CALLIMACHUS

522

δύπται δ' ἐξ ἁλὸς ἐρχόμενοι
ἔνδιοι καύηκες

523

τὸ δ' ἐκ μέλαν εἶαρ ἔδαπτεν

524

Εἰνατίην ὁμόδελφυν ἐπ' ὠδίνεσσιν ἰδοῦσα

ᵃ ἐπ' ὠδίνεσσιν might mean " while in labour," when it
must refer to Hebe, the sister of Ilithyia (goddess of birth),
watching Ilithyia give birth to Eros, who according to a rare
version of the myth was her son ; or it might mean " beside

526

οὐδὲ βοὴ κήρυκος ἐλίνυσεν

527 A

ὄν τε μάλιστα βοῶν ποθέουσιν ἐχῖνοι

530

χολῇ δ' ἴσα γέντα πάσαιο

533

ΛΑΟΙ Δευκαλίωνος ὅσοι γενόμεσθα γενέθλης
πουλὺ θαλασσαίων μυνδότεροι νεπόδων

ᵃ Fr. 496 Pf., which with fr. 533 Pf. forms an elegiac
couplet ; *cf.* J. Irigoin, *Rev. des Ét. gr.* lxxiii (1960), pp.

FRAGMENTS OF UNCERTAIN LOCATION

522

. . . diving terns, coming at midday from the sea.

523

. . . and he devoured the black blood.

524

. . . having seen Ilithyia, her sister, while in labour.[a]

another woman who was in labour," and might then refer to Leto, or even to Hebe herself, who bore sons to Heracles. Εἰνατίη was a Cretan epithet of Ilithyia.

526

. . . nor did the voice of the herald rest.

527 A

. . . which the stomachs of the oxen especially desire.[a]

> [a] The fragment may come from the *Hecale.*

533

WE, the race of stones, who are descended from Deucalion, much more silent than the children of the sea.[a]

439 f. There is a deliberate ambiguity in ΛΑΟΙ, for it means both " stones " (λᾶοι) and " people " (λαοί).

CALLIMACHUS

534

καί ῥα παρὰ σκαιοῖο βραχίονος ἔμπλεον ὄλπιν

ᵃ Visitors to the baths or the gymnasium took with them

538

Μουσέων δ᾽ οὐ μάλα φιδὸς ἐγώ

539

φιαρὴ τῆμος ἄνεσχεν ἕως

544

⏔ – ⏑ – ⏔ – ⏑] τοῦ μεθυπλῆγος
φροίμιον Ἀρχιλόχου.

ita div. Maas. trim. choliamb. et hemiepes.

546

κρήνη

λευκὸν ὕδωρ ἀνέβαλλεν

547

ὑδάτινον καίρωμα ⟨⏑ –⟩ ὑμένεσσιν ὁμοῖον

lac. ind. Pf., ⟨φέρειν⟩ vel sim.

549

ἔχοιμί τι παιδὸς ἐφολκόν

ἔχοιμι δέ τι cod. : δέ del. Bentley.

FRAGMENTS OF UNCERTAIN LOCATION

534

. . . and from the left arm a full flask.[a]

a flask of oil. This fragment may belong to the *Acontius and Cydippe* aetion (frs. 67-75).

538

I AM not at all miserly of my songs.

539

. . . then the bright dawn rose.

544

. . . the prelude of wine-stricken Archilochus.

546

. . . (the) fountain was throwing up white water.

547

. . . a transparent web . . . like a membrane.

549

. . . may I have something to entice a boy.

CALLIMACHUS

550

ὃ πρὸ μιῆς ὥρης θηρίον οὐ λέγεται

551

καὶ τὸν ὃς αἰζηῶν ἔγραε κηδεμόνος
⟨ἧπαρ⟩

1 τόνος cod. dist. Bergk, Wil.: γόνος—κηδεμόνα codd. v.l.
2 suppl. Maas.

552

Βριλησσοῦ λαγόνεσσιν ὁμούριον ἐκτίσσαντο

λαγόνεσσιν ὁμούριον ἐκτίσσαντο Bentley: λαγόνες εἰσὶ νόμου
ὃν ἐκτήσαντο codd.

553

καὶ κυάμων ἄπο χεῖρας ἔχειν, ἀνιῶντος ἐδεστοῦ,
κἠγώ, Πυθαγόρης ὡς ἐκέλευε, λέγω

---

[a] The followers of Pythagoras, the Samian philosopher
who migrated to Croton in the late sixth century B.C.,

554

Τόν με παλαιστρίταν ὀμόσας θεὸν ἑπτάκις φιλήσειν

---

[a] Hermes is the god of the palaestra. This is probably

264

FRAGMENTS OF UNCERTAIN LOCATION

550

. . . the animal which is not mentioned before the first hour.[a]

[a] The ape, if mentioned at night, was thought to bring bad luck. The first hour was c. seven o'clock in the morning

551

. . . and him who devoured the liver of the protector of mankind.[a]

[a] The eagle which devoured the liver of Prometheus.

552

. . . bordering on the flanks of Brilessos [a] they built.

[a] Mountain of Attica. The fragment may come from the *Hecale.*

553

. . . and to keep hands off the beans, a vexatious food, I too command as Pythagoras ordered.[a]

abstained from certain food, including beans. The κύαμοι here may be the lots by which public officers were elected.

554

HAVING sworn that he would kiss me (?) the god of the palaestra, seven times.[a]

the beginning of an epigram in " Archilochian " metre, in which the effigy of the god speaks.

CALLIMACHUS

556

νυμφίε Δημοφόων, ἄδικε ξένε

ᵃ Demophon, son of Theseus, when returning from the
Trojan war met in Thrace the princess Phyllis, who fell in
love with him. He left her, promising to return when he had

557

εἴτε μιν 'Αργείων χρῆν με καλεῖν ἀάτην

571

αἴθε γάρ, ὦ κούροισιν ἐπ' ὄμματα λίχνα φέροντες,
    'Ερχίος ὡς ὑμῖν ὥρισε παιδοφιλεῖν,
ὧδε νέων ἐρόῳτε· πόλιν κ' εὔανδρον ἔχοιτε

572

ἀρότας κύματος 'Αονίου

ᵃ The Boeotian Sea. The Boeotians were called Aones.
The furrowers of the sea are probably fishermen.

586

εἰ θεὸν οἶσθα,
ἴσθ' ὅτι καὶ ῥέξαι δαίμονι πᾶν δυνατόν

587

ἑπτὰ σοφοὶ χαίροιτε—τὸν ὄγδοον, ὥστε Κόροιβον,
    οὐ συναριθμέομεν—

FRAGMENTS OF UNCERTAIN LOCATION

556

. . . bridegroom Demophon,[a] unjust guest.

settled his affairs in Athens; but she, weary with waiting, hanged herself, and was turned into an almond tree, which put forth leaves when later Demophon came back and embraced it.

557

. . . or I should have called her (?) [a] the ruin of the Greeks.

[a] Probably Helen.

571

. . . would that you, who cast lewd eyes upon boys, might make love to the young in the manner ordained by Erchios.[a] You would have a city of noble men.

[a] Erchios is otherwise unknown.

572

. . . furrowers of the Aonian [a] wave.

586

. . . if you know a god, know also that it is possible for a god to achieve everything.

587

. . . seven sages, hail—the eighth like Coroebus,[a] we do not include—

[a] Coroebus, son of Mygdon, a Phrygian hero of the epic cycle, was proverbial for his stupidity.

588

πάλαι δ' ἔτι Θεσσαλὸς ἀνήρ
ῥυστάζει φθιμένων ἀμφὶ τάφον φονέας

591

τεθναίην ὅτ' ἐκεῖνον ἀποπνεύσαντα πυθοίμην

592

χἠ Παλλάς, Δελφοί νιν ὅθ' ἱδρύοντο Προναίην

593

μέσφα Καλαυρείης ἦλθεν ἐς ἀντίδοσιν

597

θηρὸς ἀερτάζων δέρμα κατωμάδιον

599

ἀντὶ γὰρ ἐκλήθης Ἴμβρασε Παρθενίου

ᵃ A river of the island Samos. The river was called Par-

601

ἐν Δίῃ· τὸ γὰρ ἔσκε παλαίτερον οὔνομα Νάξῳ
268

FRAGMENTS OF UNCERTAIN LOCATION

588

. . . and still, as in ancient times, the Thessalians drag the murderers round the tomb of the dead.

591

. . . may I die, when I learn that he has expired.

592

. . . and Pallas, when (?) the Delphians were setting her (statue) up as Pronaea.

593

. . . until he came to exchange Calauria.[a]

  [a] The island off the East Argolid, now known as Poros.

597

. . . hanging on his shoulder the skin of the wild beast.[a]

  [a] Probably Heracles, who hung the lion-skin on his shoulder.

599

. . . for you were called Imbrasos, instead of Parthenios.[a]

thenios because Hera, we are told, bathed in it when still a maiden.

601

. . . in Dia ; for this was the earlier name for Naxos.[a]

  [a] Possibly to be connected with frs. 3-7.

CALLIMACHUS

602

δέσποιναι Λιβύης ἡρωΐδες, αἳ Νασαμώνων
αὖλιν καὶ δολιχὰς θῖνας ἐπιβλέπετε,
μητέρα μοι ζώουσαν ὀφέλλετε

[a] The local Libyan nymphs and goddesses are invoked.

604

νόθαι δ' ἤνθησαν ἀοιδαί

[a] It may refer to the music which the composers of dithyrambs are said to have corrupted.

607

μὴ σύ γε, Θειόγενες, κόψας χέρα Καλλικόωντος;

[a] Callicoon is said to have betrayed the city of Samos (or Miletus) to Priene (according to others the island of Syros to the Samians), and the butcher Thiogenes, a native of the

611

Καλλιχόρῳ ἐπὶ φρητὶ καθέζεο παιδὸς ἄπυστος

ἄπαυστος codd. : corr. Naeke.

[a] Demeter, when searching for her daughter Persephone, who had been abducted by Hades, sat at the well Callichoron

612

ἀμάρτυρον οὐδὲν ἀείδω

FRAGMENTS OF UNCERTAIN LOCATION

602

. . . heroines, mistresses of Libya,[a] who watch over the home and the far-stretching shores of the Nasamones,[b] make greater my flourishing mother.[c]

[b] The Nasamones lived to the south-west of Cyrene along the shores of the Great Syrtis.
[c] Cyrene, the motherland of Callimachus.

604

. . . and bastard songs flourished.[a]

607

. . . was it really you, Thiogenes, who cut the hand of Callicoon ? [a]

betrayed city, cut off the traitor's hand when buying meat at his shop, saying : " You will betray no other city with this hand."

611

. . . you sat at the well Callichoron, without news of your child.[a]

of Eleusis. There the women of the city are said to have first formed a chorus and sung to the goddess.

612

I SING nothing that is not attested.[a]

[a] One more proof of the " erudite " nature of the Callimachean poetry.

CALLIMACHUS

618

Ῥήγιον ἄστυ λιπὼν Ἰοκάστεω Αἰολίδαο

---

^a Iocastos, son of Aeolus, was the founder of Rhegium.

620

ἄγνωτον μηδὲν ἔχοιμι καλόν

ἄγνωστον vel ἀνάγνωστον v.ll. codd.

620 A

ἔσκεν ὅτ᾽ ἄζωστος χἀτερόπορπος ἔτι

---

^a An " ungirdled girl " was 9 years old.
^b Spartan girls wore a short dress with their right shoulder

621

εἰμὶ τέρας Καλυδῶνος, ἄγω δ᾽ Αἰτωλὸν Ἄρηα

---

^a Probably the beginning of an epigram in which a shield speaks, describing the picture of the hunt of the Calydonian boar. Artemis, to whom Oeneus, king of Calydon in Aetolia,

625

ἠβαιὴν οὔ τι κατὰ πρόφασιν

626

τῶν οὐκ ἀγαθῶν ἐρυσίπτολιν

⟨φω⟩τῶν Lobeck : ⟨καὶ⟩ τῶν Schneider.

272

FRAGMENTS OF UNCERTAIN LOCATION

618

. . . having left Rhegium, the city of Iocastos, son of Aeolus.[a]

620

. . . may I not keep concealed anything that is good.

620 A

. . . when (she) was still ungirdled,[a] and wearing a short dress with one buckle.[b]

free. This may be also a reference to the habit of leaving the right shoulder free, when training at the gymnasium.

621

I AM a Calydonian portent, and I bring Aetolian war.[a]

had not sacrificed, sent a wild boar to ravage the country. Meleager, the son of Oeneus, gathered huntsmen and hounds from many cities and killed the boar. There are various versions of this myth.

625

. . . not on a small pretext

626

. . . defender of the city of the wicked.[a]

[a] Probably about a hero or a daemon, not about Athene, to whom the epithet ἐρυσίπτολις is usually attributed.

CALLIMACHUS

628

ἄνωγε δὲ πορθμέα νεκρῶν

630

κρηνέων τ' Εὐρώπῃ μισγομένων ἑκατόν

637

χαλεπὴ μῆνις ἐπιχθονίων

ἔπι χθονίων Bergk : ἐπ⟨ε⟩ὶ χθονίων Lloyd-Jones.

638

ἵλαθί μοι φαλαρῖτι, πυλαιμάχε

639 [a]

[a] See fr. 284 A.

644

νόμον δ' ἤειδεν Ἄρηος

646

αἱ δὲ βοοκρήμνοιο παρ' ἀγκύλον ἴχνος Ἀράτθου

Ἀραίθου codd. : corr. B. Niese.

648

ἂψ ἐπὶ Θερμώδοντος ὁδεύετον

---

[a] River of Boeotia.

FRAGMENTS OF UNCERTAIN LOCATION

628

. . . do you order the ferryman of the dead.[a]

> [a] Charon, the ferryman of the dead. ἄνωγε is apparently an unusual imperative instead of ἄνωχθι.

630

. . . and a hundred fountains mingling with Europe.[a]

> [a] A fountain in Epirus.

637

. . . severe is the wrath of men.

638

. . . be propitious to me, (Athene) of the bossed helmet, defender of the city gates.

639 [a]

> [a] See fr. 284 A.

644

. . . he was singing the chant of Ares.[a]

> [a] Probably the song (elsewhere described as a paean) sung before going into battle.

646

. . . and, near the winding course of steep-banked Arathus,[a] they.

> [a] River of Epirus.

648

. . . they two were journeying back to the river Thermodon.[a]

CALLIMACHUS

650

ἔστιν μοι Μάγνης ἐννεάμυκλος ὄνος

651

μέσσαβα βοῦς ὑποδύς

652

τὴν μὲν ὅ γ' ἐσπέρμηνεν Ἐρινύι Τιλφωσαίῃ

ᵃ Despoina was born to Posidon by Demeter Erinys, worshipped in Arcadia as the water-nymph Tilphousa. Accord-

655

καὶ τριτάτη Περσῆος ἐπώνυμος, ἧς ὀρόδαμνον
Αἰγύπτῳ κατέπηξεν

658

ἐν δὲ θεοῖσιν ἐπὶ φλογὶ καιέμεν ὄμπας

669

ὃς 〈 〉 Ἰταλὴν ἐφράσαθ' ἁρμονίην

lacunam indic. Pf. ὅς τ' Böckh : ὡς Diehl.

276

FRAGMENTS OF UNCERTAIN LOCATION

650

I have a strong (?) ass from Magnesia.[a]

[a] Probably Magnesia in Thessaly. The word ἐννεάμυκλος also means " nine-years old."

651

. . . the ox having shouldered the yoke.

652

. . . he begat her by the Tilphosian Erinys.[a]

ing to another version of the myth Tilphousa was a fountain in Boeotia and not in Arcadia.

655

. . . and a third called after Perseus,[a] from which he planted a cutting in Egypt.

[a] A tree called " Mimusops " in botany, planted by Perseus in Memphis according to the myth.

658

. . . and to burn on the flame cakes made of meal and honey for the gods.

669

. . . who . . . invented the Italian scale.[a]

[a] The Western Locrian Xenocritus is said to have invented the Italian musical scale.

670

πτέρνῃ θ' ἵππος ἐλαυνόμενος

ἵπποις cod.: ἵππος Bentley (praeeunte Anna Fabri ?).

672

Κολχίδος ἐκ καλάμης

^a Colchis, at the east end of the Euxine Sea, south of the

673

ἢ ὑπὲρ αὐσταλέον Χαρίτων λόφον

αὐσταλερὸν codd. v.l.: ἀσταλέων coni. Ruhnken.

676

ζορκός τοι, φίλε κοῦρε, Λιβυστίδος αὐτίκα δώσω
πέντε νεοσμήκτους ἄστριας

^a Probably part of a conversation between Aphrodite and

677

τὸ δὲ σκύλος ἀνδρὶ καλύπτρῃ
γιγνόμενον, νιφετοῦ καὶ βελέων ἔρυμα

^a This probably refers to the lion-skin Heracles wore. As
the owner is here called a " man," it can either be part of a

FRAGMENTS OF UNCERTAIN LOCATION

670

. . . and the horse driven by the heel.[a]

[a] Possibly the potter's wheel is here the horse, driven (turned) by the foot.

672

. . . of Colchian [a] flax.

Caucasus mountains, according to an ancient tradition a colony of the Egyptians.

673

. . . or over the rough hill of the Graces.[a]

[a] Probably a hill in the Cyrenaica.

676

I WILL give you at once, dear boy, five newly-polished knuckle-bones of a Libyan gazelle.[a]

Eros, in which the mother is promising her son this gift in order to wound somebody with his arrows.

677

. . . and the skin serving as a cover to the man, a protection against snow and missiles.[a]

speech in which Heracles speaks about himself, or of a speech by Omphale, in which case ἀνδρὶ would mean " to my husband."

680

ὑπεὶρ ἅλα κεῖνος ἐνάσθη,
Ἀλκαθόου τίς ἄπυστος

ᵃ Son of Pelops and Hippodamea, a king and hero of

681

νηφάλιαι καὶ τῇσιν ἀεὶ μελιηδέας ὄμπας
λήτειραι καίειν ἔλλαχον Ἡσυχίδες

ᵃ The Eumenides, the Furies, to whom no libations in
wine were made.

682

τί δάκρυον εὖδον ἐγείρεις;

687

δαῖμον, τῇ κόλποισιν ἐπιπτύουσι γυναῖκες

δαίμων cod.: δαῖμον Bentley, cf. fr. 384. 9 et Ap. Rh. iv.
1579.

688

ἐπὶ τρύγα δ' εἶχεν ἐδωδῇ

ἐδωδήν codd.: ἐδωδῇ coni. Schn.

689

Πὰν ὁ Μαλειήτης τρύπανον αἰπολικόν

FRAGMENTS OF UNCERTAIN LOCATION

680

. . . he was obliged to live beyond the sea, one who knew not Alcathoos.[a]

Megara. We do not know who the man was " who knew not Alcathoos." τίς is here used in the sense of a relative pronoun.

681

. . . and those [a] to whom the sober [b] Hesychian [c] priestesses had the duty always to burn sweet sacrificial cakes.

[b] The priestesses who offered libations of water and not of wine are called " sober," like the water-libations themselves.
[c] The " Hesychidae " were a family of Athens.

682

. . . why do you wake up dormant tears ?

687

. . . goddess, for whom the women spit on their bosoms.[a]

[a] Women exorcized Nemesis by spitting on their bosoms.

688

. . . and he had new wine to accompany his food.

689

PAN of Mount Malea,[a] the goatherd's screw.[b]

[a] Probably the Arcadian mountain.
[b] To be taken in an obscene sense.

690

ἰύζων δ' ἀν' ὄρος

694

ἀεὶ δ' ἔχον ἔντομα σηκοί

695

πιπρήσκει δ' ὁ καλὸς πάντα πρὸς ἀργύριον

κακὸς cod. v.l.

---

[a] Cf. fr. 193 ; Epigr. xxx. (xxxii L.C.L.) 1, and probably

701

δέδαεν δὲ λαχαινέμεν ἔργα σιδήρου

705

εἰς Ἀσίνην Ἄλυκόν τε καὶ ἆμ πόλιν Ἑρμιονήων

---

[a] These three cities of the Argolid can either be connected with the μετοικισμός forced on the Dryopes by Heracles (cf.

713

ἔνθ' ἀνέμων μεγάλων κῦμα διωλύγιον

714

κουφοτέρως τότε φῶτα διαθλίβουσιν ἀνίαι,
ἐκ δὲ τριηκόντων μοῖραν ἀφεῖλε μίαν,

2 ἀφῆκε cod. v.l.

FRAGMENTS OF UNCERTAIN LOCATION

690

. . . crying out on the mountain.

694

. . . and the sanctuaries always had victims.

695

. . . the handsome sell everything for money.[a]

Epigr. xxviii and xxxi (xxx and xxxiii L.C.L.), from which it appears that Callimachus was himself a poor lover.

701

. . . and taught how to dig (the) iron (metal).[a]

> [a] *Cf.* fr. 110. 49 f. and fr. 115. 12 f.

705

. . . to Asine and Alycos and about the city of Hermione.[a]

fr. 24/5), or with the *Hecale*, where cities of the Argolid are also mentioned.

713

. . . there, the far resounding wave, caused by strong winds.

714

. . . worries then weigh less on a man, and of thirty parts one is removed, when he blurts out his troubles

ἢ φίλον ἢ ὅτ' ἐς ἄνδρα συνέμπορον ἢ ὅτε κωφαῖς
ἄλγεα μαψαύραις ἔσχατον ἐξερύγῃ

4 εξερρύη codd. : em. Pf.

715

ὁ δρόμος ἱερὸς οὗτος 'Ανούβιδος

ᵃ The path leading to the temple.

716

Καλλίστη τὸ πάροιθε, τὸ δ' ὕστερον οὔνομα Θήρη,
μήτηρ εὐίππου πατρίδος ἡμετέρης

719

θεῷ τ' ἀλάλαγμα νόμαιον
δοῦναι

ᵃ We do not know about which god Callimachus is speak-

724

πτωχῶν οὐλὰς ἀεὶ κενεή

οὖλαι vel οὐλαὶ codd. : οὐλὰς Hecker. κεναί codd. : κενεή
Porson.

284

FRAGMENTS OF UNCERTAIN LOCATION

to a friend, or a fellow-traveller, or even finally to the deaf gusts of wind.

715

. . . this is the sacred drive *a* of Anubis.*b*

b An Egyptian god with the head of a dog, who was identified with Hermes by the Greeks.

716

. . . of old called Calliste, her later name Thera, mother of our fatherland of good horses.*a*

a Cyrene, the poet's motherland, was a colony of Thera, the island of the Aegean, to-day called Santorin.

719

. . . to offer the god *a* the usual cry.

ing. It could be Ares, or Zeus, or Dionysus or even other less important gods.

724

. . . the wallet of the poor is always empty.*a*

a A proverbial saying about the greedy.

CALLIMACHUS

725

καὶ ὡς λύκος ὠρυοίμην

731

τὴν θεῦν Ἄρτεμιν οἷ᾽ ἔπαθεν

^a See fr. 31 ʙ

784

οὐδ᾽ ὅσσον μυίης στυγερῶν ἐμπάζετο μύθων

^a Probably Heracles.

FRAGMENTS OF UNCERTAIN LOCATION

725

. . . and may I howl like a wolf.

731

. . . the goddess Artemis, what she suffered [a] . . .

784

Nor did he [a] heed in the very least [b] the loathsome words.

       [b] Literally : " as much as a fly."

MUSAEUS
HERO AND LEANDER

PREFACE

My interest in Musaeus' poem was awakened when I observed that the poet, in narrating the sad romance of Hero and Leander, not only, as a true follower of Nonnus, made verbal borrowings from the authors who comprised the educational background of a γραμματικός of this late period, but also shaped the course and motivation of whole scenes by modelling them on famous antecedents to which he made clear allusions. Among these antecedents in particular he used the meeting of Odysseus and Nausicaa in the *Odyssey* and the encounter of the lovers in Plato's *Phaedrus*. As he was also found to cite the *Hymns* of Proclus, it was easy to guess that he was familiar with the interpretations in the light of which Homer and Plato were understood and employed in late Neoplatonism, and therefore that his allusions to these authors and his significant blending of this pair of authorities—exactly what we find in the poems of Proclus himself—amounted to more than merely external literary borrowing. So the question posed itself whether the poem had an allegorical meaning expressed through these allusions in the manner we already knew well from Proclus. As a proposal for research during my residence at the Center for Hellenic Studies in Washington in 1966–1967 I set myself to extend my researches into Christian Neoplatonism. This was even more urgent because Musaeus in his poem made considerable use of Nonnus' *Paraphrase of St. John's Gospel* and sporadic use of the *Paraphrase of the Psalms* by Pseudo-Apollinarius. The catalogue drawn up by Johannes Golega of the literary authorities used in this latter paraphrase coincided remarkably closely with those used by Musaeus. At that time I was not thinking of publishing a text of my own; I had merely put together for my own use a selection of readings based on the variants recorded by Arthur Ludwich.

Then, through the kind intervention of the Director of the Center, Prof. Bernard M. W. Knox, I received an invitation from the Loeb Classical Library to prepare the present edition for this series, in which Musaeus had not yet appeared. At first it seemed that an adequate text for ordinary reading of the 343 frequently reprinted lines could be relatively quickly prepared on the basis of available information. But it then became clear that the language and style of Musaeus and his use of literary authorities had not yet been independently examined, but only treated in passing as an afterthought to research on Nonnus and his school. The readings and the stemmatic relations of the MSS. had been thoroughly dealt with by Ludwich, but deeper investigations were still needed to establish adequate criteria, when there were textual difficulties, for judging the individual characteristics of Musaeus in his own distinct place in the school of Nonnus. The results of my research on this topic have been published in *Museum Helveticum*, for which I am grateful to the editors. This research could not have been completed without the generous assistance of Prof.

PREFACE

John H. Finley, who as Master welcomed me on two visits to Eliot House in Cambridge, Massachusetts, and made it possible for me to consult the rich stocks of the Widener Library of Harvard University ; nor without the generosity of the directors of the Byzantine departments of Dumbarton Oaks, Washington D.C., who granted me unlimited access to the fine library of their magnificent Institute. I owe especial thanks to Professor Ihor Ševčenko, to the late Romilly J. H. Jenkins of Dumbarton Oaks, and to Professor William M. Calder III of Columbia University, New York, who invited me to read a paper at both their institutions and discuss it with them ; they have given me further help with valuable references. I have also gratefully used information generously put at my disposal by Professor Martin Sicherl, Münster i.W. (at that time at the Institute for Advanced Study, Princeton, N.J.) concerning his unpublished research on the Latin translations of Aldus Manutius, and by Professor Alan Cameron of King's College, University of London, concerning an unpublished papyrus of Triphiodorus.

It has been a great pleasure to work with Professor Cedric H. Whitman of Harvard University, who undertook the difficult task of translation. His elegant verses subtly reproduce the preciosity of the late antique original, and for the English reader will be the special attraction of this edition. I am indebted to him for admirable observations on the meaning of the text ; moreover he has been prepared to be totally un-selfassertive and, in the frequent cases where the meaning was only loosely discernible and the rendering could be doubtful, to accept my conception in the interest of a unity of interpretation. Accordingly if despite every precaution inaccuracies remain, the responsibility falls on me. Finally I owe special thanks to my fellow-student at the Center for Hellenic Studies, David B. Robinson of the University of Edinburgh, who out of friendship took upon himself the task of improving the style of the part of my introduction that was written in English, and of translating into English by far the greater part of it, and also all of the notes.

My remarks on the allegorical interpretation of the poem in the Introduction and the Notes are kept apart from the remainder of the interpretation of the poem, in such a way that the reader who wishes to give his attention entirely to the literary presentation of this famous romance can skip them without more ado, and enjoy without hindrance the poem as a work of literature.

ZÜRICH. *March* 1969

Shortly before I had completed the preparation of this edition in Zürich the edition of Pierre Orsini (Paris 1968) appeared. It was still possible for me to include in my text his results and the points of difference. At that time however an immediate start could not be made with the printing, and as the opportunity has now presented itself, the editor of the Loeb Classical Library has kindly allowed me to take into account in addition the work that has since been published. This was all the more necessary, since among the reviews of Orsini's edition two especially weighty contributions have appeared, those of Rudolf Keydell and Giuseppe Giangrande (both 1969), who have brought in their turn new

opinions and new material to bear on the constitution
and the explanation of the text. Further the first
fascicle of the *Lexikon zu den Dionysiaka des Nonnos*,
which is being prepared under the direction of
Werner Peek, has since then been published; this
work, together with the Index verborum to Augustin
Scheindler's edition of the *Metabole of the Gospel of
St. John* (Leipzig 1881), will constitute an indispen-
sable tool for all research in the field of later Greek
Epic.

Finally the monumental *Commentary on Musaeus* of
Karlheinz Kost has also now appeared (Bonn 1971).
It is the fruit of an extraordinarily wide-ranging and
industrious effort extending over more than ten
years. The study of this bulky volume, slowed by the
pressure of my other work, necessitated a further
delay in the completion of this edition. Kost deals
comprehensively with all questions concerning the
poet's identity and date, his material, his means of
expression, his style, his sources, and associated
topics, as well as with the history and interpretation
of his text in modern times, and his influence through
the Middle Ages up to the present day. He has
collected, for the history of the majority of words,
expressions, concepts and motifs used by Musaeus,
parallels and illustrations beginning with Homer and
continuing far beyond the time of Musaeus, together
with references to modern discussions, and has dealt
with several in a number of excursuses. The little
that I was able to take over from it, within the scope
of this edition, in order to supplement and amend
the introduction, apparatus criticus and explanatory
notes, can give no adequate impression of the wealth
of the material there offered.

MUSAEUS

Unfortunately, precisely in the field which is of most concern in such an edition as this, even after the latest efforts of these three learned interpreters, we are still far from a generally accepted consensus of opinion. Their suggestions for the solution of a relatively large number of specific problems of textual criticism and of interpretation of meaning lead to conclusions which are somewhat frequently widely divergent. This shows only how insufficient, in the final analysis, our material is for textual criticism in the case of unique or peculiar expressions in this short poem, and there is no immediate possibility of this situation being improved. Therefore I have not felt myself prompted to make substantial changes in the constitution of my text as against the suggested solutions which I have discussed and argued for in my *Bemerkungen*. On the other hand I have in the apparatus criticus gone beyond the material adduced to support my own conclusions and considerably increased the references to different solutions and to the parallels on which these are based, so as not to mislead the reader by the deceptive semblance of a certainty beyond dispute.

For his help in the translation into English of the additional notes, in the preparation of the final text of the introduction and in proof-reading I wish to thank Mr. Jean Parry, assistant in the department of classics in Bern.

THOMAS GELZER

BERN, *April* 1972

INTRODUCTION

I. THE POET AND HIS WORK

The Poet

WE have no biographical information about the epic
poet Musaeus[a] beyond the fact that in the super-
scriptions of some manuscripts[b] he is called γραμ-
ματικός. In the fifth and sixth centuries A.D. this
title was borne by several authors whose works, in
verse and in prose, we still possess. They are scholars
and teachers learned in the rhetoric, poetics and
philosophy of their time, and expert in the scholarly
interpretation of the classical prose- and verse-
authors, in particular of Homer, the orators and the
philosophers.

Clues for dating Musaeus can be gathered from
the comparison of his poem with other surviving
writings.[c] The most striking clue is the use that he

[a] Most of the topics discussed here have been treated by
me in more detail in an article, " Bemerkungen zu Sprache
und Text des Epikers Musaios," *Mus. Helv.* 24 (1967), 129-
148 and 25 (1968), 11-47. I refer to this below as " *Bemer-
kungen.*"

[b] All the material is in A. Ludwich, *Ueber die Handschrif-
ten des Epikers Musäos* (Vorlesungsverzeichnis, Königsberg
Sommer 1896), 5.

[c] On this see R. Keydell, "Musaios 2," *Real-Encyclopädie,*
16, 1 (1933), 767-769 ; L. Castiglioni, " Epica Nonniana,"
Rend. Ist. Lomb. Torino, ser. 2, vol. 45 (1932), 309-337.

INTRODUCTION

made of the *Dionysiaca* and of the *Paraphrase of St.
John's Gospel* by Nonnus of Panopolis. He takes over
from Nonnus near-complete verses, parts of verses,
words, constructions and modes of expression, so
that his poem almost gives the impression of being a
cento of Nonnus.[a] The *Paraphrase* by Nonnus can be
dated on theological grounds certainly later than
A.D. 428, probably later than 451.[b]

In essential aspects of his poetic technique, on the
other hand, Musaeus diverges from Nonnus. These
are the use he makes of rhetorical ornament and of
grammatical learning.[c] Besides Nonnus he demon-
strably imitated other authors,[d] from whose works in

[a] *Cf.* L. v. Schwabe in his edition, iv sq. ; A. Wifstrand,
Von Kallimachos zu Nonnos (=Skrifter . . . Vetenskaps
Societeten i Lund, 16, 1933), 193.

[b] J. Golega, *Studien über die Evangeliendichtung des
Nonnos von Panopolis* (= Breslauer Studien z. histor. Theo-
logie, 15, 1930), 106 sq., 144.

[c] A. Wifstrand, *op. cit.*, analysed and recorded the similar-
ities and divergences between Nonnus and his successors, in
particular Musaeus, in all important points of metre and
style ; on Musaeus see esp. pp. 193-198.

[d] The following authors for certain : (1) poets : Homer,
Iliad and *Odyssey*, *Hymn to Aphrodite*, *Batrachomyomachia* ;
Hesiod, *Theogony* and *Erga* ; Bacchylides ; Aeschylus ;
Euripides ; Aratus ; Lycophron, Apollonius Rhodius,
Callimachus and the Bucolici (besides Theocritus : Moschus,
Ps.-Theocritus 27, the " Oaristys ") ; the Manethoniana ;
Dionysius Periegetes and Dionysius Bassaricus ; Oppian,
Halieutica ; Quintus Smyrnaeus ; St. Gregory Nazianzenus.
(2) Prose authors : Plato ; New Testament ; Achilles Tatius
and probably Aristaenetus. Proofs and references : Kost
43 sq. ; for Sappho, Pindar, other lyric poets and those of the
Anthologia and for other epigrammatists see Kost's commen-
tary *passim*, and, for Ps.-Apollinarius, the following note.
Of special interest for the interpretation of Musaeus are the
borrowings from Aratus, St. Gregory Nazianzenus (also used

298

the same way he took over expressions and parts of verses. Among these other works is the *Paraphrase of the Psalms* of Pseudo-Apollinarius, which can be dated, again on theological grounds, to the period 460–470.[a] Musaeus therefore probably wrote at the earliest in the last third of the fifth century A.D. The list of the authors quoted by the paraphrast of the Psalms shows a remarkable coincidence with those quoted by Musaeus ; this is a clear indication of Musaeus' cultural background. This paraphrast is in turn used by other poets who at the same time also quote Musaeus (these include Colluthus, Christodorus and Johannes Gazaeus).

Musaeus was probably a Christian.[b] Not only did he borrow from St. Gregory Nazianzenus and the two Bible paraphrases ; he also alludes to the Gospels (Mus. 139 ~ Luke 11. 27 ; Mus. 183 sq. ~ Matth. 10. 26 ~ Mark 4. 22 ~ Luke 8. 17 ~ Nonn. *met. Jo.* 18. 97), to the Epistle to the Romans (Mus. 228 ~ Rom. 4. 11) and to a Canonical prohibition of the Church (Mus. 178).[c] He also knows Plato and the *Hymns* of Proclus (Mus. 56 ~ Procl. *Hy.* 7. 31).[d] He was

---

by Nonnus in his *Dionysiaca*), Lycophron (following C. v. Holzinger) and the Manethoniana which Kost has discovered or to which he has assigned their proper significance.

[a] J. Golega, *Der homerische Psalter* (Studia Patristica et Byzantina, 6, 1960), 25 sq., 104. This paraphrase quotes Nonnus too. That it is earlier than Musaeus is not proved, but is likely.

[b] Doubted only by J. Geffcken, *Der Ausgang des griechisch-römischen Heidentums* (Heidelberg 1929), 305, Anm. 155 ; but he does not deny it and produces no arguments.

[c] For establishment of this point, for which I must thank the late R. J. H. Jenkins, see the evidence in *Bemerkungen,* 136 sq. ; see Explanatory Notes below, on line 177.

[d] A. Ludwich, " Musaios und Proklos," *Jahrbb. f. class.*

probably therefore a Christian Neoplatonist. Thus he has much in common with the circle of poets, orators and philosophers of the time of Anastasius I (491–518). Procopius (c. 465–528) and his followers in the school of Gaza show an especially large number of stylistic similarities to Musaeus.[a] Among the authors of that period the Egyptian Colluthus quoted Musaeus[b]; so did Christodorus of Coptus (about 500) in his descriptions. Procopius and the Gazaeans,

---

Philologie, 133 (1886), 246–248, established the relation of the passages but reversed the chronological order; less striking parallels are Mus. 275, cp. Procl. *Hy.* 1. 26 ; Mus. 330, cp. Procl. *Hy.* 7. 34 ; see Explanatory Notes to line 56. Proclus is also cited by Nonnus in his *Metaphrasis* and by the paraphrast of the Psalms.

[a] Good survey in K. Seitz, *Die Schule von Gaza* (Diss. Heidelberg 1892), especially 37 sq.

[b] That Colluthus used Musaeus, and not vice versa, is almost certainly proved by Kost, 17 sq., who shows that the former's allusions point to various parts of the latter's poem, whereas in his own they are confined to three clearly defined passages, *i.e.* Helena's reception scene (Colluth. 254 sq.: 255 ∽Mus. 260-263, 257 ∽Mus. 78, 265-266 ∽Mus. 172-173), the second part of Paris' speech (Colluth. 293 sq.: 293 ∽Mus. 83, 295 ∽Mus. 203, 296 ∽Mus. 142, 297 ∽Mus. 157) and the transition (Colluth. 303-305 ∽Mus. 160-172). That Musaeus should have picked out just these few lines of Colluthus in order to quote them at various places in his whole poem is very unlikely. Besides, Colluthus " trivializes " the pointed use of Musaeus' wording. Triphiodorus also has parts of verses in common with Musaeus (listed in Ludwich's edition). Since Wernicke (1819), who noted the frequent coincidences of phrasing in Triphiodorus and Nonnus, it has been assumed that Triphiodorus was a follower of Nonnus and in his turn was copied by Colluthus. Now Prof. A. Cameron has called my attention to an unpublished papyrus of Triphiodorus which on purely palaeographical grounds would be dated to the third or fourth century A.D. Triphiodorus' many divergences from Nonnus' metrical rules have long been noticed

like Christodorus, are also Christians and Neoplaton-
ists, and, in so far as they wrote verse, followers of
Nonnus. Several of them have the title γραμματικός,
as has also Philoponus, the Christian Neoplatonist of
the Alexandrian school, who wrote a work attacking
Proclus, probably about 529.[a] Musaeus would be
quite at home in this learned company, and so it is
very likely that he is identical with the addressee
of two letters which we possess by Procopius of Gaza
(Nos. 147 and 165 ed. Garzya-Loenertz). Procopius
in another letter (No. 1) quotes the poem about
Alpheus and Arethusa (*A.P.* 9. 362) which is modelled
in its turn on the epyllion of Musaeus.[b] Procopius
addresses Musaeus as an honoured master and thanks
him (No. 147) for a book which he, apparently by his
interpretations, has turned into a work " inspired by
the Muses " in the Neoplatonic sense (cp. Proclus,
in Remp. 1. 180 sq.). It seems that this must have been
a Neoplatonic commentary or paraphrase, now lost
to us ; to have written a work of this kind would

and brought Wifstrand (*op. cit.* 75) to the conclusion :
" Were it not for the numerous phrases and parts of verses
which he has clearly taken from the *Dionysiaca*, one would
even be inclined to place him earlier than Nonnus." The
possibility therefore arises, though it is unlikely on other
grounds, that this papyrus makes both Nonnus and Musaeus
followers of Triphiodorus. But the dating of papyri purely
on palaeographical grounds has in many cases proved at least
as uncertain a criterion as the establishment of a relative or
absolute chronology on grounds of allusions and adoptions
of formulae. [See now Pap. Oxy. 2946, vol. 41.]

[a] L. G. Westerink, *Anonymous Prolegomena to Platonic
Philosophy* (Amsterdam 1962), xiii, xx.

[b] R. Holland, " De Alpheo et Arethusa," in : *Commenta-
tiones Otto Ribbeck* (Leipzig 1888), 412-414. The writer of
this poem, like Colluthus and Triphiodorus, followed the
metrical rules of Nonnus less rigidly than Musaeus.

correspond well with Musaeus' training and interests. Procopius had correspondents in Alexandria, where he had studied in his youth. He may have met Musaeus there. If that is correct, then Musaeus was probably somewhat older than Procopius and an already recognized authority in the circle of scholars and orators of the time of Anastasius I. Under Justinian (527–565) Musaeus is quoted by Johannes Gazaeus, Paulus Silentiarius, epigrammatists such as Agathias and Macedonius Thessalonicensis II, and later by many Byzantine authors.

The Story of Hero and Leander

The lover who swims over water to join a beloved whom for some reason he cannot otherwise reach, and who finally meets his death in this way, is the subject of an ancient and widely distributed legend; its origin of course can hardly be pinpointed. But in the version about Hero and Leander it is a typical local legend,[a] tied to the special circumstances of its location on the Hellespont. In antiquity the narrowest point of the Hellespont was between Sestos and Abydos, although today this is only the second narrowest point as a result of coast-erosion. Strabo (64 B.C.–A.D. 19) in his *Geography* (13. 22. 591) describes the currents at that point.[b] Admittedly

---

[a] Fundamental is L. Malten, *Motivgeschichtliche Untersuchungen zur Sagenforschung III, Hero und Leander, RhM,* 93 (1949), 65-81, excepting only that he takes over without proof the *fable convenue* of a " Hellenistic source " and regards the rise of the story as likely in the third century B.C.

[b] Of these in Musaeus the only remaining mention is in the name Ἑλλήσποντος ἀγάρροος (208), which is a literary reminiscence of *Iliad* 2. 845 (*cf.* 12. 30); see explanatory note on line 4. On Musaeus' lack of observed detail see below.

INTRODUCTION

in the poetic versions as we have them by Ovid and
Musaeus the local topography is completely ignored,
except in one characteristic detail. The story takes
place at the tower of Hero. Strabo mentions this
tower, although in his time it was already a ruin
(Antipater, *A.P.* 7. 666. 2 sq.).[a] If there were perhaps
at an earlier date beacon-lights on various of the
promontories of the Hellespont (some of which were
crowned with temples), then the story of Hero is
especially linked with this tower because it was a
beacon-tower (Mus. 23 sq.). There is still today a
lighthouse at Abydos. The first lighthouse in anti-
quity was built about 280 B.C. on the Pharos off
Alexandria. Others were built later. Our story,
therefore, in the version we have, at least, seems to
stem at the earliest from the third century B.C. It is
moreover unlikely that the story arose as soon as the
lighthouse was built ; it is much more likely that
when the beacon on the lighthouse, like Hero's lamp,
had gone out, and the tower was abandoned, then a
new αἴτιον could be invented to explain the tower's
purpose, preserving only a rather vague memory
of its former beacon-fire. The story of Hero and
Leander may have become known to a poet from the
description of the abandoned tower by a local histor-
ian or a geographer ; the poet was on the look-out
for new material. The story is like those which
Parthenius collected in his small book for Cornelius
Gallus as material for poetic treatment (sometime
after 50 B.C.).

[a] What is now called " Leander's Tower " is on the Bos-
porus. It can only have been erroneously linked with this
story much later, when " Hero's Tower " was no longer
standing. For Antipater see below.

The earliest evidence for the story,[a] the Greek evidence included, all points to the Rome of the end of the Republic and the reign of Augustus. Virgil (*Georg.* 3. 258 sq.) and Horace (probably ; *Epist.* 1. 3. 3 sq.) allude to the story without naming Hero and Leander. They assume that the story is known to their readers. The first certain mention of the story in Greek poetry occurs in two epigrams about the Hellespont by Antipater of Thessalonica (*A.P.* 7. 666 ; 9. 215), who from about 13 B.C. was *cliens* of L. Calpurnius Piso Frugi, to whose sons Horace probably dedicated his *Ars poetica*.[b] Strabo too several times spent considerable periods in Rome between 44 B.C. and 7 B.C. The first detailed treatment of the story preserved is in Ovid's *Heroides* (Epistles 18 and 19).

In contrast to a few small differences in the detail of the narrative, there are some surprisingly close similarities of wording between Ovid and Musaeus. Since it is not likely that Musaeus used Ovid, scholars have wished to infer the existence of a common Hellenistic antecedent which both poets followed.[c] But most of the completely certain coincidences are

[a] The testimonia are collected and reprinted in H. Färber's edition, 30-91.

[b] C. Cichorius, *Römische Studien* (Leipzig/Berlin 1922), 325-332, and G. W. Bowersock, *Augustus and the Roman World* (Oxford 1965), 124 sq.

[c] This " reconstruction " was expressly described as such by E. Rohde, *Der griechische Roman und seine Vorläufer* (Leipzig 1876), 133 sq. ; then it was taken to greater lengths by J. Klemm, *De fabulae quae est de Herus et Leandri amoribus fonte et auctore* (Diss. Leipzig 1889) and G. Knaack, " Hero und Leander," in : *Festgabe F. Susemihl* (Leipzig 1896), 46-82, who tried to foist their " reconstructed " poems onto an Alexandrian poet (Callimachus). Later " reconstructions " rest on these, as, *e.g.*, that of E. Sittig, " Hero," *Real-Encyclopädie*, 8 (1913), 914 sq.

confined to the field of conventional elements in erotic narrative, and belong not to the content of this story but to usages found in love-stories elsewhere, which the two authors may easily have come upon independently.[a] So far no traces of this story are to be found in any known Hellenistic poet. Two severely damaged papyrus fragments of the Imperial period do not permit conclusions to be drawn about any older poem used as a model.[b] If then we must

---

[a] G. Schott, *Hero und Leander bei Musaios und Ovid* (Diss. Köln 1957), 80 sq., shows that Musaeus did not model himself on Ovid, and so does Kost, 19 sq. Among the coincidences between Ovid and Musaeus the most striking (Ov. *Epist.* 18. 148 " idem navigium, navita, vector ero " ⌣ Mus. 255, where however Musaeus also uses another known model, *i.e.* Nonn. *met. Jo.* 6. 83) certainly cannot be simply interpreted away, and so others also may point to a common model. But, considering the basic difference in literary genre between Ovid's elegiac letters and Musaeus' epyllion, from the few detailed points no further conclusions can be drawn about the nature of an original, which in any case is hardly to be looked for in genuine Hellenistic circles, but among Greek literati in Rome at the end of the Republic. Musaeus can hardly be used as evidence in its " reconstruction," not least because he has evidently completely transformed the story following other, known models ; see below. Schott indicates (pp. 113 sq.) that Musaeus did use many Hellenistic poets, in particular bucolic poets, as a source of verse-formulae ; these poets however nowhere mentioned Hero and Leander, any more than did Musaeus' other models. Even so Schott still seems to believe in a " Hellenistic " poem as a common model.

[b] In Pap. Oxy. 864 Fr. 6 (Vol. 6, p. 172), probably third century A.D., containing florilegia from various authors, none of the stories can be identified for certain ; the trimeters included should therefore not be ascribed to any given poet ; see R. Keydell, *Prolegomena*, 2 (1953), 139 sq. In Pap. Rylands 486 (Vol. 3, p. 98), probably first century A.D., there are incoherent scraps of ten hexameters (reprinted in Färber,

INTRODUCTION

reckon with a poetic treatment of the theme as the common source for familiarity with the content of the story of Hero and Leander, and for some of the formal coincidences of presentation in later Latin and Greek versions, then its author presumably was one of those Greeks, such as Parthenius, Antipater, Strabo, Dionysius of Halicarnassus and Caecilius of Calacte, who in the second half of the first century B.C. resided in Rome as guests or clients of members of refined society ; this may then account for the fact that it quickly came to the notice already of those Roman poets, such as Virgil, Horace and Ovid, who frequented the same circles.

The further witnesses for the story down to the second century A.D. are all Latin authors : the geographer Pomponius Mela, the poets Ovid, Lucan, Silius Italicus, Statius, Martial and the orator Fronto.

---

p. 30). The widely differing attempts at reconstruction by Roberts, Snell, Page, Colonna, Pasquali, and the suggestions of R. Merkelbach in Schott, *op. cit.* 56-69, are totally uncertain, and almost all start from the postulate that there was a " Hellenistic " Hero-Leander poem which must be reconstructed. It is certain that a character called Λάανδρος is twice mentioned ; he is addressed in the vocative (VV. 6, 9, *cf.* Mus. 86, 301) ; the Evening Star is also addressed in the vocative (V. 5 ; it is merely mentioned by Mus. at 111) ; the word τηλέσκοπος appears (V. 10, Mus. 237). Whether the form Λάανδρος, which is nowhere else used for the Leander of our poem (Λέανδρος, Λείανδρος ; note the etymology Λά-ανδρος from λᾱϜός : Bechtel, *Die historischen Eigennamen des Griechischen*, Halle 1917, 279), is a pseudo-archaism or an error of the scribe (C. H. Roberts, ed. pr.), or even whether it can be certain that it denotes our Leander, is impossible to decide. Certainly it was not a model for any version of the story known to us. (The form Λήανδρος occurs on coins of Severus Alexander (A.D. 222–235) : Kost 573, n. 54.)

INTRODUCTION

Latin authors also predominate as later witnesses down into the Middle Ages. Greek poets (as opposed to prose authors) [a] take up the story again only after Musaeus.[b] Knowledge of the story seems to have spread from Rome. Probably at the games given by Titus in A.D. 80 for the dedication of the Flavian Amphitheatre an aquatic mime was performed including Leander's swim (Mart. *Liber spectac.* 25),[c] and Fronto speaks to Marcus Aurelius of a "fabula histrionibus celebrata," clearly a popular mime, which did not please him (*Epist.* V. 241 v. d. Houten). The first pictorial representations [d] are in some houses of the "fourth style" (from the time of Nero) at Pompeii. Then follow individual scattered representations on small objects. Hero and Leander are more frequently shown on later imperial coins of the cities of Abydos and Sestos, and also on medallions and gems. By comparison with the well-known stories of the best of classical literature, the diffusion of the story is limited, and, as far as literary treatment is concerned, clearly restricted to a circle of connoisseurs and otherwise to interested inhabitants of the story's locality.

[a] There is mention of a Philostratus in the *Argumenta to Ovid's Heroides* of Antoninus Volscus (arg. xviii : 15th century, Färber, p. 84). On Ps.-Hippolytus Romanus see below.

[b] The *Cento* of Homer, *A.P.* 9. 381, ascribed by Stadtmüller to Leon Philosophus (*c.* A.D. 900), is certainly later than Musaeus (*cf.* V. 11 and Mus. 286).

[c] *Cf.* L. Friedländer, *M. Val. Martialis Epigrammaton Libri mit erklärenden Anmerkungen*, vol. 1 (Leipzig 1886), 134 sq.

[d] Now collected by C. Carcopino, Art. "Leandro" in *Enciclopedia dell'arte antica classica e orientale*, vol. 4 (1961), 515-517, and by Kost on Mus. 25, 246, 252, 254 sq., with notes.

INTRODUCTION

The Presentation of the Story in Musaeus' Poem

Unlike Ovid, Musaeus presents his story in a very straightforward manner. He uses none of the traditional artifices of epic composition (reminiscence, prediction, blended or parallel narratives), which were also especial favourites of love-literature ; he uses only pure narrative and direct speech. No secondary character is individualized ; the chronological sequence of events is strictly preserved without sudden transitions or overlapping.

The arrangement is transparently logical and orderly. An elaborate prooemium in two parts (1-15, 16-27) is followed by a treatment of the story in three parts (28-231, 232-288, 289-343) ; each of these three parts is divided in turn into a longish introduction (28-54, 232-255, 289-309), a main section (55-220, 256-283, 309-341) and a short conclusion (221-231, 284-288, 342-343). The transitions are not hidden but clearly marked by the formulas of introduction and conclusion.

In contrast to the practice of Nonnus,[a] Musaeus in the scene of the meeting of the two lovers uses direct speech to give them two pairs of speeches (123-127, 135-157 and 174-193, 203-220), following the traditional Homeric manner of representing a conversation, just as Quintus Smyrnaeus did before him and Colluthus after him. In addition he models the individual scenes of his love-story on literary antecedents which he fuses into a combined development. As for Imperial love-literature, there are striking adaptations from Achilles Tatius, whom Nonnus had used earlier. In this way too Musaeus

---

[a] *Cf.* Wifstrand, *op. cit.* (in note *a*, page 298), pp. 141-151; Triphiodorus too has the " Homeric " pairs of speeches.

clothes borrowings from Achilles' theory of love in Nonnian words. Achilles' influence can be seen particularly in the description of Hero's beauty (55–57 ∼ Ach. Tat. 1. 4. 2, cp. 4. 1. 8), in the development of the effects of love (92–98 ∼ Ach. Tat. 1. 4. 4), in the schematism of the description, contained there in the words of advice given by the slave Satyros, of the stages of their coming together (112 sq. ∼ Ach. Tat. 2. 4. 3 sq., cp. 4. 7. 8), in the reaction of the girl (120 sq. ∼ Ach. Tat. 1. 10. 6) and in the example of Omphale (150 sq. ∼ Ach. Tat. 2. 6. 1 sq.), even though Musaeus may perhaps have derived some of his adaptations indirectly through Nonnus.[a] But he uses Aristaenetus as well, and, like the parallels with passages in other ancient novels,[b] all confined to this first scene, most of these are stock motifs of love-literature which are so very common that it is difficult to infer the intentional echo of any particular work. For Hero's fall to her death he goes back to Lycophron's equally short account of the *Liebestod*

[a] *Cf.* Schott, *op. cit.* (in note *a*, page 305, above), 113 sq. Far more allusions than the ones quoted here can be found throughout Kost's commentary.

[b] Musaeus has in common with the schema of ancient novels only the first scene, the meeting of the lovers at a festival, for which Plato provided the common motifs. All the certain coincidences of wording with the commonplaces of love-literature are confined to this scene. The other motifs typical of the novel—forcible separation of the lovers, separate adventures, testing of the woman's chastity, ultimate union and marriage—are absent from Musaeus. His lovers come together without interruption right from the beginning, but end in death. On the common conception of love see Schott, *op. cit.* 118 sq., and note *b*, page 310. Parallels from other erotic literature are given by Ludwich on ll. 93 sq. and by Kost *passim*.

of Oenone (341 sq. ~ Lycophr. 65 sq.). But of the antecedents to which he expressly alludes by quotation there are two in particular that Musaeus used directly for the portrayal of his two characters and for his treatment of the story. The first is the arrival of Odysseus at the island of the Phaeacians in the *Odyssey* (Books 5 and 6).[a] Musaeus adapts his model with the events in a reversed sequence to suit his story : the meeting of Hero and Leander (Odysseus and Nausicaa)—Leander's swim (Odysseus in the sea)—the Storm. The second model is provided by the encounter and the experiences of the two lovers in Plato's *Phaedrus* (249 D sq.), to which already his erotic models point back in the portrayal of the effect of beauty, by way of the eyes, on the soul (Mus. 94 sq., cp. Ach. Tat. 1. 4. 4 etc., Pl. *Phaedr.* 251 B). Leander takes the role of the lover, Hero of the beloved. The reaction of the beloved as described by Plato (*Phdr.* 255 E) is the backbone of the story : " Like the lover [Mus. 84 sq.], though less passionately [Mus. 158 sq.], he desires to see his friend [Mus. 63 sq., 101 sq., 169 sq.], to touch him [Mus. 114 sq.], kiss him [Mus. 133] and lie down by him [Mus. 221 sq.]."[b] Musaeus alludes clearly and in detail to

[a] For more material on this see *Bemerkungen*, 31 sq., where also the grammatically learned " Homerisms " are collected ; and see below in the Explanatory Notes.

[b] Compare the schema of the " quinque lineae amoris " (in Greek the ἡδονῆς κλῖμαξ), significantly not precisely followed in Leander's case : visus, allocutio, tactus, osculum sive suavium, coitus ; E. R. Curtius, *Europäische Literatur und lateinisches Mittelalter* (2. Aufl., Bern 1954), 501. Plato's theory of love, with variations, is the basis of the novels, and in its turn itself goes back to older formulations ; *cf.* F. Lasserre, ἐρωτικοὶ λόγοι, *Mus. Helv.* 1 (1944), 169-178.

both his models at central points in his poem (Mus. 90 sq. ~ *Phdr.* 250 B sq., 255 C ; Mus. 135 sq. ~ *Od.* 6. 149 sq.). He plays upon or paraphrases further passages of his models at many other points. Where these two stories yield nothing to help his narrative, he falls back on other passages of his authors ; for example, for the union of the lovers (Mus. 260 sq.) he falls back on Odysseus and Penelope (*Od.* 23. 205 sq.) and Zeus and Hera (*Iliad* 14. 342 sq.), and for the self-sacrifice for love (Mus. 338 sq.) on the *Symposium* (Pl. *Smp.* 179 B sq.). He modelled especially on Plato his description of the experiences of the awakening and the growth of love, although he also uses words and expressions from Homer, the lyric poets, the tragedians, and later erotic literature up to, and including, Nonnus. Clearly Musaeus took over the story of Hero and Leander only in general outline, and then himself shaped it to a plan of his own based on these other literary antecedents.

The sections into which he breaks up his presentation of the story are strikingly disproportionate. He takes up 203 lines, almost two thirds of the whole poem, for the first section, the awakening of love (28 sq.), with the first meeting (30-108) and the conversation of the lovers (109-231). The second section, the union of the lovers, has only 56 lines, the third, with the successive deaths of the pair, only 54. He gave the lion's share to the least dramatic section, the first, which ends with mutual understanding but without direct action, while the most pathetic section, the third, is little more than sketched. The awakening of love is presented four times, in the first section in the young men (69 sq.), in Leander (86 sq.) and in Hero (158 sq.), in the second section again in Leander (239 sq.), while the emotions appropriate to the union of the lovers (266 sq.) and to the drowning of Leander (324 sq.) are not mentioned at all, and Hero's feelings before her suicide are barely hinted at (335 sq.).

Musaeus' Language and Style

The language in which Musaeus tells his story is highly elaborate and literary, but his turns of phrase are only in very few places original. That is intentional and corresponds to the literary taste of the time ; it is a learned style, and as such an entirely artificial mixture of elements which Musaeus drew from Nonnus and his other models and blended with each other. It includes words, forms and constructions which at this time were long since dead. For this reason, just as in Nonnus, a degree of uncertainty appears in the use of cases and moods, and occasional involuntary Byzantinisms escape Musaeus just as they escaped Nonnus. He proves himself to be a γραμματικός by the introduction of Homeric words in lost senses and of " glosses " based on recondite learned explanations.[a] His sentence-structures also seem

---

[a] I accept (against Schwabe and others until Kost) for πλῶε 229 the meaning " swam " and take this to be a conscious Homerism. Homer uses πλώειν only in the sense of " swim " as against πλέειν " to sail " (W. Schulze, *KZ*, 40 (1907), 120 sq.), whereas in later authors (including Nonn. *D.* 4. 115, 4. 244, 26. 177, 31. 91) πλώειν is used for sailing. Accordingly πλωτήρ 2 means " swimmer," not " sailor," as also in Opp. *H.* 2. 196 (fishes) and in Nonn. *D.* 23. 296 sq. (a dolphin), 23. 305 (a bull), and in those places where with swimming corpses (*D.* 25. 73, 39. 229) and swimming armour (*D.* 23. 107) he clearly hints at the sense of πλῶον in *Il.* 21. 302, although πλωτήρ means also " seaman " ; see Aristoph. *Eccl.* 1087.

occasionally to follow rare Homeric peculiarities. He
goes further in this than Nonnus. The ambition of
these *poetae docti* is never to introduce new words and
constructions except according to the recognized
rules, and their success, in which Musaeus richly
participated, was for these to be accepted and taken
over by later authors. Verbal citations were marks
of respect (Horace, *Ars poetica* 47 sq.).

In metre Musaeus is the most devoted follower of
Nonnus, whose intricate metrical rules he breaks
occasionally precisely at places where he is either
quoting models word for word, Homer above all,
or aiming at a special figure of style or assonance.
The metrical system of Nonnus, first reconstructed
step by step with laborious counter-checking by
modern scholars,[a] is an extension of the rules of the
refined Hellenistic metrics already practised in
Alexandria. In the late Imperial form of this metri-
cal system it is already the case that rules based on
accentuation hint at the changes in the pronunciation
of the spoken word which made themselves felt in
the historical development of the Byzantine and
Modern Greek languages. But essentially—like the
puristic but in the same way linguistically question-
able metrics of the "syllable-marking" Meister-
singer, or the much greater virtuosity of Baudelaire
and the young Verlaine—it is an artificial, pedantic
discipline modelled on classical works that reflected
an earlier state of the language; a discipline to
which poets of the importance of Crinagoras of
Mytilene, the creator of "court poetry" under Au-
gustus, and the epic poet Quintus of Smyrna did

[a] For the literature see *Bemerkungen*, 133 sq.; for the sys-
tem itself see page 329, note *b*, below.

not submit themselves, probably from choice. To this extent this metrical discipline is a peculiarity of a " school " of *poetae docti* who employed it with ostentatious pride as one weapon among others in their armoury of education peculiar to a γραμματικός. In a hexameter bound by these rules very few standardized metrical variations remain possible. " Overlong " composite words steadily gain the upper hand.[a] In the end, for all the euphony sought for and achieved, the result of the extreme regimentation is a striking monotony.

The shape of Musaeus' writing is dominated by his effort to adorn his diction with figures of style and assonance. Other considerations seem to be to a large extent subordinated to this. He cultivates devices for external assonance, anaphora, repeated words at sentence-, verse-, or colon-beginnings, alliteration, rhyming colon-, sentence- and verse-endings. He especially loves figures in word-order such as hyperbaton and chiasmus, and syntactical figures such as antithesis, parenthesis, and asyndeton in the speeches. Following a fashion of the period of Anastasius I which is especially strongly marked in Colluthus, the sentence is chopped into short cola in order to facilitate the introduction of these figures. Long sentences are produced by stringing short cola one on to another, their monotony being avoided by variations

---

[a] With H. Fränkel in his edition of Apollonius Rhodius and with P. Friedländer in his Paulus Silentiarius I think now (as against *Bemerkungen* 144, n. 90), that it is correct to write 67 περιπολλόν, 213 ὀψεδύοντα as one word, and accordingly 41 πυριπνείοντας, 216 and 309 βαρυπνείοντας (-τες), 333 ἐπαγρύπνοισιν. Perhaps even 204 πυριπαφλάζοιτο ought to be taken as one word. See the corresponding notes in the apparatus to the text.

in construction (*cf.* Mus. 1-13, 44-54, 84-89, 274-286).
The construction and intelligibility of a sentence are
often sacrificed to the decoration of details. In its
use of figures, its peculiarities of syntax and its spe-
cific commonplaces of love-literature, Musaeus' poem
strikingly resembles the *Declamations* of Procopius and
the display-speeches and poems of the other Ga-
zaeans.[a] Musaeus shares with them a manner in
which rare metaphors and similes are seldom so
thought out as to present a picture from life, but are
often combinations of disparate antecedents, and con-
sequently almost incomprehensible (*cf.* Mus. 56-66).[b]

A general lack of vividness and clarity is a domi-
nant feature of Musaeus' style, which is in sharp
contrast to the markedly naturalistic Hellenistic
epyllion and to the rhetorically detailed descriptive
passages of Nonnus, and is particularly striking when
his handling of such themes is compared with that
of his immediate antecedents in erotic literature.
Admittedly Musaeus employs long sections of his
short poem on descriptions of persons and things :
Hero (twice : 30-41, 55-68), the secret union (274-
283), winter (293-299) and the storm (309-319). Even
so there is not a single instance of a vivid detail. Of
Hero one hears only that she is radiant, roseate (a
mere simile) and lovely. In addition she is of dis-
tinguished descent (30), and her parents, who have
destined her to be a priestess, are three times men-
tioned (125, 180, 190)—but who are they ? We never
actually hear their names. Leander is made to give
his name and country (185) ; he confines himself to
doing just that (209, 220) though the reader knows

---

[a] Material in : *Bemerkungen*, 137 sq., 17, 21 sq.
[b] *Cf.* Seitz, *op. cit.* (in note *a*, page 300), 41 sq.

both already, with no extra information about his father or his family. Of Abydos, Sestos, the festival, the temple of Aphrodite, the tower and the chamber of Hero, the Hellespont and its shores we are given not the slightest picture. Leander, who takes part in the festival as a " citizen of neighbouring Abydos " (50, 208 sq.), is subsequently, despite this information, described without correction as " a wanderer, a stranger and not to be trusted " (177 sq.) and " a roaming alien" (181, cf. 337); all this fitted Odysseus better. The Hellespont, which is narrow enough to allow Leander to see the lamp on the opposite shore and to swim across (238 sq.), is regularly described as the " sea " (16, 32, 190, 206, 234, 245 etc.), and at the end Hero searches for him " over the broad back of the sea " (336=Il. 2. 159). The description of the night of love in the tower consists solely of a lengthy enumeration of all that is lacking to make it a true marriage (274-283).

The Poem as a Christian Neoplatonist Allegory

Several of the features of this poem that are strange from a poetic point of view—the logical schematism of the arrangement, the disproportion of the parts, the total lack of vividness in the presentation and the frequent repetitions and variations of the same motifs—are probably to be explained as technical requirements for the conveyance of a " higher " meaning which Musaeus concealed allegorically beneath the surface of the love-story he narrated. This is not the place to justify this interpretation or even to present it in detail ; a full-scale commentary would be necessary.[a] A few hints must suffice.

In using a love-story for the symbolic representation of transcendental truths Musaeus stands in a long tradition, richly documented at an early date on pagan and Christian sarcophagi. A literary witness, not far removed in time, is the anonymous Christian-Neoplatonist interpreter of Heliodorus' novel about the lovely Chariclea ; his work is cast in the form of a reported " Platonic " dialogue.[b] In the " Ovidius moralizatus " of the Latin Middle Ages Ovid's frivolous love-stories are given an edifying interpretation which makes them suitable for the adornment of Christian cathedrals.[c]

Hero and Leander appear first to figure in allegory in a list of mythological names contained in an account of the vulgar-gnostic Christian sect of the Perates given in the *Refutatio Omnium Haeresium* which used to be ascribed to Hippolytus Romanus (p. 110. 8-13 Wendland).[d] These names are associ-

[a] I am preparing a book on this subject.

[b] Text : " Fragmentum Marcianum " ed. R. Hercher, *Hermes*, 3 (1869), 382-388 ; see K. Praechter, *Die Philosophie des Altertums* (Ueberweg-Praechter, 12. Aufl. 1926), 671 sq. ; *cf.* H. Dörrie, " Die griechischen Romane und das Christentum," *Philologus*, 93 (1938), 273-276.

[c] On the depiction of the story of Pyramus and Thisbe (Ov. *Met.* 4. 55-166) on the capital of a column in the ambulatory of the Münster at Basle (end of the twelfth century) see A. Goldschmidt, *Der Albanipsalter in Hildesheim und seine Beziehung zur symbolischen Kirchenskulptur des XII. Jahrhunderts* (Berlin 1895), 72 sq. ; O. Immisch, " Pyramus und Thisbe " in Roscher's *Mythologisches Lexikon* 3. 1 (1897–1909), 3340. Thisbe=the soul, Pyramus=the healer, the wall=original sin, the lion=the devil ; and a life is sacrificed for love.

[d] This work, which was ascribed first to Origen, then to

317

ated with Ἔρως as " intermediary " (δύναμις μέση)
in the heavenly hierarchy. As a Christian Neoplaton-
ist Musaeus belongs to a line whose most consider-
able representatives in Alexandria were Clement,
Origen and Synesius, and in which the Pseudo-
Dionysius Areopagita took his place probably not
much later. The name Musaeus is otherwise rare,
but is that of the mythical singer from Eleusis often
mentioned by Plato and regarded by the Neoplaton-
ists as the pupil or son of Orpheus ; it could be a
deliberately chosen pseudonym.[a]

Musaeus used Homer and Plato as models in the
composition of his poem. We have good information
about the contemporary Neoplatonic interpretation
of these authors, in particular from the commentary
of Proclus on Plato's *Republic*, which goes into detail
on Homer, and from the commentary of Hermias of
Alexandria on Plato's *Phaedrus*. How Homer and
Plato under their Neoplatonic interpretations were
in turn used in the poetic presentation of Neopla-

Hippolytus (antipope against Callistus in A.D. 218), is
probably not by the latter, but was used by him in the
composition of a work of his own of which a fragment
survives ; see P. Nautin, *Hippolyte contre les hérésies,
fragment, étude et édition critique* (=ét. et textes pour
l'histoire du dogme de la trinité 2, Paris 1949), 19-39.

[a] This was suggested to me in conversation by the late
P. Von der Mühll of Basle. From Kost, p. 16, n. 22, who
does not approve of the suggestion, I learn now that it had
already been made by Guil. Canter, *Novarum lectionum libri
VIII* (Antwerp 1571), 55 sq., and later by U. v. Wilamowitz-
Moellendorff, *Die griechische Literatur und Sprache* (Leip-
zig/Berlin 1912), 219, E. Sittig, *op. cit.* (in note c, page
304), 910, and F. Norwood, *Hermathena*, 50 (1937), 240
and *Phoenix*, 4 (1950), 9. Testimonia in O. Kern, *Orphi-
corum Fragmenta* Berlin 1922), 50 sq., 166-172.

tonic doctrine can be seen from the *Hymns* and *Epigrams* of Proclus.[a]

Allegorical composition rests on the theory accepted already by Origen, that every serious text must be interpreted on three levels of understanding. Beyond the superficial level, the second is the " moral " level. On that level love is interpreted as the love found in marriage (*cf.* Mus. 220, 274 sq.). Plutarch in his *Amatorius* had already re-interpreted Plato's *Phaedrus* in this way. But the highest and most important level is the " theoretical," that is to say, theological, interpretation. On this level, the three sections of the poem represent the life of a philosophical soul—Leander—according to the pattern which the Neoplatonists found in the *Phaedrus*. The first part (28-231) represents the soul's life in heaven before birth, in which it is by its original vision of its own god chosen and called to follow him in the heavenly procession ; the second part (232-288) is its life on earth, where recollection effected through love leads it to exaltation and mystic union with its god ; the third part (289-343) is its release from the chains of the body and the foreshadowing of its reward in the afterlife in the highest and culminating union with God. Neoplatonically interpreted this refers to the " first birth " (πρώτη γένεσις ; Mus. 44 sq.) from the " origin " (ἀρχή) to the place of the " allotting " (λῆξις) of the god whom the soul follows (Mus. 55 sq.), where it follows him first in its " abiding " (μονή ; Mus. 84 sq.), then is brought to its real " birth " (γένεσις) into the material world in his

[a] Parallels in the hymns in E. Vogt, *Procli Hymni* (=Klassisch-philologische Studien, 18, Wiesbaden 1957), in the epigrams in T. Gelzer, *Mus. Helv.* 23 (1966), 1-36.

INTRODUCTION

" procession " (πρόοδος ; Mus. 227 sq.) ; from the material world, through the " inspiration " (ἐνθουσιασμός) which comes with " recollection " (ἀνάμνησις ; Mus. 232 sq.), it can return to the " reversion " (ἐπιστροφή ; Mus. 251 sq.) which consists in a mystic vision (Mus. 272 sq.) until in the end it achieves complete and final unity with its origin—" reinstatement " (ἀποκατάστασις ; Mus. 289 sq., 343 ; cf. Procl. in Tim. 3. 291. 6 sq. ; Herm. in Phdr. 89. 8 sq.). Musaeus clearly takes these experiences of the soul from the life of the Christian " inspired philosopher " as it is lived by an ascetic monk, according already to Macarius the Egyptian († c. 390), St. Gregory of Nyssa († 394) and later on to Nylus of Ancyra († c. 430), Theodoretus of Cyrrhus († 438) and others. The call (42 sq.), the choosing (84 sq.), the instruction (123 sq.), the illumination (234 sq.), baptism with fire and water (244 sq.), consecration (256 sq.), mystic exaltation (268 sq.) and redemption (293 sq.) are thus represented with the help of a system of complicated equivalences produced by exegesis between concepts and formulae of very diverse origins ; these equivalences cannot be fully expounded here.

The central point is naturally the meaning of love. Other important notions include the light (Mus. 224, cf. St. John 1. 4 sq.) that shines in the darkness (Mus. 211, 227 sq., 238 sq., 309 sq.), represented here by Hero's lamp (Mus. 6 sq., 210 sq., 236 sq.). All the events take place by night (3, 109 sq., 230 sq., 282 sq., 309 sq.) ; day rules only at the beginning (44 sq., the " origin ") and at the end (335 sq., the " redemption "). The lamp guides Leander's life (25, 218, 239 sq., 256 sq.) and as a witness (1, 223, 236 ; μαρτυρίη) it spreads the message (6 sq., 222, 235 sq. ;

ἀγγελίη) of heavenly love (8 sq., 40). The catalogue of those who flock together from all over the world to the festival represents the mass of the Called (Mus. 44 sq. ~ Ps.-Apollinarius, *met. Psalm. προθ.* 63 sq., the catalogue of the peoples on the occasion of the miracle of Pentecost). Many young men fall in love with Hero (Mus. 69 sq.), but only one, Leander (86 sq.), finds his love returned (221 sq.). He is the soul " which best follows after God and is most like him " (Pl. *Phdr.* 248 A i sq., cp. Mus. 112 sq.) and at its first birth " is to be a philosopher and a lover of beauty " (*Phdr.* 248 D 1 sq.). Alone among that number he is initiated into the highest mysteries and admitted to the supreme vision (*Phdr.* 249 C 3 sq., Herm. *in Phdr.* 172. 5 sq., Mus. 272 sq.), as, in the parable of the wedding-feast that represents the Kingdom of Heaven (Matth. 22. 2 sq., cp. Mus. 42 sq.), it is said of those invited to the feast (Matth. 22. 9 sq., cp. Mus. 44 sq.) " For many are called, but few are chosen " (Matth. 22. 14, cp. Pl. *Phaedo* 69 c). The other young men are " the other souls " who " follow after [cp. Mus. 72], all yearning for the upper region but unable to reach it " (Pl. *Phdr.* 248 A, cp. Mus. 80 sq.). The marriage that is not a marriage (274 sq.) signifies the mystery of this love (142 sq.). The mystic ineffability of this union which is set in the highest region and is perceptible only to the pure *Noûs* is represented by means of a precise imitation of the paradoxes through which St. Gregory Nazianzenus expresses the mystic double nature of Christ (Mus. 274 sq. ~ Greg. Naz. *carm.* 1. 1, 2, 62 sq., *P.G.* 37. 406, cp. Matth. 22. 42 sq.).[a] The

---

[a] This immediate model, which is especially interesting for the Christian-Neoplatonic interpretation of this poem, was

321

tower by the water (Mus. 24 sq., 32, 187 sq., 335 sq.)
is the Church (*Pastor Hermae*, vis. 3. 2. 4 sq.), and
on the top of the tower, in the height of heaven
(187, 260), the vision of the *unio mystica* in the realm
of the mind (νοῦς) of God (273) is represented as a
ἱερὸς γάμος (Mus. 272 sq., *cf.* *Il.* 14. 342 sq. with
Proclus, *in Remp.* 1. 132-141). The three interme-
diaries, ἔρως (Mus. 240 sq.), the light of truth (Mus.
234 sq., *cf.* Pl. *Rep.* 508, 532 B, *Tim.* 39 B, cp. Procl.
in Alc. 33. 14 sq., 153. 4 sq.) and silence, the symbol
of belief (Mus. 261, 280, *cf.* Procl. *Theol. Plat.* 4. 9,
p. 193. 52 sq.) lead the soul purified of all that is
material (Mus. 264 sq.) to the vision in the place
ruled by night, the symbol of truth in the " region
above the heavens " (Pl. *Phdr.* 247 c sq. ; Mus. 282,
cf. Herm. *in Phdr.* 147. 16 sq.). At the redemption
the last coverings fall away, namely love, the light
of belief, and the soul, which are all only " interme-
diaries " (Mus. 14 sq., 329 sq. ; *cf.* Procl. *in Alc.* 30.
18 sq., 43. 7 sq., 51. 8 sq.), so that only the highest,
most primordial and godlike element of the soul
remains (Herm. *in Phdr.* 157. 5 sq.). The help given
by God to this ὁμοίωσις θεῷ (Pl. *Theaet.* 176 B, cp.
Herm. *in Phdr.* 101. 16) is represented by the ἐπ-
αποθνήσκειν (Pl. *Smp.* 179 D sq.) of Hero, who like-
wise strips herself of her last covering χιτών (340 sq.,
cf. Procl. *in Alc.* 138. 12) before the two finally reach
their culminating union (342 sq., *cf.* Procl. *in Alc.*
247. 9 sq.).

---

discovered by Kost, 484, who, by adducing it, explained the
use, foreign to Nonnus' practice, of the two ἀλλ' in the same
verse (see note *d*, page 298, above). We can now understand,
I think, why Musaeus chose to follow this example in spite
of the metre.

INTRODUCTION

The Influence of Musaeus in Modern Times [a]

Musaeus' poem already enjoyed very high esteem in Italy in the fifteenth century, as the large number of manuscripts from that period demonstrates. It was often used as an introduction to Greek literature.[b] Musaeus was often identified, as he himself probably intended, with the archaic poet of Eleusis. In Venice Aldus deliberately printed Μουσαῖον τὸν παλαιότατον ποιητήν before all the other classical authors.[c] Julius Caesar Scaliger, in his famous rationalistic *Poetics*, set Musaeus far above Homer and Orpheus.[d] But Isaac Casaubon and then Scaliger's son Joseph rightly placed him with Nonnus and Paulus Silentiarius. Two printings, one by Aldus with a Latin translation of his own,[e] one by Fran-

---

[a] Bibliography on the later influence of Musaeus since M. H. Jellinek, *Die Sage von Hero und Leander in der Dichtung* (Berlin 1890) is given in her edition by E. Malcovati, v sq., xvi–xxiii, with additions by her in *Athenaeum*, n.s. 40 (1962), 368 sq., by R. Keydell, *Prolegomena*, 2 (1953), 140, V. Galiano, *Emerita*, 19 (1951), 328 sq. (Spanish literature), H. Färber in his edition 98 sq., Orsini xxv sq., Kost 69–85 and throughout his commentary.

[b] Cf. D. J. Geanakoplos, *Greek Scholars in Venice* (Cambridge, Mass. 1962), 40 sq., 117, 120 sq., 237 sq.

[c] A. Firmin-Didot, *Alde Manuce et l'hellénisme à Venise* (Paris 1875), 55 sq., and note *e*, below.

[d] J. C. Scaliger, *Poëtices libri VII* (Leyden 1561), 214; Scaliger compares many individual passages or lines, among them rightly Mus. 135 sq. with *Od.* 6. 149 sq.

[e] Prof. M. Sicherl informs me that the Latin version is not the work of Marcus Musurus, as has been hitherto assumed (*e.g.* by Geanakoplos, *op. cit.* (in note *b*, above), pp. 120 sq.); the MS. sent to the printers, which is now among the papers of Beatus Rhenanus at Sélestat (101, 2), is demonstrably the translator's own draft, and the handwriting shows it is by Aldus Manutius himself. On the printing of this edition see note *a*, page 342, below.

cesco de Alopa in Florence with a text by Janus
Lascaris, secured a rapid distribution for the poem
before the end of the fifteenth century. The story
had long been known from Ovid, and is preserved in
medieval vernacular versions in Italian, Dutch and
German. But from the sixteenth century onwards
translations and adaptations of Musaeus appear in
most European literatures. There appeared almost
simultaneously in Spain a " Historia de Leandro y
Hero " by Juan Boscán Almogáver (1540), in France
a free adaptation by Clément Marot (1541) and in
Germany the rhyming tale by Hans Sachs " Die
unglückhafft Lieb Leandri mit Fraw Ehron " (1541).
In Italy Bernardo Tasso, the father of Torquato,
published a paraphrase in 1555. Towards the end of
the century in England Christopher Marlowe began
a baroque poem of enormous conception, " Hero and
Leander," of which by 1592 he had completed two
cantos. After his death George Chapman completed
it with four more " Sestiads " (2376 lines altogether)
and published it in 1598. In subsequent periods the
theme was treated in a great variety of poetic forms :
ballads, epics, plays, and also in parodies and traves-
ties [a] ; in musical form in operas, cantatas, melo-
dramas, ballets ; and finally in the visual arts. In
Italy it became fashionable to publish versions of
Musaeus on the occasion of great weddings.

But of the countless treatments in all languages a
few works by celebrated poets may be selected for
mention. Friedrich Schiller in 1801 composed a
Ballade of 260 lines, " Hero und Leander," rhetori-
cally ornamented with learned trimmings. The

[a] Cf., e.g., E. Segal on Góngora's satirical poem, Com-
parative Literature, XV. 4 (1963).

INTRODUCTION

tragedy in five acts, " Des Meeres und der Liebe Wellen " (Waves of the Sea and of Love : 1831), into which Franz Grillparzer interwove many religious and philosophical themes of his own, alludes in its title to its origin in Musaeus (Mus. 245 sq.). Lord Byron made the story famous in another way. To match Leander himself, he swam the Hellespont in an hour and ten minutes on 3 May 1810, though admittedly by day and in the direction of Leander's return crossing, already noted by Strabo to be the easier direction. He displayed his pride in this sporting achievement in a poem " Written after Swimming from Sestos to Abydos," in several letters, and in allusions in his " Bride of Abydos " (canto 2, stanza 1) and " Don Juan."

Hermann Koechly used Latin to express a careful judgement on Musaeus' poem [a] which elegantly appraises the charm of the story as it is handled by Musaeus. The last part of this has been quoted countless times since : " Though the poem is not free from the faults of its time, nor from the empty bombast of the school of Nonnus, nevertheless it has great charm and life, and breathes an air of the frenzy of passionate love. It may not unjustly be called the last rose of the fading garden of Greek literature."

Far below the heights of literature, the theme of the rash swimmer who against all odds sought his beloved across the water occupied the imagination of composers and singers in almost all tongues throughout Europe from Sweden to Italy and from

[a] H. Koechly, *De Musaei grammatici codice Palatino* (Festgabe Philologenversammlung Heidelberg 1865=Opuscula philologica I (Leipzig 1881), 447-468), vii.

Ireland to the Ukraine. In the broad stream of traditional folk-poetry dependence on Musaeus can of course no longer be demonstrated. The German ballad traceable from the sixteenth century inspired Engelbert Humperdinck to compose his fairy-opera " Die Königskinder " (with libretto by E. Rosner), which had its world première in New York in 1910.

II. Transmission, Treatment and Editing of the Text

The Transmission of the Poem

Modern editions are based on the collations of : Hermann Koechly, who described the ms. P and thereby cleared up most of the problems of the poem's orthography [a] ; Carl Dilthey, who for his edition employed collations of 16 mss. (partly made by others) and based his text on four of them (B, V, NP) ; Arthur Ludwich, who described 26 mss. and two *editiones principes* (likewise partly from other scholars' collations), classified them in a *stemma* [b] and published a selection of their readings in his edition (1912) ; and recently of P. Orsini, who was able to verify from photographs some uncertain readings of four mss. (BVNA), and of K. Kost who collated again two mss. (VH) and the *editiones principes*.[c] The present edition is not based on any collations of my own. A. Ludwich published the Scholia in B from a collation by T. W. Allen.[d]

Ludwich's classification of the mss. is now gener-

[a] H. Koechly, *op. cit.* (in note *a*, page 325, above).

[b] A. Ludwich, *op. cit.* (in note *b*, page 297, above), p. 11.

[c] P. Orsini in his edition, xxxv sq., K. Kost, 64.

[d] A. Ludwich, *Scholia Graeca in Musaei carmen* (Vorlesungsverzeichnis, Königsberg Sommer 1893).

ally accepted ; he showed that the older MSS. represent a three-branched tradition, as follows : (1) B with its copy F1 (lines 250-343) ; (2) P and N, which are copies of a common ancestor ; (3) V. None of these branches gives the whole poem ; in none of them do the lines that each transmits stand in the same order as in any other branch.[a] The readings of the archetype must be reconstructed so far as possible from these older MSS. There are also a greater number of humanist MSS. of the fifteenth and sixteenth centuries.[b] These are all contaminated from different branches of the tradition. Some of them show considerable agreements with the Aldine *editio princeps* ; this whole group goes back essentially to the B-branch. Others go back to a damaged ancestor (lines 1-245 only) which was closely related

[a] Nevertheless PN and V have lines 331 sq., which are missing in B, while B has 325, which is missing in PN and V. PN and V therefore, which are also all written with two lines of the poem to each line of the MS., go back eventually to a common *hyparchetype*. This is not recognized in Kost's sketch of a stemma, p. 57. Kost gives in addition (pp. 63 sq.) throughout his apparatus criticus (although not in his commentary) only the readings of P, and not those of N, on the ground that these two witnesses are very similar. But there is no sufficient ground for preferring either one of these certainly very similar but not identical manuscripts, which represent together one common ancestor. In order to make the apparatus criticus more lucid one ought to indicate the common readings of P and N by a *siglum* denoting this common ancestor, and probably those of PN and V by one denoting the *hyparchetype*. But this will be possible only when all three of them have been systematically recollated for that purpose.

[b] Since Ludwich's researches a few additional *mutili* have come to light ; see *Bemerkungen*, 132, n. 25. Kost (p. 580, n. 173) gives a list of twelve MSS. which were not yet known to Ludwich.

to V. Lascaris' *editio princeps* shows influences of both the B and the PN group. Finally there is a whole series of MSS. copied from ancestors that are preserved, whether from MSS. or from early printings. The *eliminatio codicum* proves therefore that the text must be based on the readings of MSS. B, PN and V as representatives of the three branches of the tradition. Carl Dilthey and Enrica Malcovati have maintained this correctly. The contaminated humanistic MSS. and the *editiones principes* cannot be used to reconstruct the archetype ; their good readings are nevertheless humanists' conjectures which deserve mention as such [a] ; these MSS. must therefore be reported selectively so far as they are known. The copies of preserved ancestors can be left completely aside.

The tradition is bad. At least 25 errors in the

[a] R. Keydell, *Prolegomena*, 2 (1953), 138 and *Gnomon*, 41 (1969), 738 sq., and K. Kost, 56, emphasize that the " good readings " of the later MSS. and of the editions of Aldus and Lascaris which do not appear in BPNV could not all be treated as conjectures but should be based on independent tradition. They assume thereby that these improvements imply a knowledge of Nonnus which is more than one could expect from scholars of the XVth century. But the minutiae on which this assumption rests seem to me in themselves insufficiently good evidence. In addition the relative interdependence of these late witnesses is still too little understood for us to be able to ascertain, even approximately, at what point such readings as are independent of the four old manuscripts could perhaps have entered the tradition as we have it, or even for us to be able to characterize as such a supposed independent branch of the tradition. Until greater clarity can be achieved on this point we must in any case continue to use the same eclectic procedure as before in the selection of such variants, whether it is a question of humanist conjectures or perhaps after all of an older independent tradition.

archetype must be reckoned with in 343 lines. Errors become especially frequent towards the end of the poem ; the archetype seems to have been unreadable or damaged here. But the scribes of the older MSS. seem in most cases to have let the errors stand as they found them, so that the presence of the error can be detected and the error relatively easily corrected. The most essential tool for correction is comparison with the other authors whom Musaeus cites or who cite Musaeus. Next in importance is recognition of Musaeus' special learning as a γραμματικός; its influence can often be detected in his use of strikingly learned points.[a] Part of this learning is Nonnian metrics, though Musaeus diverges from the Nonnian rules on identifiable grounds.[b] Recourse

---

[a] Some material in *Bemerkungen*, 33 sq. G. Giangrande, *JHS*, 89 (1969), 139 sq., pays special attention to this question also, but I do not feel myself able to follow him in all his conclusions.

[b] The metrical rules of Nonnus are now comprehensively described by R. Keydell, *Nonni Panopolitani Dionysiaca* vol. 1 (Berlin 1959), 35*-42* ; *cf.* A. Scheindler, " Metrische und sprachliche Untersuchungen zu Musaios' ' de Hero et Leandro,' " *Ztsch. f. die österr. Gymnasien*, 28 (1877), 161-177 ; for divergences of Musaeus from Nonnus see Wifstrand, *op. cit.* (in note *a*, page 298), 131 sq., 193 sq. and *passim*. The presentation of the rules takes up about eight pages in Keydell. The most important, given according to the terminology of P. Maas, *Griechische Metrik* (3rd ed. Leipzig 1929 ; translated as *Greek Metre* by H. Lloyd-Jones, Oxford 1962, corrected reprint 1966), are as follows. For the calculation of word-lengths not only single words, but also " word-groups " with internal relationships, such as preposition and noun, or epithet and proper name, must be taken into account. There are no lines with spondees in the fifth foot. Every line has a principal caesura, usually " feminine " ; where there is a " masculine " caesura there is a secondary caesura after the fourth longum or after the fourth

biceps or after both, but not after the fifth longum ; where there is a feminine caesura there is seldom a secondary caesura after the fourth or the fifth longum. In the first half of the line words that begin before the second longum, where there is a masculine caesura never, and where there is a feminine caesura, seldom, end after the first syllable of the second biceps where this is disyllabic. Monosyllables stand at the end of the line only when a bucolic diaeresis precedes. Word-end is generally avoided after the first brevis of the fourth dactyl and after the second and fourth biceps if these consist of a single syllable. Disyllables with two long syllables seldom stand with their second syllable as a longum ; not at the second longum when the first is a noun, virtually never at the fourth. Two spondaic words can only follow each other in the same line if they are separated by the masculine caesura. Words consisting of a single long syllable stand neither in a biceps, nor at the third, fourth or sixth longum ; at the first longum only when there is a secondary caesura before the principal caesura, at the fifth when there is punctuation after the bucolic diaeresis. Words of more than one syllable at the end of the line usually have long final syllables. Words of two or more syllables at the end of the line are paroxytone or perispomena, never proparoxytone or oxytone (except αὐτός, αὐτόν). Before the masculine caesura stand as a rule paroxytones, seldom perispomena ; before the feminine caesura no oxytone stands unless there is a secondary caesura after the second longum. Lengthening of short final syllables by position never occurs in the biceps, never in third or fifth longum, seldom in the sixth, in the second and fourth never after a monosyllabic biceps, and after a disyllabic biceps only occasionally in words of three or more syllables. Nouns in -οι and -αι are similarly treated except at the beginning of the line. Short final vowels with a consonant are never lengthened by position in any biceps except the first, though in monosyllabic words also in the second ; in the longum seldom after a monosyllabic biceps except in trisyllabic oxytones and perispomena at the beginning of the line. Νῦ ephelkustikon is almost never used for position-making. Hiatus, shortening of vowel before vowel, and elision are limited to a few traditional examples. Nonnus himself breaks these rules when he quotes classical predecessors such as Homer *et al.* and on other determinate grounds.

to the relevant parallels and learned interpretations is therefore essential for the restoration of the text, and occasionally even for the simple comprehension of it. The parallels and learned interpretations are often more important than the variants in the MSS.

Editions

Since the Renaissance Musaeus has been very frequently republished ; at least 77 editions, to my knowledge, appeared before the edition by C. Dilthey.[a] E. Patzig investigated the relationships between the older editions.[b] After the two *editiones principes* by Aldus Manutius and Janus Lascaris the following are the most important :

Demetrius Dukas, Cretensis, Alcalá (Complutum) 1514.

Johannes Froben, Basle 1518 (with Latin translation).

Henricus Stephanus, Geneva 1566 (in : *Poetae Graeci principes heroici carminis et alii nonnulli*, pars 2, 419-427, with variants in the margin ; his text is based on the Lascaris edition and is the foundation of all later editions).

He treats the rules less strictly in his *Paraphrase of St. John* than in the *Dionysiaca*. Musaeus diverges from them occasionally according to principles of his own. I have discussed the individual cases in *Bemerkungen* ; literature is cited there pp. 135 sq. ; on Musaeus' metrics see *ibid.* pp. 38 sq. ; and page 343, note *b*, below, and Kost 53 sq.

[a] Kost, 592 sq., counts 52 editions and 81 additional printings of texts before Dilthey in a list which completes mine but itself contains a few omissions by comparison with mine.

[b] M. J. E. Patzig, *De Musaei grammatici emendatione* (Diss. Leipzig 1870), 4-12.

INTRODUCTION

Andreas Papius, Antwerp 1575.

Daniel Pareus, Frankfurt 1627 (with Latin translation, detailed commentary with parallel passages from other poets, especially Nonnus, and index).

David Whitford, London 1655 (and 1659) (Musaeus with Bucolic poets, with Latin translation).

Joh. Heinrich Kromayer, Halle-Magdeburg 1721 (2nd ed. Leipzig 1725, 3rd ed. Gotha 1731) (Musaeus with the Ovidian letters with an introduction, notes by C. Barth, Weitz, Voëtius, Heumann, Schoettgen, Gesner, Bergler, Groebel, and an index ; collected results of earlier scholarship).

Matthias Röver, Leyden 1737 (introduction, Latin translations [by several hands], notes, scholia printed for the first time, readings from seven MSS. [often falsely reported, according to Dilthey], and index).

Joh. Schrader, Leeuwarden 1742 (2nd, enlarged edition by Gottfr. Heinr. Schaefer, Leipzig 1825) (with conjectures by Peter Francius, notes, animadversiones ; text based on Röver).

Ludw. Heinr. Teucher, Leipzig 1789 (2nd ed. Leipzig 1795, 3rd ed. Halle 1801).

Carl Friedrich Heinrich, Hanover 1793 (with notes ; text based on Röver).

Franz Passow, Leipzig 1810 (introduction, fragments of the Eleusinian Musaeus, German translation, critical notes ; text based on Heinrich).

F. S. Lehrs, Paris 1840 (2nd ed. 1862), publ. by A. Firmin Didot (in : *Hesiodi carmina* etc., with Latin translation ; text based on Passow, with corrections by other scholars).

INTRODUCTION

A broader basis of MSS. classified according to modern scholarly methods is employed in the following scholarly editions (listed with some important reviews) :

Carl Dilthey, Bonn 1874, with a complete index. (The preface, written after the printing of the text, contains many additional proposals for emendations. Review : K. Lehrs, *Jenaer Literaturzeitung*, 1 (1874), 508 sq.)

Ludwig v. Schwabe, Tübingen 1874 (=*Festgabe Philologenversammlung " De Musaeo Nonni imitatore liber "* ; text based on Dilthey with emendations of Schwabe's own ; introduction ; huge collection of parallel passages from Nonnus and others ; excellent observations on language, metre, word-formation etc. Review : E. Rohde, *Jenaer Literaturzeitung*, 4 (1877), 206 sq.)

Arthur Ludwich, Bonn 1912 (photog. reprint Berlin 1929) (=Kleine Texte für Vorlesungen und Uebungen, hsg. v. H. Lietzmann, 98) (introduction, text with select variants and scholia ; much other material ; Ovid's two Epistles. Review : H. Tiedke, *BPhW*, 33 (1913), 1185 sq.)

Enrica Malcovati, Milan 1947 (introduction, text with Italian translation and notes. Review : R. Keydell, *Prolegomena*, 2 (1953), 137 sq.)

Hans Färber, Munich 1961 (with German translation ; text without apparatus but with brief critical notes based on Ludwich and Malcovati ; complete collection of testimonia for the Hero-Leander story ; abundant notes. Review : H. Hunger, *AAHG*, 15 (1962), 224 sq.)

Pierre Orsini, Paris 1968 (introduction, text with

French translation, notes ; verbose and not always trustworthy but with some good details. Reviews : R. Keydell, *Gnomon*, 41 (1969), 738 sq. and G. Giangrande, *JHS*, 89 (1969), 139 sq.)

Karlheinz Kost, Bonn 1971 (with introduction, text, and German translation, commentary, appendix with bibliography and list of earlier editions, 612 pp.).[a]

---

[a] No review of Kost's edition has yet been published ; I propose therefore to make on his text and apparatus a few points of significance for its use in the preparation of this edition. His text is not meant to be a substitute for a new critical edition, but only to constitute a basis for his interpretation ; it does not quite reach the standard of his commentary. He too has not carried out a new collation of all the MSS., and gives in his apparatus only a selection of manuscript variants according to the principles of Dilthey and Malcovati, but even more limited than theirs. In the classification (see note *a*, page 327) and evaluation (see note *a*, page 328), of the manuscripts he comes in a few points to different conclusions from those suggested here. He deliberately keeps his apparatus short. In the apparatus not all the readings are reported which he then quotes and discusses in his commentary, so that one must always look there too. In particular the following important readings which are reported by Ludwich (or Orsini) do not appear in his apparatus : on l. 228 μή τι Ω μήδε B μὴ δὲ T μὴ PN (only p. 429 μήδε B μὴ PN) ; on l. 270 δ' Ω (δὲ T) θ' E τ' Ald. (only p. 476 his choice " τ' mit Ald. (θ' E ; δὲ T) " but nowhere δ' Ω, while otherwise he always carefully indicates the variations between τε and δέ) ; on ll. 319 sq. Ludwich's indication that ll. 319-321 in PN are after 328, with Orsini's additional information that 319-320 are missing and 321 is written after 328 in N[1] ; on 325 from Ludwich's and Orsini's note " om. PNVU " he gives only " om. PV," and precisely this transposition and this omission are not even mentioned in his discussion of the disputed order of the lines 319 sq. (pp. 525 sq.), whereas otherwise he lists throughout his apparatus verses which are missing or transposed in the MSS., and even

INTRODUCTION

There is also a new Index :

Domenico Bo, *Musaei Lexicon*, Hildesheim 1966.

Bibliography

The literature up to 1912 is summarized in the introduction to Ludwich's edition, and to 1931 by R. Keydell in *JAW*, 230 (1931), 123-125 ; the results of work up to 1970 are included in the commentary of Kost. Many suggestions for the improvement or understanding of the text are scattered in commentaries on other authors or in discussions of late Greek Epic.[a] In addition to those already cited the following works contain useful contributions :

---

missing single words ; on l. 336 ἐς PN ἐπ᾽ Ω, not mentioned in the commentary either. Further divergences are occasionally to be found in his text and apparatus from what he then accepts in his commentary : l. 178 he prints in his text ἐμοὶ φιλότητι μιγείης without any indication in his apparatus, while on p. 373 he prints and prefers ἐμῇ but in turn without quoting any manuscript reading ; perhaps it is only through a misprint that in l. 216 βαρυπνείοντες is printed in the text (but l. 309 βαρὺ πνείοντας) which is contrary to his decision to divide into two words on p. 418 ; the decision for δαμάζει in l. 198 is rightly denoted as Graefe's choice on p. 395 while in the apparatus ad loc. only Ludwich is mentioned, and similarly the addition of < δ᾽ > in l. 333 is correctly attributed to Dilthey on p. 539 while in the apparatus again only Ludwich's name appears. Apart from divergences in individual cases (they are to be found in the list on pp. 338 sq. below) he has come to different decisions from my own in the following matters. He divides some words which were probably thought of at this time as compounds (see note *a*, page 314), and he reckons with lacunae in the tradition after ll. 33, 46, 286, 333 but not with transpositions of lines in ll. 319 sq., 331 sq. Line 79 is forgotten in his translation.

[a] Works on later Greek epic are very fully listed by R. Keydell, *op. cit.* (in note *b*, page 329), 29*-35*.

INTRODUCTION

L. Castiglioni, " Museo, Ero e Leandro," *BFC*, 27 (1920), 68.

C. F. Graefe, " Coniectanea in Musaeum " (Programme St. Petersburg 1818, printed in *Coluthi Raptus Helenae* ed. J. D. v. Lennep, 2nd ed. by H. Schaefer, Leipzig 1825, 259 sq).

H. v. Herwerden, " Ad poetas Graecos," *Mnemosyne*, n.s. 14 (1886), 28-32.

J. D. v. Lennep (" animadversiones ad Coluthum aliosque scriptores veteres," in his edition 1747, reprinted in Schaefer, *l.c.* 133-147).

A. Ludwich ; his writings down to 1912 listed in his edition p. 9 ; in addition : " Zu Musaios," *RhM*, 69 (1914), 569 sq. and " Nachwort zu Musaios " in : *Hundert Jahre A. Marcus und E. Webers Verlag 1818–1918* (Bonn 1919), 101-104.

T. W. Lumb, " Hero and Leander," *CR*, 34 (1920), 165 sq.

P. Maas, " Nonniana," *Byz.-neugr. Jahrb.* 3 (1922), 130-134 and 4 (1923), 12 sq.

L. Mader, " Zu Musaios' Hero und Leandros," *BPhW*, 40 (1920), 1006-1008.

E. Merone, " Omerismi sintattici in Museo," *GIF*, 8 (1955), 299-313.

M. Schmidt, " Verbesserungsvorschläge . . .," *RhM*, n.s. 26 (1871), 182 sq.

F. A. Wernicke, (Commentary on) Τρυφιοδώρου ἅλωσις Ἰλίου, ed. Leipzig 1819, *passim*.

M. L. West, " Zu Musaios," *Philologus*, 106 (1962), 315 and 110 (1966), 167.

A. Wifstrand, *Eranos*, 28 (1930), 103 sq.

A. Zimmermann, *H. u. L., ein Epos des Grammatikers M.* (with Ovid's Epistles), in German with critical notes on the text (Paderborn 1914).

INTRODUCTION

Text and Textual Notes of this Edition

1. The notes to this text are not conceived as representing a full apparatus criticus ; that, with our present knowledge, would be an impossible undertaking without a new comprehensive scrutiny of the manuscripts. These notes give only a selection of manuscript readings, conjectures and references to parallels of form or content in other authors ; this is meant to achieve a double purpose ; first to indicate the origin of the readings and conjectures here chosen and to adduce the material necessary for their justification and explanation, and secondly to draw the reader's attention to problems and uncertainties in the constitution of the text and, in a selection of instances, to offer in addition the basis for the substantiation of conclusions other than those here arrived at. Consequently no notes will be found on passages where the indubitably correct reading is preserved in at least one of the older manuscripts, or where a trivial corruption of the tradition has been in my opinion removed beyond dispute. In cases where verses are missing or transposed in single manuscripts and branches of the tradition, the fact is recorded only in those instances in which the order is, in my opinion, rightly disputed and this information could contribute to the justification of divergences from the traditional order of lines (ll. 319 sq., ll. 331 sq.).[a] Similarly reference to the sometimes far-

---

[a] Omissions and transpositions are noted by Ludwich, *op. cit.* (in note *b*, page 297, and in his edition, as well as, partly on the basis of their own collations of manuscripts, by Orsini and Kost. But nowhere are these indications reliably complete throughout. That justifies for this edition

337

reaching assumptions made by earlier editors about
lacunae, interpolated lines and necessary transposi-
tions is made not in the apparatus but in the following
list.   On the other hand references to parallels,
models, or imitations are freely added where they are
essential, as is frequently the case, to substantiate
decisions on stylistic grounds.

2. In order to disencumber the notes the variants
of the seven most recent scholarly editions are put
together in a synoptical list which at the same time
affords an easy review of their scope and achieve-
ments. The following compilation aims at a complete
enumeration of all the instances where this edition
departs from the text of the editions by Dilthey 1874
(D), Schwabe 1876 (S), Ludwich 1912 (L), Malcovati
1947 (M), Färber 1961 (F), Orsini 1968 (O), Kost 1971
(K).   Again neglected are purely orthographic
variants (including capitalization) based mostly on
changing conventions in the rendering of Greek texts,
different punctuations, and obvious misprints. Also
excluded are emendations and different readings
suggested by the same editors in their apparatus or
published elsewhere, but not actually printed in their
texts. These will be produced, together with their
other emendations if they seem still relevant, at
their place in the notes to the text.

4 γάμον ἔννυχον : -ος -ος DSO ‖ 5 νηχόμενόν : οἰχόμ- DS, σμυχόμ-
L ‖ 5 τε : δὲ DS ‖ 12 δ' ἐφύλαξεν : τε φύλ- O, τ' ἐφύλ- K ‖ 13
χαλεπὸν : -αῖς DSLFO ‖ 17 ἀνὰ : ἴσα DSMK, ἐὰ LFO ‖ 18
ξυνέηκεν : ξύνωσεν DSLFOK ‖ 32 ἀπὸ : † ἀπὸ S ‖ 33 τε : δὲ
SLMFOK ‖ lac. after l. 33 LK ‖ 38 Ἀφροδίτην : † Ἀφρ- S, μετ'
Ἀθήνην L ‖ 41 πυριπνείοντας : πυρὶ πνείοντας K ‖ 45 ναιετάε-

a selection of those few which are relevant for the constitution
of the text.

σκον: -τάασκον SLMFOK ‖ lac. after l. 45 LK ‖ whole l. 46
† S ‖ l. 47 put after l. 50 D ‖ 53 ἀθανάτων ἀγέμεν: -τοισιν
ἄγειν DSLMFK, -τοισιν ἀγέμεν O ‖ 54 lac. after ὅσσον, and
< μοῦνον > with the rest of l. 54 as l. 54a D ‖ 54 ἀγειρόμενοι:
-μένων LMFOK ‖ 58 χιονέης ... παρειῆς: -έων ... -ῶν O ‖ 66
εὔρατο: -ρετο D ‖ 67 περιπολλόν: περὶ πολλόν LMFK ‖ 67
ἀριστεύουσα: -σασα O ‖ 69 ἀνδρῶν: αὐτῶν DSLMFK ‖ 74
ἄστυ: ἄστρον LF ‖ 77 ᾖ: καὶ D ‖ 81 ἡμετέρην: -ροις D ‖ 83
ὀπάσσοις: -σαις DSLMF ‖ 84 ἄλλοθεν: -οθε δ' MK, -οτε
δ' LF ‖ 91 ἀνικήτου: ἀνηκέστου D ‖ 94 ἀπ' ὀφθαλμοῖο βολάων:
δι' ὁ. πυλάων D ‖ 98 ἄριστον: ἄπιστον DS ‖ 101 ἐλέλιζεν:
-ξεν O ‖ 104 ἀγλαΐησιν: ἀγγελί- L ‖ 106 ἐπαγγέλλουσα:
-γγελέουσα O ‖ 118 θαρσαλέη: -λέως O ‖ 124 κέλευθον:
κέλευσον DLO, κάλεσσον S ‖ 125 ἀπόειπε: ἀλέεινε DSLMFO
‖ 126 οὔ σοι ἔοικε: οὐκ ἐπέοικε DSLF ‖ 129 θηλείης: θηλυ-
τέρης DO ‖ 131 ἀπειλήσωσι: -λείουσι DSLMFOK ‖ 134
βεβολημένος: δεδονημένος S ‖ 138 μήτηρ: γαστήρ D ‖ 143
Ἀφροδίτη: Κυθερείη LMFK ‖ 146 Κυθέρειαν: Ἀφροδίτην
SLMFK ‖ 148 ἱκέτην: ἐπέτην D ‖ 151 ἐκόμισσεν: -ιζεν
D ‖ 155 χολωσαμένης: χολωομ- DSLMFK ‖ 158 ἀναινομένην:
-μένης DSLMFOK ‖ 159 ἐνὶ: ἔο DSL ‖ 162 ἔξεσεν: -εεν
DLMFOK ‖ 166 καὶ: δὲ DSLMFK ‖ 173 ἀποστάζουσα:
ἀπαυγάζ- L ‖ 178 ἐμοί: ἐμῇ DSO ‖ 179 question mark after
ἀμφαδόν O ‖ 181 πολύφοιτος: περίφ- S ‖ 186 ἐμοί: ἔχω
DSLMFK ‖ 187 ἀμφιβόητος: ἀμφιδόν- D ‖ 188 μούνῃ: -νη
F ‖ 193 ἠνεμόφωνος: -μόφοιτος S ‖ 193 ἠχή: ἠχώ DS ‖
198 δαμάσσας: -μάζει SLMF ‖ 199 ἀκέσσεται: ἀκείεται
DSL ‖ 204 πυρὶ παφλάζοιτο: περιπαφλά- LO ‖ 204 ἄπλοον:
εὔπλ- DS ‖ 205 χεῖμα: χεῦμα O ‖ 210 ἕνα: τινα DSLOK ‖ 213
ὀψεδύοντα: ὀψὲ δύοντα DSLMFOK ‖ 215 πατρίδος: Κύπριδος
DSLF ‖ 216 βαρυπνείοντας: βαρὺ πνείοντας S ‖ 217 θυμὸν:
μοῦνον L ‖ l. 218 put after l. 212 S ‖ 218 ἡγεμονῆα: ἡνιοχῆα
DSL ‖ 219 εἰ ἐτεόν δ': εἰ δ' ἐτεόν γ' O ‖ ll. 224-229 excluded
D ‖ 225 ἀνέσαντες: ἀνύσ- D, ὁμόσ- S, ὁρίσ- LMF ‖ 227 ἐόν:
ἔβη SLF ‖ l. 228 excluded S ‖ 228 μηδὲ: μή τι DSLMFOK ‖
228 πύργου: πυρσοῦ D ‖ 229 δῆμον: πορθμὸν DS ‖ 235
φαεινομένην: -νων DSLMFK ‖ 236 πολυκλαύτοιο: -κλαύστοιο
M (not 334) O, -λλίστοιο DS ‖ 237 τηλέσκοπον: -σκόπον
DLMFK ‖ 243 ἀείρας: ἀγείρας D ‖ 244 τοίοις ἦν: τοίοισι
DSM, τοίοισιν O, τοίοις οἱ LF ‖ 246 ἐστὶν: στεινὸν O ‖ 247
λάζεο: ἄζεο DSLFOK ‖ 253 ἐξ ὦρτο: ἐξῶρτο DSMFOK,
ἐξᾶλτο L ‖ 255 αὐτόματος (cp. 327): -μάτη DSLK ‖ 257

INTRODUCTION

λεπταλέαις: λευγαλέης M ‖ 263 ἔπι: ἐπὶ D ‖ 266 βαθυστρώτοις
ἐνὶ λέκτροις: β-ων ἐπὶ λ-ων DS ‖ 267 φιλήνορας: -ήτορας
DLF ‖ 270 τ’: δ’ DSLMO ‖ 272 τάδ’ ἔειπεν: † ταῦτ’ εἶπεν
S, παρέπεισεν LFO ‖ 273 ἀριστονόου: ἀρεσσινόου D, ἀκεσ-
σιπόνου S ‖ 276 ἤστραψε: -πτε DSLMFK ‖ 276 εὐήν: -νήν
MFO ‖ 278 ἄεισε: -δε DSLMFOK ‖ l. 281 excluded D,
put after 273 S ‖ 283 ἀριγνώτοις ἐνὶ λέκτροις: ἐνστρώτων
ἐπὶ λ-ων D, † ἀριγνώστων ἐπὶ λ-ων S ‖ 285 ἐννυχίων: παν- D ‖
lac. after l. 286 DSLK ‖ 293 καὶ τότε: ἀλλ’ ὅτε DLMFO ‖
293 lac. after ἀλλ’ ὅτε, and < δὴ τότε > with the rest of l. 293
as l. 293a D ‖ 296 χειμέριοι: -ιον S ‖ 297 τυπτομένης: -νην
SFO ‖ lac. after l. 297 LM ‖ 298 διψάδι: διχθάδι DO ‖ 301
πύργου: λύχνου DS ‖ 309 βαρυπνείοντες: βαρὺ πνείοντες SK
(not 216) ‖ 310 χειμερίας πνοιῇσιν: -ίης πνοιῆσιν M, -ίοις
ῥοθίοισιν D ‖ 310 ἀέλλας: ἀῆται S, ἰωὰς LMF ‖ 312 δὴ τότε
καὶ: καὶ τότε δὴ DSLMF, δὴ τότε δὴ ‖ 315 ἠχὴ: ἠχὼ DS ‖
317 ἐφέηκεν: ἀφ- DS ‖ lac. after l. 321 SL ‖ l. 322 after
l. 321 DSLMFOK ‖ 324 ὁρμῇ: ὁλκῷ DSLF, ὀργῇ O ‖ 326 ἀν-
όνητον: ἀδόν- MK ‖ 326 ἀκοιμήτων: ἀκινήτ- D, ἀνικήτ- S ‖ 327
αὐτόματος (cp. 255): -μάτη LK ‖ lac. after l. 330 DSLOK ‖
330a < Ἡρὼ > . . . O ‖ ll. 331-332 excluded MF ‖ 332 θέ-
σπισσε Λεάνδρου: -ισσεν ἀκοίτου O ‖ 333 εἰσέτι: ἡ δ’ ἔτι MF ‖
333 ἐπαγρύπνοισιν: ἐ-σι δ’ LK, ἐπ’ ἀγρ-σι δ’ DS, ἐπ’ ἀγρ-σιν
O ‖ 334 πολυκλαύτοισι: -κλύστ- D, -κλαύστ- O ‖ ll. 335-336
after l. 334 DSLMFOK ‖ 335 ἤλυθεν: -θε δ’ LMFOK ‖ 336
ἐς: ἐπ’ DSMOK ‖ 342 κὰδ δ’ Ἡρὼ: κὰδδ’ Ἡ. DMFOK, καὶ
διερῇ L ‖.

3. The manuscripts of Musaeus,[a] so far as we can
see from the more or less precise investigations
which have been made so far, fall into three groups
of different value for the establishment of the text :
(a) the older manuscripts up to the XIVth c., all in
codices miscellanei, representing three lines of the

[a] Full details in Ludwich, *op. cit.* (in note b, page 297),
1-4 ; on the classification see *Bemerkungen*, 131 sq., and
above, pp. 326 sq. Orsini in his edition (xxxii sq.) is astonish-
ingly unclear. On Kost's classification and use of the mss.
see note a, page 327 and note a, page 334 ; for additional
mss. see note b, page 327.

340

transmission, of which two (PN and V) on their side go back to a common *hyparchetype*. [a]

B   Barocc. 50, Bodleian., Oxford, first half of the Xth c., with scholia

F1 Estensis II–C–12, Modena, early XIVth c. (cont. ll. 250-343, derived, perhaps indirectly, from B)

N   Neapolitan. II–D–4, bibl. Naz. Napoli, XIVth c.

P   Palatin. Gr. 43, Heidelberg, XIVth c.

V   Vatican. Gr. 915, Roma, early XIVth c.

The readings of B, PN, V are presented in the notes as completely as possible (within the limitations given above).

(b) the humanist manuscripts of the XVth (and XVIth) c., dividing into two groups :

H E (XVth c.), T (XVIth c.), all closely connected but not identical with the Aldine edition

A G I J L Q R X, *codices mutili* (cont. ll. 1-245 with omission of 101 s.), all XVth c., whose text is derived from an exemplar closely connected with V and included (in Italy) in the expanded *corpus hymnorum* [b]

C F2, *codices mutili* (cont. ll. 1-245) more closely connected with V (F3, ll. 246-249 added by a later hand in order to connect F2 and F1)

The good readings of these manuscripts are most

---

[a] See note *a*, page 327 above. If the source of the scholia in B is considered as an independent line of the tradition (see Ludwich, introduction to his edition, p. 9), there are even four represented in the older mss.

[b] For references, and four further *mutili* from the *corpus hymnorum*, see *Bemerkungen*, 132, n. 25.

probably humanist conjectures, mostly anonymous, which will be referred to in the notes as " hum.," mostly without mentioning manuscript sigla.
(c) the late manuscripts (XVth to XVIIIth c.) copied from two kinds of still extant originals :
  copies of manuscripts : U V⁰ (of V), K (of F = F2 + F3 + F1)
  copies of printed texts : D S W (of the Aldine), O Y (of Dukas' ed. 1514), Z (XVIIIth c., probably of Portus' ed. 1629).
The readings of these manuscripts are neglected.

In addition to the manuscripts there exist two *editiones principes* :

Aldina (Ald.), printed by Aldus Manutius in Venice, before the 1st of Nov. 1495 (with a Latin translation by himself in later copies, added not before 1497).[a]

Laskarina (Lask.), printed by Francesco de Alopa in Florence between 1494 and 1496 (its text assigned almost certainly to Janus Lascaris).[b]

These two editions were obviously prepared independently, as the Aldina goes with the group of B, the Laskarina also with that of PN in characteristic points. Which of them was earlier cannot be determined now and is irrelevant.

Indirectly transmitted are eight verses found in the *Historiarum Variarum Chiliades* by Jo. Tzetzes (2nd

[a] For the Latin translation by Aldus himself see page 323, note *e*, above. It is printed in a type not met before 1497 in such a way that it corresponds to the Greek text page by page and can be bound between the pages of the Greek ; see V. Scholderer, *Catalogue of Books Printed in the XVth Century now in the British Museum*, part V (London 1924), 552 sq.

[b] See V. Scholderer, *op. cit.* part VII (London 1930), 667.

INTRODUCTION

half XIIth c.), *i.e.* Mus. 63-65 (*Hist.* 10. 520-522) and
Mus. 148-152 (*Hist.* 2. 438-442). Tzetzes follows
closely B or a manuscript very similar to it, but he
tries to correct mistakes by conjectures of his own
(cp. 151 note). Further, one verse is found in an an-
onymous late rhetorical treatise, *i.e.* Mus. 1 (Anon.
π. τῶν τοῦ λόγου σχημάτων, *Rhet. Gr.* VIII 657. 21
Walz).[a]

4. Emendations accepted in the text or mentioned
in the notes are to the best of my knowledge assigned
to those who first proposed them, whereas later
assenters are mentioned only in special cases. The
options made by the editors since 1874 are shown in
the preceding list. Those emendations which, so far
as I know, are original to me are indicated by the
initials T. G.

5. In the notes the following abbreviations are used
with a special connotation :

hum. = reading of one or more of the humanist manu-
scripts of the XVth (or XVIth) c. (= anony-
mous humanist conjecture, see 3(*b*)).

mss. = reading common to all the manuscripts B, PN,
V, except the one(s) separately designated
in the same note (see 3(*a*)).

schol. = scholion in B (see 3(*a*)).

The indication "metre" is added, where conjec-
tures or manuscript readings are chosen or refuted
for metrical reasons.[b]

THOMAS GELZER

[a] This quotation is indicated by Kost, p. 90.
[b] See page 323, note *b*, above, and notes below on Mus. 13,
38, 54, 74, 146, 204, 213, 225, 327, 342.

ΜΟΥΣΑΙΟΥ ΓΡΑΜΜΑΤΙΚΟΥ

ΤΑ ΚΑΘ' ΗΡΩ ΚΑΙ ΛΕΑΝΔΡΟΝ

Εἰπέ, θεά, κρυφίων ἐπιμάρτυρα λύχνον ἐρώτων
καὶ νύχιον πλωτῆρα θαλασσοπόρων ὑμεναίων
καὶ γάμον ἀχλυόεντα, τὸν οὐκ ἴδεν ἄφθιτος Ἠώς,
καὶ Σηστὸν καὶ Ἄβυδον, ὅπη γάμον ἔννυχον[1]
   Ἡροῦς
νηχόμενόν τε Λέανδρον ὁμοῦ καὶ λύχνον ἀκούω,   5
λύχνον ἀπαγγέλλοντα διακτορίην Ἀφροδίτης,
Ἡροῦς νυκτιγάμοιο γαμοστόλον ἀγγελιώτην,
λύχνον, Ἔρωτος ἄγαλμα, τὸν ὤφελεν αἰθέριος Ζεὺς

---

[1] γάμον ἔννυχον Ludwich, constr., cp. 75 and pap. Oxy. 2.
214 r. 10 s.: -ος -ος mss. (with full stop after Ἡροῦς).

---

[a] "Goddess"=the Muse (*cf.* Nonn. *D.* 1. 1 ∽*Il.* 1. 1).

[b] The lamp as witness of secret love is a long-standing
motif in love-stories ; *cf.*, *e.g.*, Aristoph. *Eccl.* 1 sq.; *A.P.* 5.
4 sq.

[c] Sestos, a town on the Thracian Chersonese (the Gallipoli
peninsula) and Abydos in Mysia, Asia Minor, both lie near
the entrance to the Hellespont (the present-day Dardanelles),
Sestos a little nearer to the Sea of Marmara. Both towns are
already mentioned together in the *Iliad* (2. 836). The
distance across at the narrowest point is today 1350 metres.
The currents out of the Sea of Marmara are very rapid,
and soon made a sorry sight of Xerxes' bridge structures
(Hdt. 7. 36). One did not, therefore, in practice strike directly
across. The crossing-points are a little outside the towns ;

344

MUSAEUS

HERO AND LEANDER

TELL of the lamp, O goddess,[a] the witness of hidden
 loves,[b]
And of the one who swam by night, to sea-borne
 spousals,
And the darkling marriage-bond, unseen by death-
 less Dawn.
And Sestos and Abydos,[c] where I hear of the mid-
 night bridals
Of Hero, of Leander swimming, and thereto of the
 lamp,   5
The lamp that beaconed forth Aphrodite's ministry,
Courier of night-wed Hero, furnisher-forth of
 wedding,
The lamp, love's glory ; would Zeus of the aether
 had brought it,

from Abydos one crossed from a point eight stades N.E.
above the town in the direction of the Sea of Marmara (Polyb.
16. 29. 13 sq.). From Sestos one went to Hero's tower, S.W.
of the town, and let oneself be carried by the current from
there. From Abydos the swim was more difficult because
one had to cross the currents (Strabo 13. 1. 22 C. 590 sq.) ;
cf. Malten, *op. cit.* (in note *a*, page 302), pp. 71 sq.
According to Antipater of Thessalonica (*A.P.* 7. 666. 3), in
Augustan times only ruins of Hero's tower were left. A
corresponding tower on the other shore near Abydos is
mentioned by Horace (*Epist.* 1. 3. 4 ; cp. Strabo, *loc. cit.*).

ἐννύχιον μετ' ἄεθλον ἄγειν ἐς ὁμήγυριν ἄστρων
καί μιν ἐπικλῆσαι νυμφοστόλον ἄστρον Ἐρώτων,   10
ὅττι πέλεν συνέριθος ἐρωμανέων ὀδυνάων,
ἀγγελίην δ'[1] ἐφύλαξεν ἀκοιμήτων ὑμεναίων
πρὶν χαλεπὸν[2] πνοιῇσιν ἀήμεναι ἐχθρὸν ἀήτην.
ἀλλ' ἄγε μοι μέλποντι μίαν συνάειδε τελευτὴν
λύχνου σβεννυμένοιο καὶ ὀλλυμένοιο Λεάνδρου.   15

Σηστὸς ἔην καὶ Ἄβυδος ἐναντίον ἐγγύθι πόντου.
γείτονές εἰσι πόληες· Ἔρως δ' ἀνὰ[3] τόξα τιταίνων
ἀμφοτέραις πολίεσσιν ἕνα ξυνέηκεν[4] οἰστὸν
ἠΐθεον φλέξας καὶ παρθένον· οὔνομα δ' αὐτῶν
ἱμερόεις τε Λέανδρος ἔην καὶ παρθένος Ἡρώ.   20
ἡ μὲν Σηστὸν ἔναιεν, ὁ δὲ πτολίεθρον Ἀβύδου,
ἀμφοτέρων πολίων περικαλλέες ἀστέρες ἄμφω,
εἴκελοι ἀλλήλοισι. σὺ δ', εἴ ποτε κεῖθι περήσεις,

---

[1] δ' hum. (apographa of Ald.) Dilthey : τ' V Kost, τε
φυλ- PN Orsini, om. B.
[2] χαλεπὸν BV, adjective as 129, 147, 285, 290, 296, 340
Wifstrand, or adverb as 88, 311 : -πῇσι P, -ποῖσι N ; -παῖς
Koechly with the assent of Tiedke (metre).
[3] ἀνὰ mss., cp. Opp. H. 2. 90 : ἐὰ Lehrs, cp. 149, Nonn.
D. 16. 2 ; ἴσα Dilthey, cp. Rufin. A.P. 5. 97. 1, Nonn. D.
41. 420 ; ἅμα Graefe.
[4] ξυνέηκεν mss., cp. Il. A 8 and Eustath. ad l. (ed. Rom.
p. 21. 40 ss., cp. p. 22. 8 s.) : ξύνωσεν Dilthey, cp. Nonn.
D. 35. 134 s., 5. 560 s. etc.

---

[a] Turning (the lamp) into a star, καταστηρισμός, is an old
motif ; its most famous use is in the *Coma Berenices* in Bk.
IV of Callimachus' *Aitia* (fr. 110 Pfeiffer), translated by
Catullus (66) ; for the love-lamp as a star see Callimachus,
Epigr. 56. Here the lamp is the " guiding star " of
Leander's life (212, 218). *Cf.* this vol., pp. 80-85.

After the nightlong struggle, to the congress of the
    stars,[a]
And named it for invocation, bride's escort, star of
    loves,   10
For it was fellow and helper of maddened love's
    anguish,
And watched over the message of sleepless
    hymenaeals,
Before the enemy wind blew, harsh with its gales.
But come, and, with my singing, sing of the end they
    shared,
The quenching of the lamp and Leander's perishing. 15
Sestos there was and Abydos opposite, near to the
    sea.
Neighbouring cities they are ; and Love, upstraining
    his bow,
Shot forth a single shaft into both cities together,
Kindling a youth and maiden ; and their names were
    these :
He was Leander, quickener of desire, and the
    maiden, Hero.   20
She dwelt in Sestos, and he in the city of Abydos,
Of each of their two cities each the fairest star,[b]
Like to each other ; but you,[c] if ever you journey
    thither,

[b] The " stars " of their towns are described on the model
of Callimachus' Acontius and Cydippe (*Aitia* IV, fr. 67.
5 sq.), ὁ μὲν ἦλθεν Ἰουλίδος, ἡ δ᾽ ἀπὸ Νάξου, καλοὶ νησάων ἀστέρες
ἀμφότεροι—see on vv. 200 sq. and pp. 50-51 of this vol.

[c] Vv. 23-27. The reader is addressed, in the same way as
the traveller in some epigrams on gravestones (or on a
cenotaph for people drowned at sea) ; for such epigrams see,
e.g., the one by Antipater of Thessalonica on Hero and
Leander's tomb (*A.P.* 7. 666, see n. on v. 4 above) and *A.P.* 7.
236 sq. ; but at 86 and 301 Leander is addressed, which is
quite different ; see on v. 86.

MUSAEUS

δίζεό μοί τινα πύργον, ὅπῃ ποτὲ Σηστιὰς Ἡρὼ
ἵστατο λύχνον ἔχουσα καὶ ἡγεμόνευε Λεάνδρῳ·
δίζεο δ' ἀρχαίης ἀλιηχέα πορθμὸν Ἀβύδου
εἰσέτι που κλαίοντα μόρον καὶ ἔρωτα Λεάνδρου.

Ἀλλὰ πόθεν Λείανδρος Ἀβυδόθι δώματα ναίων
Ἡροῦς εἰς πόθον ἦλθε, πόθῳ δ' ἐνέδησε καὶ αὐτήν;

Ἡρὼ μὲν χαρίεσσα Διοτρεφὲς αἷμα λαχοῦσα
Κύπριδος ἦν ἱέρεια· γάμων δ' ἀδίδακτος ἐοῦσα
πύργον ἀπὸ προγόνων παρὰ γείτονι ναῖε θαλάσσῃ,
ἄλλη Κύπρις ἄνασσα, σαοφροσύνῃ τε[1] καὶ αἰδοῖ.
οὐδέ ποτ' ἀγρομένῃσι συνωμίλησε γυναιξίν,
οὐδὲ χορὸν χαρίεντα μετήλυθεν ἥλικος ἥβης
μῶμον ἀλευομένη ζηλήμονα θηλυτεράων—
καὶ γὰρ ἐπ' ἀγλαΐῃ ζηλήμονές εἰσι γυναῖκες—,
ἀλλ' αἰεὶ Κυθέρειαν ἱλασκομένη Ἀφροδίτην[2]
πολλάκι καὶ τὸν Ἔρωτα παρηγορέεσκε θυηλαῖς

---

[1] τε mss. Linge Graefe, cp. Paul. Sil. Soph. 995, Pl. Phdr.
253 D 7 : δὲ hum. Ald. Lask. most modern editors (with
stop before σαοφροσύνῃ Schwabe, or lac. after 33 Ludwich).

[2] Ἀφροδίτην mss., for the hiatus cp. Il. I 389, Od. θ 337,
Hom. hy. Ven. 1 etc., Q. S. 13. 343 : conjectures, e.g. φρεσὶ
Κύπριν Graefe ; μετ' Ἀθήνην Ludwich.

---

[a] " Kypris " and " Kythereia " are titles of Aphrodite
already found in Homer, taken from her cult-centres in
Cyprus (46) and Cythera (47). Hesiod (Theog. 188 sq.)
describes how Aphrodite was born from the foam (ἀφρός)
which had formed around the genitals of Uranus (Οὐρανίη,
40) which Kronos had cut off and thrown into the sea
(Θαλασσαίη, 249 sq., 320), and how she first went to Cythera
(hence the title Κυθέρεια), then to Cyprus (hence the title
Κύπρις). Herodotus (1. 105) describes the sanctuary of
Aphrodite Urania in Askalon as the oldest, and those in
Cyprus and Cythera as Phoenician foundations from there ;

Seek me a tower out, where once Hero of Sestos
Stood, holding the lamp, and pointed the way for
    Leander ;   25
And seek the sea-resounding strait of ancient
    Abydos,
Which still laments, I fancy, Leander's fate and
    love.
But whence did it arise that Leander, who dwelt at
    Abydos,
Came to desire for Hero, and bound her too in
    desire ?
Hero the beautiful, heiress of Zeus-engendered
    blood,   30
Was priestess of Aphrodite,[a] and being unschooled
    in love's ways
Dwelt by the neighbouring sea in an ancestral tower,
A second Cyprian goddess,[b] in chastity and shame-
    fastness.
Never did she mingle among the gatherings of
    women,
Nor enter the graceful dance of young girls of her
    years,   35
Shunning the word of blame,[c] the envious word of
    women,
For always at sight of beauty women are envious.
Yet ever as she appeased Aphrodite the Cytherean
Often she would assuage Love too with sacrifices

cf. M. P. Nilsson, *Geschichte d. griech. Religion* (3rd ed. Munich 1967), 519 sq.

  [b] Hero is first (33, 67 sq.) compared with Aphrodite and described as excelling the other women, then is addressed herself as such by Leander (135 sq.), just as Nausicaa is first compared with Artemis and later addressed as such (*Od.* 6. 102 sq., 149 sq.).

  [c] Hero, like Nausicaa, averts μῶμος (*Od.* 6. 273 sq.).

MUSAEUS

μητρὶ σὺν Οὐρανίῃ φλογερὴν τρομέουσα φαρέτρην. 40

ἀλλ' οὐδ' ὡς ἀλέεινε πυριπνείοντας[1] οἰστούς.

Δὴ γὰρ Κυπριδίη πανδήμιος ἦλθεν ἑορτή,

τὴν ἀνὰ Σηστὸν ἄγουσιν Ἀδώνιδι καὶ Κυθερείῃ.

πασσυδίῃ δ' ἔσπευδον ἐς ἱερὸν ἦμαρ ἱκέσθαι,

ὅσσοι ναιετάεσκον[2] ἁλιστεφέων[3] σφυρὰ νήσων, 45

οἱ μὲν ἀφ' Αἱμονίης,[4] οἱ δ' εἰναλίης ἀπὸ Κύπρου·

οὐδὲ γυνή τις ἔμιμνεν ἀνὰ πτολίεθρα[5] Κυθήρων,

οὐ Λιβάνου θυόεντος ἐνὶ πτερύγεσσι χορεύων,

---

[1] πυριπνείοντας hum. Ald. most modern editors, cp. note on l. 204 : πυρὶ πνείοντας mss. (πνέον- P¹N) Schwabe, cp. Nonn. *D.* 42. 200.

[2] ναιετάεσκον mss., a regular v.l. in Homeric mss. (cp. ad *Il.* B 539, *Od.* ο 385 etc., Meister, *homer. Kunstsprache*, 65), cp. Mus. 39, 291, Keydell with hesitation ; this verb is not in Nonn. : -άασκον Lask. later hum. Lobeck all modern editors since Schwabe.

[3] ἁλιστεφέων hum. Casaubonus, cp. Nonn. *D.* 13. 455 : ἀλ(λ)ιτρεφέων mss., ἁλιστρεφέων hum.

[4] Αἱμονίης mss., cp. Nonn. *D.* 44. 2, Coluth. 17, 219 : Αἰολίης Sittig, cp. Nonn. *D.* 13. 388.

[5] ἀνὰ πτολίεθρα (πολ- P¹) NP² Lask., cp. A. R. 1. 825 : ἐνὶ πτολίεσσι other mss.

---

[a] Οὐρανίη, an epithet of Aphrodite (see on 31), is connected by Plato with heavenly Ἔρως (*Symp.* 180 D sq.) in contrast with Aphrodite Πάνδημος and earthly love (" vulgivaga ").

[b] Adonis divided the course of the year between the two goddesses who loved him, Aphrodite in the upper world and Persephone in the underworld. His festivals celebrated his death and his return. There is a famous description of the festival for his death in Theocritus, *Idyll* 15 ; the celebrations in Alexandria for his return are described by Jerome, Origen and Cyril ; *cf.* A. S. F. Gow, *Theocritus* vol. 2 (Cambridge 1952), p. 264. On Kythereia see on v. 31.

[c] All the places in the following list have famous cults of

Together with his Heavenly mother,[a] fearing his
 quiver of flame.   40
But still she did not escape the fire-breathing arrows.
For lo, the public festival of the Cyprian goddess
 was come
Which they celebrate in Sestos to Adonis and
 Cythereia.[b]
And in full host they hastened to come to the sacred
 day,
All those whose dwellings lay at the feet of the sea-
 crowned islands,   45
Some from Haemonia,[c] some from Cyprus that lies
 in the sea ;
Neither was there woman who tarried in the cities
 of Cythera,
Nor dancer in the winged heights of incense-bearing
 Lebanon [d] ;

Aphrodite. Haemonia is a literary name for Thessaly after
its mythical king Haemon, father of Thessalos (Strabo 9. 5.
23 C. 443 sq.). In Thessaly various places, *e.g.* Larisa,
Pharsalos, and Metropolis, had old cults of Aphrodite ; see
M. P. Nilsson, *Griechische Feste von religiöser Bedeutung*
(Leipzig 1906), 378 and Kost, 214 ; on Cyprus and Cythera
see on v. 31 above.

 [d] Libanos, today Mt. Lebanon, is the highest mountain in
central Syria, famous in the Old Testament for its cedars and
their fragrance (e.g. LXX, Hosea 14. 6 sq. ; Cant. 4. 14 sq.) ;
the Greek geographers down to Strabo give surprisingly
inaccurate descriptions of it (Strabo 16. 2. 16 sq. C. 754 sq.).
On its slopes, east of Byblos, stood the famous sanctuary of
Aphrodite of Aphaka on the river Adonis (Lucian, *Syr. D.*
8 sq.) ; after its destruction by Constantine its cult was still
being secretly continued in Helioupolis under Anastasius I
(*Suda*, s.v. Χριστόδωρος X 525). At the end of antiquity
Lebanon was a place of refuge for the heathen ; see Honig-
mann, " Libanos 2," *Real-Encycl.* 13. 1 (1926), 1-11. For
Adonis and Aphrodite's dance on Mount Lebanon see Nonn.
D. 4. 81 sq.

οὐδὲ περικτιόνων τις ἐλείπετο τῆμος ἑορτῆς,
οὐ Φρυγίης ναέτης, οὐ γείτονος ἀστὸς Ἀβύδου,   50
οὐδέ τις ἠιθέων φιλοπάρθενος· ἦ γὰρ ἐκεῖνοι
αἰὲν ὁμαρτήσαντες, ὅπῃ φάτις ἐστὶν ἑορτῆς,
οὐ τόσον ἀθανάτων[1] ἀγέμεν[2] σπεύδουσι θυηλάς,
ὅσσον ἀγειρόμενοι[3] διὰ κάλλεα παρθενικάων.

Ἡ δὲ θεῆς ἀνὰ νηὸν ἐπώχετο παρθένος Ἡρὼ   55
μαρμαρυγὴν χαρίεσσαν ἀπαστράπτουσα[4] προσώπου
οἷά τε λευκοπάρῃος ἐπαντέλλουσα Σελήνη·
ἄκρα δὲ χιονέης φοινίσσετο κύκλα παρειῆς[5]
ὡς ῥόδον ἐκ καλύκων διδυμόχροον· ἦ τάχα φαίης
Ἡροῦς ἐν μελέεσσι ῥόδων λειμῶνα φανῆναι·   60
χροιὴ γὰρ μελέων ἐρυθαίνετο· νισσομένης δὲ
καὶ ῥόδα λευκοχίτωνος ὑπὸ σφυρὰ λάμπετο κούρης.
πολλαὶ δ᾽ ἐκ μελέων χάριτες ῥέον· οἱ δὲ παλαιοὶ

---

[1] ἀθανάτων mss. Ald. Lask.: ἀθανάτοισιν V most modern editors.

[2] ἀγέμεν B Ald. Lask., cp. 288, Il. Η 418, 471 etc.: ἄγειν mss. most modern editors.

[3] ἀγειρόμενοι mss. schol. ἀθροιζόμενοι, cp. Il. Π 207, Od. δ 686 etc., constr. 286 : ἀγειρομένων hum. Ald. Lask. some editors with the assent of Tiedke (metre); ἀγείρονται Schwabe.

[4] ἀπαστράπτουσα BV schol. ἀπαστράπτουσα τῷ προσώπῳ, cp. Procl. hy. 7. 31: ἐπ- PN (with προσώπῳ N), cp. Nonn. D. 18. 74.

[5] παρειῆς Wernicke, cp. 161, Nonn. D. 10. 180 etc.: -ῶν mss. (but with χιονέης mss., corr. with χιονέων hum.).

---

[a] Phrygia several times changed its size and its frontiers in antiquity. The part here mentioned seems to be the Φρυγία ἡ πρὸς Ἑλλήσποντον (Xen. Cyr. 2. 1. 5 etc.) or " Little Phrygia," the western part which was separated from the eastern part of Phrygia at the end of the Vth century B.C. (cp. Strabo 12. 4. 2 sq., C. 563 sq. and W. Ruge, Real-Encycl. 20. 1 (1941), 801 sq.). To this region belongs the Trojan Aphrodite, who is the ancestor of the Aeneadae (cp. Hom. Il. 352.

Neither did any of those dwelling round then miss the festival,

No dweller in Phrygia,[a] no citizen of neighbouring Abydos,   50

Nor yet any of the youths who loved maidens ; for they,

Following always wherever there is rumour of festival,

Are eager, not so much to make sacrifice to the immortals,

As to foregather for sake of the maidens' beauty.

But she through the goddess' temple was passing, maiden Hero,   55

Flashing a lightning of lovely radiance from her face,[b]

Even as Selene of the fair white cheeks, when she is rising.

And crimson shone, high on the curves of her snowy cheek,

As the rose from the bud comes twy-coloured ; ah, you might wellnigh

Say that a meadow of roses appeared in Hero's limbs ; 60

For the flesh of her limbs blushed, and as she moved roses

Flashed also from round the ankles of the white-robed girl.

Many the graces that flowed from her limbs ; the men of old

5. 311 sq., 20. 180 sq., 302 sq. ; *Hymn to Aphrodite* 196 sq.) ; for the Aeneadae in Scepsis in the Troad see Strabo (13. 1. 52 sq., C. 607 sq.).

  [b] " Radiance," μαρμαρυγή = the light of the truth (Pl. *Rep.* 515 c, 518 A) ; the " lightning," which is a quotation from Proclus, *Hy.* 7. 31 (there from the face of Athena), is the radiance of the beloved (Pl. *Phaedr.* 254 B) which recalls the vision of κάλλος ; see on v. 94.

τρεῖς Χάριτας ψεύσαντο πεφυκέναι· εἷς δέ τις
   Ἡροῦς
ὀφθαλμὸς γελόων ἑκατὸν Χαρίτεσσι τεθήλει.   65
ἀτρεκέως ἱέρειαν ἐπάξιον εὕρατο Κύπρις.

   "Ὡς ἡ μὲν περιπολλὸν[1] ἀριστεύουσα γυναικῶν,
Κύπριδος ἀρήτειρα, νέη διεφαίνετο Κύπρις.
δύσατο[2] δ' ἠιθέων ἁπαλὰς φρένας, οὐδέ τις ἀνδρῶν[3]
ἦεν, ὃς οὐ μενέαινεν ἔχειν ὁμοδέμνιον Ἡρώ.   70
ἡ δ' ἄρα, καλλιθέμεθλον ὅπη κατὰ νηὸν ἀλᾶτο,
ἑσπόμενον νόον εἶχε καὶ ὄμματα καὶ φρένας ἀνδρῶν.
καί τις ἐν ἠιθέοισιν ἐθαύμασε καὶ φάτο μῦθον·
   "Καὶ Σπάρτης ἐπέβην, Λακεδαίμονος ἔδρακον
   ἄστυ,[4]
ᾗχι μόθον καὶ ἄεθλον ἀκούομεν ἀγλαïάων·   75
τοίην δ' οὔ ποτ' ὄπωπα νέην ἰδανήν θ'[5] ἁπαλήν τε·
ἦ τάχα Κύπρις ἔχει Χαρίτων μίαν ὁπλοτεράων.
παπταίνων ἐμόγησα, κόρον δ' οὐχ εὗρον ὀπωπῆς.

---

[1] περιπολλὸν Schwabe, cp. A. R. 2. 437, 2. 472, 3. 427: περὶ
πολλὸν V : π. πολλῶν mss.

[2] δύσατο mss., cp. A. R. 4. 865, Nonn. *met. Jo.* 13. 115,
Pl. *Phdr.* 255 c 3 : δήσατο Teucher, cp. 29.

[3] ἀνδρῶν mss., cp. 72 s.: αὐτῶν Dilthey, cp. Nonn. *met. Jo.*
7. 112, most modern editors.

[4] ἄστυ mss., cp. *Il.* B 801 etc.: ἄστρον Ludwich (metre,
but cp. 227).

[5] νέην ἰδανήν θ' Dilthey, cp. Call. fr. 114. 9 Pfeiffer, νέην
ἰδανῆν θ' B : other mss. various meaningless corrupt readings.

---

[a] Three Graces since Hesiod (*Theog.* 907); the play on
the word (*cf.* 307 sq.) and the related exaggeration of the
number is a stock motif of erotic writing (*cf.* Strato, *Δ.P.*
12. 181. 1 sq.; Nonn. *D.* 34. 36 sq.; Aristaenetus 1. 10 sq.
etc.). The stock motifs of two-coloured roses and graces in
the eyes are used in just the same way in Procopius' *Decla-
mations* (see *Bemerkungen*, 138, n. 61).

[b] Sparta, famous for the beauty of its women, of whom
Helen was one, already had the epithet " of beautiful

Falsely fabled three Graces born [a] ; either single
    laughing
Eye of Hero blossomed forth with a hundred Graces. 65
Cypris had verily found for herself a worthy priestess.
So she far, far excelling among women,
Priestess of Cypris, revealed herself Cypris anew.
And she entered the tender hearts of the youths, nor
    was there any
Man who was not in rage to possess Hero as bed-   70
    mate.
She then, wherever she strayed through the fair-
    founded temple,
Had following her the mind and eyes and hearts of
    the men.
And many a one of the youths marvelled and spoke
    these words :
" I have been even to Sparta,[b] seen the city of
    Lacedaemon,
Where we hear tale of the contest and battle-fray
    of beauty ; 75
But never saw I such a girl, lovely and delicate.
Ah, Cypris likely possesses one of the younger
    Graces !
As I beheld I anguished, but found no surfeit of
    gazing.

women " in the *Odyssey* (13. 412).   Heraclides Lembos
(second century B.C.) talks of the exceptional esteem accorded
to beauty at Sparta (fr. 2, *FHG* 3. 168 = Athen. 13, 566a).
Beauty contests are known to have occurred in several other
places at festivals as " Kallisteia " in honour of the gods ;
see M. P. Nilsson, *Griechische Feste von religiöser Bedeutung*
(Leipzig 1906), 57, 94, 336.   But precisely for Sparta no
Kallisteia are attested.   Here perhaps athletic contests for
girls are meant ; for such contests Sparta was famous, and
they accounted for the beauty of its girls (cp. Propert.
3. 14. 1 sq. ; Ovid, *Epist.* 16. 149 sq.).

αὐτίκα τεθναίην λεχέων ἐπιβήμενος Ἡροῦς·
οὐκ ἂν ἐγὼ κατ᾽ Ὄλυμπον ἐφιμείρω θεὸς εἶναι   8⟨6⟩
ἡμετέρην παράκοιτιν ἔχων ἐνὶ δώμασιν Ἡρώ.
εἰ δέ μοι οὐκ ἐπέοικε τεὴν ἱέρειαν ἀφάσσειν,
τοίην μοι, Κυθέρεια, νέην παράκοιτιν ὀπάσσοις."[1]

Τοῖα μὲν ἠιθέων τις ἐφώνεεν· ἄλλοθεν[2] ἄλλος
ἕλκος ὑποκλέπτων ἐπεμήνατο κάλλεϊ κούρης·   8⟨8⟩
αἰνοπαθὲς Λείανδρε, σὺ δ᾽, ὡς ἴδες εὐκλέα κούρην,
οὐκ ἔθελες κρυφίοισι κατατρύχειν φρένα κέντροις,
ἀλλὰ πυριβλήτοισι δαμεὶς ἀδόκητον ὀιστοῖς
οὐκ ἔθελες ζώειν περικαλλέος ἄμμορος Ἡροῦς.
σὺν βλεφάρων δ᾽ ἀκτῖσιν ἀέξετο πυρσὸς Ἐρώτων   9⟨0⟩
καὶ κραδίη πάφλαζεν ἀνικήτου πυρὸς ὁρμῇ—
κάλλος γὰρ περίπυστον ἀμωμήτοιο γυναικὸς
ὀξύτερον μερόπεσσι πέλει πτερόεντος ὀιστοῦ·
ὀφθαλμὸς δ᾽ ὁδός ἐστιν· ἀπ᾽ ὀφθαλμοῖο βολάων
κάλλος[3] ὀλισθαίνει καὶ ἐπὶ φρένας ἀνδρὸς ὁδεύει—.   9⟨2⟩
εἷλε δέ μιν τότε θάμβος, ἀναιδείη, τρόμος, αἰδώς·

[1] ὀπάσσοις mss., cp. Nonn. *D.* 33. 128, 42. 395, 47. 401 :
-αις Ald. Lask. most modern editors.
[2] ἄλλοθεν mss., constr. cp. Aen. Gaz. *ep.* 1. 6 ss. : -οθε δ᾽
hum. Zimmermann, cp. Q. S. 9. 176, 12. 197 : -οτε δ᾽
Ludwich, cp. Archil. fr. 7. 7 Diehl[3] (a displaced δ᾽ after ἕλκος
85 in PN Kost).
[3] κάλλος mss. Schrader, cp. 92 s., Pl. *Phdr.* 251 в 1, Ach.
Tat. 1. 4. 4 : ἕλκος hum. Ald. Lask., cp. Ov. *Epist.* 16. 276,
Ach. Tat. ibidem, Mus. 84 s.

---

[a] Leander is addressed in " epic apostrophe " (86 and
301) as is, *e.g.*, Menelaus (*Il.* 4. 146 etc.) and Eumaeus (*Od.*
14. 55, 165 etc.) ; see on v. 23, above.
[b] The eye as the way Beauty enters the soul is described by

Instantly let me die, but first mount the bed of Hero !
I would feel no desire to be a god in Olympus   80
Had I but in my house Hero for my wife.
But if it is not permitted to me to touch your
    priestess,
Send me, O Cythereia, a young wife such as she."
So said many a youth, and others from every side,
Hiding the wound, raged maddened by the girl's
    beauty.   85
But you, dread-suffering Leander,[a] when you saw
    the glorious girl,
You had no will to consume your heart with secret
    goadings,
But vanquished, all unlooked-for, by the fire-smitten
    arrows
You had no will to live in loss of lovely Hero.
Under the glance of her eyes, love's firebrand grew
    fiercer   90
And your heart seethed at the charge of indomitable
    fire—
For the far-renowned beauty of woman without flaw
Comes to mortal men keener than a winged arrow,
And its pathway is the eye[b]; out of the eye's
    glances
Beauty glides, and journeys into the hearts of men—   95
Then awe, shamelessness, tremor, shame seized him ;

Plato (*Phaedr.* 250 D sq., 255 c). κάλλος (see on v. 56) leads
to the μανία of ἔρως (249 D, *cf.* Mus. 84 sq.) ; this alone
awakens the soul to true vision (250 B sq., *cf.* Mus. 142, 145,
240 sq.).   This awakening of " love at first sight," in echo of
Plato, is a stock erotic motif (Achill. Tat. 1. 4. 4 ; 1. 9. 4
etc. ; see Rohde, *Roman* (1st ed.), 148 sq., and the Intro-
duction, pages 310 sq.).   The subsequent inner strife (Mus.
96 sq.) is decribed by Plato by the allegory of the soul as
a charioteer and pair (*Phaedr.* 253 c sq., 254 B sq.).

ἔτρεμε μὲν κραδίην,[1] αἰδὼς δέ μιν εἶχεν ἁλῶναι,
θάμβεε δ' εἶδος ἄριστον, ἔρως δ' ἀπενόσφισεν αἰδῶ.
θαρσαλέως δ' ὑπ' ἔρωτος ἀναιδείην ἀγαπάζων
ἠρέμα ποσσὶν ἔβαινε, καὶ ἀντίος[2] ἵστατο κούρης· 10
λοξὰ δ' ὀπιπεύων δολερὰς ἐλέλιζεν ὀπωπὰς
νεύμασιν ἀφθόγγοισι παραπλάζων φρένα κούρης.
αὐτὴ δ', ὡς ξυνέηκε πόθον δολόεντα Λεάνδρου,
χαῖρεν ἐπ' ἀγλαΐησιν[3]· ἐν ἡσυχίῃ δὲ καὶ αὐτὴ
πολλάκις ἱμερόεσσαν ἑὴν ἐπέκυψεν[4] ὀπωπὴν 10
νεύμασι λαθριδίοισιν ἐπαγγέλλουσα Λεάνδρῳ,
καὶ πάλιν ἀντέκλινεν. ὁ δ' ἔνδοθι θυμὸν ἰάνθη,
ὅττι πόθον ξυνέηκε καὶ οὐκ ἀπεσείσατο κούρη.

Ὄφρα μὲν οὖν Λείανδρος ἐδίζετο λάθριον ὥρην,
φέγγος ἀναστείλασα κατήιεν εἰς δύσιν Ἠώς, 11
ἐκ περάτης δ' ἀνέτελλε[5] βαθύσκιος Ἕσπερος ἀστήρ.
αὐτὰρ ὁ θαρσαλέως μετεκίαθεν ἐγγύθι κούρης,
ὡς ἴδε κυανόπεπλον ἐπιθρῴσκουσαν ὀμίχλην·
ἠρέμα δὲ θλίβων ῥοδοειδέα δάκτυλα κούρης
βυσσόθεν ἐστενάχιζεν ἀθέσφατον. ἡ δὲ σιωπῇ 11

[1] κραδίην Francius, cp. 107, 167, Ach. Tat. 1. 4. 5: -ίη or -ίη mss. (καρδ- PN).
[2] ἀντίος hum. Dilthey, cp. Il. P 31, Nonn. D. 36. 83: ἀντίον mss.
[3] ἀγλαΐησιν mss., cp. 37, [Apoll.] met. ps. 96. 2 (cp. 218 note): ἀγγελίῃσιν Ludwich.
[4] ἐπέκυψεν mss., cp. Nonn. D. 17. 346 (ms.), Pl. Phdr. 254 D 6: ἀπέκρυψεν B; ἔκρυψεν Hermann.
[5] ἀνέτελλε hum. Lask. Röver Patzig, Nonn. has only this form: ἀνέτειλε mss.; -φηνε V¹ hum., -φαινε V² hum., -βαινε d'Arnaud.

He trembled at heart, and shame possessed him to be
    so conquered.
He wondered at the surpassing form, and love
    drove out shame.
And boldly at love's command embracing shame-
    lessness,
Quietly he stepped forward and stood facing the girl ;   100
And peering sidelong, he darted quivering, con-
    spiring glances,
With voiceless gestures turning astray the heart
    of the girl ;
But she, when she recognized Leander's ensnaring
    desire,
Rejoiced in his splendid charms ; and quietly she
    also
Once and again bent on him her own love-quickening
    gaze,   105
With furtive gestures sending her message to
    Leander,
And turned away again. And his heart glowed
    within him,
That the girl knew his longing, and had not brushed it
    away.
While then Leander was seeking the hour of secrecy,
The day, furling her light, was going down to
    setting,   110
And off the horizon rose deep-shadowed the evening
    star.
But now full of boldness he came near to the girl,
When he saw the darkness leaping on in deep blue
    robe,
And gently pressing the rose-like fingers of the girl,
Sighed inexpressibly from the depths of his heart ;
    but she in silence,   115

MUSAEUS

οἷά τε χωομένη ῥοδέην ἐξέσπασε χεῖρα.
ὡς δ' ἐρατῆς ἐνόησε χαλίφρονα νεύματα κούρης,
θαρσαλέη[1] παλάμῃ πολυδαίδαλον εἷλκε χιτῶνα
ἔσχατα τιμήεντος ἄγων ἐπὶ κεύθεα νηοῦ.
ὀκναλέοις[2] δὲ πόδεσσιν ἐφέσπετο παρθένος Ἡρὼ   12
οἷά περ οὐκ ἐθέλουσα, τόσην[3] δ' ἀνενείκατο φωνὴν
θηλυτέροις ἐπέεσσιν ἀπειλείουσα Λεάνδρῳ·
" Ξεῖνε, τί μαργαίνεις; τί με, δύσμορε, παρθένον
  ἕλκεις;
ἄλλην δεῦρο κέλευθον,[4] ἐμὸν δ' ἀπόλειπε χιτῶνα.
μῆνιν ἐμῶν ἀπόειπε[5] πολυκτεάνων γενετήρων·   12
Κύπριδος οὔ σοι ἔοικε[6] θεῆς ἱέρειαν ἀφάσσειν·
παρθενικῆς ἐπὶ λέκτρον ἀμήχανόν ἐστιν ἱκέσθαι."
Τοῖα μὲν ἠπείλησεν ἐοικότα παρθενικῇσι.
θηλείης δὲ Λέανδρος ὅτ'[7] ἔκλυεν οἶστρον ἀπειλῆς,
ἔγνω πειθομένων σημήια παρθενικάων—   13
καὶ γὰρ ὅτ' ἠιθέοισιν ἀπειλήσωσι[8] γυναῖκες,

¹ θαρσαλέη Wernicke, -η V hum., cp. 120, Nonn. D. 26. 75,
36. 224 : -λέως mss.
² ὀκναλέοις V hum. Lask.=Nonn. D. 32. 265, cp. 118 :
-λέως mss.
³ τόσην Imanuel Passow= Mosch. Eur. 134=Nonn. D. 6.
345=Coluth. 169, 265, 305, 329 : τοίην mss.
⁴ κέλευθον mss., cp. 175, Xenoph. B. 7. 1, Parm. B. 2. 4,
Emp. B. 35. 15, 115. 8 Diels-Kranz⁷ : κέλευσον Koechly ;
κάλεσσον Patzig.
⁵ ἀπόειπε mss. Leuzius Patzig, cp. Il. Γ 406 and Eustath.
ad l. (ed. Rom. p. 430. 10 s.), Il. T 35 (cp. 18, 225, 244
notes) : ἀλέεινε Heinrich, cp. Od. α 433 etc., Nonn. D. 4. 66,
most modern editors ; ἀπόλειπε hum. Teucher ; ἀπάλευε Ja-
cobs.
⁶ οὔ σοι ἔοικε mss., cp. Q. S. 2. 309, 5. 227 etc., Nonn.
D. 41. 336, met. Jo. 6. 150, 18. 58 : οὐκ ἐπέοικε Dilthey, cp.
82, 143.
⁷ ὅτ' hum. Lask., cp. Nonn. D. 35. 230 : ὡς mss.
⁸ ἀπειλήσωσι hum. T. G., cp. Nonn. D. 22. 292, 29. 84 s.:

Like one who is angry, drew away her rosy hand.

But when he saw in the lovely girl the signs of
 yielding,

With bold hand he pulled at her richly broidered
 gown

Leading her into the farthest coverts of the lordly
 temple.

And on shy, tremulous feet the maiden Hero
 followed,   120

Like one who is unwilling, and she lifted her voice
 so,

Threatening Leander with words of the kind that
 women use :

" Stranger, what madness is this ? Why, wretch, do
 you drag me, a maiden ?

Come, seek you another way, and release my gown.

Shun the wrath of my parents, rich in many posses-
 sions.   125

It is unfit you touch the priestess of the goddess
 Cypris,

It is beyond contrivance to come to the bed of a
 virgin."

Such were the threats she uttered after the way of
 maidens.

But when Leander had heard the goad of her girlish
 threat,

He recognized the tokens of maidens as they sur-
 render ;   130

For so it is that whenever women threaten youths

ἀπειλήσουσι B, (ἐπ-) εχθαίρουσι MSS.; ἀπειλείουσι hum. Lask.
most modern editors ; -λείωσι Ald.

MUSAEUS

Κυπριδίων ὀάρων αὐτάγγελοί εἰσιν ἀπειλαί—·
παρθενικῆς δ' εὔοδμον εὔχροον αὐχένα κύσσας
τοῖον μῦθον ἔειπε πόθου βεβολημένος οἴστρῳ·
  "Κύπρι φίλη μετὰ Κύπριν, 'Αθηναίη μετ'
    'Αθήνην—   135
οὐ γὰρ ἐπιχθονίῃσιν[1] ἴσην καλέω σε γυναιξίν,
ἀλλά σε θυγατέρεσσι Διὸς Κρονίωνος ἐΐσκω—,
ὄλβιος, ὅς σε φύτευσε, καὶ ὀλβίη, ἣ τέκε μήτηρ,
γαστήρ, ἥ σε λόχευσε, μακαρτάτη· ἀλλὰ λιτάων
ἡμετέρων ἐπάκουε, πόθου δ' οἴκτειρον ἀνάγκην·   140
Κύπριδος ὡς ἱέρεια μετέρχεο Κύπριδος ἔργα·
δεῦρ' ἴθι, μυστιπόλευε γαμήλια θεσμὰ θεαίνης·
παρθένον οὐκ ἐπέοικεν ὑποδρήσσειν 'Αφροδίτῃ,[2]
παρθενικαῖς οὐ Κύπρις ἰαίνεται. ἢν δ' ἐθελήσῃς
θεσμὰ θεῆς ἐρόεντα καὶ ὄργια κεδνὰ δαῆναι,   145
ἔστι γάμος καὶ λέκτρα· σὺ δ', εἰ φιλέεις Κυθέρειαν,[3]

[1] ἐπιχθονίῃσιν Ald. Lask.: -νίῃς B[3] hum. Passow; -νίων mss.
[2] 'Αφροδίτῃ hum. Ald., cp. Nonn. *D.* 48. 297: 'Αφροδίτην mss.; Κυθερείῃ Ludwich (cp. 146 note).
[3] Κυθέρειαν mss., cp. Hes. *Th.* 169, A. R. 1. 742, for the metre Christod. *A.P.* 2. 386: 'Αφροδίτην Papius Ludwich (metre; L. supposed the ends of ll. 143 and 146 to be interchanged).

---

[a] Vv. 135 sq. The lover honours the beloved as a god (*Phaedr.* 251 A, 255 A). Leander's speech (135 sq.) is modelled on *Od.* 6. 149 sq. (see on v. 33). In addition there is a quotation from St. Luke's Gospel (Luke 11. 27 μακαρία ἡ κοιλία ἡ βαστάσασά σε said there to Jesus, *cf.* Luke 1. 42 said to Mary). The Gazaeans likewise quote Homer and the New Testament in the same sentence (see Seitz, *Schule von Gaza* (note a, page 300, above), p. 51).

[b] Vv. 141 sq. Leander persuades Hero to resemble her

Threatening its very self is herald of Love's converse.

And kissing the maiden's throat, fragrant and fair
 of skin,

He spoke these words, stricken with the stinging of
 desire :

" Dear Cypris next after Cypris, Athena next after
 Athena—[a]   135

For I will not call you equal of women who walk
 the earth,

But liken you to the daughters of Zeus, Cronus'
 son—

Happy is he who fathered you, happy the mother
 who bore you,

Most blessed the womb that brought you to birth !
 But give ear

To these my prayers, and take pity on desire's
 necessity ;   140

Since you are Cypris' priestess, attend to the works
 of Cypris.[b]

Come, conduct the mystery, the marriage laws of
 the goddess ;

It is not fitting a virgin attend on Aphrodite.

Cypris takes no pleasure in virgins ; if you are
 willing

To learn the amorous laws of the goddess, and her
 goodly rites,   145

Here is our couch, our wedding ; but you, if you
 love Cythereia,

personal divinity, like the lover in the *Phaedrus* (253 B ; for
the process of πείθειν *cf.* Mus. 130, 164 sq.). For this Mus.
uses a stock erotic appeal formulated by Nonnus (*D.* 42.
371 sq.) and at the same time echoes a famous passage of
Homer (*Il.* 5. 427). Love is a mystery (142, 145), just as
in the *Phaedrus* (250 B sq., 254 B) the vision leads to the
mystery of ἔρως ; see more on v. 94.

MUSAEUS

θελξινόων ἀγάπαζε μελίφρονα θεσμὸν Ἐρώτων.
σὸν δ' ἱκέτην με κόμιζε καί, ἢν ἐθέλῃς, παρακοίτην,
τόν σοι Ἔρως ἤγρευσεν ἑοῖς βελέεσσι κιχήσας,
ὡς θρασὺν Ἡρακλῆα θοὸς χρυσόρραπις Ἑρμῆς
θητεύειν ἐκόμισσεν Ἰαρδανίῃ ποτὲ νύμφῃ[1]·
σοὶ δ' ἐμὲ Κύπρις ἔπεμψε, καὶ οὐ σοφὸς ἤγαγεν
Ἑρμῆς·
παρθένος οὔ σε λέληθεν ἀπ' Ἀρκαδίης Ἀταλάντη,
ἥ ποτε Μειλανίωνος ἐρασσαμένου φύγεν εὐνὴν
παρθενίης ἀλέγουσα· χολωσαμένης[2] δ' Ἀφροδίτης,
τὸν πάρος οὐκ ἐπόθησεν, ἐνὶ κραδίῃ θέτο πάσῃ.
πείθεο καὶ σύ, φίλη, μὴ Κύπριδι μῆνιν ἐγείρῃς."

---

[1] Ἰαρδανίῃ (ιορδανίη mss.) ποτὲ νύμφῃ (-η mss.) mss.
Koechly: ιορδανίην ποτὲ νύμφην B, Ἰαρδανίην ποτὶ νύμφην
Tzetzes hum. Ald. Lask.
[2] χολωσαμένης B hum. Ald. Lask. (χοωσαμ- V hum.), cp. Il.
Γ 414 s., Opp. H. 3. 404 (after ἐρασσαμένην 3. 403, cp. Mus.
154): χολωομένης Patzig (Nonnus has only χολώομαι) most
modern editors; χωομ- NP.

---

[a] Vv. 150 sq. Mythological examples of persons who
without any intention on their part, or contrary to their
intentions, were subdued by Aphrodite; the " daughter of
Iardanus " was Omphale, Queen of Lydia. At the command
of Zeus Hermes sold Heracles to her to be her slave, as
punishment for his theft of the Delphic tripod (Apollod. Bibl.
2. 6. 2 sq.; Ach. Tat. 2. 6. 1 sq.). The contrast between ἔρως
and σοφία (152 sq.) also occurs in Procopius (Decl. 7. 50).
[b] The Arcadian huntress Atalanta guarded her virginity.
Already Euripides, in his Meleager (Fr. 530. 4 N.[2]), calls her
a Κύπριδος μίσημα. There were two main versions of the
tale of how she was nevertheless finally caught by a man.
According to the one which is used here by Musaeus the

Embrace the tender law of the heart-beguiling
    Loves,
And gather me up, your suppliant, and if you will,
    your husband,
Whom Love hunted down for you, overtaking me
    with his arrows,
As Hermes the swift of the golden staff once brought
    the bold   150
Heracles to be slave of the daughter of Iardanus.[a]
But Cypris sent me to you ; shrewd Hermes brought
    me not.
You have heard of Atalanta, the maid from Arcadia,[b]
Who on a time shunned the bed of Milanion, who
    loved her,
Careful of her maidenhood ; but Aphrodite in
    anger   155
Put him in all her heart, whom first she did not
    desire.
You too, beloved, yield ; do not wake wrath in
    Cypris."

Arcadian shepherd Meilanion served her in a self-sacrificing
manner. He was famous for his φιλοπονία which was eventu-
ally successful (Xen. *Cyneg.* 1. 6 ; cp. Ovid, *Ars am.* 2.
187 sq.). The wrath of Aphrodite is not directly attested in
connexion with this version. Also in the other, Boeotian,
version Atalanta hates marriage (Hes. Frr. 73 sq. M.-W.).
Her suitors had to engage in contests with her ; if they failed
they were killed. Hippomenes (Tzetzes, *Hist.* 12. 943
mistakenly talks of Hippomedon) while running let fall three
golden apples, which Atalanta eagerly picked up and so
lost the race (Hes. *loc. cit.*). Aphrodite had given him the
apples and suggested the plan. Although in the Boeotian
story Aphrodite's wrath is attested (Apollod. *Bibl.* 3. 9. 2 ;
Hygin. *Fab.* 185 ; Propert. 1. 1. 9 ; Ovid, *Met.* 10. 681 sq.),
Musaeus, despite Tzetzes, does not seem to follow this
version here. For possible Hellenistic antecedents see Kost,
346 sq.

Ὥς εἰπὼν παρέπεισεν ἀναινομένην[1] φρένα κούρης
θυμὸν ἐρωτοτόκοισι παραπλάγξας[2] ἐνὶ[3] μύθοις.
παρθενικὴ δ' ἄφθογγος ἐπὶ χθόνα πῆξεν ὀπωπὴν   16
αἰδοῖ ἐρευθιόωσαν ὑποκλέπτουσα παρειήν,
καὶ χθονὸς ἔξεσεν[4] ἄκρον ὑπ' ἴχνεσιν, αἰδομένη δὲ
πολλάκις ἀμφ' ὤμοισιν ἑὸν συνέεργε χιτῶνα—
πειθοῦς γὰρ τάδε πάντα προάγγελα, παρθενικῆς δὲ
πειθομένης ποτὶ λέκτρον ὑπόσχεσίς ἐστι σιωπή—,   16
ἤδη καὶ[5] γλυκύπικρον ἐδέξατο κέντρον Ἐρώτων,
θέρμετο δὲ κραδίην γλυκερῷ πυρὶ παρθένος Ἡρώ,
κάλλεϊ δ' ἱμερόεντος ἀνεπτοίητο Λεάνδρου.
ὄφρα μὲν οὖν ποτὶ γαῖαν ἔχεν νεύουσαν ὀπωπήν,
τόφρα δὲ καὶ Λείανδρος ἐρωμανέεσσι προσώποις   17
οὐ κάμεν εἰσορόων ἀπαλόχροον αὐχένα κούρης.
ὀψὲ δὲ Λειάνδρῳ γλυκερὴν ἀνενείκατο φωνὴν
αἰδοῦς ὑγρὸν ἔρευθος ἀποστάζουσα[6] προσώπου·
" Ξεῖνε, τεοῖς ἐπέεσσι τάχ' ἂν καὶ πέτρον[7] ὀρίναις.

---

[1] ἀναινομένην mss., cp. Pl. Phdr. 253 c ss.: -μένης hum.
Ald. Lask., cp. (Π. N 788) Nonn. D. 24. 170, 35. 31 etc.,
most modern editors.

[2] παραπλάγξας (-άξας) mss., cp. Od. τ 187, Opp. H. 2. 236,
Mus. 154, 155 : -πλάζων Dilthey, cp. 102, Nonn. D. 14. 161,
42. 322.

[3] ἐνὶ mss., cp. Nonn. D. 31. 280, A. R. 3. 549, Castiglioni :
ἕο Koechly, cp. Nonn. D. 8. 369, 22. 322, Mus. 185, 210, 212.

[4] ἔξεσεν V Schwabe, cp. Nonn. D. 47. 189, 34. 287 : -ξεεν
mss. most modern editors.

[5] καὶ BV, cp. 39, 201 : δὲ καὶ PN ; δὲ Koechly most
modern editors.

[6] ἀποστάζουσα (ὑπό- PNV) mss., cp. Joh. Gaz. 2. 301
(Christod. A.P. 2. 146), Greg. Naz. carm. 2. 2. 6. 77 (P.G.
37. 1548), Aesch. Suppl. 578, Call. hy. Ap. 39 Kost, Pl.
Phdr. 251 B, 255 C: ἀπαυγάζουσα Ludwich, cp. Nonn. D. 48.
319.   [7] πέτρον hum.: -ραν mss.

---

[a] Vv. 160 sq. Love now awakens in Hero as it did in

So he spoke and persuaded the girl's heart, though
    denying,
Leading her spirit astray with love-engendering
    words.
Speechless, the maiden fixed her gaze upon the
    ground,[a]   160
Modestly abashed, hiding away her flushing cheek,
And with her feet she smoothed the ground's surface,
    again
And again chastely closing her gown about her
    shoulders ;
For these are all harbingers of compliance, and a
    girl's
Silence, when she is won, is her promise to the couch
    of love.   165
Now she too had felt the Loves' bitter-sweet sting,
And the maiden Hero glowed in her heart with sweet
    fire,
And trembled at the beauty of Leander, quickener
    of desire.
So as she kept her eyes drooping toward the earth,
Leander also the while, his countenance mad with
    love,   170
Wearied not with gazing at the girl's soft-skinned
    throat.
Then at last she lifted up her sweet voice to Leander,
Letting fall slowly the moist blush of shame from
    her face :
" Stranger, likely with your words you might rouse
    even a stone.

Leander (86 sq.), just as in the *Phaedrus* (255 A sq.), where
the beloved when he is treated like a god (see on v. 135)
overcomes his shame and " possesses that counter-love which
is the image of love " and " feels a desire like the lover's, yet
not so strong " (255 D sq.).

MUSAEUS

τίς σε πολυπλανέων ἐπέων ἐδίδαξε κελεύθους;   17.
ὤμοι,[1] τίς σε κόμισσεν ἐμὴν εἰς πατρίδα γαῖαν;
ταῦτα δὲ πάντα μάτην ἐφθέγξαο· πῶς γὰρ ἀλήτης
ξεῖνος ἐὼν καὶ ἄπιστος ἐμοὶ[2] φιλότητι μιγείης;
ἀμφαδὸν οὐ δυνάμεσθα γάμοις ὁσίοισι πελάσσαι·
οὐ γὰρ ἐμοῖς τοκέεσσιν ἐπεύαδεν· ἢν δ' ἐθελήσῃς 18.
ὡς ξεῖνος πολύφοιτος ἐμὴν εἰς πατρίδα μίμνειν,
οὐ δύνασαι σκοτόεσσαν ὑποκλέπτειν Ἀφροδίτην·
γλῶσσα γὰρ ἀνθρώπων φιλοκέρτομος, ἐν δὲ σιωπῇ
ἔργον ὅ περ τελέει τις, ἐνὶ τριόδοισιν ἀκούει.
εἰπὲ δέ, μὴ κρύψῃς, τεὸν οὔνομα καί σεο πάτρην· 18.
οὐ γὰρ ἐμόν σε λέληθεν, ἐμοὶ[3] δ' ὄνομα κλυτὸν
    Ἡρώ.
πύργος δ' ἀμφιβόητος ἐμὸς δόμος οὐρανομήκης,
ᾧ ἔνι ναιετάουσα σὺν ἀμφιπόλῳ τινὶ μούνῃ[4]
Σηστιάδος πρὸ πόληος ὑπὲρ βαθυκύμονας ὄχθας
γείτονα πόντον ἔχω στυγεραῖς βουλῇσι τοκήων. 19.
οὐδέ μοι ἐγγὺς ἔασιν ὁμήλικες, οὐδὲ χορεῖαι
ἠιθέων παρέασιν· ἀεὶ δ' ἀνὰ νύκτα καὶ ἠῶ
ἐξ ἁλὸς ἠνεμόφωνος ἐπιβρέμει οὔασιν ἠχή."

[1] ὤμοι Ludwich : οἴμοι MSS.
[2] ἐμοὶ hum. van Herwerden, cp. Il. Z 165, Od. τ 266:
ἐμῇ (-ῆ) MSS. (cp. Hom. hy. Ven. 150, where also this is
only an iotacism of the late MSS. of the corpus hymnorum).
[3] ἐμοὶ V = Od. τ 183, cp. Mus. 220 : ἔχω MSS.
[4] μούνῃ MSS., cp. Od. ψ 227 : -νη PN Francius.

---

[a] Vv. 177 sq. As " a vagabond, a stranger and not to be
trusted " Leander may not marry Hero against the will of
her parents. Mus. here paraphrases the Canonical prohibi-
tion of the Church forbidding τέκνα τῶν κληρικῶν from
marrying an ἐθνικὸς ἢ αἱρετικός (178 = ξεῖνος ἐὼν καὶ ἄπιστος) ;
see Introduction, page 299.

Who was it taught you the paths of devious utter-
    ance ?   175
Alas, who was it brought you here to my fatherland ?
You have spoken all this vainly ; for how could you,
    a vagabond,
A stranger and not to be trusted,[a] mingle in love
    with me ?
We cannot openly come into a righteous marriage,
For it was not my parents' will ; and if you should
    wish   180
As a roaming alien to come and stay in my father-
    land,
Yet you cannot conceal the love-goddess in darkness,
For the tongue of men is loving of jibes ; and that
    same deed
That a man does in silence, he hears of in the cross-
    ways.
But tell me, do not hide it, your name and your
    fatherland ;   185
Mine is no secret to you, my well-known name is
    Hero.
My house is a tower high as the heavens, and the sea
    roars round it,
And there I, making my home with a single maid-
    servant,
At the edge of Sestos' city above the deep-waved
    shore,
Have for my neighbour the sea, by my parents'
    hateful will.   190
Neither are near me girls of my age, nor any dances
Of youths at hand ; but always throughout the night
    and the dawn,
From the sea the wind-voiced sound thunders in my
    ears."

Ὡς φαμένη ῥοδέην ὑπὸ φάρεϊ κρύπτε παρειὴν
ἔμπαλιν αἰδομένη, σφετέροις δ' ἐπεμέμφετο μύθοις. 19
Λείανδρος δὲ πόθου βεβολημένος ὀξέι κέντρῳ
φράζετο, πῶς κεν ἔρωτος ἀεθλεύσειεν ἀγῶνα—
ἄνδρα γὰρ αἰολόμητις Ἔρως βελέεσσι δαμάσσας[1]
καὶ πάλιν ἀνέρος ἕλκος ἀκέσσεται[2]· οἷσι δ' ἀνάσσει
αὐτὸς ὁ πανδαμάτωρ βουληφόρος ἐστὶ βροτοῖσιν· 20
αὐτὸς καὶ ποθέοντι τότε χραίσμησε Λεάνδρῳ—.
ὀψὲ δ' ἀλαστήσας πολυμήχανον ἔννεπε μῦθον·

"Παρθένε, σὸν δι' ἔρωτα καὶ ἄγριον οἶδμα
    περήσω,
εἰ πυρὶ παφλάζοιτο[3] καὶ ἄπλοον ἔσσεται ὕδωρ.
οὐ τρομέω βαρὺ χεῖμα[4] τεὴν μετανεύμενος εὐνήν, 205
οὐ βρόμον ἠχήεντα περιπτώσσοιμι θαλάσσης·
ἀλλ' αἰεὶ κατὰ νύκτα φορεύμενος ὑγρὸς ἀκοίτης
νήξομαι Ἑλλήσποντον ἀγάρροον· οὐχ ἕκαθεν γὰρ
ἀντία σεῖο πόληος ἔχω πτολίεθρον Ἀβύδου.

---

[1] δαμάσ(σ)ας mss. Lask. Stephanus, constr., cp. 38 s.,
211 s.: -άζει B Ald. Graefe most modern editors.

[2] ἀκέσσεται mss., cp. Nonn. D. 29. 141 (34. 73) : ἀκείεται
Graefe.

[3] πυρὶ παφλάζοιτο mss., cp. Nonn. D. 24. 23, Mus. 91,
246 s. (probably one word, cp. 41, 213, Introduction, p. 314,
note a) : περιπαφλ- Ludwich (metre).

[4] χεῖμα PNV Graefe, cp. Nonn. D. 4. 116, Schwabe:
χεῦμα B mss. d'Arnaud, cp. Q. S. 5. 14, A.P. 7. 391. 1,
Nonn. D. 39. 246 ; βαθὺ χεῦμα Koechly.

---

[a] Vv. 198 sq. Ἔρως is a healer (Plato, Phaedrus 252 B,
Symposium 189 D). At the same time Musaeus paraphrases,
even in analogous verb-forms, the proverb " the injurer will
also be the healer " (ὁ τρώσας (καὶ) ἰάσεται Paroem. Gr. 2. 763
L.-Schn.), originally an oracle for Telephus, who had been
wounded by Achilles and had to be healed by the same

Thus she spoke and hid her rosy face in her mantle,
Filled once more with shame, and angry at her own
    words.   195
But Leander, stricken through with the keen goad of
    desire,
Was taking heed how he might win the struggle of
    love ;
For devious-minded Love, having conquered a man
    with his shafts,
Will cure the man's wound again [a] ; and for those
    to whom he is lord
He himself the all-conqueror is councillor for
    mortals [b] ;   200
He himself then also helped Leander in his yearning.
And at last, after distraction, he spoke words full
    of contrivance :
" Maiden, for the sake of your love I will cross even
    the wild surges,
Even should they seethe with fire, and the water be
    closed to ships.
I fear no heavy storm, journeying to your bed,   205
I would not cringe before the resounding crash of
    the sea ;
But always by night, I your husband, wet and sea-
    tossed,
Will swim the strong-flowing Hellespont ; for not far
    off
Opposite your city is mine, the city of Abydos.

weapon (Schol. Aristoph. *Nub.* 919 ; Hygin. *Fab.* 101 ;
Apollod. *Epit.* 3. 19 sq.) ; this proverb is often used in erotic
connections ; see Kost 393 sq.

   [b] Vv. 200 sq. αὐτός, here repeated, is an echo of the famous,
much imitated line of Callimachus (fr. 67. 1) αὐτὸς Ἔρως
ἐδίδαξεν Ἀκόντιον (see on v. 22) ; *cf.* also Plato, *Symp.*
179 A 7.

μοῦνον ἐμοὶ ἕνα[1] λύχνον ἀπ' ἠλιβάτου σεὸ πύργου 2

ἐκ περάτης ἀνάφαινε κατὰ κνέφας, ὄφρα νοήσας

ἔσσομαι ὁλκὰς Ἔρωτος ἔχων σέθεν ἀστέρα λύχνον,

καί μιν ὀπιπεύων, οὐκ ὀψεδύοντα[2] Βοώτην,

οὐ θρασὺν Ὠρίωνα καὶ ἄβροχον ὁλκὸν Ἁμάξης,

πατρίδος[3] ἀντιπόροιο ποτὶ γλυκὺν ὅρμον ἱκοίμην. 2

ἀλλά, φίλη, πεφύλαξο βαρυπνείοντας[4] ἀήτας,

μή μιν ἀποσβέσσωσι—καὶ αὐτίκα θυμὸν ὀλέσσω—,

λύχνον, ἐμοῦ βιότοιο φαεσφόρον ἡγεμονῆα.[5]

εἰ ἐτεὸν δ'[6] ἐθέλεις ἐμὸν οὔνομα καὶ σὺ δαῆναι,

οὔνομά μοι Λείανδρος, ἐυστεφάνου πόσις Ἡροῦς." 2

Ὣς οἱ μὲν κρυφίοισι γάμοις συνέθεντο μιγῆναι,

καὶ νυχίην φιλότητα καὶ ἀγγελίην ὑμεναίων

λύχνου μαρτυρίῃσιν ἐπιστώσαντο φυλάσσειν,

ἡ μὲν φῶς τανύειν, ὁ δὲ κύματα μακρὰ περῆσαι.

---

[1] ἕνα mss., cp. for the hiatus Il. Ψ 6, O 710, Od. μ 154 etc., for the expression Hom. hy. Merc. 284, Od. ψ 227, Nonn. D. 31. 280 s., Mus. 18, 64 : τινα Lennep most modern editors.

[2] ὀψεδύοντα taken for a compositum (metre) as Paul. Sil. H.S. 854 (Friedländer), ὀψὲ δύοντα Canter, cp. Od. ε 272 : ὄψομαι δύντα mss.

[3] πατρίδος mss. : Κύπριδος Dilthey.

[4] βαρυπνείοντας mss., cp. 309 : βαρὺ πνείοντας V hum. Lask. Dindorf Schwabe.

[5] ἡγεμονῆα mss., cp. 25, [Apoll.] met. ps. 131. 35 (cp. 104 note) : ἡνιοχῆα Dilthey, cp. Nonn. D. 24. 267.

[6] εἰ ἐτεὸν δ' mss. Graefe, cp. Nonn. D. 7. 178 etc., Mus. 90, 104, 338 for the position of δέ, for the (Homeric) hiatus Keydell, Nonnus, p. 41* : εἰ δ' ἐτεόν γ' Wakefield ; εἰ ἐτεόν γ' Passow, cp. Od. π 300, ω 259 ; εἰ δ' ἐτεῶς Zimmermann.

---

[a] Vv. 212 sq. Leander sets his own " guiding star," the lamp, in direct contrast to the stars by which Odysseus guided

Only, light me a single lamp from your lofty tower   210
Off the horizon through the dark, that when I see it
I shall become Love's vessel, with a star from you,
    your lamp,[a]
And keeping my watch on that, not on late-setting
    Boötes,
Nor bold Orion, nor the track of the Wain untouched
    by the sea,
Let me come to sweet haven in your land on the
    farther shore.   215
But, beloved, have a care of the heavily blowing
    winds,
Lest they should quench the lamp, and I forthwith
    should lose
My life—your lamp, light-bearing conductor of my
    existence.
And if you also truly desire to know my name,
Leander is my name, husband of fair-crowned
    Hero." [b]   220
Thus they made their compact to join in secret union,
And pledged their nightly love and the tidings of
    their bridals
In trust to the witnessing of the lamp, to watch over,
She to stretch forth the lamp, and he to cross the
    long waves.

himself; there is an explicit allusion to *Od.* 5. 272 sq. See
on v. 319. Aratus too (584 sq.) cited the line about the late
setting of Boötes, which occurs in autumn from the end of
September to the end of October. This would be the time,
therefore, at which the storm in the *Odyssey* occurred, and
likewise the storm in prospect of which Leander refused to
feel afraid (205, 300 sq.).

  [b] ἐυστέφανος is a standard epithet of goddesses, especially
of Aphrodite (*Od.* 8. 267 ; Hom. *Hym. Ven.* 6, 175, 287 ;
Hes. *Theog.* 196). Hero is a second Aphrodite (33, 68, 135).

παννυχίδας δ' ἀνέσαντες¹ ἀκοιμήτων ὑμεναίων   2
ἀλλήλων ἀέκοντες ἐνοσφίσθησαν ἀνάγκῃ,
ἡ μὲν ἑόν² ποτὶ πύργον, ὁ δ' ὀρφναίην ἀνὰ νύκτα.
μηδὲ¹³ παραπλάζοιτο, λαβὼν⁴ σημήια πύργου
πλῶε βαθυκρήπιδος ἐπ' εὐρέα δῆμον Ἀβύδου.
παννυχίων δ' ὄάρων κρυφίους ποθέοντες ἀέθλους   2
πολλάκις ἠρήσαντο μολεῖν θαλαμηπόλον ὄρφνην.

Ἤδη κυανόπεπλος ἀνέδραμε νυκτὸς ὀμίχλη
ἀνδράσιν ὕπνον ἄγουσα καὶ οὐ ποθέοντι Λεάνδρῳ.
ἀλλὰ πολυφλοίσβοιο παρ' ἠιόνεσσι θαλάσσης
ἀγγελίην ἀνέμιμνε φαεινομένην⁵ ὑμεναίων   2
μαρτυρίην λύχνοιο πολυκλαύτοιο δοκεύων
εὐνῆς δὲ κρυφίης τηλέσκοπον ἀγγελιώτην.
ὡς δ' ἴδε κυανέης λιποφεγγέα νυκτὸς ὀμίχλην,
Ἡρὼ λύχνον ἔφαινεν. ἀναπτομένοιο δὲ λύχνου
θυμὸν Ἔρως ἔφλεξεν ἐπειγομένοιο Λεάνδρου·   2

---

¹ ἀνέσαντες B Koechly Ludwich (*Rh. M.* 69 [1914], 569 s.),
cp. *Il.* N 657, Ξ 209 and Eustath., ad l. (ed. Rom. pp. 952. 59,
979. 5 s.), Apollon. *Soph.* 32. 13: ἀνύσαντες mss.; ἀναθέντες
Rohde; ὁμόσαντες Schwabe; ὁρίσαντες Ludwich earlier.

² ἑὸν mss., cp. 260: ἔβη Schwabe, cp. 259.

³ μηδὲ (μήδε) B, μὴ δὲ hum., cp. *Od.* θ 414, π 372, σ 147 etc.,
Triph. 150 etc.: μὴ PN; μή τι V most modern editors (with
stop before ὁ δ' or ἡ μὲν in 227).

⁴ λαβὼν (Z, XVIIIth cent.) Bergler; for the nautical
expression cp. Naum. 1. 41, 6. 39 (ed. Dain), Giangrande:
βαλὼν mss., with πύργῳ (B's reading), cp. Naum. 3. 2 and
Nonn. *D.* 14. 165, 37. 601, 48. 126 etc., Giangrande;
λαθὼν V.

⁵ φαεινομένην (φαεννο-) Nodell (φαεινο-) Passow, cp. 237
and 210 s., 230 s., 276 ss., 282 ss.: -νων mss., cp. φαεινοτέροις
ὑμεναίοις Nonn. *D.* 5. 562, Schwabe.

ᵃ Vv. 233 sq. Leander feels the same emotions as Plato's

Then pressing each other to night-long festals of
    sleepless wedlock,   225
Unwillingly, but of need, they parted from one
    another,
She up to her tower, and he through darkness of
    night.
Lest he should wander astray, he took the tower's
    landmark
And swam to the wide region of deep-founded
    Abydos.
And yearning for the secret bouts of night-long
    conversings   230
Often they prayed for the dark, their bridal atten-
    dant, to come.
And now the gloom of the night, in darkling robe,
    arose,
Bringing sleep to men, but not to yearning Leander.[a]
But all along the shores of the sea with its great
    foaming,
He was awaiting the gleaming signal, tiding of
    spousal,   235
Watching for the testimony of the much lamented
    lamp,
And the messenger seen from afar of the secret
    marriage-bed.
But when she saw light fading in the gloom of dark-
    hued night
Hero lit the lamp ; and when the lamp was illumined,
Love fired the spirit of the hastening Leander ;   240

lover when parted from his beloved (*Phaedr.* 251 E). His
racing mind cannot sleep at night for remembering the καλός
and he runs, his soul ποθοῦσα (Mus. 230, 233), to the places
where he expects to see him who has κάλλος, and only when
he sees him again (here the light of the lamp, 239 sq.) he
recovers (243 sq.).

λύχνῳ καιομένῳ συνεκαίετο· πὰρ δὲ θαλάσσῃ
μαινομένων ῥοθίων πολυηχέα βόμβον ἀκούων
ἔτρεμε μὲν τὸ πρῶτον, ἔπειτα δὲ θάρσος ἀείρας
τοίοις ἦν¹ προσέλεκτο² παρηγορέων φρένα μύθοις·
  " Δεινὸς Ἔρως, καὶ πόντος ἀμείλιχος· ἀλλὰ θα-
      λάσσης   24
ἐστὶν ὕδωρ, τὸ δ' Ἔρωτος ἐμὲ φλέγει ἐνδόμυχον
      πῦρ.
λάζεο³ πῦρ, κραδίη, μὴ δείδιθι νήχυτον ὕδωρ.
δεῦρό μοι εἰς φιλότητα· τί δὴ ῥοθίων ἀλεγίζεις;
ἀγνώσσεις, ὅτι Κύπρις ἀπόσπορός ἐστι θαλάσσης,
καὶ κρατέει πόντοιο καὶ ἡμετέρων ὀδυνάων; "   2ε
  Ὣς εἰπὼν μελέων ἐρατῶν ἀπεδύσατο πέπλα
ἀμφοτέραις παλάμῃσιν, ἑῷ δ' ἔσφιγξε καρήνῳ,
ἠιόνος δ' ἔξ ὦρτο,⁴ δέμας δ' ἔρριψε θαλάσσῃ.
λαμπομένου δ' ἔσπευδεν ἀεὶ κατεναντία λύχνου
αὐτὸς ἐὼν ἐρέτης, αὐτόστολος, αὐτόματος⁵ νηῦς.   2ε
  Ἡρὼ δ' ἠλιβάτοιο φαεσφόρος ὑψόθι πύργου,
λεπταλέαις αὔρῃσιν ὅθεν πνεύσειεν ἀήτης,

¹ τοίοις ἦν T. G., cp. _Od._ ε 355, α 5, constr. cp. A. R. 4. 833:
τοίοισι MSS.; -οισιν Hilberg; -οις οἱ Ludwich.
² προσέλεκτο B, cp. _Od._ μ 34 and Eustath. ad l. (ed. Rom.
p. 1706. 11 s.); προσλέ- προλέ- MSS.
³ λάζεο MSS., cp. 167, 204, _A.P._ 12. 132. 11 s., _A.P._ 6.
190. 1, Giangrande: ἅζεο Graefe, most modern editors.
⁴ ἔξ ὦρτο (ἐξῶρτο MSS.), cp. A. R. 1. 306 (Fränkel): ἐξᾶλτο
Ludwich.
⁵ αὐτόματος MSS., cp. 327 and Eustath. ad _Il._ Ε 749 (ed.
Rom. p. 604. 43 ss.) (Keydell αὐτὸς στόλος, αὐτόματος masc.):
αὐτομάτη Dilthey with Tiedke's assent (metre)=Nonn. _met._
_Jo._ 6. 83, cp. Antip. Thess. _A.P._ 7. 637. 4.

ᵃ Vv. 244 sq. Leander arouses " his own heart " before
the swim as Odysseus does in the water (_Od._ 5. 355 sq.,
376 sq.).
ᵇ Cypris-Aphrodite is Οὐρανίη and Θαλασσαίη (see on

He burned with the burning lamp ; and now beside
    the sea,
Hearing the far echoing thunder of the raving surf
He trembled at first, but then raising his courage up
Spoke in such words as these, comforting his own
    heart [a] :
" Dread is love, and the sea implacable ; yet is the
    water   245
The sea's, while the fire of love, lurking within,
    consumes me.
Seize the fire, my heart, fear not the full-flowing
    water.
Come then, forth to love ! What care you for the
    surge ?
Do you not know that Cypris is offspring of the sea,
And is mistress over the deep and over our suffer-
    ings ? " [b]   250
Thus he spoke, and stripped the clothes from his
    lovely limbs
With both his hands and knotted them up around
    his head,[c]
Rushed from the strand and flung his body into the
    sea.
Always he strove in his course straight on for the
    flaring lamp,
His own oarsman, his own escort, himself his ship.   255
Hero bearing the light high on her lofty tower,
From wherever the wind might blow with its subtle
    breathings

vv. 31, 40, 320). She is summoned as Εὔπλοια, Ποντία,
Λιμενία before sea-voyages or in rough seas (*A.P.* 5. 11 ;
5. 17 ; 9. 143 sq. etc.).

  [c] Vv. 252 sq. Leander ties his clothing above his head
before swimming like Odysseus (*Od.* 14. 349 sq.).

φάρεϊ πολλάκι λύχνον ἐπέσκεπεν, εἰσόκε Σηστοῦ
πολλὰ καμὼν Λείανδρος ἔβη ποτὶ ναύλοχον ἀκτήν.
καί μιν ἑὸν ποτὶ πύργον ἀνήγαγεν· ἐκ δὲ θυράων
νυμφίον ἀσθμαίνοντα περιπτύξασα σιωπῇ
ἀφροκόμους ῥαθάμιγγας ἔτι στάζοντα θαλάσσης
ἤγαγε νυμφοκόμοιο μυχοὺς ἔπι παρθενεῶνος·
καὶ χρόα πάντα κάθηρε, δέμας δ' ἔχρισεν[1] ἐλαίῳ
εὐόδμῳ ῥοδέῳ, καὶ ἀλίπνοον ἔσβεσεν ὀδμήν.
εἰσέτι δ' ἀσθμαίνοντα βαθυστρώτοις ἐνὶ λέκτροις
νυμφίον ἀμφιχυθεῖσα φιλήνορας ἴαχε μύθους·
   "Νυμφίε, πολλὰ μόγησας, ἃ μὴ πάθε νυμφίος
      ἄλλος,
νυμφίε, πολλὰ μόγησας· ἅλις νύ τοι ἁλμυρὸν ὕδωρ
ὀδμή τ'[2] ἰχθυόεσσα βαρυγδούποιο θαλάσσης·
δεῦρο, τεοὺς ἱδρῶτας ἐμοῖς ἐνικάτθεο κόλποις."
   Ὣς ἡ μὲν τάδ' ἔειπεν,[3] ὁ δ' αὐτίκα λύσατο μίτρην,
καὶ θεσμῶν ἐπέβησαν ἀριστονόου[4] Κυθερείης.

---

[1] ἔχρισεν anon. conj. in Pareus, cp. *Od.* γ 466, κ 364, 450 etc.: ἔχριεν mss., cp. *Il.* Ψ 186 etc.

[2] τ' Ald.: δ' mss.

[3] τάδ' ἔειπεν Wernicke, cp. Nonn. *D.* 5. 366, *met. Jo.* 13. 100, 18. 1, τάδε εἶπεν V : τ(οι)αῦτ' ἔειπεν PN, ταῦθ' εἶπεν B ; προσέπεισεν Schwabe ; παρέπεισεν or (*Rh. M.* 69 [1914], 570) τοῖα μὲν εἶπεν, cp. Nonn. *met. Jo.* 11. 131, Ludwich ; τὸν ἔπεισεν Zimmermann.

[4] ἀριστονόου mss., cp. Nonn. *met. Jo.* 19. 183 : ἀ(μ)ερσιν-Lehrs, cp. Nonn. *D.* 33. 67, *met. Jo.* 8. 125 ; ἀπιστον- or ἀλιτρον- Rohde ; ἀρεσσιν- Dilthey ; ἀκεσσιπόνου Schwabe ; ἀριστοπόνου Ludwich, cp. *A.P.* 9. 466. 2.

---

[a] Vv. 268 sq. Leander is twice greeted with the words πολλὰ μόγησας almost exactly as Odysseus describes himself to Nausicaa (*Od.* 5. 449, *cf.* 5. 223).

[b] The θεσμά of Aphrodite have already been described as

Sheltered often the lamp with her cloak, until
    Leander
With hard toil came to Sestos' beach, the haven of
    ships.
And she led him up to her tower, and there, before
    the portals   260
Silently folding her arms around her panting bride-
    groom,
While still he was dripping the foaming drops of the
    sea,
Led him to the deep recesses of her maiden's bridal
    chamber,
And purified all his skin, and anointed his body with
    oil
Sweetly scented with rose, and quenched the smell
    of the sea.   265
And while he still breathed hard on the bed of deep
    coverlets
Closely embracing her bridegroom she cried these
    loving words :
" Bridegroom, heavy toiler,[a] as no other bridegroom
    has suffered,
Bridegroom, heavy toiler, enough now of briny
    water
And the smell of fish from the sea with its heavy
    thunderings,   270
Here on my breasts repose the sweat of your
    labouring."
Thus she spoke these words, and forthwith he loosed
    her girdle,
And they entered into the rites of most wise
    Cythereia.[b]

mysteries (142 sq.) ; on the allegories of " Silence " and
" Night " (280 sq.) see Introduction, page 322.

ἦν γάμος, ἀλλ᾽ ἀχόρευτος· ἔην λέχος, ἀλλ᾽ ἄτερ
   ὕμνων·
οὐ Ζυγίην Ἥρην τις ἐπευφήμησεν ἀείδων,
οὐ δαΐδων ἤστραψε σέλας θαλαμηπόλον εὐνῇ,[1]
οὐδὲ πολυσκάρθμῳ τις ἐπεσκίρτησε χορείῃ,
οὐχ ὑμέναιον ἄεισε[2] πατὴρ καὶ πότνια μήτηρ·
ἀλλὰ λέχος στορέσασα τελεσσιγάμοισιν ἐν ὥραις
Σιγὴ παστὸν ἔπηξεν, ἐνυμφοκόμησε δ᾽ Ὀμίχλη,
καὶ γάμος ἦν ἀπάνευθεν ἀειδομένων ὑμεναίων.
Νὺξ μὲν ἔην κείνοισι γαμοστόλος, οὐδέ ποτ᾽ Ἠὼς
νυμφίον εἶδε Λέανδρον ἀριγνώτοις ἐνὶ λέκτροις·
νήχετο δ᾽ ἀντιπόροιο πάλιν ποτὶ δῆμον Ἀβύδου
ἐννυχίων ἀκόρητος ἔτι πνείων ὑμεναίων.
Ἡρὼ δ᾽ ἑλκεσίπεπλος ἑοὺς λήθουσα τοκῆας[3]
παρθένος ἠματίη, νυχίη γυνή. ἀμφότεροι δὲ
πολλάκις ἠρήσαντο κατελθέμεν[4] εἰς δύσιν Ἠῶ.

---

[1] εὐνῇ Graefe, cp. Nonn. D. 45. 87 : -νὴν MSS.

[2] ἄεισε Ald. Lask., cp. Od. φ 411 : ἄειδε MSS. most modern
editors.

[3] λήθουσα τοκῆας MSS., cp. Il. Ξ 296, A.P. 9. 381. 11,
constr. cp. 54 : either λήθεσκε (cp. Il Ω 13) or lac. after 286
Graefe.

[4] κατελθέμεν hum. Ald. Lask. schol. κατελθεῖν, cp. Nonn.
D. 42. 52, Mus. 231 : καθελκέμεν (μεθ- V) MSS.

---

[a] Vv. 274 sq. Partly using the same words, a similar
enumeration of all that was missing of the customary rituals
of marriage is found on a grave-epigram by Antonius Thallus
for a bride who died on her wedding-day (Garland of Philip,
about A.D. 10, A.P. 7. 188). For the quotation of the para-
doxa from St. Gregory Nazianzenus' Carm. 1. 1. 2. 62 sq.
(P.G. 36. 406) see Introduction, pages 321 sq.

[b] Ἥρη Ζυγίη (cf. Ap. Rhod. 4. 96 ; A.P. 7. 188. 4), else-

Wedding it was, but without a dance ; bedding, but
    hymnless.[a]
None glorified in song Hera the union-maker,[b]   275
Nor did the attendant gleam of torches flash on the
    bed
Nor was there any who gambolled and sprang in
    leaping dance,
Nor father nor lady-mother intoned the hymenaeal ;
But laying ready the couch in the hour of consum-
    mation
Silence made fast the bed ; Gloom was the bride's
    attendant,   280
And it was a marriage afar from the singing of
    hymenaeals.
Night was their wedding's furnisher-forth, nor did
    ever Dawn
Behold the bridegroom Leander in the well-known
    marriage-bed ;
But he swam back to the town of Abydos on the
    other shore
Still breathing unsated desire for the night's
    embraces.   285
Hero of the trailing robes, in secrecy from her
    parents,[c]
Was maiden by day, by night a wife ; and both
    lovers
Prayed again and again for the day to go down to
    setting.

where usually called Τελεία, is protectress of marriage ; cf.
M. P. Nilsson, *Geschichte der Griech. Rel.* 429 sq.

[c] Hero unites herself with Leander ἑοὺς λήθουσα τοκῆας
just like Hera and Zeus in the *Iliad* (14. 296) φίλους λήθοντε
τοκῆας. This line is cited also in the Cento Homericus, *A.P.*
9. 381. 11 for the same " secret union " ; see Introduction,
page 307, note b, and page 322.

Ὡς οἱ μὲν φιλότητος ὑποκλέπτοντες ἀνάγκην
κρυπταδίῃ τέρποντο μετ᾽ ἀλλήλων Κυθερείῃ.　　29
ἀλλ᾽ ὀλίγον ζώεσκον ἐπὶ χρόνον, οὐδ᾽ ἐπὶ δηρὸν
ἀγρύπνων ἀπόναντο πολυπλάγκτων ὑμεναίων,
καὶ τότε[1] παχνήεντος ἐπήλυθε χείματος ὥρη
φρικαλέας δονέουσα πολυστροφάλιγγας ἀέλλας,
βένθεα δ᾽ ἀστήρικτα καὶ ὑγρὰ θέμεθλα θαλάσσης　29
χειμέριοι[2] πνείοντες ἀεὶ στυφέλιζον ἀῆται
λαίλαπι μαστίζοντες ὅλην ἅλα· τυπτομένης[3] δὲ
ἤδη νῆα μέλαιναν ἐφείλκυσε[4] διψάδι[5] χέρσῳ
χειμερίην καὶ ἄπιστον ἀλυσκάζων ἅλα ναύτης.
ἀλλ᾽ οὐ χειμερίης σὲ φόβος κατέρυκε θαλάσσης,　30
καρτερόθυμε Λέανδρε, διακτορίη δὲ σὲ πύργου[6]
ἠθάδα σημαίνουσα φαεσφορίην ὑμεναίων
μαινομένης ὤτρυνεν ἀφειδήσαντα θαλάσσης,
νηλειὴς καὶ ἄπιστος. ὄφελλε δὲ δύσμορος Ἡρὼ
χείματος ἱσταμένοιο μένειν ἀπάνευθε Λεάνδρου　30
μηκέτ᾽ ἀναπτομένη μινυώριον ἀστέρα λέκτρων·
ἀλλὰ πόθος καὶ μοῖρα βιήσατο· θελγομένη δὲ

---

[1] καὶ τότε Schwabe, cp. Nonn. *met. Jo.* 10. 81, D. 4. 207
etc.: ἀλλ᾽ ὅτε MSS.

[2] χειμέριοι MSS., cp. 13, 299, 310, Nonn. *D.* 47. 361 s.:
-μέριον d'Orville, cp. 13, 88, 311.

[3] τυπτομένης (-νη V) MSS., cp. 61 : lac. after 297 Koechly ;
-μένην d'Orville.

[4] ἐφείλκυσε (ἐπέλκ-) Brunck (ἐφέλκ-) d'Arnaud (ἐφείλκ-
Dilthey, cp. 118) : ἐπέκλυσε(ν) MSS., ἀπ- hum. Lask.; ἀπέκλασε
Ald. ; ἀνέλκυσε d'Orville Lennep.

[5] διψάδι Mazzarella-Farao Brunck Schwabe, cp. Nonn. *D.*
16. 373, *met. Jo.* 21. 55 etc.: διχθάδι MSS. (-χάδι V) some
editors ; ἠθάδι Lennep, cp. 302.

[6] πύργου B Ald., cp. 210, 228, 256 : λύχνου MSS. Lask.,
cp. 6, 223, 236.

And so they, concealing the compelling need of their
    love,
Joyed with one another in their secret goddess of
    love.   290
But they lived only a little time, nor did they long
Enjoy the sleepless marriage that cost much journey-
    ing.
Then indeed the season of frosty winter came on,
Driving along the shuddering blasts in whirl on
    whirl;
The abysses were dislodged, and the wintry gales
    with their blowing   295
Steadily battered the sodden foundations of the
    sea,
With whirlwind scourging the whole brine; and the
    mariner
From its beaten flood already had drawn up his black
    ship
To dry land, shunning a wintry sea, not to be
    trusted.
But fear of the sea in winter storm did not restrain
    you,   300
Brave-hearted Leander; the ministry of the tower,
Signalling the familiar uplifted light of spousal,
Spurred you on unsparing, reckless of the maddened
    sea.
Pitiless light that failed your trust! Would that
    hapless Hero
Once winter was begun had remained far from
    Leander,   305
No longer lighting the short-lived star of the bed of
    love.
But yearning and fate forced her on; and in her
    beguilement

Μοιράων ἀνέφαινε καὶ οὐκέτι δαλὸν Ἐρώτων.
Νὺξ ἦν. εὖτε μάλιστα βαρυπνείοντες[1] ἆηται
χειμερίαις πνοιῆσιν ἀκοντίζοντες ἀέλλας[2]   310
ἀθρόον ἐμπίπτουσιν ἐπὶ ῥηγμῖνι θαλάσσης,
δὴ τότε καὶ[3] Λείανδρος ἐθήμονος ἐλπίδι νύμφης
δυσκελάδων πεφόρητο θαλασσαίων ἐπὶ νώτων.
ἤδη κύματι κῦμα κυλίνδετο, σύγχυτο δ᾽ ὕδωρ,
αἰθέρι μίσγετο πόντος, ἀνέγρετο πάντοθεν ἠχὴ   315
μαρναμένων ἀνέμων· Ζεφύρῳ δ᾽ ἀντέπνεεν Εὗρος,
καὶ Νότος εἰς Βορέην μεγάλας ἐφέηκεν[4] ἀπειλάς·
καὶ κτύπος ἦν ἀλίαστος ἐρισμαράγοιο θαλάσσης.
αἰνοπαθὴς δὲ Λείανδρος ἀκηλήτοις ἐνὶ δίναις   319
Ἀτθίδος οὐ Βορέην ἀμνήμονα κάλλιπε νύμφης[5]·   322
πολλάκι μὲν λιτάνευε Θαλασσαίην Ἀφροδίτην,   320

---

[1] βαρυπνείοντες mss., cp. 216 : βαρὺ πνείοντες V Lask.
Schwabe.
[2] ἀέλλας (V likely reading) Dilthey (ἀέλαις hum.), cp.
Nonn. D. 11. 436 s., 32. 153 s., 39. 377 s. etc., Mus. 294, 297,
Il. N 334 with Eustath. ad l. (ed. Rom. p. 935. 19 s.) : ἀήτας
mss., ἆηται hum. Ald. Lask.; ἰωὰς hum. Ludwich, cp.
Il. Λ 307 s.; ἀπειλὰς Graefe ; ἐς ἀκτὰς or ἀλίητας or ἰωκὰς
Ludwich ; ἀυτμὰς Zimmermann, cp. Q. S. 13. 329.
[3] δὴ τότε καὶ V, cp. Call. hy. 4. 307, Giangrande : δὴ τότε
mss. (with the addition of περ after Λείανδρος B Ald. Lask.);
καὶ τότε δὴ Koechly, cp. Il. Α 92, Od. ω 147, 149 ; δὴ τότε δὴ
M. L. West and T. G. (Bemerkungen 20), cp. Nonn. D. 22.
299, Orph. A. 1270 (codd.), Opp. C. 2. 271, Q. S. 10. 224
(cod. V, vulg.), but cp. Call.
[4] ἐφέηκεν BP : ἀφ- NV.
[5] Transposition T. G.: 319-321 put after 328 P, 319-320
missing and 321 put after 328 N[1].

---

[a] The three Moirai, Klotho, Lachesis and Atropos (already
in Hes. Theog. 904 sq.) are according to Plato (Rep. 617 B sq.)
daughters of Ananke (cf. Mus. 289, 307). The wedding-
torch becomes the torch of death, a stock motif in erotic
literature (cp. Ach. Tat. 1. 13. 6 : Ovid, Epist. 21. 174 etc.)

She showed forth the torch of the Fates,[a] no longer
    the Loves'.
Night came down. When most the heavily blowing
    winds,
Hurling their blasts like javelins with stormy
    breathing,   310
All together descend on the surf-edge of the sea,
Then, then also Leander, in hope of his accustomed
    bride,
Was borne on the back of the fiercely shrieking sea.
Now wave wallowed on wave, the water was all
    turmoiled,
Sea mingled with upper air, and everywhere rose the
    sound   315
Of warring winds[b]; Eurus blew hard against
    Zephyrus,
And Notus hurled mighty menacings against Boreas,
And the din was unrelenting of the loud-thundering
    sea.
Leander, dire suffering in the inexorable coils,[c]   319
Left not Boreas unmindful of the maid of Attica[d];   322
Once and again he prayed to sea-born Aphrodite,[e]   320

and in funeral epigrams (*A.P.* 7. 712. 5 sq., 7. 182. 8 sq. etc.) ;
for more parallels see Kost 511 sq.

[b] Vv. 316 sq. The four winds struggle with each other as
they do in the storm in the *Odyssey* (*Od.* 5. 295 sq., 331 sq.).

[c] Vv. 319 sq. Leander prays to the gods while swimming,
like Odysseus to the river-god (*Od.* 5. 445 sq.), but without
result—in emphatic contrast, as at 212 sq.

[d] Boreas carried off Oreithyia, daughter of Erechtheus, from
the Ilissus and carried her to his homeland of Thrace, where
she bore him Kalais and Zetes (Hdt. 7. 189 ; Pl. *Phaedr.*
229 B sq. ; Ap. Rhod. 1. 211 sq. ; Apollod. *Bibl.* 3.15.1).

[e] Aphrodite of the Sea (*cf.* 31 sq., 250) is called Θαλασσαίη
also by Nonnus (*D.* 42. 496 and frequently) and by Procopius
(*Decl.* 3. 3 sq.).

πολλάκι δ᾽ αὐτὸν ἄνακτα Ποσειδάωνα θαλάσσης, 321
ἀλλά οἱ[1] οὔ τις ἄρηγεν, Ἔρως δ᾽ οὐκ ἤρκεσε
    Μοίρας. 323
πάντοθι δ᾽ ἀγρομένοιο δυσάντεϊ κύματος ὁρμῇ[2]
τυπτόμενος πεφόρητο, ποδῶν δέ οἱ ὤκλασεν ὁρμή,[3] 325
καὶ σθένος ἦν ἀνόνητον[4] ἀκοιμήτων[5] παλαμάων.
πολλὴ δ᾽ αὐτόματος[6] χύσις ὕδατος ἔρρεε λαιμῷ,
καὶ ποτὸν ἀχρήιστον ἀμαιμακέτου πίεν ἅλμης.
καὶ δὴ λύχνον ἄπιστον ἀπέσβεσε πικρὸς ἀήτης
καὶ ψυχὴν καὶ ἔρωτα πολυτλήτοιο Λεάνδρου. 330
Ἤλυθεν[7] ἠριγένεια, καὶ οὐκ ἴδε νυμφίον Ἡρώ. 335
πάντοθι δ᾽ ὄμμα τίταινεν ἐς[8] εὐρέα νῶτα θαλάσσης,[9] 336
νείκεσε δ᾽ ὀμβριόθυμον ἐπεσβολίῃσιν ἀήτην· 331
ἤδη γὰρ φθιμένοιο μόρον θέσπισσε Λεάνδρου
εἰσέτι[10] δηθύνοντος· ἐπαγρύπνοισιν[11] ὀπωπαῖς
ἵστατο κυμαίνουσα πολυκλαύτοισι μερίμναις, 334

[1] ἀλλά οἱ Ald. Lask. hum.: ἀλλ᾽ (without οἱ) MSS.
[2] ὁρμῇ (-ῆ -η) MSS. = Nonn. *D.* 32. 156, cp. *Od.* ε 320, A. R. 2. 1118: ὁλκῷ Ludwich, cp. Nonn. *D.* 11. 459, *met. Jo.* 21. 52 etc.; either 324 ὀργῇ, or 325 ῥώμη, or ἀλκή instead of ὁρμή Graefe.
[3] L. 325 missing in PNV.
[4] ἀνόνητον Graefe, cp. Nonn. *D.* 14. 168, 20. 163, 39. 309 etc. and *Od.* ε 416 (cp. ἀνόητον V): ἀδόνητον (ἀδύνα-) MSS., cp. Paul. Sil. *H.S.* 273 Kost.
[5] ἀκοιμήτων Ald. Lask., cp. 12, 225: ἀκινήτων MSS.; ἀνικήτων Schwabe.
[6] αὐτόματος MSS.: -μάτη Dilthey with the assent of Tiedke (metre), cp. 255.
[7] ἤλυθεν MSS. Koechly, cp. 309: ἤλυθε δ᾽ B Ald. Lask.
[8] ἐς PN constr. with ὄμμα τιταίνειν Nonn. *D.* 38. 318 s., *met. Jo.* 17. 2 etc.: ἐπ᾽ BV, from the Homeric formula ἐπ᾽ εὐρέα νῶτα θαλάσσης *Il.* B 159 etc. (10 times in *Il.* and *Od.*).
[9] Transposition of ll. 335-336 T. G.: 331-332, missing in B[1], were reintegrated by Koechly, who put a lac. after 330, Hunger would insert them after 335, Malcovati and Färber reject them; Terzaghi puts 331 after 328.

Once and again to Poseidon himself, lord of the
    sea.   321
But no one helped him, and Love could not fend off
    the Fates.   323
As the wave on every side hunted him with resistless
    charge
He was beaten and hurled along, and the thrust of his
    feet grew slack,   325
And profitless was the strength of his unresting
    hands.[a]
A great gush of water of itself poured into his throat,
And he swallowed a worthless draught of the
    irresistible brine.
Then lo, a bitter gust blew out the faithless lamp,
And with it the life and love of hard-suffering
    Leander.   330
Dawn came, the early-born, and Hero saw no
    bridegroom [b] ;   335
She strained her eyes everywhere over the sea's
    broad back,   336
And with great curses reviled the wild-tempered
    wind ;   331
For already she divined the fate of Leander, perished,
Still, still delaying his coming ; with sleepless eyes
She stood, in a swelling tumult of grief and anxious-
    ness   334

---

[a] Vv. 325 sq. Odysseus also has his legs fail under him and
his strength seem to fade (*Od.* 5. 406, 416).
[b] Right from the beginning (2 sq.) it is emphasized that
the union takes place only by night (*cf.* 282 sq.)—on the
symbolism of Night and Day see Introduction, page 320.

---

[10] εἰσέτι BV, cp. 27, 266 : εἰ δέ τι PN Ald. ; ἡ δ' ἔτι Lask.
[11] ἐπαγρύπνοισιν P (cp. 213) : ἐπ' ἀ-σι (-πνίῃσιν B ἀγρίπ- N)
MSS. ; ἐπ' ἀ-σι δ' Dilthey ; ἐ-σι δ' Ludwich.

MUSAEUS

εἴ που ἐσαθρήσειεν ἀλωόμενον παρακοίτην   337
λύχνου σβεννυμένοιο. παρὰ κρηπῖδα δὲ πύργου
δρυπτόμενον σπιλάδεσσιν ὅτ᾽ ἔδρακε νεκρὸν ἀκοίτην,
δαιδαλέον ῥήξασα περὶ στήθεσσι χιτῶνα   340
ῥοιζηδὸν προκάρηνος ἀπ᾽ ἠλιβάτου πέσε πύργου.
κὰδ δ᾽ Ἡρὼ¹ τέθνηκε σὺν ὀλλυμένῳ παρακοίτῃ,
ἀλλήλων δ᾽ ἀπόναντο καὶ ἐν πυμάτῳ περ ὀλέθρῳ.

¹ κὰδ δ᾽ Ἡρὼ (κὰδδ᾽, κὰδ᾽) mss., cp. *Il.* Ω 725, Nonn. *D.*
40. 113, Triph. 228 (Mus. 241 πὰρ δὲ) : καὶ διερῷ Scheindler ;
καὶ δυερὴ or καὶ διερὴ Ludwich, cp. *Od.* ζ 201 (metre).

---

^a Leander is here once again described as " straying " (at
337 as at 177 sq. ; *cf. Od.* 5. 448) and is torn on the rocks
like Odysseus (*Od.* 5. 401 sq., 426 sq.).
^b Vv. 342 sq. In Plato those who love to the end are

Still hoping to see somewhere her husband straying,[a] 337
Now that the lamp was quenched. And when at the
    foot of the tower
She saw her husband, a dead body flayed by the tide-
    rocks,
Tearing away her embroidered robe from round her
    breasts, 340
And sweeping headlong down she fell from the lofty
    tower ;
And Hero lay in death beside her dead husband,
And they had joy of each other even in their last
    perishing.[b]

rewarded and remain united (*Phaedr.* 256 A sq., *Phaedo*
68 A). To die following the beloved's death (ἐπαποθνῄσκειν,
Symp. 179 E sq.) is especially pleasing to the gods.

CALLIMACHUS

INDEX

	PAGES	FRAGMENTS
Abdera	70 n., 71 & n.	90
Acaeos	61 & n.	75
Achaia	195	260
Acheron	107 & n., 203 n.	191
Achilles	254 n.	—
Acmon	257 & n.	498
Acontius, Acontiadae	2 n., 50 n., 51, 52 n., 53 & n., 55 n., 57, 59, 263 n.	67-75, 534 (?)
Acragas	38 n., 47 & n.	64
Acropolis	125 n., 193 & n.	260
Adonis	117 & n., 139	193
Adrastea (Nemesis)	212 n., 213	299
Adrastus	154 n.	—
Adriatic	14 n.	—
Aeacus	25 n.	—
Aedepsos	183 & n.	236
Aeëtes	13 & n.	7
Aegaeon (Posidon)	45 & n.	59
Aegaleos	185 & n.	238
Aegean (Sea)	13 n., 21 n., 61 n., 72 n., 164, 167 n., 249, 285 n.	23, 228, 399
Aegeus	131 n., 178 n., 181 & n., 183 & n., 193 & n., 195 n.	232, 233, 234, 240, 260
Aegialos	203 & n.	278 (?)
Aegina	134, 135, 137 & n.	—
Aegletes (of Apollo)	13 & n.	7
Aegyptus	74 n.	—

INDEX TO CALLIMACHUS

	PAGES	FRAGMENTS
Aenus	132, 133, 135 & n.	197
Aeolian, Aeolic	135, 145 n.	—
Aeolus	272 n., 273	618
Aesepus	213 & n.	299
Aeson	17 & n.	18
Aesop	112 n., 115 & n., 118	192
Aethalon	62 n., 63	78
Aethiopia	83	110
Aethra	178, 182 n., 225 & n.	371
Aetia	xi, xii, 11, 2-99, 179	1-112
Aetolia	272 n., 273	621
Agamemnon	139, 141 & n.	200 B
Aganippe	9 n.	—
Agias	11 n., 27 n., 49 n.	—
Agraulos	193 n., 195	260
Aiora	95 n.	—
Alalaxius (epithet of Zeus)	61	75
Albania	14 n.	—
Alcathoos	280 n., 281	680
Alcibiades	234	—
Alcinous	17 n., 18 n., 19 & n.	21
Alcmene	39 n., 42 n.	—
Alcmeon	111 & n.	191
Aletes	44 n., 45	59
Alexandria, Alexandrians	viii & n., ix, xi-xiii, 4 n., 5 n., 9 n., 49 n., 105 n., 107 n., 130 n., 143 n., 147, 163 n., 167 n., 169 & n., 177, 233 n., 237	228, 384
Alybas	75 n.	—
Alycos	282 n., 283	705
Amantine	17	12
Amarynthus	139	—
Aminias	246 n.	—
Amnisus	143 & n.	202
Amphalces	104, 109 & n.,l 11	191
Amphiaraus	111 n.	—
Amphidromia	142	—
Amphitryon	39 n.	—
Amyclae	57 & n.	75

392

INDEX TO CALLIMACHUS

	PAGES	FRAGMENTS
Amymone	49 & n.	66
Ananke	212 n.	—
Anaphe	12 n., 13, 19 n., 20 n.	7
Anatolia, Anatolians	116 n.	—
Androgeos	10 n., 76 n., 77 & n.	03
Andronicus	115 & n.	192
Anthesteria	94 n., 95	178
Anthologies, *cf.* *Palatine* and *Planudian*	—	—
Antigone (1), w. of Peleus	25 n.	—
Antigone (2), d. of Oedipus	78 n., 79	105
Antimachus	5 n., 246 n.	—
Anubis	285 & n.	715
Aonian (Boeotian)	71 & n., 267 & n.	91, 572
Apesas, Apesantian	154 n., 155	223
Aphidnae	189 & n.	253
Aphrastus	61 & n.	75
Aphrodite (Cypris)	15 n., 35 & n., 65 & n., 81 n., 83 & n., 85, 117 & n., 138, 139, 140, 160, 162 n., 163, 278 n., 279	43, 80, 110, 193, 200 A, 227
Apis (1), Egyptian god	233 & n.	383
Apis (2), Argive king	145 & n.	202
Apollo	7, 12, 13 & n., 17 & n., 19 & n., 24 n., 27 n., 37, 51 & n., 57 & n., 61, 65 n., 68-69 n., 71 n., 88 n., 89 & n., 98 n., 99 & n., 105, 107, 109 & n., 117, 121 & n., 125 & n., 127, 129 n., 134, 137 n., 141, 142 n., 145,	1, 7, 18, 43, 67, 75, 85, 86, 87, 114, 186, 191, 193, 194, 195, 202, 203, 227, 228, 229, 260, 261, 273, 302,

393

	PAGES	FRAGMENTS
	147 & n., 149, 162 n., 163, 165 & n., 168, 169 n., 171 & n., 173 & n., 176, 178, 192 n., 195 n., 197 & n., 199, 201, 213 & n., 254 n., 255	492
Apollodorus	18 n.	—
Apollonius	116 n., 126, 128 & n.	195 (?)
Apollonius Rhodius	ix-xi, xiii, 116, 136 n., 148, 179	—
Arachne	189 n.	—
Arathus	275 & n.	646
Aratus	xi	—
Arcadia	59 n., 104, 107, 109 & n., 145 n., 154 n., 155, 207 & n., 276 n., 277 n., 281 n.	191, 223, 284 A
Archemoros (Opheltes)	237 & n.	384
Archilochus	143 n., 230 n., 231, 239 & n., 263	380, 384, 544
Arctonnesus	80 n.	—
Arcturus	95 n.	—
Area	41 & n.	49 (?)
Areopagus	217 n.	—
Ares	15 n., 123, 275 & n., 285 & n.	194, 644, 719
Arete	18 n., 19	21
Argo, Argonauts	12 n., 13 & n., 15 & n., 17 & n., 18 n., 19 n., 80 n., 81 & n., 135, 136 n., 137 & n., 161	7, 11, 12, 18, 19-21, 108, 198
Argos, Argolis, Argolica, Argives	16 n., 24 n., 25 n., 26 n., 27 & n., 42 n., 43, 45 & n., 48 n., 49 & n., 74-75 n., 138-139, 145 n., 203 n., 204-205 n., 221 n., 233 & n., 237, 239 n., 269 n., 282 n., 283 n.	26, 55, 59, 65, 66, 383, 384
Argus	48 n.	—

INDEX TO CALLIMACHUS

	PAGES	FRAGMENTS
Ariadne (Ari-ede)	51 & n., 83 & n.	67, 110
Arimaspians	99 & n.	186
Arion	154 n., 155	223
Aristaeus	57 & n.	75
Aristophanes (of Byzantium)	xiii	—
Arneus, Arnus	25, 27 & n.	26, 27
Arsinoë	x, 81 n., 83 & n., 85 n., 159, 162-169 & nn., 242 & n., 243 & n.	110, 112 (?), 228, 392
Artacia	81 n.	—
Artemidorus	xiv	—
Artemis	28 n., 29 & n., 50 n., 57 & n., 64 n., 65 & n., 72 n., 73, 138, 139, 140 n., 141, 143 & n., 212 n., 213 & n., 241 & n., 272 n., 287	31 B, 75, 79, 80, 96, 200 B, 202, 302, 388, 731
Artemis of Leucas	xiv, 28, 29	31 B
Asbystae	235 & n.	384
Asclepiades	4 n.	—
Asia (Minor)	62 n., 64 n., 112 n., 119 n., 139 n., 213 n., 240 n.	—
Asine	25 & n., 282 n., 283	25, 705
Asopis	137 n.	—
Aspendus	138	—
Asterion	205 & n.	280
Athamas (Tammes)	40 n., 41 & n., 71 n.	49
Athena	29, 30 n., 31, 45 & n., 75, 80 n., 124 n., 125, 133 n., 145 & n., 147, 178, 189 & n., 193 & n., 195 & n., 197, 224 n., 229, 238 n., 239 & n., 241 & n., 258 n., 259, 269 & n., 273 n., 275	37, 57, 100, 194, 202, 253, 260, 261, 374 (?), 384, 388, 519, 592, 638

	PAGES	FRAGMENTS
Athenaeus	163 n., 234 n.	—
Athenis	106 n.	—
Athens, Athenians, Attica	viii n., xii, 41 & n., 51 n., 57 n., 73 & n., 94 n., 95 & n., 105, 107 n., 111 n., 121 n., 124 n., 125 & n., 130, 132 n., 139, 176, 178 n., 180 n., 181, 185 n., 189 n., 195 n., 199 & n., 211 n., 213 n., 214 n., 217 n., 221 n., 233 n., 239, 265 n., 267 n., 273 n., 281 n.	51, 94-95, 97, 178, 194, 230, 261, 384
Atthis, Atthido-grapher	176, 177 n.	—
Athos	83 & n., 164, 167	110, 228
Augeas	62 n.	—
Augustus	xiv	—
Ausonian Sea	185 & n.	238
Ausonians	75 n.	—
Automate	49 & n.	65, 66
Babrius	215 n.	—
Bacchus, *cf.* Dionysus	—	—
Bacchylides	51 n., 59 n., 136 n., 234 n.	—
Bacis	129 & n.	195
Barber, E. A.	xvi, 261 n.	—
Bathycles	104, 107, 109 & n.	191
Battos	vii	—
Belice, *cf.* Hypsas	—	—
Bellerophon	8 n.	—
Bentley, R.	xv	—
Berenice (1), w. of Ptolemy I	80 n.	—
Berenice (2), w. of Ptolemy III	xi, 80 n., 81 & n.-85, 230 n., 232 n., 241	110, 112, 388 (?)
Bias	104, 111 & n.	191
Boeotia, Boeo-	9 n., 37 n., 39 n., 40 n.,	91, 572

INDEX TO CALLIMACHUS

	PAGES	FRAGMENTS
tians (*cf.* Aonian)	71 & n., 129 n., 145 n., 199 n., 266 n., 267 & n., 274 n., 277 n.	
Bootes	81 n., 95 n.	—
Boreas	82 n., 83, 216 n., 217	110 (?), 321
Bouthoinas (Heracles)	23 n.	—
Branchus	121 & n., 159, 168, 169, 171 & n.	194, 229
Brennus	228 n., 229	379
Brilessos	181 n., 217 n., 265 & n.	552
Bruttium	65 n., 75 n.	—
Bull (of Marathon)	176, 177, 191 & n., 193, 205, 219 n.	258, 259, 260, 283
Bupalos	106 n., 107	191
Busiris	38 n., 39 & n.	44-46
Byne (Ino)	71 & n.	91
Byzantium, Byzantine	ix, xiii	—
Cabiri	91 n.	115
Cadmus, Cadmean	15 n., 37, 70-71 n.	43
Calauria	269	593
Callichoron	270 n., 271	611
Callicoon	270 n., 271	607
Callimachus	vii-xv, 2 & n., 3, 4-11 nn., 20 n., 25 n., 27 n., 30 n., 31 n., 41 n., 45 n., 48 n., 62 n., 64 n., 66-67 n., 70 n., 76 n., 78 n., 80 n., 87 n., 94 n., 99 n., 104 & n., 111 n., 112 n., 113, 116-119, 126, 127 n., 128, 130-133 n., 135, 136, 137, 139, 141, 142 n., 143, 146, 148, 151 n., 160, 176-179, 215 n., 228, 229, 230, 231, 233-235, 243, 245, 247 n., 271 n., 283 n., 284 n.	—

	PAGES	FRAGMENTS
Calliope	13 n., 28 n., 35, 85 n., 87 n.	7, 43
Calliste	285 & n.	716
Calydonian (Boar)	272 n., 273	621
Camarina	33 & n., 46 n., 47	43, 64
Camicus	35 n.	—
Canopus	83 & n.	110
Caria, Carians	61 & n.	75
Carthaea	61 & n.	75
Caryae (Cares)	59 & n.	75
Casian (Sea)	239 & n.	384
Castnion	138-139	200 A
Castor	16 n., 17, 47 & n., 163 & n.	18, 64, 227
Cato	2 n.	—
Catullus	80 n., 85 n.	—
Caucasus	279 n.	—
Caÿster	119 n.	—
Cean Tetrapolis	61 & n.	75
Cecrops	125 & n., 178, 193 & n., 195 n.	194, 260
Celaenae	59 & n.	75
Cenchreae	235 n.	—
Centhippe	204 n., 205	279
Ceos, Cean (1)	4 n., 46 n., 47, 50 n., 51 n., 59 & n., 61, 154 n., 155	64, 75, 222
Ceos (2), son of Apollo	61	75
Cerberus	258 n., 259 & n.	515
Cercyon	207 & n., 216 n.	284 A
Ceyx	51 n., 57, 59	75
Chalcidice	83 n.	—
Chalcis	35	43
Chalybes	83 & n.	110
Chaos	9	2
Charis	164, 167 & n., 169	228
Charitades	118, 119, 141 n.	194
Charmides	130, 133	196
Charon	203 n., 275 & n.	628
Chellon	254 n., 255	486

INDEX TO CALLIMACHUS

	PAGES	FRAGMENTS
Chilon	105, 111 & n.	191
Chios	147, 249	399
Choeroboscus	127	—
Chryso	61 & n.	75
Cimmerians	57 n.	—
Cinyps	237 & n.	384
Cinyras	117 n.	—
Cirodes	59	75
Cissousa	37 & n.	43
Clazomenae	106 n.	—
Cleobulus	105	—
Cleon	116 n., 126, 128 & n., 129	195 (?)
Cleonae	42 n., 43 n., 45 n., 221 & n.	339
Clio	28 n., 29, 35	31 B, 43
Clymenus (Hades)	208 n., 209 & n.	285
Cnossus	37 & n.	43
Cocalus	35 & n.	43
Cocles, cf. Horatius	—	—
Codrus	51 n., 57 & n., 73 n., 111 n.	75
Colaenis (Artemis)	139, 140 n., 141	200 B
Colchis, Colchians	13 n., 15 & n., 278 n., 279	7, 10, 672
Colias	221 & n.	341
Colonos (Colonae)	213 & n.	300
Colophon	5 n., 104, 149 n., 189 n., 246 n.	—
Comes	254 n., 255	486
Connarus, Connidas	140, 141	201
Conon	80 n., 81 & n.	110
Coppola	85 n., 113 n.	—
Corcyra	16 n., 17 & n.	12
Coresus	61 & n.	75
Coroebus (1), killer of Poine	25, 27 n.	26
Coroebus (2),	267 & n.	587

	PAGES	FRAGMENTS
proverbial fool		
Coronis	10 n., 197 & n.	260
Corycian (Nymphs)	59 & n.	75
Corycus	112 n., 113 n.	—
Cos, Coan	ix, 4 n.	—
Crannon	47 & n.	64
Crataemenes	35, 37	43
Crete, Cretan	4, 10 n., 11 n., 12 n., 21 n., 33 n., 35, 37 & n., 39 n., 61 n., 143 & n., 185 n., 209 n., 261 n.	43, 202
Croesus	169	—
Cromna	235 & n.	384
Cronus	37 & n., 91 n., 112 n., 115, 247	43, 192, 393
Croton	264 n.	—
Crotopus	24 n., 26 n., 27 & n., 29 & n.	26, 28
Cumae, Cumaeans	169	—
Cybele (Cybebe)	116 n., 117 & n., 127 & n.	193, 194
Cyclops	228	
Cydippe	2 n., 50 n., 51 & n., 52 n., 53 & n., 55 & n., 57, 59	67-75
Cyme	35	43
Cynthus, Cynthian	51 & n., 89 & n.	67, 114
Cypris, cf. Aphrodite	85	110
Cyprus, Cypriote	4, 38 n., 117 n., 239, 241 n.	384
Cyrenaica	235 n., 279 n.	—
Cyrene, Cyrenean	vii, viii, xiii, 7 n., 30 n., 31 n., 80 n., 85 n., 87 & n., 135, 233, 271 & n., 285 & n.	112, 602, 716
Cyrene (nymph)	7 n., 57 n., 85 n., 87 & n.	112

	PAGES	FRAGMENTS
Cyta, Cytaean, (=Colchian)	13 & n.	7
Cyzicus	80 n., 81 & n., 213 n.	108
Daedalus	21 n., 35 & n.	43
Daites	168, 171 & n.	229
Damasichthon	51 n.	—
Damasus	29	33
Damon, cf. Demonax	—	—
Danaus	48 n., 49 n., 74 n., 75 & n., 233 & n.	100, 383
Daphnephoria	69 & n.	86-87
Dawson, C. M.	103, 104 n.	—
Decelea	201	272
Deipnias	69 & n.	87
Delos, Delians	x, 17, 50 n., 51 & n., 57, 88 n., 89, 98 n., 125 & n., 145, 151 n., 169 n., 173 & n., 229, 254 n.	18, 67, 75, 114, 194, 202, 203, 229
Delphi, Delphians	17, 25 n., 51 n., 68 n., 69 & n., 107 & n., 115 & n., 121 & n., 123, 129 & n., 145 & n., 168, 171 n., 204 n., 228 n., 229, 269	18, 86, 191, 192, 194, 195, 202, 592
Delphinius (epithet of Apollo)	172 n., 173, 176 n.	229
Demeter	5 & n., 21 & n., 54 n., 55, 117 n., 154 n., 167 & n., 203 n., 208 n., 209 & n., 212 n., 213 n., 270 n., 271, 276, 277 & n.	1, 21, 75, 228, 285, 611, 652
Democritus	xii	—
Demonax	61 & n.	15
Demophon	266 n., 267	556
Deo, cf. Demeter	—	—
Deoine	212 n., 213	302
Dercylos	11 n., 27 n., 49 n.	—
Despoina	276 n., 277	652
Deucalion	533	261

	PAGES	FRAGMENTS
Dexithea	51 n., 61 & n.	75
Dia (Naxos)	269	601
Diana, *cf.* Artemis	—	—
Dicte	143 & n.	202
Didymi, Didyma, Didymean	105, 109 & n., 168, 169, 171 & n.	191, 229
Diegeseis	vii n., xiv, 3, 28 n., 63 n., 64 n., 66 n., 68, 70 n., 72–76 nn., 78–80 nn., 104, 106 n., 112, 114, 115 n., 118, 126, 132, 134, 138–140, 146, 147, 159, 160, 162, 169, 177, 227	—
Dike	147 & n.	202
Diochares	199 n.	—
Diodorus	246 n., 247 & n.	393
Dionysias (Naxos)	59	75
Dionysus	10 n., 37 n., 76 n., 95, 117 n., 214 n., 215, 285 n.	43, 305, 719 (?)
Dioscorides	241 & n.	384 A
Dioscuri (*cf.* Castor and Polydeuces)	160, 163 n., 165 & n.	228
Dodona	21 n., 99 n., 129 n., 253 & n.	186, 195, 483
Doric, Dorian	33 n., 121, 135, 141, 149	194, 203
Drepanum, *cf.* Zancle	—	—
Dryopes	23 & n., 24 n., 25 & n., 282 n.	24, 25
Echidna	259 & n.	515
Egypt, Egyptians	7, 38 n., 39 & n., 94 n., 95, 164, 169, 231, 232, 233 & n., 235 & n., 237 n., 239 n., 277 n., 279 n.	1, 44, 178, 383, 384, 655
Eilithyia (Ilithyia)	13 & n., 65 n., 143 n., 260 n., 261 & n.	7, 524

	PAGES	FRAGMENTS
Elalos	197 n.	—
Eleusis	21 n., 207 n., 217 n., 271 n.	—
Elis, Eleans	62 n., 63 & n., 130, 131, 133 & n.	77, 196
Ellopians	99 & n.	186
Emporion	162, 163 n.	—
Enceladus	9 & n.	1
Endeis	25 n.	—
Enna	167 & n.	228
Eos (Tito)	18 n., 83 n.	—
Epeus	132 & n., 135 & n.	197
Ephesus	57 n., 76 n., 77 & n., 105 n., 149 & n., 151	102, 203
Ephyra, cf. Corinth	—	—
Epigrams	245-249	393-401
Epirus	21 n., 28 n., 107 n., 253 n., 275 n.	—
Epizephyrian (Locrians), cf. Locrians		
Epopsios (epithet of gods)	67 & n.	85
Eratosthenes	xiii	—
Erchios	267 & n.	571
Erechtheus	180 n., 181 & n., 217 & n.	230, 321
Eretria	138, 139	—
Ericho, cf. Oricus	—	—
Erichthonius	178, 192 n., 193 & n., 225	260, 374
Erigone	57 n., 94 n., 95 & n.	178
Erinys (Demeter)	276 n., 277	652
Eriphyle	111 n.	—
Eros	51, 59 & n., 260 n., 279 & n.	67, 75, 676
Erotes	162 n., 163	227
Eryx	35 & n.	43
Eteocles	79 n.	—
Etesian (Winds)	57 n.	—

	PAGES	FRAGMENTS
Etruscans	79 n.	—
Euanthe	11 n.	—
Euboea	35 & n., 99 n., 139, 183 n.	43
Eudeipnos, *cf. Aiora*	—	—
Eudemos	113 & n., 115	192
Euhemerus	105 & n., 107 & n.	191
Eumaeus	191 n.	—
Eumenides	280 n., 281	681
Euphorbos	109 & n.	191
Euphraios (Euphrates)	vii	—
Eupylus	61 & n.	75
Euripides	xiii, 111 n., 161, 234	—
Europa	35 & n.	43
Europe (fountain)	275 & n.	630
Eurotas	57 n., 207	284 A
Euryclea	40 n.	49 (?)
Eurynome	11 & n., 239 & n.	6, 384
Eurystheus	23 n.	—
Euthycles	66 n., 67 & n.	84, 85
Euthydemos	116	—
Euthymus	75 & n.	98
Euxanthius	51 n., 61 n.	—
Euxine (Black Sea)	15 n., 278 n.	—
Fasti	2 n.	—
Fates	145 & n.	202
Franks	xiii	—
Gaius, *cf.* Horatius	—	—
Galatea	x, 228, 229	378, 379
Galates, Gauls	228 & n., 229 & n.	379
Gê	91 n., 123 n., 195 & n.	194, 260
Gela, Gelas (river)	33 & n.	43
Giants	91	119
Glauce (Athena)	238 n., 239	384
Graces	10 n., 11 & n., 61, 75, 85	3, 6, 61, 75,

	PAGES	FRAGMENTS
	& n., 88 n., 89, 130, 131, 133, 239 & n., 279	112, 114, 196, 673
Grapheion	230, 231	380
Greece, Greeks	x, xii, xiii n., 5 n., 8 n., 15, 35 n., 41 n., 54 n., 72 n., 79 & n., 83 n., 98 n., 99 & n., 109 n., 117 n., 133, 145 n., 201 n., 212 n., 228 n., 229, 231 n., 232 n., 233 n., 237 n., 267, 285 n.	11, 106, 186, 379, 557
Hades (*cf.* Clymenus)	55, 91 n., 105 n., 106 n., 107 n., 203 n.	75
Haemonia (Thessaly)	13 & n., 215 & n.	7, 304
Haliartus	37 & n.	43
Hamaxae	81 n., 109 & n., 165 & n.	191, 228
Harmonia	15 & n.	11
Hebe	141, 145 & n., 260 n., 261 & n.	202, 524
Hecale (Hecaline)	xi, 119, 125 n., 159, 176-225, 229, 254 n., 256 n., 261 n., 265 n., 283 n.	230-232, 240-244, 246-257, 263, 292, 342, 355
Hecate	107	191
Helen	160, 163 n., 267 & n.	257, 557
Helen's Island	233 & n.	383
Helicon	2, 8 n.	—
Helios	82 n., 83	110 (?)
Helle	40 n., 41 (?)	49 (?)
Hellenistic	viii, xv	—
Hemsterhuis	vii n.	—
Hephaestus	29, 30 n., 41 n., 91, 147 & n., 167 n., 193 & n., 195	37, 115, 202, 260
Hera	11 n., 41 n., 42 n., 43, 49 & n., 54 n., 55, 71 n., 74 n., 75 & n., 76 n., 77 & n., 145, 239 & n., 269 n.	55, 66, 75, 100, 101, 202, 384

INDEX TO CALLIMACHUS

	PAGES	FRAGMENTS
Heracles	13, 20 n., 21 n., 23 & n., 25 & n., 39 n., 42 n., 43 & n., 45 & n., 62 n., 63 & n., 76 n., 258 n., 259, 261 n., 269 & n., 274 n., 279 & n., 286 n., 287	7, 23, 24, 25, 57, 59, 77, 515, 597, 677, 784
Heraclides	129 n.	—
Heraiom	204-205 n., 239 & n.	384
Hermes	132 & n., 133, 134, 135 & n., 136, 137 & n., 139 & n., 155 & n., 264 n., 265	197, 199, 221, 554
Hermione	203 & n., 209 n., 283 & n.	278 (?), 705
Hermocrates	viii n.	—
Hermus	119 n.	—
Herodotus	137	—
Herse	193, 195, 285 n.	260
Hesiod	9 & n., 17 n., 87 & n., 116, 165 n., 195 n., 217 n.	2, 112
Hesychidae	281 & n.	681
Hipparis	35 & n.	43
Hippe	49 & n.	66
Hippocrene	8 n.	—
Hippodamea	280 n.	—
Hippomenes	72 n.	—
Hipponax	104, 105 & n., 106 n., 129 n., 149 & n.	191, 203
Homer, Homeric	xi-xiii, 95 & n., 167 n., 190 n.	178
Horae	130, 131 & n., 133 & n.	196
Horatius (Cocles)	78 n., 79 & n.	106
Hunt, A. S.	xv n.	—
Hyblaea Megara	35 & n.	43
Hydrophoria	135-137 n.	—
Hydrussa	59 & n.	75
Hylas	23 n.	—
Hylichus	154 n., 155	222

406

	PAGES	FRAGMENTS
Hyllus (1), harbour	17 & n.	15
Hyllus (2), son of Heracles	23 & n.	24
Hymettus	185 & n.	238
Hyperboreans	98 n., 99 & n., 254 n., 255 & n.	186, 492
Hyperion	82 n.	—
Hypsas (Belice, River)	140 n., 141 & n.	201
Hypsipyle	237 & n.	384
Ialysus	13 n.	
Iambi	xi, 2 n., 3, 87 & n., 103, 104-155, 159, 179	191-223
Iasis, *cf.* Io	—	—
Iasos	viii n., 246 n.	—
Ibis	ix, x & n.	—
Icarius	95 & n.	178
Icarus, Icarian, Sea, *i.e.* Aegean	21 & n.	23
Icmaeus, Icmius (epithet of Zeus)	57 & n.	75
Icos	95 & n., 97 & n.	178
Idmon	189 n.	—
Ieios, epithet of Apollo	17 & n.	18
Illyria, Illyrians	14 n., 15 & n.	11
Illyria Graeca	17 n.	—
Ilyssus	217 n.	—
Imbrasos	268 n., 269	599
Indian	147 & n., 236 n.	202
Ino (Byne)	70 n., 71	91
Io (Iasis)	48 n., 49	66
Iocastus	272 n., 273	618
Ion (of Chios)	146, 147	—
Ionians, Ionic	62 n., 64 n., 121, 139, 149, 151, 240 n.	194, 203
Iphicles (Iphiclus)	59 & n.	75
Ischys	197	260

	PAGES	FRAGMENTS
Isindus, Isindians	62 n., 63 & n.	78
Ister	99 n.	—
Isthmian (Games)	45 & n., 232, 236 n., 237	59, 384
Isthmus (of Corinth)	145 & n., 235 & n.	202, 384
Italia, Italians	237 n., 277 & n.	669
Iulls	51 & n., 59 & n., 61 & n.	67, 75
Jason	14 n., 15, 177 n.	9, 18
Kaibel, G.	vii n.	—
Laconia, Lacedaemonians	57 n., 105	—
Laomedon	18 n., 19	21
Lapithes	171 & n.	229
Larissa	69 n.	—
Leandrios	105 & n.	—
Learchus	71 n., 237 & n.	384
Lechaeon	235 & n.	384
Leda	17 n., 163 n.	—
Leleges	61 & n., 70 n.	75
Lemnos	160, 161, 167 & n., 237 n.	226, 228
Leo	81 n.	—
Leon	140, 142 n., 143	204 (?)
Leontini	35 & n.	43
Leoprepes	47	64
Lepargus	25 & n.	24
Lesbos, Lesbian	70 n., 249, 255 & n.	399, 485
Leto	125 & n., 151 & n., 261 n.	194, 203
Leucas	xiv, 28 n., 29 & n.	31 B
Libya, Libyan	2, 30 n., 31 & n., 145 n., 167, 235 n., 270 n., 271, 279	37, 228, 602, 676
Limnae	214 n., 215	305
Limone (Limonis)	73 & n.	94 & 95
Lindus, Lindians	13 & n., 20 n., 21 & n., 23 n., 33, 75 & n., 105	7, 22, 43, 100
Linus (1), son of Ismenius	23 n.	—

INDEX TO CALLIMACHUS

	PAGES	FRAGMENTS
Linus (2), son of Psamathe	24 n., 25 & n., 27 & n., 29 & n.	26, 27, 28
Lipara	70 n., 71 & n.	93
Lobel, E.	xv n., 29 n., 142 n.	—
Locrian (attribute of Arsinoë)	83 & n.	110
Locrians (Western)	66 n., 67 & n., 277 n.	84, 85, 669
Lycabettus	193 n., 199 n.	—
Lycean (Gymnasium)	199 & n.	261
Lycia	59 n.	—
Lycian (Apollo)	7 & n.	1
Lyde	5 n., 7 (?), 247 & n.	1 (?), 398
Lydia, Lydians	5 n., 116 n., 119 & n., 127 n., 189 n., 247 n.	194
Lygdamis	57 & n.	75
Maas, P.	xvi, 142 n., 222 n., 235 n.	—
Macelo	61 & n.	75
Machaereus	171 n.	—
Maera	57 & n., 95 n.	75
Magas	80 n., 230, 241	—
Magnesia	95 n., 277 & n.	650
Malea	281 & n.	689
Malis	99 & n.	186
Maloeis	254 n., 255	485
Marathon	176, 189, 191 n., 193, 199 n., 205 n., 219 n.	253, 260
Marsyas	117 n.	—
Massagetae	7 & n.	1
Mecone (Sicyon)	90 n., 91	119
Medea	13 n., 14 n., 15 & n., 18 n., 19 n., 177, 180 n., 181 & n., 224 n.	7, 232, 374 (?)
Medes	7 & n.	1
Megacles	61 & n.	75
Megara, Megarians, Megarid	26 n., 35 & n., 208 n., 246 n., 257 n., 281 n.	43

	PAGES	FRAGMENTS
Megara Hyblaea, *cf.* Hyblaea Megara	—	—
Megatime	vii	—
Melaenae	199 & n.	266
Melas	18 n., 19	19
Meleager	273 n.	—
Meleager's Garland	xiii	—
Melia	61	75
Melicertes	70 n., 71 & n., 237 & n.	91, 384
Memnon	83	110
Memphis	277 n.	—
Menelaus	109 n.	—
Merithus	185 & n.	238
Mesatma	vii	—
Messene, *cf.* Zancle	—	—
Midas	59 & n.	75
Miletus, Milesians	64 n., 65 & n., 80 n., 104, 105, 109 & n., 111 & n., 121 n., 168, 169 n., 171 & n., 172 n., 173 & n., 270 n.	80 & 82, 191, 229
Mimnermus	5 n., 7, 149 & n.	1, 203
Mimusops	277 & n.	655
Minoa	35 & n.	43
Minos, Minoan	10 n., 11, 35 & n., 51 n., 61 n., 77 n., 83 & n.	4, 5, 43, 110
Minyae (Argonauts)	13 & n., 15 n.	7
Mitylene	4 n., 105, 255 n.	—
Molorchus	42 n., 43 & n., 45 & n.	55-59
Momos	246 n., 247	393
Mousetrap	69, 91	177
Muses	2, 3, 5, 7, 9 & n., 13, 28 n., 29, 61, 69, 85 & n., 87 & n., 117, 145, 149, 153, 155, 165 & n., 203, 222, 235, 237	1, 2, 7, 31 F, 75, 86, 112, 193, 202, 218, 228
Mycenae	43 n.	—

INDEX TO CALLIMACHUS

	PAGES	FRAGMENTS
Mygdon	267 n.	—
Myrina	237 & n.	384
Myrmidons	97 & n.	178-183
Myrrha	117 n.	—
Myso-Phrygian	80 n.	—
Myus	65 & n.	80
Naios (Zeus)	99 & n.	186
Nanno	5 n., 7	1
Nasamones	271 & n.	602
Naxos	10 n., 18 n., 35 n., 51 & n., 59 & n., 83 n., 269	67, 75, 601
Neleus	65 n., 111 & n.	191
Nelson's Island, cf. Helen's Island	—	
Nemea, Nemean Games	42 n., 45 & n., 54 n., 221 & n., 232, 233 n., 236 n., 237, 239 & n.	58, 59, 339, 383, 384
Nemesis	212 n., 213, 281 & n.	299, 687
Neoptolemus	171 n.	—
Nepea	213 & n.	299
Nereid	228	—
Nestor	64 n., 65	80 & 82
Nestos	71 n.	—
Nike	xi, 133 & n., 232	196, 384
Nile	7 n., 233 n., 237 & n., 239	384
Nisa	35 & n., 257 & n.	43, 495
Nisus	208, 209 & n.	288
Oceanus, Oceanid	11 n., 85, 91 n., 123 n., 257 & n.	110, 498 (?)
Odysseus	74-75 n., 190 n.	—
Oecus (Miletus)	173 & n.	229
Oeneus	272 n., 273 n.	—
Oesydres	79	104
Olympia, Olympic Games	63 n., 66-67 & n., 123 & n., 130, 133 n., 231 n.	84, 194
Olympus	145	202
Omphale	279 n.	—
Onnes	91 & n.	115

411

INDEX TO CALLIMACHUS

	PAGES	FRAGMENTS
Opheltes - Archemoros, *cf.* Archemoros	—	
Ophion	91 & n.	177
Orestes	70 n., 95, 111 n.	178
Orgas	257 & n.	495
Oricus	17 & n.	12
Orientals	145 n.	—
Orithyia	216 n.	
Orpheus, Orphic	xiii, 118 n.	—
Ouranos	11 n., 123 n., 257 & n.	498
Ovid	x, 2 n.	—
Pactolus	127 & n.	194
Pagasae	19	18
Palatine (Anthology)	ix n., xiii, 4 n., 5 n., 9 n., 142 n.	—
Pallas, *cf.* Athena	—	—
Pamphylia	138, 139 n.	—
Pan	281	689
Pan - Athenean Games	232, 238 & n.	384
Panchaea	107 & n.	191
Pandrosos	193 n., 195	260
Pan-Ionian Festival	62 n.	—
Panormus	81 & n.	108
Parmenion	104, 106 n.	—
Parnasus	59 & n., 195 n.	75
Parnes	185 & n.	238
Paros, Parian	10 n., 11, 13, 78 n., 231 n.	3, 7
Parthenios (Pontus)	57 & n.	75
Parthenios (Samos)	268 n., 269	599
Parthenon	133 n.	—
Pasicles	76 n., 77 & n.	102
Pasiphaë	51 n.	—
Pausanias	131	—
Pegasus	8 n., 9, 87	2, 112

	PAGES	FRAGMENTS
Pelasgians	49 & n., 72 n., 73 & n., 99 & n., 137	66, 97, 186
Peleus	25 & n., 97 & n.	24, 178-184
Pellene	193 n., 195	260
Peloponnesus	24 n., 90 n., 145 n.	—
Pelops	235 & n., 280 n.	384
Pelusium	239 n.	—
Peneus	68 n., 171 n.	—
Periander	104	—
Pericles	133 n.	—
Perieres	35, 37	43
Perillos	39 & n.	46
Perpheraios (Hermes)	134 n., 135	197
Persephone	203 n., 208 n., 209, 270 n., 271	285, 611
Perseus	277 & n.	655
Persians	7 & n., 83 & n., 169 n., 241 n.	1, 110
Peucetii (Etruscans ?)	79 n.	—
Pfeiffer, R. H.	vii n., ix n., xi n., xii n., xiv & n., xv. 4 n., 69, 78 n., 103, 129, 159, 160, 179, 228, 234 n.	—
Phaeacia, Phaeacians	17, 18 & n., 19 & n.	12, 15, 21
Phalaris	38 n., 39 & n.	44-46
Phaleron	76 n.	—
Pharos	167 n., 169	228
Phasis	15 & n.	7
Phidias	131, 132 n., 133 & n.	196
Philadelphos, cf. Ptolemy	—	—
Philetadas	136, 137	—
Philetas	ix, 4 n., 5 & n.	1
Philo	112 n.	—
Philochorus	176, 177 & n.	—
Philotera	164, 167 & n., 169	228
Philton	113, 115	192
Phlegyas	197	260
Phocaea	240 n., 241	388

	PAGES	FRAGMENTS
Phocus	25 n.	—
Phoebus, *cf.* Apollo	—	—
Phoenicians	109 & n.	191
Phoenix	47 & n.	64
Phrasios	38 n., 39 n.	—
Phrygia, Phrygians	59 n., 80 n., 109, 117 & n., 267 n.	191, 193
Phrygius	64 n., 65 & n., 109	80, 82
Phthia	97	184
Phyleus	62 n., 63 & n.	77
Phyllis	266 n.	—
Physadea	49 & n.	66
Pieria	64 n., 65 & n.	80, 82
Pinakes	viii, xii	—
Pindar	231 n., 234	—
Piraeus	76 n.	—
Pirene	236 n., 237	384
Pisa	63 & n., 67 & n.	76, 84
Pittacus	105	—
Pittheus	128 n., 130 n., 131 & n., 178 n., 225 n.	195
Planudian(Anthology)	xiii, 4 n.	—
Plato	9 n.	—
Plokamos	x, xi, 3, 80-85 & nn.	110
Plutarch	176	—
Pluto	90-91 n.	119
Poeessa	61 & n.	75
Poine	27 n.	26
Polae	15 & n.	11
Polites	75 n.	—
Polybius	233	—
Polycles	134	—
Polydeuces	16 n., 17, 47 & n., 163 & n.	18, 64, 227
Polynices	79 n.	—
Pontus	57 n.	—
Poros, *cf.* Calauria	—	—
Posidippus	4 n., 9 n., 242 n.	—
Posidon	45 & n., 49, 61 & n.,	59, 66, 75,

	PAGES	FRAGMENTS
	90 n., 91, 124 n., 125 & n., 145 & n., 154 n., 195 n., 235 & n., 276 & n.	119, 194, 202, 384, 652
Praxiphanes	4 n.	—
Priam	254 n., 255	491
Priene	104, 111 n., 270 n.	—
Procles	75 n.	—
Proclus, Proclean (hymns)	xiii	—
Procyon, *cf.* Sirius	—	—
Prometheus, Promethean	115 & n., 256 n., 257, 265 & n.	192, 493, 551
Promethus	51 & n.	67
Pronaea (Athena)	269	592
Propertius	2 n.	—
Propontis	80 n.	—
Prosymna	205 & n.	279
Proteus	167 & n.	228
Prurides	70 n,	—
Psamathe (1), Nereid, m. of Phocus	25 n.	—
Psamathe (2), d. of Crotopus	24 n., 25, 27 & n.	26
Ptolemaea	232-233, 239 n.	—
Ptolemaic (papyri)	xiii n.	—
Ptolemies	viii, 87, 232, 237 n., 239 n.	112
Ptolemy I	80 n., 232, 239 & n.	384
Ptolemy II (Philadelphos)	viii-x, 162, 165, 242	228, 392
Ptolemy III (Euergetes)	81 n., 233, 241	—
Ptolemy IV & V	xi, 233	—
Pygmies	7 & n.	

	PAGES	FRAGMENTS
Pylos	65 & n.	80 & 82
Pythagoras, Pythagoreans	109 & n., 111 & n., 260 n., 264 n., 265	191, 553
Pythia	121 & n.	194
Pythian Games	121 & n., 123	194
Pytho	121 & n., 145 & n.	194, 202
Rarus, Rarian (Demeter)	21 & n.	21
Red Sea	107 n.	—
Rhadamanthys	38 n., 39	43
Rhegium	272 n., 273	618
Rhipaean (Mountains)	99 & n.	186
Rhodes, Rhodians	ix, 4 n., 13 n., 20 n., 33 n., 75 n.	—
Roberts, C. H.	xiii n.	—
Rome, Roman	78 n., 79 & n.	106
Salustius	xiv	—
Samos, Samian	74 n., 75, 76 n., 77 & n., 109 n., 264 n., 268 n., 270 n.	100, 101
Samothrace	91 n.	—
Santorin, cf. Thera	—	—
Sarapis, Sarapideum	104, 105 n., 107 & n.	191
Sardis	115	192
Saronic Gulf	235 n.	—
Scamander	132	—
Scelmis	74 n., 75, 77 n.	100
Scholia (Florentina)	xiv, 4, 10 n.	—
Scoglitti	33 n.	—
Scopadae	47 & n.	64
Scylla	208 n., 209 & n.	288
Scythian	7 n., 83 n.	—
Selene	107 n.	—
Selinus	35 n., 140, 141 & n.	—
Selloi	21 & n., 99 & n.	23, 186
Sibyl	129 & n.	195
Sicily, Sicilian	9 & n., 33 & n., 35 & n.,	1, 43, 69, 228

	PAGES	FRAGMENTS
	46 n., 47 n., 53, 71 n., 140, 141 n., 162 n., 167 & n., 185 n.	
Sicyon	4 n., 90 n., 91, 203 n.	119
Sidon, Sidonian	241 & n.	384
Silenus	51 & n.	67
Simonides	2, 46 n., 47 & n., 51 n., 59 n., 154 n., 155, 231	64, 222
Simos	116 n., 118, 119 & n.	194
Sirius	57 n., 95 n.	—
Sisyphus, Sisyphidae	235 & n.	384
Smicrus	168, 171	229
Solon	104, 111 & n.	191
Sosibios	xi, 230, 231-241	384, 384 A
Sparta, Spartan	13, 111 n.	7
Stilbe	171 n.	—
Strabo	vii n., 131, 185 n.	—
Suidas	vii & n., x & n., xii, xiv	—
Syracuse	35 n., 47 n.	—
Syrma	78 n., 79	105
Syros	270 n.	—
Syrtis	271 n.	—
Tammes, cf. Athamas	—	—
Tauromenium	141 n.	—
Telamon	25 n.	—
Telchines (1), Wizards	4 n., 61 & n.	75
Telchines (2), enemies of Callimachus	xiii, 3, 4 n., 5 & n., 148	1, 203
Telestorides	29 & n.	33
Temese (Temesa)	67 & n., 74 n., 75 n.	85
Tempe	68-69 n., 121 & n., 123	194
Tenedos	70 n.	—
Teos	41 n.	—
Tethys	11 n., 123 & n.	194
Tetrapolis (1), Attic	176, 205 n., 219 n.	—

	PAGES	FRAGMENTS
Tetrapolis (2), Cean	61 & n.	75
Teutamos	111 & n.	191
Thales	104, 105, 109 & n., 111	191
Thasos	79 & n.	104
Thebes(1), Boeotian	71 n., 78 n.	—
Thebes (2), Egyptian	167 & n.	228
Theia	82 n., 83, 221 & n.	110, 338
Themisto	40 n., 41	49 (?)
Theocritus	xi, xv, 8 n.	—
Theodaesia	37 & n.	43
Thegoenes	97	178
Theon	xiv	—
Thera (Santorin)	13 & n., 18 n., 285 & n.	7, 716
Thermodon (1), Scythian river	83 n.	—
Thermodon (2), Boeotian river	275 & n.	648
Theseus	51 n., 83 n., 119, 125 & n., 131 n., 176-225, 256 n., 266 n.	194, 232-236, 239, 240, 245, 253, 257 - 260, 262 - 263, 280 - 281, 290, 330, 345
Thesprotia	107 n.	—
Thessaly, Thessalians	13 n., 40 n., 47 & n., 69 n., 95 & n., 97, 121 n., 215 & n., 229 n., 255, 269, 277 n.	7, 178-184, 304, 488, 588
Thetis	167 & n.	228
Thiodamas	20 n., 21 n., 23 & n., 25 n.	22, 24
Thiogenes	271	607
Thoas	161	—

418

	PAGES	FRAGMENTS
Thrace, Thracian	7, 71 n., 79 & n., 95 & n., 118 & n., 132, 135 n., 160, 167, 185 n., 266 n.	1, 104, 178. 228
Thriae	195 & n.	260
Tilphousa	277 & n.	652
Timaeus	141 n.	—
Titan	11 & n., 256 n.	6
Tithonus	18 n., 19, 123 & n.	21, 194
Tito	18 n., 19	21
Tmarus	21 & n.	23
Tmolus	118, 119 & n., 127	194
Tottes	91 n.	—
Trachis	25 n.	—
Tripodiscon	26 n.	—
Triton (Tritonis), Libyan lake or river	30 n., 31	37
Tritonis (Athene)	145 & n.	202
Troezen	177, 178 n., 183, 205 n., 223 n.	235
Troilus	254 n., 255	491
Troy, Trojan	109 n., 132 n., 135 & n., 266 n.	197
Tyndareus, Tyndaridae	17 & n., 163 & n.	18, 227
Typhon	259 n.	—
Tyrrhenians	71 n., 73 & n., 136, 137	97
Ursa Major and Minor, cf. Hamaxae	—	—
Virgo	81 n., 95 n.	—
Wilamowitz, U. von	vii n., viii n., xv & n., 177, 234 n.	—
Wilcken, U.	xi n.	—
Xenocritus	277 & n.	669
Xenomedes	59 & n.	75
Xerxes	83 n.	—
Zancle (Messene)	37 & n., 107 n.	43
Zephyr	83 & n.	110

INDEX TO CALLIMACHUS

	PAGES	FRAGMENTS
Zephyritis (Arsinoë)	83 n.	110
Zephyrium	81 n., 83 n.	—
Zeus	7, 9 n., 10 n., 11 n., 16 n., 17, 21 n., 30 n., 31, 39 n., 40 n., 41, 42 n., 43 & n., 47, 54 n., 61 & n., 63 & n., 65 n., 74 n., 76 n., 85 n., 87, 90 n., 91 & n., 99 & n., 112, 115 & n., 125 n., 127, 129 n., 130, 133 & n., 143 & n., 145, 147, 155, 171, 176, 195, 212 n., 213 n., 231 & n., 249 n., 253 n., 285 & n.	1, 18, 37, 48, 55, 64, 75, 76, 77, 112, 119, 186, 192, 194, 196, 202, 223, 229, 260, 383, 400, 719
Zeus Aristaeus, Icmaeus, or Icmius	57 & n.	75
Zeus Casios	239 n.	—
Zeus Hecaleios	177	—
Zeus Panchaeus	107 & n.	191
Ziegler, K.	ix n.	—

MUSAEUS

INDEX OF PROPER NAMES

(The numbers refer to the lines of the poem.)

Abydos 4, 16, 21, 26, 28, 50, 209, 229, 284
Adonis 43
Aphrodite (see Cypris, Cythereia) 6, (Cythereia) 38, (Urania) 40, 143, 155, 182, (Thalassaia) 320
(Arcadia 153)
Atalanta 153
Athena (*bis*) 135
(Attica 322)

Boötes 213
Boreas 317, 322

Charites 64, 65, 77
(Cronus 137)
Cypris (see Aphrodite, Cythereia) 31, 33, (42), 66, (*bis*) 68, 77, 126, (*bis*) 135, (*bis*) 141, 144, 152, 157, 249
Cyprus 46
Cythera 47
Cythereia (see Aphrodite, Cypris) (38), 43, 83, 146, 273, 290

Dawn see Eos

Eos 3, 110, 282, (335)
Eros 8, 17, 39, 149, 198, 212, 240, 245, 246, 323
Erotes 10, 90, 147, 166, 308
Eurus 316
Evening-Star, Hesperus 111

Fates see Moirai

Graces see Charites

Haemonia 46
Hamaxa 214
Hellespont 208
Hera 275
Heracles 150
Hermes 150, 152
Hero 4, 7, 20, 24, 29, 30, 55, 60, 64, 70, 79, 81, 89, 120, 167, 186, 220, 239, 256, 286, 304, 335, 342
Hesperus 111

(Iardanus 151)

421

INDEX TO MUSAEUS

Lacedaemon 74

Leander 5, 15, 20, 25, 27, 28, 86, 103, 106, 109, 122, 129, 168, 170, 172, 196, 201, 220, 233, 240, 259, 283, 301, 305, 312, 319, 330, 332

Libanus 48

Love see Eros

Loves see Erotes

Milanion 154

Moirai 308, 323

(Muse 1, 14 s.)

Notus 317

Olympus 80

Orion 214

Phrygia 50

Poseidon 321

Selene 57

Sestos 4, 16, 21, 43, (189), 258

Sparta 74

Thalassaia see Aphrodite

(Thessaly, Haemonia 46)

Urania see Aphrodite

Wain 214

Zephyrus 316

Zeus 8, (30), 137

THE LOEB CLASSICAL LIBRARY

Latin Authors

AMMIANUS MARCELLINUS. J. C. Rolfe. 3 Vols.

APULEIUS: THE GOLDEN ASS (METAMORPHOSES). W. Adlington (1566). Revised by S. Gaselee.

ST. AUGUSTINE: CITY OF GOD. 7 Vols. Vol. I. G. E. McCracken. Vols. II and VII. W. M. Green. Vol. III. D. Wiesen. Vol. IV. P. Levine. Vol. V. E. M. Sanford and W. M. Green. Vol. VI. W. C. Greene.

ST. AUGUSTINE, CONFESSIONS. W. Watts (1631). 2 Vols.

ST. AUGUSTINE, SELECT LETTERS. J. H. Baxter.

AUSONIUS. H. G. Evelyn White. 2 Vols.

BEDE. J. E. King. 2 Vols.

BOETHIUS: TRACTS and DE CONSOLATIONE PHILOSOPHIAE. Rev. H. F. Stewart and E. K. Rand. Revised by S. J. Tester.

CAESAR: ALEXANDRIAN, AFRICAN and SPANISH WARS. A. G. Way.

CAESAR: CIVIL WARS. A. G. Peskett.

CAESAR: GALLIC WAR. H. J. Edwards.

CATO: DE RE RUSTICA. VARRO: DE RE RUSTICA. H. B. Ash and W. D. Hooper.

CATULLUS. F. W. Cornish. TIBULLUS. J. B. Postgate. PERVIGILIUM VENERIS. J. W. Mackail. Revised by G. P. Goold.

CELSUS: DE MEDICINA. W. G. Spencer. 3 Vols.

CICERO: BRUTUS and ORATOR. G. L. Hendrickson and H. M. Hubbell.

[CICERO]: AD HERENNIUM. H. Caplan.

CICERO: DE ORATORE, etc. 2 Vols. Vol. I. DE ORATORE, Books I and II. E. W. Sutton and H. Rackham. Vol. II. DE ORATORE, Book III. DE FATO; PARADOXA STOICORUM; DE PARTITIONE ORATORIA. H. Rackham.

CICERO: DE FINIBUS. H. Rackham.

CICERO: DE INVENTIONE, etc. H. M. Hubbell.

CICERO: DE NATURA DEORUM and ACADEMICA. H. Rackham.

CICERO: DE OFFICIIS. Walter Miller.

CICERO: DE RE PUBLICA and DE LEGIBUS. Clinton W. Keyes.

CICERO: DE SENECTUTE, DE AMICITIA, DE DIVINATIONE. W. A. Falconer.

CICERO: IN CATILINAM, PRO FLACCO, PRO MURENA, PRO SULLA. New version by C. Macdonald.

CICERO: LETTERS TO ATTICUS. E. O. Winstedt. 3 Vols.

CICERO: LETTERS TO HIS FRIENDS. W. Glynn Williams, M. Cary, M. Henderson. 4 Vols.

CICERO: PHILIPPICS. W. C. A. Ker.

CICERO: PRO ARCHIA, POST REDITUM, DE DOMO, DE HARUSPICUM RESPONSIS, PRO PLANCIO. N. H. Watts.

CICERO: PRO CAECINA, PRO LEGE MANILIA, PRO CLUENTIO, PRO RABIRIO. H. Grose Hodge.

CICERO: PRO CAELIO, DE PROVINCIIS CONSULARIBUS, PRO BALBO. R. Gardner.

CICERO: PRO MILONE, IN PISONEM, PRO SCAURO, PRO FONTEIO, PRO RABIRIO POSTUMO, PRO MARCELLO, PRO LIGARIO, PRO REGE DEIOTARO. N. H. Watts.

CICERO: PRO QUINCTIO, PRO ROSCIO AMERINO, PRO ROSCIO COMOEDO, CONTRA RULLUM. J. H. Freese.

CICERO: PRO SESTIO, IN VATINIUM. R. Gardner.

CICERO: TUSCULAN DISPUTATIONS. J. E. King.

CICERO: VERRINE ORATIONS. L. H. G. Greenwood. 2 Vols.

CLAUDIAN. M. Platnauer. 2 Vols.

COLUMELLA: DE RE RUSTICA. DE ARBORIBUS. H. B. Ash, E. S. Forster and E. Heffner. 3 Vols.

CURTIUS, Q.: HISTORY OF ALEXANDER. J. C. Rolfe. 2 Vols.

FLORUS. E. S. Forster.

FRONTINUS: STRATAGEMS and AQUEDUCTS. C. E. Bennett and M. B. McElwain.

FRONTO: CORRESPONDENCE. C. R. Haines. 2 Vols.

GELLIUS. J. C. Rolfe. 3 Vols.

HORACE: ODES and EPODES. C. E. Bennett.

HORACE: SATIRES, EPISTLES, ARS POETICA. H. R. Fairclough.

JEROME: SELECTED LETTERS. F. A. Wright.

JUVENAL and PERSIUS. G. G. Ramsay.

LIVY. B. O. Foster, F. G. Moore, Evan T. Sage, and A. C. Schlesinger and R. M. Geer (General Index). 14 Vols.

LUCAN. J. D. Duff.

LUCRETIUS. W. H. D. Rouse. Revised by M. F. Smith.

MANILIUS. G. P. Goold.

MARTIAL. W. C. A. Ker. 2 Vols. Revised by E. H. Warmington

MINOR LATIN POETS: from PUBLILIUS SYRUS to RUTILIUS NAMATIANUS, including GRATTIUS, CALPURNIUS SICULUS, NEMESIANUS, AVIANUS and others, with "Aetna" and the "Phoenix." J. Wight Duff and Arnold M. Duff. 2 Vols.

MINUCIUS FELIX. Cf. TERTULLIAN.

NEPOS, CORNELIUS. J. C. Rolfe.

OVID: THE ART OF LOVE and OTHER POEMS. J. H. Mozley. Revised by G. P. Goold.

OVID: FASTI. Sir James G. Frazer. Revised by G. P. Goold.

OVID: HEROIDES and AMORES. Grant Showerman. Revised by G. P. Goold.

OVID: METAMORPHOSES. F. J. Miller. 2 Vols. Revised by G. P. Goold.

OVID: TRISTIA and EX PONTO. A. L. Wheeler. Revised by G. P. Goold.

PERSIUS. Cf. JUVENAL.

PERVIGILIUM VENERIS. Cf. CATULLUS.

PETRONIUS. M. Heseltine. SENECA: APOCOLOCYNTOSIS. W. H. D. Rouse. Revised by E. H. Warmington.

PHAEDRUS and BABRIUS (Greek). B. E. Perry.

PLAUTUS. Paul Nixon. 5 Vols.

PLINY: LETTERS, PANEGYRICUS. Betty Radice. 2 Vols.

PLINY: NATURAL HISTORY. 10 Vols. Vols. I.–V. and IX. H. Rackham. VI.–VIII. W. H. S. Jones. X. D. E. Eichholz.

PROPERTIUS. H. E. Butler.

PRUDENTIUS. H. J. Thomson. 2 Vols.

QUINTILIAN. H. E. Butler. 4 Vols.

REMAINS OF OLD LATIN. E. H. Warmington. 4 Vols. Vol. I. (ENNIUS AND CAECILIUS) Vol. II. (LIVIUS, NAEVIUS PACUVIUS, ACCIUS) Vol. III. (LUCILIUS and LAWS OF XII TABLES) Vol. IV. (ARCHAIC INSCRIPTIONS).

RES GESTAE DIVI AUGUSTI. Cf. VELLEIUS PATERCULUS.

SALLUST. J. C. Rolfe.

SCRIPTORES HISTORIAE AUGUSTAE. D. Magie. 3 Vols.

SENECA, THE ELDER: CONTROVERSIAE, SUASORIAE. M. Winterbottom. 2 Vols.

SENECA: APOCOLOCYNTOSIS. Cf. PETRONIUS.

SENECA: EPISTULAE MORALES. R. M. Gummere. 3 Vols.

SENECA: MORAL ESSAYS. J. W. Basore. 3 Vols.

SENECA: TRAGEDIES. F. J. Miller. 2 Vols.

SENECA: NATURALES QUAESTIONES. T. H. CORCORAN. 2 VOLS.

SIDONIUS: POEMS and LETTERS. W. B. Anderson. 2 Vols.

SILIUS ITALICUS. J. D. Duff. 2 Vols.

STATIUS. J. H. Mozley. 2 Vols.

SUETONIUS. J. C. Rolfe. 2 Vols.

TACITUS: DIALOGUS. Sir Wm. Peterson. AGRICOLA and GERMANIA. Maurice Hutton. Revised by M. Winterbottom, R. M. Ogilvie, E. H. Warmington.

TACITUS: HISTORIES and ANNALS. C. H. Moore and J. Jackson. 4 Vols.

TERENCE. John Sargeaunt. 2 Vols.

TERTULLIAN: APOLOGIA and DE SPECTACULIS. T. R. Glover. MINUCIUS FELIX. G. H. Rendall.

TIBULLUS. Cf. CATULLUS.
VALERIUS FLACCUS. J. H. Mozley.
VARRO: DE LINGUA LATINA. R. G. Kent. 2 Vols.
VELLEIUS PATERCULUS and RES GESTAE DIVI AUGUSTI. F. W. SHIPLEY.
VIRGIL. H. R. Fairclough. 2 Vols.
VITRUVIUS: DE ARCHITECTURA. F. Granger. 2 Vols.

Greek Authors

ACHILLES TATIUS. S. Gaselee.
AELIAN: ON THE NATURE OF ANIMALS. A. F. Scholfield. 3 Vols.
AENEAS TACTICUS. ASCLEPIODOTUS and ONASANDER. The Illinois Greek Club.
AESCHINES. C. D. Adams.
AESCHYLUS. H. Weir Smyth. 2 Vols.
ALCIPHRON, AELIAN, PHILOSTRATUS: LETTERS. A. R. Benner and F. H. Fobes.
ANDOCIDES, ANTIPHON. Cf. MINOR ATTIC ORATORS Vol. I.
APOLLODORUS. Sir James G. Frazer. 2 Vols.
APOLLONIUS RHODIUS. R. C. Seaton.
APOSTOLIC FATHERS. Kirsopp Lake. 2 Vols.
APPIAN: ROMAN HISTORY. Horace White. 4 Vols.
ARATUS. Cf. CALLIMACHUS.
ARISTIDES: ORATIONS. C. A. Behr.
ARISTOPHANES. Benjamin Bickley Rogers. 3 Vols. Verse trans.
ARISTOTLE: ART OF RHETORIC. J. H. Freese.
ARISTOTLE: ATHENIAN CONSTITUTION, EUDEMIAN ETHICS, VICES AND VIRTUES. H. Rackham.
ARISTOTLE: GENERATION OF ANIMALS. A. L. Peck.
ARISTOTLE: HISTORIA ANIMALIUM. A. L. Peck. Vols. I.–II.
ARISTOTLE: METAPHYSICS. H. Tredennick. 2 Vols.
ARISTOTLE: METEOROLOGICA. H. D. P. Lee.
ARISTOTLE: MINOR WORKS. W. S. Hett. On Colours, On Things Heard, On Physiognomies, On Plants, On Marvellous Things Heard, Mechanical Problems, On Indivisible Lines, On Situations and Names of Winds, On Melissus, Xenophanes, and Gorgias.
ARISTOTLE: NICOMACHEAN ETHICS. H. Rackham.
ARISTOTLE: OECONOMICA and MAGNA MORALIA. G. C. Armstrong (with METAPHYSICS, Vol. II).
ARISTOTLE: ON THE HEAVENS. W. K. C. Guthrie.
ARISTOTLE: ON THE SOUL, PARVA NATURALIA, ON BREATH. W. S. Hett.
ARISTOTLE: CATEGORIES, ON INTERPRETATION, PRIOR ANALYTICS. H. P. Cooke and H. Tredennick.

ARISTOTLE: POSTERIOR ANALYTICS, TOPICS. H. Tredennick and E. S. Forster.

ARISTOTLE: ON SOPHISTICAL REFUTATIONS.
On Coming-to-be and Passing-Away, On the Cosmos. E. S. Forster and D. J. Furley.

ARISTOTLE: PARTS OF ANIMALS. A. L. Peck; MOTION AND PROGRESSION OF ANIMALS. E. S. Forster.

ARISTOTLE: PHYSICS. Rev. P. Wicksteed and F. M. Cornford. 2 Vols.

ARISTOTLE: POETICS and LONGINUS. W. Hamilton Fyfe; DEMETRIUS ON STYLE. W. Rhys Roberts.

ARISTOTLE: POLITICS. H. Rackham.

ARISTOTLE: PROBLEMS. W. S. Hett. 2 Vols.

ARISTOTLE: RHETORICA AD ALEXANDRUM (with PROBLEMS. Vol. II). H. Rackham.

ARRIAN: HISTORY OF ALEXANDER and INDICA. Rev. E. Iliffe Robson. 2 Vols. New version P. Brunt.

ATHENAEUS: DEIPNOSOPHISTAE. C. B. Gulick. 7 Vols.

BABRIUS and PHAEDRUS (Latin). B. E. Perry.

ST. BASIL: LETTERS. R. J. Deferrari. 4 Vols.

CALLIMACHUS: FRAGMENTS. C. A. Trypanis. MUSAEUS: HERO AND LEANDER. T. Gelzer and C. Whitman.

CALLIMACHUS, Hymns and Epigrams and LYCOPHRON. A. W. Mair; ARATUS. G. R. Mair.

CLEMENT OF ALEXANDRIA. Rev. G. W. Butterworth.

COLLUTHUS. Cf. OPPIAN.

DAPHNIS AND CHLOE. Thornley's translation revised by J. M. Edmonds: and PARTHENIUS. S. Gaselee.

DEMOSTHENES I.: OLYNTHIACS, PHILIPPICS and MINOR ORATIONS I.–XVII. and XX. J. H. Vince.

DEMOSTHENES II.: DE CORONA and DE FALSA LEGATIONE. C. A. Vince and J. H. Vince.

DEMOSTHENES III.: MEIDIAS, ANDROTION, ARISTOCRATES, TIMOCRATES and ARISTOGEITON I. and II. J. H. Vince.

DEMOSTHENES IV.–VI.: PRIVATE ORATIONS and IN NEAERAM. A. T. Murray.

DEMOSTHENES VII.: FUNERAL SPEECH, EROTIC ESSAY, EXORDIA and LETTERS. N. W. and N. J. DeWitt.

DIO CASSIUS: ROMAN HISTORY. E. Cary. 9 Vols.

DIO CHRYSOSTOM. J. W. Cohoon and H. Lamar Crosby. 5 Vols.

DIODORUS SICULUS. 12 Vols. Vols. I.–VI. C. H. Oldfather. Vol. VII. C. L. Sherman. Vol. VIII. C. B. Welles. Vols. IX. and X. R. M. Geer. Vol. XI. F. Walton. Vol. XII. F. Walton. General Index. R. M. Geer.

DIOGENES LAERTIUS. R. D. Hicks. 2 Vols. New Introduction by H. S. Long.

DIONYSIUS OF HALICARNASSUS: ROMAN ANTIQUITIES. Spelman's translation revised by E. Cary. 7 Vols.

DIONYSIUS OF HALICARNASSUS: CRITICAL ESSAYS. S. Usher. 2 Vols.
EPICTETUS. W. A. Oldfather. 2 Vols.
EURIPIDES. A. S. Way. 4 Vols. Verse trans.
EUSEBIUS: ECCLESIASTICAL HISTORY. Kirsopp Lake and J. E. L. Oulton. 2 Vols.
GALEN: ON THE NATURAL FACULTIES. A. J. Brock.
GREEK ANTHOLOGY. W. R. Paton. 5 Vols.
GREEK BUCOLIC POETS (THEOCRITUS, BION, MOSCHUS). J. M. Edmonds.
GREEK ELEGY AND IAMBUS with the ANACREONTEA. J. M. Edmonds. 2 Vols.
GREEK LYRIC. D. A. Campbell. 4 Vols. Vols. I. and II.
GREEK MATHEMATICAL WORKS. Ivor Thomas. 2 Vols.
HERODAS. Cf. THEOPHRASTUS: CHARACTERS.
HERODIAN. C. R. Whittaker. 2 Vols.
HERODOTUS. A. D. Godley. 4 Vols.
HESIOD AND THE HOMERIC HYMNS. H. G. Evelyn White.
HIPPOCRATES and the FRAGMENTS OF HERACLEITUS. W. H. S. Jones and E. T. Withington. 7 Vols. Vols. I.–VI.
HOMER: ILIAD. A. T. Murray. 2 Vols.
HOMER: ODYSSEY. A. T. Murray. 2 Vols.
ISAEUS. E. W. Forster.
ISOCRATES. George Norlin and LaRue Van Hook. 3 Vols.
[ST. JOHN DAMASCENE]: BARLAAM AND IOASAPH. Rev. G. R. Woodward, Harold Mattingly and D. M. Lang.
JOSEPHUS. 10 Vols. Vols. I.–IV. H. Thackeray. Vol. V. H. Thackeray and R. Marcus. Vols. VI.–VII. R. Marcus. Vol. VIII. R. Marcus and Allen Wikgren. Vols. IX.–X. L. H. Feldman.
JULIAN. Wilmer Cave Wright. 3 Vols.
LIBANIUS. A. F. Norman. 2 Vols..
LUCIAN. 8 Vols. Vols. I.–V. A. M. Harmon. Vol. VI. K. Kilburn. Vols. VII.–VIII. M. D. Macleod.
LYCOPHRON. Cf. CALLIMACHUS.
LYRA GRAECA, III. J. M. Edmonds. (Vols. I.and II. have been replaced by GREEK LYRIC I. and II.)
LYSIAS. W. R. M. Lamb.
MANETHO. W. G. Waddell.
MARCUS AURELIUS. C. R. Haines.
MENANDER. W. G. Arnott. 3 Vols. Vol. I.
MINOR ATTIC ORATORS (ANTIPHON, ANDOCIDES, LYCURGUS, DEMADES, DINARCHUS, HYPERIDES). K. J. Maidment and J. O. Burtt. 2 Vols.
MUSAEUS: HERO AND LEANDER. Cf. CALLIMACHUS.
NONNOS: DIONYSIACA. W. H. D. Rouse. 3 Vols.
OPPIAN, COLLUTHUS, TRYPHIODORUS. A. W. Mair.
PAPYRI. NON-LITERARY SELECTIONS. A. S. Hunt and C. C. Edgar. 2 Vols. LITERARY SELECTIONS (Poetry). D. L. Page.

PARTHENIUS. Cf. DAPHNIS AND CHLOE.

PAUSANIAS: DESCRIPTION OF GREECE. W. H. S. Jones. 4 Vols. and Companion Vol. arranged by R. E. Wycherley.

PHILO. 10 Vols. Vols. I.–V. F. H. Colson and Rev. G. H. Whitaker. Vols. VI.–IX. F. H. Colson. Vol. X. F. H. Colson and the Rev. J. W. Earp.

PHILO: two supplementary Vols. (*Translation only*.) Ralph Marcus.

PHILOSTRATUS: THE LIFE OF APOLLONIUS OF TYANA. F. C. Conybeare. 2 Vols.

PHILOSTRATUS: IMAGINES; CALLISTRATUS: DESCRIPTIONS. A. Fairbanks.

PHILOSTRATUS and EUNAPIUS: LIVES OF THE SOPHISTS. Wilmer Cave Wright.

PINDAR. Sir J. E. Sandys.

PLATO: CHARMIDES, ALCIBIADES, HIPPARCHUS, THE LOVERS, THEAGES, MINOS and EPINOMIS. W. R. M. Lamb.

PLATO: CRATYLUS, PARMENIDES, GREATER HIPPIAS, LESSER HIPPIAS. H. N. Fowler.

PLATO: EUTHYPHRO, APOLOGY, CRITO, PHAEDO, PHAEDRUS. H. N. Fowler.

PLATO: LACHES, PROTAGORAS, MENO, EUTHYDEMUS. W. R. M. Lamb.

PLATO: LAWS. Rev. R. G. Bury. 2 Vols.

PLATO: LYSIS, SYMPOSIUM, GORGIAS. W. R. M. Lamb.

PLATO: REPUBLIC. Paul Shorey. 2 Vols.

PLATO: STATESMAN, PHILEBUS. H. N. Fowler; ION. W. R. M. Lamb.

PLATO: THEAETETUS and SOPHIST. H. N. Fowler.

PLATO: TIMAEUS, CRITIAS, CLEITOPHON, MENEXENUS, EPISTULAE. Rev. R. G. Bury.

PLOTINUS: A. H. Armstrong. 7 Vols.

PLUTARCH: MORALIA. 16 Vols. Vols. I.–V. F. C. Babbitt. Vol. VI. W. C. Helmbold. Vols. VII. and XIV. P. H. De Lacy and B. Einarson. Vol. VIII. P. A. Clement and H. B. Hoffleit. Vol. IX. E. L. Minar, Jr., F. H. Sandbach, W. C. Helmbold. Vol. X. H. N. Fowler. Vol. XI. L. Pearson and F. H. Sandbach. Vol. XII. H. Cherniss and W. C. Helmbold. Vol. XIII. 1–2. H. Cherniss. Vol. XV. F. H. Sandbach.

PLUTARCH: THE PARALLEL LIVES. B. Perrin. 11 Vols.

POLYBIUS. W. R. Paton. 6 Vols.

PROCOPIUS. H. B. Dewing. 7 Vols.

PTOLEMY: TETRABIBLOS. F. E. Robbins.

QUINTUS SMYRNAEUS. A. S. Way. Verse trans.

SEXTUS EMPIRICUS. Rev. R. G. Bury. 4 Vols.

SOPHOCLES. F. Storr. 2 Vols. Verse trans.

STRABO: GEOGRAPHY. Horace L. Jones. 8 Vols.

THEOCRITUS. Cf. GREEK BUCOLIC POETS.

THEOPHRASTUS: CHARACTERS. J. M. Edmonds. HERODAS, etc. A. D. Knox.

THEOPHRASTUS: ENQUIRY INTO PLANTS. Sir Arthur Hort, Bart. 2 Vols.

THEOPHRASTUS: DE CAUSIS PLANTARUM. G. K. K. Link and B. Einarson. 3 Vols. Vol. I.

THUCYDIDES. C. F. Smith. 4 Vols.

TRYPHIODORUS. Cf. OPPIAN.

XENOPHON: CYROPAEDIA. Walter Miller. 2 Vols.

XENOPHON: HELLENICA. C. L. Brownson. 2 Vols.

XENOPHON: ANABASIS. C. L. Brownson.

XENOPHON: MEMORABILIA and OECONOMICUS. E. C. Marchant. SYMPOSIUM and APOLOGY. O. J. Todd.

XENOPHON: SCRIPTA MINORA. E. C. Marchant. CONSTITUTION OF THE ATHENIANS. G. W. Bowersock.